Wittgenstein, Mind and Meaning

M000191558

"*Wittgenstein, Mind and Meaning* represents one of the most subtle and sustained developments available of the communitarian or social reading of Wittgenstein's later work."

Mind

"a remarkably clear and immensely rewarding book."

Philosophical Investigations

"Meredith Williams' engagement with various themes in Wittgenstein's later writings is highly original, and her arguments should stimulate all of us who work in these areas of inquiry. This is a truly superb contribution to current philosophical debates."

Jeff Coulter, Boston University

"Meredith Williams' work sacrifices nothing in terms of rigour or sensitivity to textual detail, but manages to turn the discussion in such a way that issues of real significance are once again on the philosophical agenda."

David Bloor, University of Edinburgh

Wittgenstein, Mind and Meaning

Toward a social conception of mind

Meredith Williams

London and New York

First published 1999
by Routledge
11 New Fetter Lane, London EC4P 4EE

Simultaneously published in the USA and Canada
by Routledge
29 West 35th Street, New York, NY 10001

First published in paperback 2002

Routledge is an imprint of the Taylor & Francis Group

© 1999, 2002 Meredith Williams

Typeset in Baskerville by Taylor & Francis Books Ltd
Printed and bound in Great Britain by
TJ International Ltd, Padstow, Cornwall

British Library Cataloguing in Publication Data
A catalogue record for this book is available from the British Library

Library of Congress Cataloging in Publication Data
A catalog record for this book is available from the Library of Congress

ISBN 0–415–18908–X (Hbk)
ISBN 0–415–28756–1 (Pbk)

For my mother and in memory of my father

For my wife and in memory of my father

Contents

Preface

Over the last twenty years, I have worked in two areas in contemporary philosophy: the later philosophy of Ludwig Wittgenstein and the foundations of cognitive science. Wittgenstein's critical views concerning philosophical theories and their illusions and his positive views concerning the normative structure of our language games conflict deeply with the reductionist aspirations of many contemporary cognitivist theories of mind. Behind cognitive science as it interests philosophers is a firm commitment to naturalism, to the idea that our cognitive capacities require a naturalistic explanation of mental content, logical relations, indeed the whole logical space of reasons. Philosophers have looked primarily to computational theories, Darwinian functionalist theories, and information-processing theories to provide this naturalistic account. Wittgenstein too seeks a naturalism with respect to the mind as the formation of a second nature through acculturation into our normatively structured language games.

Wittgenstein, both in his early work and his later work, is a seminal figure in the development of analytic philosophy, in promoting the idea that natural language use is key to understanding the nature of the mind. Wittgenstein is notable, however, for his rejection of the positivists' celebration of science. The cognitivist movement of the second half of the twentieth century, on the other hand, repudiates the linguistic turn while identifying its naturalistic project with a defense of the hegemony of science. Cognitivist theories of mind are rife with nativist theories of rules, concepts, theories, and beliefs; with psychologically real cognitive processes, structures, and concepts, all of which ride free of a dependence upon (natural) language mastery. This philosophical movement is identified in large part by its return to realist theories of thought and cognition. It is only to be expected that Wittgenstein's later views of language and mind must conflict in profound ways with the current cognitivist movement in the philosophy of mind.

This book is directed towards trying to understand and evaluate this conflict. This requires both gaining a full understanding of Wittgenstein's later ideas, a task that has been greatly enriched by the availability of his *Nachlass* and by the revival of philosophical interest in his ideas, and an understanding of cognitivist theories of mind. The chapters here do not cover the full range of cognitivist theories, but are restricted to one of the most influential, namely, the computational theory of the mind. By bringing this work on Wittgenstein and cognitivism together, we can appreciate the intersection of Wittgenstein's views on representation and rules and criticisms of cognitivism's naturalistic approach to these same normative phenomena. Though originally written independently of each other over a fifteen-year period, these ten chapters, together, create a strikingly coherent book, one that I hope contributes both to enriching our understanding of the later Wittgenstein and to raising questions about the foundations of cognitivism.

Meredith Williams
January 1998

Acknowledgments

All of the chapters here have been previously published and are reprinted with only minor revisions and corrections. I have added a Postscript to Chapter 4, "Language learning and the representational theory of mind." This chapter is a critical examination of J.A. Fodor's language of thought hypothesis as presented and defended in *The Language of Thought*. Since that time Fodor has gone on to develop a much more sophisticated semantic theory for mental representations. The Postscript is an examination of these subsequent developments. Also, I have enriched the notes of "Wittgenstein, Kant, and the 'metaphysics of experience'" in order to acknowledge the ways in which P.M.S. Hacker modified his views in the second edition of *Insight and Illusion*. His current views are now much closer to the interpretation I defend in that paper.

The author and publisher wish to thank the editors, journals, and publishers who gave permission to reprint these articles: to the *Canadian Journal of Philosophy* for "Wittgenstein on Representations, Privileged Objects, and Private Languages" (1983) and "The Philosophical Significance of Learning in the Later Wittgenstein" (1994); to *International Philosophical Quarterly* (1994) for "Private States and Public Practices"; to Walter de Gruyter for "Wittgenstein, Kant, and the 'Metaphysics of Experience'" in *Kant-Studien* (1990); to *Journal for the Theory of Social Behavior* (1985) for "Wittgenstein's Rejection of Scientific Psychology"; to *Synthese* (1984) for "Language Learning and the Representational Theory of Mind"; to Notre Dame University Press for "Narrow Content, Norms, and the Individual" published in *Midwest Studies in Philosophy* XV (1990); to Oxford University Press for "The Etiology of the Obvious" from T. McCarthy, ed., *Wittgenstein in America* (Oxford University Press: forthcoming); and to *Harvard Educational Review* (1989) for "Vygotsky's Social Theory of Mind." "Rules, Community, and the Individual" first appeared in Klaus Puhl, ed., *Meaning–Scepticism* (Berlin/New York: Walter de Gruyter, 1991).

Most of these papers (or earlier versions) were presented at various conferences and universities. I wish to thank all those who offered criticism and comment on those occasions. Also, my special thanks go to Joe Rouse for his helpful comments on "Private States and Public Practices"; to Donald Gustafson and Richard Rorty for their criticisms of an earlier version of "Wittgenstein's Rejection of Scientific Psychology"; to Barbara von Eckardt and Jeff Poland for pressing criticisms of "Language Learning and the Representational Theory of Mind"; to Crispin Wright for his incisive comments on "Rules, Community, and the Individual"; and to James Wertsch, Stephen Toulmin, and Addison Stone for stimulating discussions of Vygotsky. I also wish to thank those anonymous reviewers for journals who read my papers. Their comments and criticisms were almost invariably to the point and helpful. Finally, my greatest thanks go to Michael Williams who offered that invaluable combination of criticism, support, and humor.

List of abbreviations

Below are the abbreviations used to refer to Wittgenstein's writings. They are listed in chronological order.

TLP (1971) *Tractatus Logico-Philosophicus*, trs. D.F. Pears and B.F. McGuinness, London, Routledge and Kegan Paul.

BB (1958) *The Blue and Brown Books*, Oxford, Basil Blackwell.

RFM (1978) *Remarks on the Foundations of Mathematics*, Revised Edition, ed. G.H. von Wright, R. Rhees, G.E.M. Anscombe, tr. G.E.M. Anscombe, Cambridge, MA, The MIT Press.

PI (1953) *Philosophical Investigations*, tr. G.E.M. Anscombe, New York, The Macmillan Company.

Z (1967) *Zettel*, tr. G.E.M. Anscombe, Oxford, Basil Blackwell.

OC (1969) *On Certainty*, tr. D. Paul and G.E.M. Anscombe, Oxford, Basil Blackwell.

Introduction

Two major critical moments define Wittgenstein's later philosophy, his critique of denotational theories of meaning, as found in Frege's and his own earlier conception of language, and his critique of the Cartesian theory of mind, particularly as expressed in the introspectionist/phenomenalist treatments of mind by Russell and William James. Of these two moments, Wittgenstein's ideas about language continue to be influential. By contrast, his criticism of the Cartesian theory of mind seems to be of interest only for historical reasons. As this book will make clear, this is a mistake, and for two important reasons.

First, philosophers who downplay Wittgenstein's critique of Cartesianism do so because they take Wittgenstein's target to be the introspectionist conception of consciousness, which theoretically we have moved far beyond. However, contemporary cognitivist theories of mind are continuous with the Cartesian tradition in various respects, in particular, in their commitment to the *explanatory* role of mental processes and mental representations. Wittgenstein is at least as interested in the explanatory significance of psychological vocabulary as he is in consciousness. (Not that the critique of consciousness is out of date.)[1]

Second, Wittgenstein's rejection of the Cartesian model of mind – including those elements that lie within contemporary cognitivism – cannot be easily detached from his philosophy of language. The interpenetration of the structure of language and the structure of mind is such that his conception of language cannot but have deep implications for his conception of mind. This is also true of Chomsky and Fodor. What is at stake is the direction of explanation. Where Wittgenstein argues that there is no thought without language, no thinking in addition to its linguistic expression, Chomsky and Fodor argue for the priority of thought, rules, and mental representations over natural language usage.

In the light of these considerations, this book explores the connection between Wittgenstein's criticisms of the Cartesian theory of mind, his conception of language, and his understanding of mind. Some of the essays are directly on Wittgenstein's work and some are directed towards current issues in the philosophy of mind in which I use Wittgensteinian arguments and considerations. Taken together, they lay the foundation for a social conception of mind, a conception that emphasizes the social basis of rule-following and the philosophical significance of language learning.

Part I "Against the philosophic tradition" consists of five chapters, each taking on an important aspect of Cartesianism, both in its modern and contemporary forms. Chapter 1, "Wittgenstein on representations, privileged objects and private languages" and Chapter 2, "Private states and public practices," are directed against the Cartesian conception of mind as the subjective starting place for meaning and belief. One of the innovations that Descartes introduced in his conception of mind was to treat the contents of sensory perception and the contents of belief and reasoning as the same sort of thing, namely, as ideas interior to the mind and operated upon within the various faculties of the mind. In this way, he brought the immediacy of consciousness and the intentionality of belief together in the idea of the self-illuminating or transparent nature of mental substance. For Descartes, both immediacy and intentionality are explained in terms of the special infallible knowledge that the thinker has of the contents of his own mind. This epistemological mark of the mental privileges the subjective over the public and/or social as the starting place for language, belief, and knowledge, an emphasis retained in the theories of early-twentieth-century philosophers. This commitment bridges the divide between analytic and continental philosophy. It is found not only in the sense-data theories of Russell and others within the positivist movement, but also in the work of adherents of the phenomenological tradition, such as Husserl and Schutz. Schutz, whose official project is to understand everyday social life, nonetheless tries to ground our intentional public practices in individual subjective consciousness. "Private states and public practices" draws out just how and why Schutz's explanatory resources are inadequate to the task.

The relation between the public and the private is further explored in Chapter 3, "Wittgenstein on representations, privileged objects and private languages." This chapter, which focuses on the private language argument, shows that this argument does not reduce, as many have objected, to a form of verificationism. The verificationist reading takes the fundamental problem to be an epistemological one that focuses attention on the problem of other minds. But Wittgenstein's concern is to show the inadequacy of the Cartesian picture from the first-person perspective. These passages (PI §243–315) presuppose and draw upon earlier arguments that Wittgenstein has made in the *Investigations*. Not just the rule-following passages, but, more importantly I argue, the early critical discussion of ostensive definition and the role of object as a means of representation. The central point that Wittgenstein is making in the private language argument is that a private act of ostension can no more set a standard of use for a term than a public act of ostensive definition can. He argues this by showing that the Cartesian theory is self-defeating in that it renders the sensation irrelevant to its expression in behavior or report even for the subject, making "it" irrelevant to the life of the subject.

Wittgenstein's critiques of denotational theories of meaning and the Cartesian theory of mind identify a single deep philosophical problem – "the problem of normative similarity," as I call it. It concerns our most basic judgments of identity and reidentification over time. It emerges in three forms in Part I of the *Investigations*, giving rise to the three most discussed passages and arguments in Wittgenstein's work. These are the semantic role of ostensive definition and so reference more generally; the interpretation of rules and so rule-following more generally; and finally the identification of sensations and so consciousness more generally. Seeing these as forms of the same problem enables us to recognize that Wittgenstein develops a distinctive new method of argumentation in dealing with them. This new form of argumentation is designed to show that the very philosophical theories that purport to provide the best solutions to the problem of normative similarity, in its various guises, destroy the possibility of making those very judgments of sameness. The theories are self-defeating, not because the speaker is caught in a pragmatic contradiction, but because the theories destroy the very phenomena that they were designed to explain. The private language argument and the paradox of interpretation are just such arguments.

There is a justifiable temptation to read Wittgenstein as developing a Kantian response to the overly simplistic, and so vulnerable, Cartesian theory of experience. On this reading, Wittgenstein's grammatical propositions and propositions that hold fast (in *On Certainty*) are akin to Kant's a priori synthetic judgments, expressing the necessary applicability of concepts to sensory experience and action. Though there are important affinities between Wittgenstein and Kant, this standard way of characterizing them mislocates them. In "Wittgenstein, Kant, and the 'metaphysics of experience,'" I argue that it is a mistake to read him as offering such a transcendental philosophy and in particular a mistake to attribute to him a Kantian theory of concepts and experience. Wittgenstein is fundamentally opposed to the picture of mind according to which experience or knowledge is some kind of amalgam of given sensory data and active mental construction or operation. Wittgenstein repudiates the metaphysics of both a Cartesian and a Kantian variety. Grammar, rules, concepts are not the a priori metaphysical or epistemological conditions for the possibility of experience, judgment, and action. Grammatical propositions, rules, and concepts can be abstracted from our ongoing practices, from our language games, but they do not ground those games.

The last two chapters of Part I bring Wittgensteinian themes and arguments to bear on contemporary theories of mind. Chapter 4, "Language learning and the representational theory of mind," is directed to Fodor's language of thought hypothesis and his key argument that language acquisition requires an innate language of thought. Since that paper was published in 1984, I have added an addendum in which I examine subsequent attempts on Fodor's part to evade the difficulties that beset this theory. Two problems in particular command Fodor's attention since his initial articulation of the representational theory of mind. These are the problem of background belief and the problem of mental content. While he accepts a holistic conception of belief, he insists upon an atomistic theory of meaning for mental representations. His task is one of showing his representational theory of mind and the language of thought hypothesis can successfully accommodate these two views. What is especially striking is that Fodor is led increasingly to acknowledge the explanatory work done by the environment within which the subject acts rather than by the cognitive machinery of the subject. Not only are there the causal relations that the individual has to properties instantiated in the world, causal relations that are held to fix the semantic content of Mentalese, there is the social environment. Even the most austere version of the representational theory of mind is forced to turn important explanatory work over to the natural and social environments, explanatory work that initially was to be provided by the individual's cognitive machinery.

The argument of Chapter 5, "Social norms and narrow content," is continuous with the criticisms of the representational theory of mind offered in Chapter 4. It looks closely at the difficulties in maintaining an internalist and individualist conception of mental states and their content. These difficulties have led advocates of cognitivism to the introduction of a distinction between narrow mental content and wide mental content. Narrow content is "in the head" content, content that is available as the local cause of behavior. Wide content implicates the semantic relations that mental representations have to the world. Two strategies, one atomistic and the other holistic, have been developed in the attempt to preserve a role for mental content in the explanations of behavior. One of these is Fodor's atomistic causal theory of denotation and the other is the holistic conceptual-role semantics as defended by Ned Block and Brian Loar. Both strategies fail, suggesting that there is something wrong in principle with attempts to understand mental content in a wholly individualist and internalist manner. But the point of this chapter is not just to show the difficulties facing narrow content, but to defend a richer conception of the semantic relations implicated in the notion of wide content. This makes Tyler Burge's argument against individualism especially interesting and important. Burge has argued that the semantic properties of mental content include not only reference and truth conditions but social norms as well as the linguistic division of labor. This chapter defends this conclusion while nonetheless criticizing the thought experiments Burge uses to reach it. Thought experiments can be used or interpreted in more than one way. What matters is the explanation given for the semantic "facts" that the thought experiment is held to reveal.

Burge's explanation is that social norms of understanding are required to individuate the beliefs that individuals hold. This can be shown, Burge argues, by considering how beliefs are individuated under differing social conditions. A person and his doppelganger can be molecule-for-molecule identical and yet hold beliefs that differ in their semantic value solely in virtue of differences in their community. Both might believe, for instance, that sofas are religious artifacts, yet for one this is false and he holds idiosyncratic views about certain pieces of furniture while for the other this belief is true, for in his community sofas really are religious artifacts. This, however, does not provide a satisfying explanation of why social norms are necessary to the individuation of an individual's beliefs nor why one couldn't preserve a place for narrow content in terms of the way in which the individual understands the expressions he uses, the "cognitive value," as Burge puts it, that the individual places on his conception of sofas. Why couldn't an individual have a fully idiosyncratic set of beliefs that would set him at odds with his community and make communication difficult? Looking at the matter in this way might well lead one to think that social norms are, in effect, homophonic and converging cognitive values placed by the individual members of the community on their conceptions of things.[2] Such convergence would certainly be necessary for communication and so for social life, but it doesn't seem to eliminate a substantial explanatory role for cognitive value, or narrow content. Burge's failure to close off this construal of the relation between the individual and the community is a serious weakness in his defense of the social dimension of mental content.

Wittgenstein's criticisms of both denotational theories of language and Cartesian theories of mind lead him to identify, as a fundamental philosophical error, the failure to recognize the normative dimension of language and mind. On his diagnosis, philosophers have mistakenly treated norms as metaphysical claims. This is how otherwise banal ordinary statements can be transformed into metaphysical pictures of a deep underlying reality hidden behind the everyday surface. The crucial divide, for Wittgenstein, is not between different kinds of objects, minds, and bodies or meanings and words, but between events and actions that are normatively structured and those that are not and between norms and empirical propositions. This is the real point of continuity between Wittgenstein and Kant, the distinction between "is" and "ought," between norms and facts. Language and mind are normatively structured. Learning to participate in language games is acquiring a human mind. Our psychology is not the workings of an autonomous interior arena.

Part II "A new direction" turns to the positive picture of language and mind that grows out of Wittgenstein's diagnosis of philosophical illusion. Many commentators find this description of what Wittgenstein is doing objectionable. By his own metaphilosophical remarks, he offers no theses, only criticism and diagnosis of fallacious or misplaced forms of theorizing. I think, however, the view that his work is purely critical and negative is a mistake. He does not offer theories of language and meaning, of mind or of knowledge. None of these can be made the subject of theory. Nonetheless, a positive, and alternative, picture of our situation in the world and the use of language emerges through his critiques of the tradition and the diagnoses and descriptions he arrays in his attempts to undermine particular philosophical theories. Wittgenstein is struck, it seems to me, by the extent to which we are like his builders (despite their unrealistically impoverished language game) rather than logicians or scientists. The complex and sophisticated normative structure of the language games of the logician and scientists rests on a bedrock of shared primitive techniques acquired through training. Wittgenstein, I argue in the chapters of Part II, identifies both a social dimension of language games and initiate learning (that is, the training of the complete novice) as elements critical to a full understanding of language and mind.

The opening chapter of Part II, "Rules, community and the individual," provides the kind of argument and explanation that is lacking in Burge's account for why there is a social dimension to language. Here I argue that Wittgenstein defends a version of the so-called "community view" of rule-following, a position I now prefer to call a "social view" in order to distinguish it from those versions of the community view that are overly reductionist. Such reductionist versions state that the normativity of a practice, that is, the very distinction between correct and incorrect moves in the language game, is a matter of what the majority of the community do and say, as a matter of fact. This "majoritarian" view can be understood in different ways. As an epistemological thesis, it states that the correctness of judgments is to be justified by appeal to majority practice. As a semantic claim, it states that the meaning of judgments is to be given in terms of how the majority speak. The semantic claim is obviously false, and is one that Wittgenstein goes out of his way on several occasions to disavow (cf. RFM III.65; VI.23, 49). There is clearly a difference between saying that $12 \times 12 = 144$ and saying that most people agree that $12 \times 12 = 144$. We do not mean, by what we say, that the majority would agree with it. Neither is Wittgenstein saying that the correctness of a judgment is warranted by its being in agreement with what the majority says or does. How we go about justifying or assessing a judgment is not by whether it conforms to the majority practice. Conformity is not a justification, but conformity within bedrock practices is necessary for the possibility of engaging in the language games of justification and knowledge.

Though such strongly reductionist versions are mistaken, nonetheless there is an ineliminable social dimension to rule-following, or at least "bedrock" rule-following. Wittgenstein's response to the Paradox of Interpretation is that there are certain ways of going on that are not a matter of interpretation but of acting as a matter of course or blindly (not, that is, from one's conception or interpretation of a rule or principle). Such matter-of-course behavior acquires its normative dimension in being shared with others to constitute an obvious way of judging and acting. Such a shared background of bedrock practices is logically necessary for the possibility of genuine disagreement, hypothesis formation and justification, or idiosyncratic belief. Without a background of certain agreement, there is logically no space for justification, doubt, challenge, or dispute. Without some things taken for granted, as beyond dispute, there is no logical space for making a substantive claim, forming a desire or intention, entering a challenge, citing evidence, and the like. This is not a psychological claim about us. It is a logical claim about what is required for the concepts of "claim," "desire," and the rest to have an application. Wittgenstein's grammatical investigations are inquiries into the background against which, and in virtue of which, our normatively structured actions and judgments can be made. The background consists in our shared judgments of normative similarity with respect to salient objects and properties in the world, going on in the same way over time, and experiencing sensations. "This agreement of humans that is a presupposition of logic," Wittgenstein maintains, "is not an agreement in opinions, much less in opinions on questions of logic" (RFM VI.49; also see RFM III.70; VI.21; VII.9). Agreements in bedrock practices and judgments are not to be understood as widely held hypotheses about the nature of logic or mathematics or naming. Conformity and agreement in our bedrock judgments (of acting with right though without justification) is indispensable, because, first, it constitutes the bedrock certainty that is logically required for any normative action, and second, as part of Wittgenstein's critique of the Cartesian model of mind, the individual in isolation hasn't the cognitive and epistemic resources to provide this bedrock for herself.

The other side of this "social view" of rule-following and meaning is that language must be learned. Chapter 7, "The philosophical significance of learning in the later Wittgenstein," argues for just this claim and the claim that the process of language learning itself is constitutive of what the individual learns. To understand these claims properly, it is necessary to distinguish between what I call "the domain of the novice" and "the domain of the master" in Wittgenstein's discussions of naming, rule-following, and experiencing. As I have already brought out in this Introduction, Wittgenstein does distinguish between bedrock practices and the more sophisticated practices that presuppose bedrock practices. More sophisticated practices include all second-order practices, such as naming, justifying, or evaluating actions and judgments, describing sensations, doubting claims, forming hypotheses or interpretations. The importance of mentioning these practices as "more sophisticated" ones is that philosophers often construe some or all of these as foundational to all linguistic practices or constitutive of all practices. Wittgenstein's view is clearly otherwise. These are the sorts of things that a fully competent master of the language can engage in. They belong to the domain of the master of language. The domain of the novice, that is, the individual who has not acquired a language, who is an initiate learner, cannot make use of such devices as these, for they all already presuppose the very mastery that is the goal of the initiate learner. The novice is trained in the very techniques of application that provide the cognitively substantive background against which hypotheses can be formed, names can be given, interpretations evaluated, and sensations described. Since these techniques of application themselves can only be shown, that is, they cannot be described by a set of explicit rules or propositions, learning through training, that is, learning to act before acquiring understanding, is acquiring the background skills and judgments presupposed by our sophisticated practices. The process of learning is training in techniques, and in this sense the process of learning is constitutive of what is learned. Wittgenstein's numerous, and increasingly frequent, appeals to child learning is thus more than a heuristic or expository device for laying bare the grammar of our concepts. Learning plays an explanatory role as well as a constitutive one with respect to our bedrock practices and concepts.

Mastery of language requires that we mutually acknowledge necessary connections among our judgments and actions. The nature of necessity, that is, the "hardness of the logical must," and its relation to the obvious is the subject of Chapter 8, "The etiology of the obvious." One of the disquieting features of the later Wittgenstein, at least from a Quinean perspective, is his continued insistence on a philosophically important distinction between grammatical propositions and empirical propositions and with this the recognition of a place for necessity that is not merely pragmatic. Wittgenstein draws this distinction in various ways, as between conceptual matters and empirical matters, between grammar and moves within a language game, between what is necessary ("what must be the case") and what is experiential. And though none of these is the distinction between analytic truths and empirical truths, their affinity to this distinction is patent.

No one with Quinean scruples about analyticity can be very happy about Wittgenstein's insistence on these distinctions and their centrality in his conception of the philosophical endeavor. "The etiology of the obvious" takes up this conflict between the later Wittgenstein and Quine, bringing out important similarities in their argumentative strategies that suggest that one should find greater similarities in their conceptions of language and mind. Yet that is not the case. Both offer indeterminacy arguments. Both repudiate Cartesianism and metaphysics in general. But the significance of these critical points differs in striking ways for these two philosophers. The differences need to be understood in terms of the philosophical myth each introduces to illuminate the working of language. Quine's myth of the situation of the radical translator must be contrasted with that of Wittgenstein's builders. There is a certainty in the builder's language game that forever eludes the radical translator (and we are all in the situation of the radical translator). For Wittgenstein, necessity is not just a well-entrenched or highly favored empirical hypothesis, but part of the normative constraints without which language games cannot exist. As the reader can easily guess by now, my reading of Wittgenstein seeks to explain the distinctions aligned above in terms of a fundamental distinction between a norm and an empirical claim (or other move within a language game). Quine rejects metaphysics, meaning, and necessity in favor of a homogeneous and unitary system of empirical beliefs, where items are distinguished only in terms of how entrenched they are within the system.[3] Wittgenstein rejects metaphysical explanations of meaning and necessity, but retains what he sees as a legitimate place for each. Meaning is not a special kind of object but the way in which we can explain the use of words. Necessity is not a metaphysical connector nor a merely psychological or pragmatic feature of language use, but integral to the character of norms or normatively structured practices.

Wittgenstein's hostility to metaphysics and philosophical theorizing extends to psychological theorizing as well, at least psychological theorizing that purports to be scientific. Wittgenstein clearly does not think that problems about the mind that were created by bad philosophical theories can now be adequately addressed through empirical scientific means. Chapter 9, "Wittgenstein's rejection of scientific psychology," focuses on his scepticism about such an empirical project. It is clear that Wittgenstein was influenced by certain psychologists, notably Wolfgang Kohler, William James, and Freud, and was interested in the psychological theories of the day. And, though he held that empirical psychological explanations can be given of our behavior, nonetheless he did not think that psychology was a science. Psychological theory remains too enmeshed in the Cartesian model of mind and so inherits the same conceptual difficulties as that philosophical theory, and its subject matter, on Wittgenstein's view, is not of the right sort for the application of scientific method. Its normative structure does not allow for the successful application of the experimental method. Nor can it allow for the control of a fixed array of variables, the *sine qua non* of the experimental method. In Chapter 9, I pursue one strand in Wittgenstein's criticism of scientific psychology. This concerns the consequences of accepting a holistic conception of belief (or if not holistic, at least a non-atomistic conception). Many philosophers acknowledge the force of anti-atomistic arguments, but they do not all draw the same moral from these arguments. The issue then is to identify what further commitments Wittgenstein has that lead to his scepticism about psychology rather than to a different conception of what scientific psychology can achieve. One obvious commitment is his rejection of mental processes (except for rather shallow instances, like calculating in one's head) and their causal efficacy.

A full treatment, which is not possible in a single chapter, would need to examine Wittgenstein's grounds for this rejection, so counterintuitive to so many. What that full examination would reveal is that such mental-process accounts draw on certain misconceived propositions, such as sensations are private, acts of imagination are voluntary, people act on their intentions and beliefs, and so on. These propositions are misconceived, according to Wittgenstein, because they are taken as empirical claims describing interior states and causes of behavior. In fact, their status as grammatical propositions reveals them to be norms of our psychological language games. They are propositions like "The bishop in a game of chess moves diagonally." This proposition expresses a rule of the game, not an empirical claim about how bishop-shaped figurines move in the world. Sometimes they roll off the table.

The final chapter turns to the psychological theory of concepts and concept development of the Russian psychologist Lev Vygotsky. The interest here lies with the fact that Vygotsky pursued an empirical, scientific understanding of the mind while agreeing with much that can be found in Wittgenstein. So far as we know, the two men, though contemporaries, did not know each other's work. Vygotsky shares with Wittgenstein a suspicion of denotational theories of meaning and language, a rejection of the Cartesian transparency of mind, an emphasis on learning and the developmental character of cognition, and the interpenetration of mind and language, extending his account to include a constitutive role to be played by formal education. Yet Vygotsky retains a place for the psychological reality and causal efficacy of inner mental processes. Indeed Vygotsky was an early cognitivist in his rejection of associationist and behaviorist theories in psychology in favor of cognitively enriched characterizations of higher mental processes.[4] His work inevitably raises an important question for Wittgenstein's nihilistic conclusion with respect to scientific psychology. If one accepts a thoroughgoing critique of traditional theories of language and the Cartesian theory of mind, has one thereby accepted a critique of the possibility of scientific psychology? That is a disturbing implication for many who feel that psychology is now well established as a respectable scientific endeavor. No final resolution of this important matter can be reached in this book. Indeed even the way in which the question is raised is open to justifiable suspicion since it suggests that the expression "psychology" designates a unitary subject matter held to a single explanatory theory or model. Psychology has always been fragmented, and the proper explanatory domain of scientific psychology has always been contested. What we can see from Wittgenstein's suspicions about scientific psychology is that he thought that the normative structuring he identifies in our language games cannot but inform the human mind. It is this normative dimension of the mind as well as his hostility to inner mental processes that lies behind his scepticism. The conceptual confusions that arise from mistaking normative properties for metaphysical ones cannot be resolved or even properly understood through the application of the experimental method.

Part I

Against the philosophic tradition

1 Wittgenstein on representations, privileged objects, and private languages

In this chapter, I shall investigate Wittgenstein's private language argument, that is, the argument to be found in *Philosophical Investigations* §243–315. Roughly, this argument is intended to show that a language knowable to one person and only that person is impossible; in other words, a "language" which another person *cannot* understand isn't a language. Given the prolonged debate sparked by these passages, one must have good reason to bring it up again. I have: Wittgenstein's attack on private languages has regularly been misinterpreted. Moreover, it has been misinterpreted in a way that draws attention away from the real force of his arguments and so undercuts the philosophical significance of these passages.

What is the private language hypothesis, and what is its importance? According to this hypothesis, the meanings of the terms of the private language are the very sensory experiences to which they refer. These experiences are private to the subject in that he alone is directly aware of them. As classically expressed, the premise is that we have knowledge by acquaintance of our sensory experiences. As the private experiences are the meanings of the words of the language, *a fortiori* the language itself is private. Such a hypothesis, if successfully defended, promises to solve two important philosophical problems: It explains the connection between language and reality – there is a class of expressions that are special in that their meanings are given immediately in experience and not in further verbal definition. More generally, these experiences constitute the basic semantic units in which all discursive meaning is rooted. I shall refer to this solution as the thesis of semantic autonomy.[1] This hypothesis also provides a solution to the problem of knowledge. For the same reason that sensory experience seems such an appropriate candidate for the ultimate source of all meaning, so it seems appropriate as the ultimate foundation for all knowledge. It is the alleged character of sensory experience, as that which is immediately and directly knowable, that makes it the prime candidate for both the ultimate semantic and epistemic unit. This I shall refer to as the thesis of non-propositional knowledge (or knowledge by acquaintance).

However, the idea that sensory experiences are supposed to constitute the meanings of the terms of a private language needs explicating, for on the face of it, it is difficult to understand how a red flash, tickle, or pain could *be* a meaning. A clearer way to express this is to say that the sensory experience is *directly* correlated with a term. Making this correlation generate a rule of meaning actually masks two assumptions which explicate how we are to understand such peculiar rules: (1) the *Naming Assumption*: to fix meaning, ostensive baptism of a sensory experience must occur; and (2) the *Consistency Assumption*: in subsequent use, the objects referred to by the term in question must be of the same kind as the object originally baptized.

Wittgenstein's attack on the possibility of a private language focuses on the legitimacy of such rules of meaning. The upshot of his challenge is that this empiricist solution to the problem of relating language to reality and to the problem of knowledge cannot succeed. The mind, Wittgenstein argues, is not the privileged source of either meaning or knowledge. Roughly, Wittgenstein's strategy is a three-stage affair: an attack on the traditional role that ostensive definition is alleged to play in language acquisition, an attack on the idea that representation requires the existence of special privileged objects, and an attack on the attempt to substitute "reference" for "meaning" as the link between the world and ourselves. If Wittgenstein is correct, reference is no better a philosophical tool for solving the problem of our epistemic relation to the world than was meaning. Both founder on a misconception of representation and knowledge.

These are ambitious aims, with far-ranging implications for theory of language, the character of sensory experience, and the structure of knowledge. Meanings aren't "in the head"; sensory experience isn't transparent and simply "given" to the subject; knowledge isn't grounded in sensory experience. These large philosophical claims aren't established by the private language argument alone as an argument separable from the rest of the *Investigations*. As I shall show, the private language argument draws on some of the general arguments concerning the nature of language that are developed much earlier in the *Investigations*. Thus, the rubric "private language argument" is something of a misnomer. Yet the standard interpretation of these passages in the *Investigations* treats the private language argument as a relatively self-contained argument, fit to join the canon of other great philosophical arguments such as the Ontological Argument or Zeno's Paradoxes. As I shall now argue, the private language argument treated in this way loses its philosophical persuasiveness and becomes embroiled in a debate that leads us away from the important issues and into a blind alley.

1 A blind alley: the Consistency Assumption

Norman Malcolm's early interpretation of the private language argument gives clear expression to the idea that private language fails because it only gives seeming rules for consistent usage (cf. Malcolm 1966). The fundamental error of this interpretation lies in casting Wittgenstein's argument against the Consistency Assumption. Not only is this an incorrect interpretation, it cannot demonstrate the inadequacy of a private language.

The standard empiricist approach to the question of private languages is to claim that the subject can ostensively define his primitive terms and proceed to use them in accordance with the private rule, "I shall call this same thing 'S' whenever it occurs." Both the empiricist and his critic agree that a term cannot be a means of representation unless it can be consistently used. The critic charges that it is impossible to determine whether a private term is being used consistently. The best way to characterize this charge against the empiricist is to let the critic – in this case Malcolm – speak for himself:

> Now how is it to be decided whether I have used the word consistently? What will be the difference between my having used it consistently and its *seeming* to me that I have? Or has this distinction vanished? "Whatever is going to seem right to me is right. And that only means that here we can't talk about 'right'" (258). If the distinction between "correct" and "seems correct" has disappeared, then so has the concept *correct*. It follows that the "rules" of my private language are only impressions of rules (259). My impression that I follow a rule does not confirm that I follow the rule, unless there can be something that will prove my impression correct. And the something cannot be another impression—for this would be "as if someone were to buy several copies of the morning paper to assure himself that what it said was true" (265). The proof that I am following a rule must appeal to something *independent* of my impression that I am.
>
> (Malcolm 1966: p. 68)

Malcolm's argument is intended to show that the Consistency Assumption can be satisfied only if there is some independent check on the application of the rule in question – independent, that is, of the subject's say-so. And that is precisely what the private-language user, *ex hypothesi*, cannot have: He can only check his seeming to follow a rule correctly by another *seeming*. But, in this case, the difference between a word's *seeming* to be correctly applied and its *being* correctly applied collapses.[2] With this collapse goes the possibility of determining whether the private "rule" is used consistently.

The well-known empiricist answer is to argue that the subject's memory provides an adequate check on the correct, hence consistent, application of a private term. Against this, Malcolm argues that one must be able to distinguish genuine memory from ostensible memory, and if the is/seems distinction collapses at this level, it likewise collapses at the lower level. If such a distinction cannot be drawn, then (citing Wittgenstein for support) "whatever is going to seem right to me is right. And that only means that here we can't talk about 'right'" (PI §258). The rejoinder of the empiricist is to claim that this objection brings into question the reliability of memory itself, a move which equally undercuts his opponent's position since the general reliability of memory must be presupposed whether the checks in question are the subject's own memory or public checks.

A common response to this defense is to argue that the issue is not the reliability of memory but whether uncheckable checks are checks at all. In other words, the critic raises the question, can the subject's memory, which cannot be checked, serve as a check on his application of rules in his private language?[3]

In the end, this line of argument against memory as an adequate check fails. It fails because, first, it raises the threat of scepticism concerning the reliability of memory. A public language has no greater safeguard against this kind of scepticism than a private language.[4] Second, the position taken concerning "uncheckable checks," namely that these are not genuine checks, makes a stronger demand on the empiricist than many would require of their own position. Many critics of the empiricist agree that, in any justificatory context, the quest for reasons must eventually come to an end. They do not insist that every reason or justification – to be a genuine reason – must itself be susceptible to some independent check. Within any given inquiry there will be assumptions which confer reasonableness on some other belief within that inquiry, but which cannot themselves be justified within that context. This is the bedrock of justification – we finally come to reasonless reasons. The point here is that the critic of the empiricist does not impose such rigid strictures on what is acceptable or justificatory on himself and thus should not object to the empiricist's appeal to uncheckable checks.

This line of debate leads up a blind alley – it diverts attention from the real force of Wittgenstein's arguments without really damaging the empiricist's position.[5] By concentrating on the Consistency Assumption, philosophers have implicitly conceded the more important Naming

Assumption. Yet it is primarily against the Naming Assumption that Wittgenstein directs his attack.

2 Ostensive definition: the Naming Assumption

Wittgenstein's actual strategy is to argue that the Consistency Assumption cannot be satisfied because it is contentless – not because it appeals to uncheckable checks.

In accordance with the Naming Assumption, the empiricist maintains that it is possible for the subject to individuate a particular mental entity – sensation or impression – concentrate his attention on it, and label it. It is then merely a matter of correctly applying the same expression whenever a qualitatively similar entity is present to the subject's consciousness. The empiricist thinks that an act of "private ostensive definition" can fix meaning and set a standard for correct use in the future. The meaning of a symbol is given by that sensation or impression with which it is associated by the subject.

Earlier I separated two strands in this empiricist program, viz. the existence of non-propositional knowledge and the independence of the private terms. These theses are mutually supporting and crucially bound up with the notion of acts of ostension as fundamental to concept formation. Non-propositional knowledge (or knowledge by acquaintance) is that knowledge we acquire of mental states just in virtue of having them. Nothing is known about them; rather they are directly known themselves. They are the basic epistemic units *and* the basic semantic units, for they provide the meanings of primitive terms. This guarantees the independence of these terms. They need not be embedded in a larger linguistic practice in order to be meaningful; no other knowledge or grasp of concepts is required for the acquisition of these expressions. It may be discovered that certain logical relationships hold between these terms (such as, nothing can be red and green in the same place and at the same time), but knowledge of these relationships is irrelevant to grasping the full meaning of a term. For the full meaning is given in an act of pure ostension. Thus, the plausibility of these two theses (non-propositional knowledge and semantic autonomy) is bound up with the plausibility of the claim that ostension is fundamental to concept formation and acquisition.

The argument of PI §259–61 where this issue is taken up has frequently been misconstrued by commentators as attacking the Consistency Assumption in the ways discussed in section 1. The real point of Wittgenstein's argument is to demonstrate that the notion of consistently applying an expression of a private language is *contentless*.

According to the empiricist, the rule for reapplication is generated by the act of private baptism, an act which can be accomplished wholly independently of any knowledge or concept other than the awareness of the particular sensory experience to be labeled. The crucial part of Wittgenstein's argument against this has already been established earlier in the *Investigations* in the attack on the appeal to ostensive definition as basic to determining meaning (PI §28–38). What he intends to show in his critique of private languages is that *private* ostensive definition as a means for generating a language is as *much* a myth as is public ostensive definition. That is, Wittgenstein offers a *general* critique of ostensive definition which he then applies explicitly to private ostension.[6]

This pattern is wholly in keeping with his general strategy for dealing with philosophical problems. The same theses can arise and seem to find support from various sources; this fact requires that any philosophical problem be approached from different perspectives if it is finally to be laid to rest. So in the present case, although the notion that ostensive definition is fundamental to concept formation and language acquisition has already been shown to be mistaken, we are tempted to believe that it must work for our private sensations. Sensations seem to have features which make ostensive definition especially appropriate. Wittgenstein intends to show that this is mere illusion.

Naming and pointing or inwardly concentrating one's attention are sophisticated acts that can only be successful within a context in which much else is known. When one says "He gave a name to his sensation" one forgets that a great deal of stage setting in the language is presupposed if the mere act of naming is to make sense (PI §257). I shall not review the familiar arguments that Wittgenstein brings against ostension beyond reiterating their conclusion: the use of ostension presupposes linguistic competence and so cannot be the source of that competence.

Having reminded us of the difficulties with ostension and thus already undermined the claim for the autonomy of private terms, Wittgenstein addresses the problem of a private language directly. He shows that the possibility of a private rule for correct application of an expression is an illusion by showing that a private rule is empty. It is empty just because no standard for subsequent namings has been set at the outset, and thus no sense can be made of the claim to continue to use the expression correctly – this is true even if our memory is infallible. Wittgenstein gives this argument in PI §258, a passage which has often been construed as denying that we could tell when a private rule has been correctly applied:

A definition surely serves to establish the meaning of a sign.—Well, that is done precisely by the concentration of my attention; for in this way I impress on myself the connexion between the sign and the sensation.–But "I impress it on myself" can only mean: *this* process brings it about that I remember the connexion right in the future. *But in the present case I have no criterion of correctness* (my emphasis).

(PI 258)

In other words, an act of ostension can neither give meaning to a sign nor generate a standard for reapplication. Without such a criterion or standard, the notion of getting the connexion right is empty. The Naming Assumption degenerates into idle ceremony.

As one can now see, this argument has nothing to do with the reliability of memory or the need for independent checks. Even more significantly, these grounds for rejecting a private language have nothing to do with the privacy of the language per se. He is showing that private ostension is no exception to his general critique of ostension.

The strength of Wittgenstein's critique of ostensive definition lies not only in the criticisms he makes but also in his explanation of why ostension appears to be such a plausible mechanism for acquiring language. In the interest of giving such an explanation, he distinguishes between *ostensive definition* and *ostensive teaching* (PI §6). As has been stated, far from providing the basic mechanism for fixing meaning and generating a language, ostensive definition doesn't play this role, so how is the acquisition to language to be explained? Wittgenstein suggests that the role traditionally attributed to ostensive definition is actually played by ostensive teaching:

> An important part of the training [in the master of language] will consist in the teacher's pointing to the objects, directing the child's attention to them, and at the same time uttering a word....(...I say that it will form an important part of the training, because it is so with human beings; not because it could not be imagined otherwise.) This ostensive teaching of words can be said to establish an association between the word and the thing.

(PI §6)

In other words, ostensive teaching is a causal process which brings about an association between an object and a sign. Animals as well as human beings are susceptible to this kind of teaching. The result of this teaching (or conditioning) is the ability to parrot, but it does not (in itself) effect an understanding of the sign. For this, ostensive teaching must be coupled with a training in the use of the sign. And the use of a sign is determined by the practice or custom in which the sign is embedded. Thus, ostensive teaching, which helps effect understanding, also presupposes a public language, though the child does not know it. The success of ostensive definition, on the other hand, does require individual mastery of a language: "One has already to know (or be able to do) something in order to be capable of asking a thing's name" (PI §30). Thus, both ostensive definition and ostensive training presuppose communal practices and customs, though in different ways.

The explanation for the mistaken role of ostensive definition should be patent. Empiricists conflated ostensive definition and ostensive teaching. As ostensive teaching can be characterized as a kind of stimulus–response training, instances of this can be isolated from any mention of social conventions or customs. Also the pupil need have no knowledge of these customs. This permits the autonomy the empiricists require. On the other hand, in explaining how this in itself allegedly generates meaning, competence-presupposing ostensive definition is smuggled in. In this way, causal and semantic features have been mismatched. Ostensive teaching does not locate the place of use for a word though it may be used as a teaching aid in training the child to master a practice; ostensive definition, on the other hand, fixes the place, but it cannot explain naive language acquisition nor how the place was prepared. Both, however, in different ways, presuppose a context of language mastery.

3 "Subjective justification": the role of samples

Despite the criticism of ostensive definition, its allure is great. It still seems that mental phenomena are special in a way that would exempt their ostensive baptism from the general objections to ostensive definition. In pressing the argument against the specialness of mental phenomena (i.e., their alleged epistemic transparency as a mark of their peculiar nature), Wittgenstein does seem to argue that any genuine justification for applying an expression must be independent of the subject's memory; in other words, that a "subjective justification" is not only not special, it isn't even a justification. This argument seems to appear in the notoriously troubling PI §265:

> But justification consists in appealing to something independent.—
> "But surely I can appeal from one memory to another. For example, I don't know if I have remembered the time of departure of a train right and to check it I call to mind how a page of the time-table looked. Isn't it the same here?"—No; for this process has got to produce a memory which is actually *correct*. If the mental image of the time-table could not itself be *tested* for correctness, how could it confirm the correctness of the first memory?
>
> (PI §265)

Quite rightly, I think, this passage has puzzled commentators. Wittgenstein seems to have abandoned his usual modes of argument and to have cast doubt on the reliability of memory.[7] However, for a number of reasons which I shall make clear shortly, I do not think that this is the correct interpretation, although I grant that it is the most obvious. It is so out of step with the rest of the *Investigations* that alternative interpretations must at least be examined.[8]

The key to an alternative interpretation of Wittgenstein's rejection of memory as the standard of correctness is PI §56, where he first introduces memory as a check:

> "And if we bear it in mind thus it comes before our mind's eye when we utter the word. So, if it is always supposed to be possible for us to remember it, it must be in itself indestructible."—But what do we regard as the criterion for remembering it right?—When we work with a sample instead of our memory there are circumstances in which we say that the sample has changed colour and we judge of this by memory. But can we not sometimes speak of a darkening (for example) of our memory-image? Aren't we as much at the mercy of memory as of a sample? (For someone might feel like saying: "If we had no memory we should be at the mercy of a sample.")...Suppose that the colour struck you as brighter on one day than on another; would you not sometimes say: "I must be wrong, the colour is certainly the same as yesterday"? This shows that we do not always resort to what memory tells us as the verdict of the highest court of appeal.
>
> (PI §56)

There is a striking similarity between PI §265 and PI §56 – both raise the issue of appealing to memory as a way of justifying the use of a word; both concern the role of the memory-image as a means of representation (or standard for correctness); both are preceded by a discussion of the view that the bearer of a word is the meaning of the word, a view which (as we have seen) gives pre-eminence to the role of ostensive definition. Thus, there is reason to believe that an examination of PI §56 may well shed light on PI §265.

Although the critique of ostensive definition as basic to language acquisition shows that an object does not bear a linguistic role on its face, this does not mean that an object cannot play a linguistic role. Objects can, though this fact has generated some of the more critical mistakes made by philosophers concerning the nature of representation. A color chart (cf. PI §51), the standard meter in Paris (cf. PI §50), or a leaf schema (cf. PI §73–4) all can serve as a means of representation; that is, as a standard for the correct application of a term. To say that an object is a means of representation (or a sample) rather than what is *represented* is to give that object a symbolic function and to give it a special epistemic status. Wittgenstein's main point is that a color chart or the standard meter has this role in virtue of the way it is used in a language game,[9] *not* in virtue of any peculiar properties intrinsic to this piece of cardboard (a color chart) or to this piece of metal (the standard meter). The mistake is to think that this piece of cardboard (with its colored squares) must have certain special properties without which it could not be a means of representation but only something to be represented.

It is claimed that in order to be a means of representation, the sample must be indestructible, otherwise the meaning of "red," "black" etc. would vaporize in a flame. This inference, Wittgenstein argues, is fallacious: It is the result of turning a truism into an apparently deep metaphysical truth. It involves a move from the truism that if this particular piece of cardboard did not exist, we couldn't use it as a means of representation, to the metaphysical truth that this piece of cardboard must be indestructible. (Of course, nothing so mundane and obviously combustible as a piece of cardboard can be indestructible, and so we are led to hypothesize Tractarian objects or we turn away from destructible physical objects to mental entities.) But this truism is a comment, not on the indestructibility of this color chart, but on our method of representation. This piece of cardboard is a means of representation and as such is part of our language:

> And to say "if it did not *exist*, it could have no name" is to say as much and as little as: if this thing did not exist, we could not use it in our language-game—What looks as if it *had* to exist, is part of the language. It is a paradigm in our language-game; something with which comparison is made. And this may be an important observation; but it is none the less an observation concerning our language-game—our method of representation.
>
> (PI §50)

To understand fully the point Wittgenstein is making here we need to understand the metamorphosis whereby a truism is converted into a profound metaphysical truth. This metamorphosis is achieved through a deep-seated commitment to the thesis that the ultimate units of meaning (like ultimate epistemic units) are autonomous and self-contained. Indeed this is one of the theses distinguished above as involved in a theory of private meaning. Once again we see that a private language is just a special case of certain claims about language.

It is this deep-seated commitment that Wittgenstein is intent on exposing and debunking. This began with the critique of ostensive definition and continues with the examination of the role samples play. An object can only play this linguistic role if it is used as such within a language game. It is only within a language game – a public communal practice – that an object can take on a representative function, and precisely what that function is can only be shown by how the object is used. This is what Wittgenstein is drawing attention to when he claims that the truism says something about our method of representation and not about the nature of the object itself. This is further buttressed by pointing out that the very same object could play quite different roles in a language game, e.g. the piece of cardboard used as a color chart or as a pattern for mosaics or as a list of colors no self-respecting artist would use or...(PI §53); and the role it does play could be achieved by other means, e.g., simply learning to make correct color judgments in appropriate circumstances (PI §54). Thus, the object used as a sample is neither sufficient nor necessary for the practice; no object is special or privileged in and of itself.

But it may be felt that these objections show that the indestructible source of meaning cannot be a physical object, that we must look to the mind, and in particular to memory, for the source of the indestructible bearers of meaning. Wittgenstein's immediate response is that the memory-image is in no different or better position than public objects: "...we do not always resort to what memory tells us as the verdict of the highest court of appeal," he concludes in PI §56. The mistake was not in misidentifying the privileged objects (memory-images rather than cardboard samples are privileged), but in believing that there must be privileged objects at all, a "highest court of appeal." The difficulty with the memory-image as the privileged means of representation is not the problem of the reliability of memory (a sceptical argument), but the illusory search for an indestructible bearer of meaning which functions as the point at which all justification must terminate. That a memory-image is in no better position than any ordinary sample is shown by the commonplace that under certain circumstances ostensible memory claims can be overridden – memory is neither especially vulnerable nor especially strong.

This, it seems to me is important background for understanding the argument of PI §265–8. As PI §56 suggests, our *ordinary* use of memory indicates no intrinsic epistemic specialness which makes memory the natural place to terminate all chains of justification. Despite these mundane considerations, philosophers have perennially thought the mind a special place with special privilege. In PI §265ff., Wittgenstein takes up the issue of the alleged privilege of the memory-image as a means for representation. Just as Wittgenstein argued that private ostension is no better than public ostension (an attack on the thesis of non-propositional knowledge), so he argues that a private sample, or means of representation, is no better than a public sample (an attack on the thesis of semantic autonomy). Indeed if we artificially isolate the memory-image and the role it can play in understanding and justification, not merely is it not stronger than a public sample, it cannot play the role of representation at all.

An object is used as a means of representation if it plays a certain role in a language game – a role which can only be understood within its proper context. In attempting to characterize the memory-image as privileged, the proponents of private language strip away the very context that would enable the memory-image to function as a representation. Wittgenstein's point is not that memory is especially vulnerable (that would transform his argument into a general sceptical attack on the reliability of memory), but that the memory-image, when so abstracted from any context, cannot function as a means of representation and so a standard of correctness. The object does not carry this special role within itself, as it were, but only in a context of use. It is for this reason that the memory-image cannot be a test for correctness. This point is elaborated in PI §266:

> I can look at the clock to see what time it is: but I can also look at the dial of a clock in order to guess what time it is; or for the same purpose move the hand of the clock till its position strikes me as right. So the look of a clock may serve to determine the time in more than one way.
>
> (PI §266)

Here Wittgenstein doesn't deny that the look of a clock can be used to determine the time; he does deny that the look of the dial itself determines *only* one way to use it. The second point that he is making is that certain of the uses are derivative, and can only serve to determine the time because of their relation to the basic use of the clock to tell time. In the same way, the memory-image could be used in more than one way and more than one memory could be used to the same end (imagining the time-table or seeing the platform clock as the train pulls out in one's mind's eye). There is nothing intrinsic to the memory-image that ensures its serving a particular role.

What, then, does transform an object, or a memory-image, into a sample, a part of language? Ostensive definition cannot achieve this; and we now see that there are no privileged objects. For Wittgenstein, the answer has already been developed. In the absence of objects with mystical properties and magical acts of pure ostension, there are only human practices and ways of acting. It is our interaction with each other and the world that provides the context in which objects can be used as samples. The important consequence of this for the use of memory-images as samples is that the use must be derivative, i.e., there must be a public standard, one that is expressed in our actions and practices. Thus, using the look of a clock to guess the time (PI §266), imagining justifying the choice of dimensions for a bridge (PI §267), and remembering the look of a time-table (PI §265) all are parasitic on public practices.

This line of thought can easily be confused with the more familiar sceptical line of reasoning. Perhaps it could be argued that Wittgenstein himself has not adequately distinguished them. Nevertheless, these two lines of argument – the sceptical argument and the attack on epistemically privileged objects – are distinct, and the attack on memory as privileged is not only consonant with these troublesome passages (PI §265ff.), but it is in harmony with the whole tenor of the *Investigations*.

4 "Not part of the mechanism": the appeal to reference

The arguments of sections 2 and 3 point to the same general conclusion: Public practices are fundamental. Without a public practice, ostension is futile gesturing. Without a public practice, a "sample" is a meaningless piece of cardboard or a passing image. The natures of understanding and representation preclude the possibility of a private language.

Nevertheless, the philosopher is still drawn to the idea that such a language is possible, at least in a modified sense. The modified version acknowledges the force of the arguments against semantic autonomy, arguments against the idea that there could be private unteachable meanings; it refuses, however, to give up the idea that the individual subject has non-propositional knowledge of his inner life, that the referent of the sensation-term is knowable to him alone, even though the meaning is fixed by public and social criteria. As one defender of this view puts it, "the word 'pain' simply means 'sensation of a type which has such and such teaching links'" (Donagan 1966). So if, unknown to us, and perhaps unknowably to us, the same teaching links pointed to different kinds of sensation in different people, those differences would not be picked up in the meaning of the word "pain."[10]

Wittgenstein introduces this modified version for examination by asking:

> Or is it like this; the word "red" means something known to everyone; and in addition, for each person, it means something known only to

him? (or perhaps rather: it refers to something known only to him).

(PI §273)

What Wittgenstein attempts to show (PI §270–315) is that this appeal to private reference, despite appearances to the contrary, is as vacuous as the appeal to private meaning: "a wheel that can be turned though nothing else moves with it, is not part of the mechanism" (PI §271). To show that private reference is "not part of the mechanism," he must show that it is rooted in a profoundly misguided conception of sensations. The argument of these passages, it seems to me, moves through three stages: First, Wittgenstein shifts the burden of proof to those who think appeal to private reference is obviously helpful:

> Of course, saying that the word "red" "refers to" instead of "means" something private does not help us in the least to grasp its function; but it is the more psychologically apt expression for a particular experience in doing philosophy. It is as if when I uttered the word I cast a sidelong glance at the private sensation, as it were in order to say to myself: I know all right what I mean by it.
>
> (PI §274)

Second, he gives a characterization of sensations that undercuts the alleged imaginability of many Cartesian thought experiments, thought experiments that are intended to show that reference is indeed private. Finally, he shows that what made these thought experiments seem possible is what renders the private referent completely vacuous. In all of this, he combats the idea that sensation can be disassociated from behavior and the reactive context in which the sensation is embedded.

Talk of reference is not ordinarily troublesome and is perfectly useful (e.g., "I was referring to the vase in the corner, not that one"). But ordinary reference, like ordinary meaning, occurs in a context of mutually accepted practices and beliefs, and can only be understood by looking at the concrete circumstances in which it occurs. There is no general theory of ordinary reference. There are particular explanations (which may, of course, involve generalizations) about particular acts of referring: Reference may be achieved through the use of a definite description, through pointing, through raising an eyebrow, through insinuation, through knowledge of the person referring (*she* must have meant...), and so on. In these respects, ordinary reference is just like meaning. But the defenders of the modified version, then, are not concerned with ordinary reference, but with private reference, with the idea that there is always space for a purely private referring, rooted in the subject's direct unsharable acquaintance with the sensation itself. On Wittgenstein's view, all there is is ordinary reference. The idea that something has eluded capture and can be pinned down only by private reference is an illusion.

If we grant that our experiential expressions have a public use (that is, their ordinary use), then, Wittgenstein asks, "what right have [we] to speak in this sense [i.e., of a private reference as well] of a representation or piece of information – if these words were rightly used in the first case?" (PI §280). This question demands an answer, as one has to work to create the climate in which the need for a private language is felt:

> Look at the blue of the sky and say to yourself "How blue the sky is!"—When you do it spontaneously—without philosophical intentions—the idea never crosses your mind that this impression of colour belongs only to you. And you have no hesitation in exclaiming that to someone else.
>
> (PI §275)

These reminders apply not only to color and other "secondary qualities," but also to paradigmatic sensations such as pain. Just as we react to the color of the sky, so we react to the pain of the person. The natural home of sensations and feeling is the person who is fully part of the public domain. But these remarks simply won't satisfy the adherent of private sensations, for such claims really seem to be but a thinly disguised version of behaviorism. So long as there can be pain without pain-behavior and the behavior without pain, it seems that there must be room for private reference. It is this that Wittgenstein challenges.

The central claim in Wittgenstein's account of pain (and so sensation generally) is that pain is *part of a reactive context*. This reactive context includes behavioral, psychological, and circumstantial factors. These factors are all constitutive of pain – they are not external, *accidentally* associated features. Yet on the thesis that sensations are private, even on the modified version, all these features can only be accidentally related to the sensation itself. Since this view does not accord with our ordinary experience with pain (whether our own or another's), some grounds must be given. And these grounds are the alleged imaginability of pain's separability from all these "external, public" factors:

> Couldn't I imagine having frightful pains and turning to stone while they lasted?
>
> (PI §283)

Such thought experiments are crucial to sustaining the idea that mental phenomena are essentially private. They form an indispensable part of Descartes' argument for mind–body dualism and for the epistemological dualism (between the certain and the probable, the given and the inferred) with which it is closely connected. Descartes tells us that:

> I shall consider myself as having no hands, no eyes, no flesh, no blood, nor any senses, yet falsely believing myself to possess all these things...
>
> (Descartes 1972: p. 148)

> I consider that I possess no sense; I imagine that body, figure, extension, movement and place are but the fictions of my mind.
>
> (Descartes 1972: p. 149)

The tradition of using such imaginings in philosophical arguments continues unabated: Imagine that you are a brain in a vat, imagine that you see through someone else's eyes, imagine that a stone feels frightful pains. Well, can I really imagine such things?

Wittgenstein calls into question these imaginings; his point is that they are not so easy as is supposed. And the difficulty in imagining these arises not only from the third-person perspective but from the *first-person perspective* as well. The two are closely connected and in displaying the difficulties in imagining a stone to feel frightful pain, Wittgenstein discloses the difficulties in imagining a stone in pain. Difficulties for the third-person perspective have their reverberations in the first-person perspective.

The persuasiveness of these thought experiments turns, to a great extent, on the fact that they are so seriously underdescribed. I am asked to imagine that a stone feels the same pain as I do when I miss a nail and smash my thumb with the hammer. The stone does not jerk its hand away, dropping the hammer; it does not feel weakened and nauseated; tears do not come to its eyes; a cry isn't torn from its throat – it just feels the pain. The pain is the essential thing, all the rest merely the external accoutrements of pain. But once all these "accoutrements" have been stripped away, what am I to imagine? It is not sufficient merely to say the words "The stone feels pain." Is it supposed to be like experiencing pain even though one is paralyzed; but even here there will be internal organic change, tears brought to the eyes, a constriction of the throat and jaws, etc. And if we say that the person is so severely paralyzed that there are no physiological or behavioral reactions at all, this case will be as difficult as that of the stone. The only recourse at this point is to maintain that it is obvious what is meant, that it requires no elaboration – the stone feels what I feel when I am in pain. But this is not as helpful as it looks, for to assert identity between what a stone feels and what I feel, I must eliminate all that is constitutive of the ordinary pain situation. I must make myself like a stone in order to establish some point of similarity between myself and the stone. This leads into the same difficulties that appeal to this obvious "truth" was supposed to solve. The pain is something completely disconnected from the ordinary ways in which we talk about it and experience it. But "if I assume the abrogation of the normal language game with the expression of a sensation, I need a criterion of identity for the sensation" (PI §288). I need some extraordinary means of identifying the pain, as only this will make it something that could sensibly be attributed to a stone, namely, to that which involves the total "abrogation of the normal language game." That extraordinary means is pure reference. The result of this, Wittgeinstein argues, is to render the sensation *irrelevant to the person who has it*. The "sensation" is reduced to a "mere ornament." This is the argument of the "beetle in the box" passage.

The "beetle in the box" language game exemplifies the modified version of the private language. The word "beetle" has a public use but the object referred to is private to each individual. Here is the passage:

> Suppose everyone had a box with something in it: we call it a "beetle". No one can look into anyone else's box, and everyone says he knows what a beetle is only by looking at *his* beetle.—Here it would be quite possible for everyone to have something different in his box. One might even imagine such a thing constantly changing.—But suppose the word "beetle" had a use in these people's language—If so it would not be used as the name of a thing. The thing in the box has no place in the language-game at all; not even as a *something*; for the box might even be empty.—No, one can "divide through" by the thing in the box, it cancels out, whatever it is.
>
> That is to say: if we construe the grammar of the expression of sensation on the model of "object and designation" the object drops out of consideration as irrelevant.
>
> (PI §293)

Traditionally, commentators have interpreted Wittgenstein to be endorsing the view that the experience of pain "drops out as irrelevant," that this expresses *his own* view of pain. But it is not Wittgenstein's view of consciousness that threatens to eliminate sensations, but the Cartesian theory. The "paradox" of the Cartesian theory of consciousness, as Wittgenstein calls it (PI §304), is that by giving pre-eminence to the private sensation, the theory eliminates sensations. The "beetle in the box" passage displays this self-defeating character of the Cartesian position.

Following a typical argumentative strategy, Wittgenstein offers a simplified language game that captures the relevant features of the philosophical theory in question. In PI §293, we are asked to consider a language game in which the word "beetle" refers to something known and knowable to the subject alone while nonetheless having a public use. The beetle–"beetle" relationship is held to be that of the "object and designation" model. Indeed the "object and designation" model is necessary to support the idea that the beetle is an object in its own right separately from the circumstances of which it is only accidentally a part. Yet upon closer examination, it becomes clear that this model cannot apply to the beetle case. Precisely because the beetle itself is wholly disassociated from the use of the word "beetle," what is the beetle or isn't is irrelevant to the use: It "drops out of consideration." That it is wholly disconnected is shown by the fact that the beetle can be anything or nothing without affecting the use of the word; but this is just a way of saying that it is irrelevant to the meaning of "beetle." What this shows is that it cannot be correct to construe the "beetle" language game on the model of "object and designation." On this model, the object is crucial to the use of the designating expression; it makes a difference to the use. So where the putative object makes no difference to the use of a term, it makes no sense to insist that the grammar of the term is that of a designator.[11]

The same internal collapse occurs on the Cartesian theory, based as it is on the "object and designation" model. Wittgenstein very carefully structures the beetle-in-the-box game to exemplify the structure of the modified version of Cartesianism. "Pain," like "beetle," has a public, social use while the pain itself, like the beetle, is known to the individual subject alone. As the argument of PI §293 shows, this very attempt to preserve the special integrity of the pain itself paradoxically results in eliminating pain. The object pain drops out as irrelevant just as the beetle does: It makes no difference whether the pain is an enduring entity, constantly changing, or nothing at all. But if a nothing serves as well as a something, then the object of designation, i.e., that which is supposed to make a difference (indeed all the difference) to the designation, is eliminated. By transforming sensations into such mysterious objects, they are removed from human life.

It is important to note that the pain is eliminated, is rendered irrelevant, not only to others, but to the subject himself. There may be nothing in the box; but whether there is something or nothing makes no difference *even to the person whose box it is*! It is not Wittgenstein who is denying the reality of sensations, but the Cartesian who attempts to construe sensations as isolable entities, the objects of pure reference (or designation). As such objects, the relation between the pain and the array of responses (withdrawal, attempt to flee, wincing, rapid heartbeat) must be purely contingent; all these responses could be removed, and yet pain in all its awfulness remains. This is what Wittgenstein argues can't be so. The attempt to make such private mental entities objects of pure reference renders them "idle," "not a part of the mechanism."[12]

According to Wittgenstein, what lies at the bottom of this is a misguided application of the "object and designation" model. It cannot apply to sensations. Sensations are not objects (which disappear when stripped of their accoutrements), but states of living organisms, states characterized by an array of distinctive responses and reactions. And without the "object and designation" model of sensations, the Cartesian thought experiments cannot be generated; and without the thought experiments, we have no grounds for thinking pain is essentially private and disconnected from circumstances, behavior, physiology, and our natural reactions. The conclusion, then, as Wittgenstein tells us,

> was only that a nothing would serve just as well as something about which nothing could be said. We have only rejected the grammar which tries to force itself on us here.
>
> The paradox disappears only if we make a radical break with the idea that language always functions in one way, always serves the same purpose: to convey thoughts – which may be about houses, pains, good and evil, or anything else you please.

(PI §304)

2 Private states and public practices

Wittgenstein and Schutz on intentionality

According to Schutz, phenomenological investigation tells us that "[i]t is only from the face-to-face relationship, from the common lived experience of the world in the We, that the intersubjective world can be constituted" (Schutz 1967: p. 171). Only through this original shared world do we understand how and why another acts and experiences as he does; or indeed how and why we act as we do. This basic We-relationship is given in the mere fact of being born into the world of directly experienced social reality (Schutz 1967: p. 165). Such comments about a shared everyday world seem to echo Wittgenstein's remarks that "[w]hat has to be accepted, the given, is – so one could say – *forms of life*" (PI II.xi, p. 226) and that human beings "...agree in the *language* they use. That is not agreement in opinions but in form of life" (PI §241).

Here we seem to have philosophers from divergent traditions led to strikingly convergent outlooks. Both find the lived reality of the ordinary social world philosophically central. Wittgenstein's emphasis on the community, on the importance of everyday life, on the notion of a form of life that cannot be captured by any set of principles or propositions, on the importance of context and circumstances in explicating meaning all seem to be reflected in Schutz's descriptions of the face-to-face relationship as constituting a common realm of shared meaning, his emphasis on context and on lived experiences as opposed to what is captured in any set of propositions, and his denial that direct involvement with others involves judgment or inference of any kind. These descriptions of social life suggest a harmony of philosophical outlook. Even so, I shall argue, this striking convergence is only skin deep. Their descriptions of social life are grounded on radically different accounts of intentionality. For Schutz, the intentionality of the social is to be sought beneath the surface; for Wittgenstein, the surface is all there is.

Schutz takes as his project explaining the intentional character of everyday social life in terms of the intentional acts of the individual. Public meaning-contexts are created out of essentially private individual meaning-contexts. He hopes to combine an individualistic conception of meaning and intentionality with a commitment to a communal world of shared meanings. Schutz's account of meaning and intentionality is signifi-cant because it highlights inescapable difficulties for *any* attempt at grounding intersubjectivity on a radical individualism. Indeed Schutz himself acknowledges more than once that he can give no adequate account of how the intentional acts and meaning-conferring acts of the individual make possible a direct face-to-face relationship with another person (cf. Schutz 1967: pp. 97–8 and 165).

Whereas Schutz sets this problem aside, never really confronting it, Wittgenstein would argue that it is ineliminable and insoluble. My purpose, then, is to develop Wittgenstein's critique of this individualistic conception of meaning and intentionality, and for two reasons. First, to bring out how Wittgenstein's original line of argumentation punctures the attractiveness of the individualist assumption. And, second, to show how this critique of individualism prepares the way for an account of intentionality that avoids the conflicts inherent in Schutz's view or any like it. In this way, I hope to make plausible Wittgenstein's view that in this area of philosophy skin-deep is deep enough – nothing has been left out.

1 Schutz's view

For Schutz, all social interaction is ultimately grounded in a basic We-rela-tionship, that is, a living face-to-face relationship in which each partner has "pure awareness of the *presence* of another person" (Schutz 1967: p. 168). What Schutz means by this is that the originating and original social rela-tion is between two people who mutually acknowledge the agency and consciousness of the other through a shared environment and a shared framework of meaning. This shared world grows out of the private experi-ences of each partner that nonetheless "merge" in some sense to create a unity:

> the pure We-relationship, which is the very form of every encounter with another person...is lived through. The many different mirror images of Self within Self are not therefore caught sight of one by one but are experienced as a continuum within a single experience. Within the unity of this experience I can be aware simultaneously of what is going on in my mind and in yours, *living through* the two series as one series – what we are experiencing together.
>
> (Schutz 1967: p. 170)

All other forms of social interaction as well as an intersubjective world presuppose this shared environment and shared framework of meaning, for it is only "from the common lived experience of the world in the We that the intersubjective world can be constituted" (Schutz 1967: p. 171).

For Schutz, then, the We-relationship is the "foundation" for the mundane world and for all social interaction, but this relationship itself, he maintains, is founded upon the subjective, and in two important ways. The first is that, although we are able to observe another's lived experience (Schutz 1967: p. 102), we do so by utilizing "an already established code of interpretation directing us through the bodily movement to the underlying lived experience" (Ibid.: p. 101). What Schutz hopes to convey by this is that though your lived experiences are accessible to me, "the meaning I give to your experiences cannot be precisely the same as the meaning you give to them when you proceed to interpret them" (Ibid.: p. 99). The second grounding in the subjective is that for Schutz all meaning is based upon subjective reflection that is private to the individual.[1] The meaning I give to your experiences in a face-to-face relationship originates within my mind through an act of reflection upon an undifferentiated stream of consciousness.[2] It is this account of meaning that needs elaboration.

Schutz develops his account of meaning in three stages. He begins with the notion of consciousness as a stream of undifferentiated experience passively given. Such experience is literally meaningless. Primordial meaning, i.e., originating meaning, occurs in a spontaneous act of reflection directed toward some part of past passive experience. The very act of reflection confers meaning upon that part of experience that now is differentiated from the rest, seen as "already finished and done with" (Schutz 1967: p. 52). Using these definitions of experience and reflection, Schutz offers a very telling definition of behavior: "'behavior'," he tells us, is "an experience of consciousness that bestows meaning through spontaneous Activity" (Schutz 1967: pp. 55–6) on behavior that otherwise would be meaningless.[3] As I shall bring out later, this is a point of significant contrast with Wittgenstein, for whom the meaning of the behavior is given through its being situated within a specific context and backed by relevant prior socialization.

Next, in his elaboration of behavior, Schutz introduces the notion of a "frame of interpretation." The act of reflection is treated as involving the use of a frame of interpretation: "The 'meaning' of experiences is nothing more, then, than that frame of interpretation which sees them as behavior" (Schutz 1967: p. 57). I think that there is good internal reason for Schutz to introduce this phrase, for it does important philosophical work. The picture that Schutz has given his reader thus far is of meaning as a kind of "spotlight" wherein the spontaneous activity of reflection confers meaning just by "lighting up" a part of experience. Such a picture is highly static; the dynamic and projective aspect of meaning is missing. Just this projective aspect is captured by the notion of a "frame of interpretation," suggestive as it is of an organizing principle or rule of application. What I want to emphasize for now is that the notion of a frame of interpretation is not just another way to talk about the act of reflection. It brings in the projective element necessary to meaning, by providing an interpretation or application for that which is highlighted by reflection.

The final stage of Schutz's account of meaning is a discussion of what he calls "meaning-context," the construction of an object. The meaning-context is a "higher stage of unity within experience" (Schutz 1967: p. 75), in which the separate acts of reflection are synthesized producing an object. Primordial meaning thus provides the basis for developing a meaning-context. A meaning-context, Schutz tells us, is a set of "lived experiences," "lived through in separate steps…" and "then constituted into a synthesis of a higher order, becoming thereby united objects of monothetic attention" (Ibid.: p. 75). This Kantian phrasing is not elaborated upon.

The structure of intentional action mirrors and builds upon that of meaningful experience. Intentional action differs, however, in two important ways from meaningful experience: First, in being spontaneous activity *oriented toward the future*, rather than the active freezing of an element from the past; and, second, in implying a contrast between the action as identified by the intended goal and the completed act itself, a contrast unlike that of the relation between primordial meanings and the construction of meaning-contexts. Each difference points to an element distinctive of action. The first highlights the fact that an intentional state anticipates the future; the second highlights the fact that the intentional state need not be fulfilled (the intentional inexistence of the intentional object).

An action is oriented toward the future in positing a projected act, an act that is to occur. This projected act, or intentional content, is, Schutz tells us, a "phantasy," an "intuitive representation," a "picture in the mind" – different terms with different connotations. All terms are associated with a kind of spontaneous activity of the mind, as though these were *sui generis* productions. The intentional object is a mental picture of some future state of affairs that is produced spontaneously. Each term does its own special work in fleshing out the notion of the intentional object. Calling it a "phantasy" highlights the intentional inexistence of the object, as a phantasy concerns realizing in imagination what has not been achieved in reality. Calling it a "picture of the mind" highlights its being an isolable mental entity fully describable in its own right. And calling it an "intuitive representation" highlights the projective character of the object, that it spontaneously and concretely represents a possible state of affairs.

Just as the act of reflection was incomplete in telling us how meaning was to be conferred upon passive experience (and so a frame of interpretation was introduced to fill the gap), so we need to understand how a mental picture stands in a *projective* relation to a possible future state of affairs. Just what is the relation between the mental picture that is the content of an expectation or intention and a future state of affairs. As with meaning, Schutz introduces a dynamic structure, this time through the metaphor of "map-consulting." Our intentional action is a form of map-consulting wherein we compare our actions as they occur with the instructions given by the map, our phantasy image (Schutz 1967: pp. 63–4). Schutz identifies such map-consulting with conscious action. Unconscious, or non-reflective, "action" is mere behavior, including paradigmatically such things as reflexes (Schutz 1967: p. 57). This reveals Schutz's commitment to the intellectualist idea that meaningfulness is tied to some act of thought such as providing an interpretation or reading a map. So just as Schutz identified being meaningful with having been interpreted (and so was forced to conclude that "mere" experience was meaningless), so he identifies intentional action with interpreted action, or action that has been planned (concluding that all other behavior is something like mere reflex).

To complete the picture Schutz gives us, the intentional state (that is, this state of phantasizing) is the basis on which a meaning-context of action is determined. That higher level meaning-context of conscious action is the act that *actually* fulfills the intentional project itself. It is the completed act that satisfies the phantasy; in satisfying the intentional project, the completed deed thereby "gives unity to all the intentional Acts and all the actions involved in its performance" (Schutz 1967: pp. 75–6). The intentional Acts are the acts of imaging an outcome and the actions are the steps actually taken to realize that outcome. Interestingly what gives meaning to this complex as a whole is not the projected outcome *qua* mental picture but the actual outcome. This makes it even more needful for Schutz to account for the way in which the projected outcome (the phantasy) anticipates (or is otherwise related) to the actual outcome, especially since the projected outcome need not occur at all. Does this mean that the totality of actions taken to realize the goal (though without doing so) are thereby rendered meaningless?

In sum, primordial meaning lies with a spontaneous act of the mind, an act having two aspects. There is the static aspect, in which an element of consciousness is highlighted or a mental picture occurs, and the dynamic aspect, in which the highlighted element is interpreted or the picture applied in action. The more complex meaning-contexts are constructed out of these spontaneous acts, the first through synthesizing separate meaningful experiences into an object and the second through successfully acting in accord with the phantasized map.

2 Wittgenstein's criticisms

The heart of Wittgenstein's criticisms of a Schutz-like conception of meaning and intentionality comes in the central passages of the *Philosophical Investigations*, the passages focusing on private languages and rule-following. I am going to direct these criticisms to the three stages of Schutz's account of primordial meaning. First, Wittgenstein's critique of ostensive definition and private languages tells against Schutz's account of primordial meaning. Second, Wittgenstein's "paradox of interpretation" tells decisively against the role assigned "the frame of interpretation" or "interpretive schemes" by Schutz. Finally, Schutz's views of meaning and intentional action involve certain philosophical illusions, the most impor-tant of which is that "the shadow of the object," as Wittgenstein expresses it, can somehow do what the object cannot.

Meaning

At the core of Wittgenstein's private language argument is his criticism of the idea that a mental act of ostensive definition could fix the meaning of a word and so set the standard for future use. Yet Schutz's "spontaneous act of reflection," which is needed to primitively confer meaning upon experience itself by the very act of differentiating a part of experience is supposed to do just this. It is a clear example of what Wittgenstein sees as an idle ceremony:

> But still I can give myself a kind of ostensive definition.—How? Can I point to the sensation? Not in the ordinary sense. But I speak, or write the sign down, and at the same time I concentrate my attention on the sensation–and so, as it were, point to it inwardly.—But what is this ceremony for? for that is all it seems to be! A definition surely serves to establish the meaning of a sign.—Well, that is done precisely by the concentration of my attention; for in this way I impress on myself the connexion between the sign and the sensation.—But "I impress it on myself" can only mean: this process brings it about that I remember the connexion *right* in the future. But in the present case I have no criterion of correctness. One would like to say: whatever is going to

seem right to me is right. And that only means that here we can't talk about "right."

(PI §258)

The focus of the private language argument is on the very idea that an act of attention could fix meaning at all. But such an act is precisely what Schutz appeals to. The stream of consciousness itself is undifferentiated and meaningless; even to call it a stream of consciousness or experience is misleading, for that is to ascribe a certain significance to it. It is, as Schutz says, ineffable (Schutz 1967: p. 53).

This primordial, meaning-conferring act of reflection cannot, therefore, be an ordinary act of reflection. An ordinary act of reflection requires that we have already distinguished the object or subject matter to be reflected upon, whereas the primordial act is what brings it into being. It does this by differentiating some aspect of our otherwise ineffable "experience," thus implicitly setting a standard of identity for whatever has been singled out (fished, so to speak, from the stream of consciousness). But to set a *standard* of identity is to establish correct and incorrect means of identification and, according to Wittgenstein, nothing in a private act of reflection establishes such a standard or criterion. Meaning has an ineliminable normative dimension. In picking something out, we determine whether subsequent reidentifications can be counted correct or incorrect. What is hard to see is how the sort of acts Schutz describes could constrain future thought or action. Schutz has himself already acknowledged that nothing *in the stream of consciousness* sets a standard. Wittgenstein adds that nothing in an isolated act of mental concentration could set a standard either. Nothing is altered by calling the act an "act of reflection." We will think we have made progress only if we think of this phrase as denoting some mysterious, *sui generis* act about which nothing more can be said. But our inability to say anything further about this act does not arise from its being somehow self-illuminating (for we have no idea of what that is at all), but from the more banal fact that this whole way of thinking about meaning leaves nothing to be said. The whole approach falls apart if pressed; the illusion of signifi-cance can be maintained only by silence (see PI §107, §111, and §196).

What diminishes this sense of the inexplicable character of acts of reflection is that Schutz introduces, without any signposting or explanation, the notion of a "frame of interpretation." Acts of reflection confer meaning upon the meaningless flow of experience in accord with a frame of interpretation. This adds a broadly Kantian flavor to Schutz's account of meaning and in fact changes it. The move is from conceiving of the mind as actively (but inexplicably) shining the light of attention upon a meaning-less flow, and thereby conferring meaning just in the act of distinguishing some part, to conceiving of the mind as having a frame of interpretation which is imposed upon the meaningless, thereby conferring meaning.[4]

But how does this frame of interpretation help us? We are given no idea of what it is, of how it is supposed to be applied, and how in being applied it confers meaning. What it adds, that is wholly missing from the act of reflection account, is an idea of how a standard or norm is to be applied. The very phrase "the frame of interpretation" suggests a dynamic cognitive dimension that hints at the fact that a norm or standard of meaning must guide or direct our actions. The arbitrary quality of spontaneous reflective activity, in which aspects of the flow of "experience" are highlighted without rhyme or reason, is removed or ameliorated by the suggestive phrase "frame of interpretation."

This shift from a more passive conception of meaning to a more dynamic one is crucial and is internal to the character of meaning itself. What is being pointed to in the use of such contrasts as "the living use of language" as opposed to "a dead word," to quote Wittgenstein, or Husserl's distinction between indication as mere mark and expression as meaningful sign is the dynamic character of meaning, that what is meaningful guides and in some way warrants or explains what is done. A spontaneous act of reflection as Schutz introduces it, neither guides nor warrants; it is arbitrary in the extreme and guides to no greater extent than the presumably meaningless flow of consciousness itself. It thus becomes crucial that the act either be supplemented, as by the appeal to the interpretive scheme, or else viewed as a mysterious process, somehow containing within itself the dynamic element indispensable to meaningfulness. I shall take up this second suggestion later.

But can the frame, or scheme, of interpretation provide the standard of application that Schutz is looking for? Before I examine more fully Wittgenstein's arguments against this view of meaning as interpretation, let me draw attention to an internal problem concerning the role of the interpretive scheme. Schutz gives us a classic picture of language:

> There exists between the sign and that which it signifies the relation of representation....[That] signitive relation is...a particular relation between the interpretive schemes which are applied to those external objects here called "signs." When we understand a sign, we do not interpret the latter through the scheme adequate to it as an external sign but through the schemes adequate to whatever it signifies.
>
> (Schutz 1967: pp. 118–19)

The word, or sign, stands in representative relation to the object it denotes, or signifies, through the mediation of schemes (or frames) of interpretation.

The meaning of the word is that scheme of interpretation that is adequate to what is denoted by the word. The object, on this view, no longer directly provides the meaning of the word, but only indirectly via the interpretive scheme. Here I want to focus, not on the signitive relation between the sign (word) and the interpretive scheme, but on the relation between the interpretive scheme and "whatever it signifies." Schutz holds that the object, namely, whatever is signified, provides the *standard for assessing* the adequacy of the interpretive scheme. As a standard it must be independent of the interpretive scheme itself. Yet on Schutz's own account of the object as the *synthesis* of a series of lived-through experiences the object seems to be a product of interpretation rather than the standard for interpretation. This means that the object, or that which is signified by the sign, to use Schutz's terminology, simply cannot figure, even indirectly, in the signitive relation. So given Schutz's own views about experience and objects, what seemed the most important feature in relationships of representation, namely, what is signified, drops out altogether. The object cannot provide the standard for assessing the adequacy of an interpretive scheme.

But what if we eliminate the idea of an independent object's setting up the standard of adequacy, for that now seems to be a hollow notion, and rest content with the sign's relation to the scheme of interpretation? The scheme of interpretation alone, we may be tempted to suppose, provides the meaning of the sign. This view of the matter falls afoul of Wittgenstein's "paradox of interpretation," now so much discussed (cf. Kripke 1982). The conclusion Wittgenstein draws from his "paradox of interpretation" is that the very notion of an interpretive scheme collapses, collapses because there is no way to distinguish accord or conflict with the scheme:

> This was our paradox: no course of action could be determined by a rule, because every course of action can be made out to accord with the rule. The answer was: if everything can be made out to accord with the rule, then it can also be made out to conflict with it. And so there would neither be accord nor conflict here.
>
> (PI §201)

Wittgenstein's argument for drawing this conclusion is summarized in PI §198 where he says that "any interpretation still hangs in the air along with what it interprets, and cannot give it any support. Interpretations by themselves do not determine meaning." Just as we saw that the object itself cannot fix a standard of meaning because it is always compatible with more than one method of projection, with more than one interpretation, so it is with the method of projection or interpretation as well. The interpretation itself can be variously interpreted, such that on one reading a certain action would be in accord with the interpretation and on another reading that very same action would be in conflict with the interpretation.

Let us consider a concrete example. Cube A and its interpretation give us the meaning of "cube." Suppose the scheme of interpretation is that one must be able to draw lines from the four points of the pictured cube to four points of the object in question. Taking that interpretation of the pictured cube, we could say that the following object is indeed a "cube," on the ground that we can draw the four lines to four points (see figure 2.1). But equally we could say that the object in question is not a "cube" on the grounds that the correct interpretation of the *scheme* requires that we project lines from the top of the cube to a single point on all corresponding objects. We would then get the objects in figure 2.2 as appropriate members of the class of cubes.

Thus, depending on the interpretation of the scheme of interpretation, our original object can be seen as a member of the class of cubes and not a member of the class of cubes. So we need to know why one interpretation of the scheme is preferable to other interpretations.[5] Otherwise we are in the paradoxical situation that Wittgenstein describes because "every course of action can be made out to accord with the rule." Since, as we have already seen, Schutz can appeal neither to the object signified nor to the stream of consciousness nor to an act of reflection to ground one scheme of interpretation over others, he faces a regress of interpretations which no resources within his position can stop.

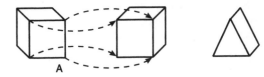

Figure 2.1

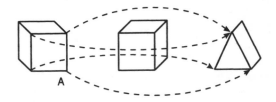

Figure 2.2

Intentional action

It might be thought that an examination of intentional action might reveal the key to addressing the problems raised about meaning, for an account of intentional action must elucidate and explain its dynamic element, that is, how the intentional state anticipates a future state of affairs. Intentional action, like meaning, is based upon spontaneous activity of the mind but, unlike meaning, that activity is directed not towards the past but towards the future. The meaning of an intentional state is the projected future act, that is, the intentional object. There are thus two central questions that any account of intentionality must address: to state clearly what the intentional object is; and to characterize the relations among the intentional object, the intentional state, and the relevant possible state of affairs in the world. These questions reflect the same philosophical structuring of intentionality that was present in Schutz's discussion of meaning. There Schutz looked for the "object" of primordial meaning and sought to characterize a tripartite relation within his theory of meaning, viz. the relation among the sign, the interpretive scheme, and the object. Not surprisingly, Wittgenstein's account of meaning and intentionality involves the rejection of both these questions.

Let us recall that, for Schutz, the intentional object is a spontaneously produced mental picture of some future state of affairs. I shall begin with Wittgenstein's arguments against the idea that a mental picture (or indeed any picture) can serve as a normative standard in itself. The shift that Schutz makes from a static conception of the intentional object as a picture to an active conception as a blueprint for action is necessary for an adequate account of intentionality. But these two conceptions are at odds with each other, and represent different underlying commitments. The adherence to the static view (the mental picture) grows out of Schutz's starting point. All meaning and intentionality must derive from the individual's private stream of consciousness. But intentionality just as much as meaning, requires a dynamic element, the projective normative element that both sets a goal or content and guides action. To bring these two demands into harmony requires that a picture be projective and normative. And just this idea comes under telling attack from Wittgenstein in his discussion of rule-following.

In PI §139, Wittgenstein asks "What really comes before our mind when we *understand* a word? – Isn't it something like a picture? Can't it *be* a picture?" The first objection he raises directly touches on Schutz's attempt to find a dynamic role for the intentional object, for it shows that the picture itself cannot guide or pick out a particular state of affairs. This picture does not reveal how it is to be used:

Well, suppose that a picture does come before your mind when you
hear the word "cube", say the drawing of a cube. In what sense can
this picture fit or fail to fit a use of the word "cube"?—Perhaps you
say: "It's quite simple;—if that picture occurs to me and I point to a
triangular prism for instance, and say it is a cube, then this use of the
word doesn't fit the picture."—But doesn't it fit? I have purposely so
chosen the example that it is quite easy to imagine a *method of projection*
according to which the picture does fit after all.

(PI §139)

Schutz, in his discussion of intentionality, uses the very metaphors that
Wittgenstein is taking issue with. The intentional object "fits" the state of
affairs given its projective relation to the world. But Wittgenstein questions
the very idea that the picture in any way determines its method of projection. Any picture can be so interpreted as to be seen to "fit" many different
things or states of affairs. A mental picture is in no wise different. He
acknowledges that, of course, "[t]he picture of the cube did indeed *suggest* a
certain use to us, but it was possible for me to use it differently," and that is
the point here. There is no necessary connection between a picture and a
particular method of projection. Converting the picture into the map or
blueprint, as Schutz attempts to do, requires an argument independent of
an appeal to the picture to show why one method of projection, or interpretation, is preferable to others. Wittgenstein's insight is to see that this is
not self-evident.

We could perhaps see Schutz's notion of an "intuitive representation"
as an attempt (unrecognized as such) to provide a self-interpreting formula
(or privileged interpretation of a mental picture), and so convert the
mental picture into a map or blueprint for action. This then takes us to
Wittgenstein's criticisms of the idea that the formula in some sense
contains within it all the applications to come. In an intentional state, we
might suppose, the self-interpreting content must contain within itself the
future state of affairs. That is what it is to anticipate the future: namely, the
future is anticipated when it or its surrogate is contained in something in
the present.

The central objection made by Wittgenstein to such a suggestion is that
we can make no sense of this idea of containment. We are working with a
picture that we can't really apply:

your idea was that the act of meaning the order had in its own way
already traversed all those steps; that when you meant it your mind as

it were flew ahead and took all the steps before you physically arrived at this or that one.

(PI §188)

It is "the result of the crossing of different pictures" (PI §191), object *qua* symbol and object *qua* object. He develops this in PI §193 where he introduces the notion of the machine-as-symbol (cf. Fogelin 1976: pp. 139–41). *We* can take an actual machine to represent or symbolize a particular action or sequence of actions. When we do this, it seems as though the symbolized action were somehow in the machine itself. With this metaphor of containment, "we are inclined to compare the future movements of the machine in their definiteness to objects which are already lying in a drawer and which we then take out" (PI §193). Yet at the same time this machine-as-symbol is not subject to all the vagaries that affect an actual machine; its parts cannot wear out, malfunction, slip, or anything else of the kind. This idealization leads to the idea that the parts or actions are contained far more perfectly in the machine than is true of the actions of any actual machine. The combination of these two ideas can only lead to the thought that "the possible movements of a machine are already there in it in some mysterious way" (PI §194).

And this leads to the search for some "superlative fact" (PI §192) in which we find a "super-strong connexion…between the act of intending and the thing intended" (PI §197), or a shadow-object that mediates between our words and the world. We feel most strongly the need for the intentional state to *contain* its object precisely because the object of an intentional state need never be realized:

> I see someone pointing a gun and say "I expect a report." The shot is fired.—Well, that was what you expected; so did that report somehow exist in your expectation?
>
> (PI §442)

The picture that lies behind this description is that of every meaningful word standing for something. There must be some thing with which the sign is related. One suggestion is that "there is some kind of agreement between your expectation and what occurred" (PI §442). But this won't do, for then, since the actual noise itself was not contained in your expectation, that noise only contingently and even accidentally coincided with the fulfillment of your expectation. This completely mischaracterizes the relation between the noise itself and the expectation, for the noise *is the fulfillment* of the expectation, not an accidental accompaniment.[6] To sever the internal connection between the event that fulfills and the expectation formed prior to the event is to transform intentional states like expectation into states of dissatisfaction such that what satisfies them is a matter for discovery. But then a cool breeze might just as well satisfy the expectation of a report as the noise of the report itself. Such a view is a dismantling of intentionality itself. So if the relation between the expectation and that which satisfies it is not contingent and external, what is the relation? There is a temptation to think that the relation must, then, be necessary. But this is clearly unacceptable, for what actually occurs need not be what is expected. It might be that the report was not so loud as expected or that the report never occurred at all. And so "haven't we an analogous case with the propositions 'Here is a red patch' and 'Here there isn't a red patch'? The word 'red' occurs in both; so this word cannot indicate the presence of something red" (PI §443). These two demands on intentionality, namely, that we need a necessary relation between the expectation and the event and that an actual satisfying event need not occur, make plausible the idea of a shadow-event, an event which stands in a necessary connection to the expectation itself and exists even if an actual satisfying event never occurs:

> The feeling is as if the negation of a proposition had to make it true in a certain sense, in order to negate it.
>
> (The assertion of the negative proposition contains the proposition which is negated, but not the assertion of it.)
>
> (PI §447)

> Again: if I say 'I have no pain in my arm', does that mean that I have a shadow of the sensation of pain, which as it were indicates the place where the pain might be?
>
> In what sense does my present painless state contain the possibility of pain?
>
> (PI §448)

But the idea of a shadow-object does not solve the problems it was intended to solve. First, it does not provide an account of the relation between the expectation and the actual event that satisfies it. We now have the expectation related to a shadow-object, an image, which is the content of that expectation, but we do not have an account of the relation of this complex state to that state of affairs that actually fulfills the state. Is that relation a necessary or a contingent one? If necessary, in virtue of what is it necessary, given that the state of affairs need not occur at all? So we are right back to where we began when we introduced the idea of a shadow-object. Perhaps we shall appeal to some notion of the shadow-object "fitting" a particular state of affairs. If we use this metaphor, and that is all that it is thus far, it is incumbent upon us to say what we mean by it. Until some such account is given, we simply have no understanding of what the relation is supposed to be, and certainly no account of why introducing the shadow-object is supposed to help. We have merely reduplicated the problem at a different level.

There is a further problem with the appeal to the shadow-object. And that is that it only gives the illusion of making intentionality intelligible. For Wittgenstein, it is a perpetuation of a very simple, but compelling, picture of language, and that is that meaning is the object for which the word stands. This, for Wittgenstein, is the greatest illusion of all:

> We do not realize that we *calculate*, operate, with words, and in the course of time translate them into one picture, sometimes another.—It is as if one were to believe that a written order for a cow which someone is to hand over to me always had to be accompanied by an image of a cow, if the order was not to lose its meaning.
>
> (PI §449)

Applied to expectation, this picture carries with it the idea that one can perceive the expectation, can perceive what is being expected: "Anyone who perceived my expectation would necessarily have a direct perception of *what* was being expected" (PI §453). "But to say that someone perceives an expectation *makes no sense*" (PI §453). It makes no sense for the same reasons that it makes no sense to suppose that one can perceive meaning in an object, whether that object be an ordinary physical object or a picture image. An object has meaning only in the way that it is used by living human beings: "The arrow points only in the application that a living being makes of it. This pointing is *not* a hocus-pocus which can be performed only by the soul" (PI §454). In these discussions, Wittgenstein is clear about his aim, and that is "...to teach you to pass from a piece of disguised nonsense to something that is patent nonsense" (PI §464). Schutz's accounts of meaning and intentionality are just such disguised nonsense.

Whether we examine an object, a mental picture, a formula or an intentional state we can find nothing in any of these that literally contains future steps or applications. And so we are inclined to think that the steps are "in some *unique* way predetermined, anticipated – as only the act of meaning can anticipate reality" (PI §188). But when we look for what this act of meaning is, we find nothing. For Wittgenstein, here is a clear case of acting upon a pervasive philosophical temptation, and that is that "[w]here our language suggests a body and there is none: there, we should like to say, is a *spirit*" (PI §36). As he elaborates on this aphorism in the same passage, "because we cannot specify any *one* bodily action which we call pointing to the shape (as opposed, for example, to the colour), we say that a *spiritual* [mental, intellectual] activity corresponds to these words." And this is precisely what Schutz does: Meaning and intentionality are both inexplicable mental activities that confer meaning "in some unique way."

The point of Wittgenstein's objection, both in his discussion of private languages and in his discussions of rule-following and intentionality, is that appeals to "spirit" occur where we have reached a philosophical blank. It is not that we have found the most rarefied and mysterious of processes or states but that we are confronting nothing at all and invoking the honorific title of "spirit" to disguise the truth of our situation. It is what he calls the search for a "superlative fact," but as he says, "[y]ou have no model of this superlative fact, but you are seduced into using a super-expression. (It might be called a philosophical superlative.)" (PI §192). "Intuitive representation" and "spontaneous activity of primordial meaning" are just such super-expressions. They can be recognized as such by the fact that though they are intended to carry most of the philosophical work of accounting for meaning and intentionality, nothing can be said of them. We are reduced to silence, a silence necessitated by the fact that the phrases are empty, refer to nothing at all.

But why does a "something about which nothing can be said" seem to satisfy certain of our philosophical urges? The answer is to be found, Wittgenstein suggests, in the fact that "[w]e fail to get away from the idea that using a sentence involves imagining something for every word" (PI §449). In other words, Wittgenstein is maintaining that even with sophisticated or esoteric theories of meaning and language, the guiding ideal is very simple. It is the one he describes in the opening paragraph of the *Investigations*: "Every word has a meaning. This meaning is correlated with the word. It is the object for which the word stands" (PI §1).

3 Wittgenstein on intentionality

Wittgenstein's views on the two central problems I am addressing in this paper, namely, the problem of projection (of how a word is meaningfully applied and how an intentional state anticipates the future event) and the problem of the intentional object, are summarized in the following three passages:

"Then can whatever I do be brought into accord with the rule?"—Let me ask this: what has the expression of a rule—say a sign-post—got to do with my actions? What sort of connexion is there here?—Well, perhaps this one: I have been trained to react to this sign in a particular way, and now I do so react to it.

(PI §198)

But it might now be asked: what's it like for him to come?—The door opens, someone walks in, and so on.—What's it like for me to expect him to come?—I walk up and down the room, look at the clock now and then, and so on.—But the one set of events has not the smallest similarity to the other! So how can one use the same words in describing them?—But perhaps I say as I walk up and down: "I expect he'll come in"—Now there is a similarity somewhere. But of what kind?!

(PI §444)

It is in language that an expectation and its fulfillment make contact.

(PI §445)

Let me take up the first passage which addresses the problem of projection. This is a problem both for meaning in general and for intentionality in particular. How can an object – whether a signpost, a word, or a mental picture – represent something? Schutz takes it that an act of reflection or the occurrence of a mental picture just does establish a method or technique (to use a favorite word of Wittgenstein's) for differentiation and projection. The spotlight of attention creates a standard and a mental image captures a projected future event. But we have already seen the very serious obstacles that stand in the way of this assertion. Wittgenstein argues – successfully to my mind – that the alleged explanatory notions themselves (attention and mental image), far from fixing a standard or a project, lose all purchase on normativity. So, far from grounding meaning or intentionality, appeals to reflection or a mental picture dissolve meaning and intentionality. But where do we look, if not within the mind of the individual, for a solution to the problem of projection?

The answer is: we do not look behind the scenes, but at the scene itself. The answer to the paradox of interpretation is that there is a way of going on that is not a matter of interpreting a standard or a method of projection. That way of going on is obeying the rule blindly, where blind obedience is understood as going on *as a matter of course*. What is taken as a matter of course depends upon how the individual is trained. Training is acculturation into a social practice. So it is the social practice that constitutes the structure reflectively described as a rule.

Wittgenstein is developing *in concreto* a functionalist theory of meaning.

Meaning, for most words, is a function of how the word is used; that structured use, for Wittgenstein, can only be found within a community of practitioners. A radically isolated individual cannot create a *use* for a word *ab initio* in the requisite sense, namely, a use that distinguishes correct from incorrect applications.

Use cannot be identified with regularity though it requires regularity. It requires what I shall call "normative regularity," that is, regularity that reflects a correct and incorrect way of going about things. Normative regularities are conventionally sustained, and so cannot be identified with natural regularities. Normative regularity, for Wittgenstein, is displayed in the de facto agreement and harmony of actions of a community of people.[7] Agreement in judgment and action is fundamental to normative practice. Deviance is possible only against the background of such harmonious agreement. Deviance, then, is the derivative notion. Out of agreement, which allows for the possibility of deviance, comes the very distinction between correct and incorrect. So for Wittgenstein the projection that is part of an intention or expectation is possible only against a background of what the community does and how it judges. It is not the result of a mental act of intending or expecting, as Shutz argues. Nevertheless, in saying that intentionalist projection depends on this background of what people do and how they judge, we are not saying that *what we mean* by something is that people so act and speak. Wittgenstein's community view of rules holds that meaning is a *function* of communally structured uses into which members of the community are trained; it does not hold that *what* we mean in using an expression is that members of the community so use it.

What we mean is given in how we explain the meanings of words, and we do not explain the meaning of a word by appealing to the fact that we all agree in a certain use. However, the explanation is such only in virtue of our agreeing on a certain use as a matter of course. The use is displayed in what we do and maintained through the process of learning, a process in which individuals come to speak and act in certain ways as second nature. Thus, on Wittgenstein's view, meaning as use, naive or initiate learning, and community agreement are intertwined in ways that make the social dimension of meaning (and mind) salient. The social dimension is not derivative, hence dependent upon the prior assignment of meaning by the individual mind, but basic. This view runs counter to both the individualism and the intellectualism in Schutz's phenomenological account.[8] If Wittgenstein is right, Schutz's whole project of seeking a phenomenological grounding for theories of social practice is radically misguided.

This has important implications for our understanding of intentionality. For Schutz, an intention is characterized by the active positing of a future state of affairs, pictured mentally. This mental picture provides a map which is consulted in guiding and assessing actions leading towards the desired end. This mental picture is related to reality via a representative projection, such that the picture can be said to anticipate the future (as yet unrealized) state of affairs and be satisfied by that state of affairs should it obtain. As we have already seen, every crucial explanatory notion – mental picture, representative projection, satisfaction – is empty, giving only the illusion of explanation. So what is Wittgenstein's account of representative projection and satisfaction? How does the intentional state anticipate the future? And what is the connection between that state and some particular state of affairs? I focus on that aspect of the problem of intentionality rather than the status and character of the intentional object because we have already seen that Wittgenstein rejects the idea of a mental picture in itself constituting meaningful content. However, Wittgenstein's way of dealing with the problem of projection provides insight into how to think about the intentional object, that is, the content of the intentional state. Wittgenstein's account of intentionality is contextualist and dynamic, as is his account of meaning. There are three stages to explicating his notion, all contained, capsule-like in PI §444 quoted above. In the first stage:

> One may have the feeling that in the sentence "I expect he is coming" one is using the words "he is coming" in a different sense from the one they have in the assertion "He is coming". But if it were so how could I say that my expectation had been fulfilled? If I wanted to explain the words "he" and "is coming", say by means of ostensive definitions, the same definitions of these words would go for both sentences.
>
> (PI §444)

The meaning of the phrase "he is coming," Wittgenstein insists, is the same whether it occurs to describe a state of affairs in the world or to identify the intentional content of an expectation. This is quite important for his position. And it differs from Schutz's account. On Schutz's account, the meaning of the phrase "he is coming" when used to specify the intentional content is given in a mental picture of someone's walking through a door. This picture is the product of spontaneous mental activity. When the same phrase is taken to mean a state of affairs in the world, the meaning involves a tripartite relation among sign, interpretive scheme and referent of sign. We have already seen that this tripartite relation is incoherent, but I want to emphasize here that Schutz tacitly takes the phrase "he is coming" (and any other) to be systematically ambiguous depending upon whether it "names" an intentional object or refers to a state of affairs in the world. The latter requires an interpretive scheme the adequacy of which is determined *by the actual state of affairs* which is the referent of the sign. Thus, the real-world referent indirectly provides the standard of meaning. The intentional object however, requires a mental picture which directly provides the meaning of the phrase. Both founder on Wittgenstein's critique of the idea that meaning can be fixed by a referent whether mental or physical.

In the context of this discussion, we see a further internal problem for Schutz: How is the intentional object to provide a blueprint for action in bringing about the desired state of affairs, when the meanings of the signs referring to the intentional object and the real state of affairs are distinct? Schutz's attempt to find an internal and necessary connection between the intention and its object by postulating a shadow-object has led him to externalize the relation between the fully contentful intention and that state of affairs that satisfies it. So we are left with only the vague metaphor of satisfaction. Given that the meaning of "he is coming" differs depending on whether the phrase refers to the intentional object (a mental picture) or an actual state of affairs (a man's walking through a door), how can the latter be said to satisfy the former? The problem of representational projection re-emerges here as strongly as ever. Indeed the problem is worse. In this case, Schutz cannot appeal to an interpretive scheme to mediate, as it were, between the intentional object and the actual state of affairs. This is because the adequacy of the interpretive scheme was fixed by a real-world state of affairs; such an adequacy condition runs directly counter to the intentional inexistence of the intentional object. So Schutz is left with no way of filling in what can be meant by the notion of satisfaction.

Wittgenstein, however, does have an account. The first stage, to repeat, states that there is no systematic ambiguity in the meaning of the phrase "he is coming." The explanation of the meaning of the phrase or the words constituting the phrase is the same. In the second stage, Wittgenstein asks:

> what's it like for him to come?—The door opens, someone walks in, and so.—What's it like for me to expect him to come?—I walk up and down the room, look at the clock now and then, and so on.—But the one set of events has not the smallest similarity to the other! So how can one use the same words in describing them?
>
> (PI §444)

Whereas Schutz explained the difference between the object of my expectation and the state of affairs that satisfies it as a difference in the referents of the phrase "he is coming," and so a systematic ambiguity in this phrase, Wittgenstein characterizes the difference as one between the expecting and the doing.[9] The meaning of the phrase isn't different; that is, how one would explain the meaning of "he is coming" would be the same whether it was used in the context of expecting or the context of asserting. But what *goes on* in the use of the phrase in these two contexts is quite different. It is also important to note that the difference is not that expectation is inner and mental while his coming is public. For Wittgenstein, both the expecting and the doing are public. But the expecting which consists in walking up and down, looking at the clock and so on is altogether different from the event expected, namely, his opening the door and walking in. Expecting is not a matter of being related to a shadow of the real thing, as is suggested by Schutz. Nor can it be a matter of being related to the state of affairs of his coming into the room, for that is only a possible state of affairs. The problem is one of identifying just where the connection lies between the expecting and his coming. At this stage of the argument, two features come into prominence: first, the dissimilarity between the expecting and the coming; and second, and equally important, "if you see the expression of an expectation, you see what is being expected" (PI §452). As Wittgenstein says in another place, "nothing is hidden" (PI §435). Take away all expression of expectation, and expectation itself disappears. To alter slightly another passage, "what is essential to [expecting], however, was not hidden beneath the surface of [this] case, but this 'surface' was one case out of a family of [expectings]" (PI §164). In other words, what is expected is displayed in the actions and context; it is not something private to the individual alone.

We are now ready for the final stage of the explication in which Wittgenstein locates the connection, or similarity as he puts it, between the expecting and the coming:

> But perhaps I say as I walk up and down: "I expect he'll come in"—Now there is a similarity somewhere. But of what kind?!
>
> (PI §444)

> It is in language that an expectation and its fulfilment make contact.
>
> (PI §445)

It is the use of the same words that connects the two. The similarity is not between a shadow and its object or a hole and its cover, but a sameness in words or signs. The same words are used to describe the object of the expectation and the event that fulfills that expectation.[10] The connection, then, lies not between the expecting and some shadow event that is "necessarily" attached to the expecting but in the fact that only what we describe in the same way as we described the object of the expectation *counts* as fulfilling or satisfying the expectation. This, as Wittgenstein says, is a grammatical remark (PI §458). It is not a remark either about a feeling of satisfaction (PI §460) or about some mysterious entity that is there whether or nor the expectation is realized in the world (PI §462). In saying "I expect he'll come in," I am not reporting on a psychological state or a shadow entity; rather saying this is part of the expecting behavior along with walking up and down the room and looking at the clock. It is part of the activity of expecting, an important part, for it sets the standard against which fulfillment is judged. It sets the standard in the way that it is used in this context, not because it describes a special metaphysical entity nor because it predicts that a certain state of affairs will induce a feeling of satisfaction. It sets the standard because the only thing we will count as satisfying this expectation is that which is described in the same way. Whether or not anything will occur that will be so described is wholly an open matter. It does not anticipate the future by bringing about the future. One may have good reasons for the expectation and those reasons provide equally good grounds for predicting that future state of affairs, but these grounds and predictions do not explicate how the expectation anticipates the future. The anticipation of the future event lies only in the potential applicability of the same description for the future event that one uses to describe one's current expectation.

There are three features of Wittgenstein's account of intentionality that I want to emphasize: contextualism, primacy of action, and the significance of learning. I want to conclude this chapter with a brief discussion of each.

Contextualism

An expectation is imbedded in a situation.

(PI §581)

What is happening now has significance—in these surroundings. The surroundings give it its importance.

(PI §583)

Wittgenstein's contextualism is, of course, the other side of the coin to his critique of meaning or intentional content as object. As Wittgenstein emphasizes throughout his later thought, nothing carries its significance within itself. Whether he is discussing an ordinary object, a mental state, a formula, or any other candidate for fixing a standard, the conclusion he draws is that any candidate for playing the privileged role of setting a standard or fixing meaning or telling us how to continue or anticipating the future plays such a role only in virtue of how we use it. Its status lies in the use that we make of it as a standard or paradigm. Wittgenstein's contextualism is pervasive. Not only does it apply to our understanding of representation and rules, it applies to how anything is identified. It is only within certain surroundings that covering my ears expresses my expecting a report; and equally for any other action, feeling, or experience that I might engage in or undergo. That these actions and feelings are part of expecting the report depends upon the circumstances. It is for this reason that no individual action or feeling or thought or experience can be said to be *the* expectation. All are part of the expecting – within these surroundings. I could act, feel, and think exactly the same ways within a different context, but I would not thereby be expecting a report. Just as transporting the ceremony of a coronation to another setting in which gold is vulgar, the fabric of the robes cheap, and a crown a parody of a hat not only devalues the activity but changes its identity (PI §584), so it is with expectation and any other intentional state. The significance of this is striking, for it runs directly counter to the individualist assumption that Schutz makes. He assumes from the outset that meaning and intention must be purely individual private matters.

Primacy of action

"When one means something, it is oneself meaning"; so one is oneself in motion. One is rushing ahead and so cannot also observe oneself rushing ahead. Indeed not.

(PI §456)

Yes: meaning something is like going up to someone.

(PI §457)

For Wittgenstein, meaning something is doing something. Clearly this goes hand in hand with his contextualism. It too runs against the two central assumptions of Schutz's position, namely, the individualistic assumption and the assumption of meaning or intentional content as object. Just as a tool is a tool only in the context of use, so a sign is meaningful only in a context of use. Meaning is not passively given and then acted upon.

Meaning is manifested in the acting itself. Meaning is shown in what is done.

This emphasis on meaning-in-motion sheds light on an interesting claim of Schutz, for Schutz is, of course, sensitive to the dynamic character of meaning. But his commitment to individualism leads him to misidentify the dynamic element. Schutz insists that the stream of consciousness itself cannot be meaningful, for it is simply passively experienced. He draws two interesting conclusions from this. It is only through a spontaneous act of reflection that meaning is conferred; we have already seen how he elaborates that to include a more dynamic Kantian element. The other conclusion is that I never know what I mean while I am acting or experiencing, for observation or self-awareness can only occur reflectively and it is only through such reflection that meaning is conferred. This is a peculiar view, leading again to internal strains for Schutz. My actions and experiences are meaningless as they occur though subsequently they can be endowed with meaning. This alienates my actions and experiences quite significantly from myself, and indeed makes the entire model Schutz has developed for intentional action quite opaque. After all, he had claimed that the intentional object provides a map to guide our action; yet he also tells us we cannot identify our actions as meaningful actions (i.e., actions guided by a map) except retrospectively. So in what sense are they guided or even legitimately described *as actions while they occur?*

On Wittgenstein's view these tensions are resolved. He would agree with Schutz that reflection is incompatible with doing, but would strongly disagree with Schutz's explication of this. For Schutz, the account is to be given in terms of the meaninglessness of the doing as it occurs. Wittgenstein holds the opposite view. To so act in these circumstances just is meaningful. I don't *observe* what I mean (an idea that goes with the assumption that meaning is an object); rather I act meaningfully. So whereas Schutz locates the incompatibility of reflecting and doing with the meaninglessness of doing and the meaning-conferring power of reflection, Wittgenstein locates meaningfulness in its primary sense in the doing within a structured context. We may reflectively describe the meaning; but we do not thereby confer meaning on what was done. The meaning of what we do does not lie wholly within the individual's power to determine; indeed it mostly lies outside the individual's power. This is a consequence of the primacy of action. What we do in the circumstances carries a significance that cannot reflectively be altered.

The significance of learning

> By nature and by a particular training, a particular education, we are
> disposed to give spontaneous expression to wishes in certain circum-
> stances....Suppose it were asked "Do I know what I long for before I
> get it?" If I have learned to talk, then I do know.
>
> (PI §441)

If Schutz were to answer the question, how do I know what I long for? or
how do I know what I mean?, he would answer I just do in virtue of the
spontaneous *sui generis* activity of reflection and projection. It is interesting
that Wittgenstein also appeals to the spontaneous expression of wishes (or
expectation or intention), but he locates and explains that spontaneity
quite differently. To understand what is done spontaneously, or blindly as
he puts it in connection with rule-following, he appeals to how we learn to
talk; in other words, to initiate learning. Learning to talk for Wittgenstein is
a matter of mastering skills, of being initiated into techniques of usage.
What is spontaneous is not a metaphysical matter, but a matter of how the
individual is trained, what comes as a matter of course, without prompting
or inference, and what seems natural, inevitable, even necessary. Learning
to talk is learning to *say and do* certain things in certain circumstances. Part
of learning to wish is learning to express what is wished for; it is learning
that to say these things in this situation just is to make a wish. Indeed a
child first learns wishing in a stylized manner: "Star light, star bright. First
star I see tonight. I wish I may; I wish I might Have this wish I wish
tonight" followed by *saying* what one wants. In saying these words in this
context, one has thereby wished. So if the child says "I want a dog," that is
what he wishes for. And so if he has learned to talk, he does indeed know
what he wishes for. If the child later thinks that he really wished for a
sandbox rather than a dog, or if he is confused about what he wished for,
he simply hasn't learned to talk properly about dogs or sandboxes or
wishes. Again, there is an important element in wishing, personal though
the activity is, that is not under the control of the individual. The individual is free to wish for what he likes, but he is not free to make that wish
into whatever he likes. To wish for a dog is not to wish for a sandbox, and
if the child thinks that it is or could be, he hasn't yet learned the language.

Each of these three elements in Wittgenstein's dynamic conception of
meaning involves a social and environmental component. This is clear
with contextualism. But it is also true for the primacy of action and the
significance of learning. What an action is, or the meaning of an action, is
not something conferred upon the action by the subject, but is shown

through the contextualized acting itself. What that action is is simply not up to the individual to determine although whether he so acts is. Learning also is social for Wittgenstein; it is a matter of being initiated into a practice and in being so initiated acquiring the skills and techniques that constitute mastery of that practice.

4 Conclusion

Though Wittgenstein and Schutz clearly share a mutual regard for everyday experience, for the role of context, and for the inadequacy of capturing human life in a set of principles, I have argued here that something like Wittgenstein's account of meaning and intentionality is required to account for social life. Though Schutz has much of interest to say on the topography of social ideals and on the differences between experienced social reality and the observation of social reality, his attempt to ground mundane social reality phenomenologically is a radically misguided project. Social reality and practice are not grounded in the phenomenology of subjective experience. We need to say with Wittgenstein (OC §402), quoting Goethe,

> and write with confidence
> "In the beginning was the deed."

3 Wittgenstein, Kant, and the "metaphysics of experience"

For Kant, the categories of the Understanding embody transcendental constraints on the form of all possible thought. Many have thought that for Wittgenstein the facts of "grammar" play a similar role. I shall argue that this is not so. There are superficial similarities between Kant and Wittgenstein, but they mask deep differences.

One of the difficulties with the Kantian interpretation of Wittgenstein's later work is getting a clear statement of what a "transcendental" philosophy is. However, in the many attributions of "transcendental" to Wittgenstein, there emerge two central ideas, one substantive and one methodological. The substantive idea is that there are limits or boundaries to what is intelligible. Transcendental philosophy is concerned with the limits of intelligibility, and the later Wittgenstein is seen to be involved in this same project. The "grammatical statements" of the *Philosophical Investigations* and the "propositions that hold fast" of *On Certainty* are held to be the counterparts to Kant's a priori synthetic judgments that are the result of the schematized categories. I shall argue that more than a concern with nonsense is required to warrant the attribution of "transcendental" to Wittgenstein; what more is required is that the limits of sense be positive limits. The methodological idea is that one cannot reach and characterize the limits of sense by empirical means. A special form of argumentation is required whereby one comes to the limits of all that is possible by a consideration of what is actual. Here too I shall argue that more than the rejection of straightforward empirical inquiry is needed to justify calling Wittgenstein a transcendental philosopher; Wittgenstein's ways of arguing must be seen to parallel Kant's transcendental deduction.

Reading Wittgenstein as a transcendental philosopher creates a sense of vertigo that is not easily allayed. David Pears expresses this vertigo as "a kind of oscillation" in which we seek to understand the limit of language by trying to "cross [that limit and, in failing,] return to language in its ordinary human setting" (Pears 1969: p. 126). We oscillate between the empirical and the transcendental. Karsten Harries sees two incompatible models of language – a transcendental one and a realistic one – the incompatibility never resolved (Harries 1968). Bernard Williams gives ambivalent acceptance to reading Wittgenstein as a "transcendental idealist" (Williams 1974). Jonathan Lear keeps this transcendental reading, and so the problem of oscillation, alive, holding that Wittgenstein "wants, as a philosopher, to communicate transcendental insights, but he recognizes that there is no language in which to communicate them" (Lear 1982). This problem of oscillation which many have "found" in Wittgenstein is, I shall argue, an artifact of the Kantian interpretation, but one that very naturally arises when one tries to make a transcendental reading fit the text.

To summarize, in section 1, I shall sketch the alleged parallels between Kant and Wittgenstein; in section 2, I shall focus on the idea that Wittgenstein develops a method of arguing appropriate to the transcendental task; in section 3, I shall take up the substantive issue of whether Wittgenstein's appeal to grammar is a kind of linguistic Kantianism; and finally I shall turn to the problem of oscillation.

1 The parallels

As I have pointed out, a number of commentators argue that the later Wittgenstein gives us a subtle and imaginative form of Kantian critical philosophy. Wittgenstein's conception of the task he has set for himself and of the way to achieve this goal, it is said, are distinctively Kantian. Both Wittgenstein and Kant are convinced that perennial philosophical problems result from profound confusions. Philosophy's true task is to disclose these confusions and diagnose their roots, thereby displaying the illusory character of philosophical perplexity. In this way philosophy, or metaphysics anyway, can be brought to an end.

For Kant, the way in which metaphysics can be shown to be confused and misguided is by showing that epistemology won't allow it: By solving the problem of knowledge, the problems of metaphysics are dissolved. The philosophical task is, to use the Lockean phrase, to uncover "the scope and limits of human knowledge," thereby drawing a boundary around all possible knowledge. In doing this, we shall not only characterize the nature and structure of knowledge, we shall have uncovered the source of philosophical illusion. For illusion and error arise when we unwittingly step beyond these bounds. Metaphysics is the attempt to acquire knowledge where knowledge cannot be had. The "scope and limits" project, then, is to develop a theory of knowledge that gives us the conditions and constraints that any particular knowledge claim must meet.

Though Kant inherits the project, he transforms the way in which we understand it. All experience and all knowledge are conditioned by the very structure of the mind, a structure that can be revealed through the method of transcendental argument. Philosophy falls into illusion when it attempts to know the unconditioned – such knowledge is impossible.

On the Kantian interpretation of Wittgenstein, Wittgenstein too is concerned to delimit the bounds of sense in order to display the source of philosophic error. But for Wittgenstein these boundaries are to be found within language, not within the mind. Wittgenstein's substantive break with Kant is not over the task or method, broadly construed, of philosophy, but over where one looks for the conditions of knowledge. As Pears puts it, Wittgenstein's philosophy "was a critique of language very similar in scope and purpose to Kant's critique of thought....His purpose was not merely to formulate what cannot be said in language, but also to succeed in understanding the structure of what can be said" (Pears 1969: pp. 2–3).[1] Wittgenstein, it is argued, adopts the Kantian approach to the main problem: The end of philosophy can be realized only by determining the limits and structure of language. Our knowledge, experience, and understanding are conditioned by the structure of language. Just as examination of the structure and function of the Understanding gives us the pure categories and a priori synthetic truths which condition and make possible all experience, so examination of the structure and function of language gives us the grammatical truths of the *Investigations*. The a priori synthetic truths of the Kantian system play a special epistemic role – they provide the universal and necessary conditions in terms of which all the particular moves in the acquisition of empirical knowledge are legitimized. Wittgenstein's grammatical statements seem to carry this same epistemically privileged status and so also to provide the background conditions which legitimize any of the particular moves we make in a language game. For Kant, the structure of the mind conditions experience; for Wittgenstein, "the apparent 'structure of reality' is merely the shadow of grammar," as Hacker expresses it (Hacker 1972: p. 145).[2] Language imposes the constraints.

This line of interpretation allows, of course, important differences between the two philosophers, differences beyond the fact that one looks to the structure of the mind, the other to the structure of language. Clearly their respective means for uncovering the conditions for the possibility of experience differ. Where Kant is systematic, Wittgenstein clearly is not. Where Kant looks for (and purports to find) an exhaustive list of the necessary conditions for all experience, Wittgenstein takes a piecemeal approach, mapping out the contours of particular areas of discourse. Where Kant looks for the universal principle, Wittgenstein looks at the concrete case. Where Kant locates the source of these principles, or rules, constitutive of experience in the very nature of the rational mind, Wittgenstein locates the source in human convention (what Hacker calls his "extreme voluntarism" (Hacker 1972: p. 139) and Williams his "constructivism" or "plural idealism" (Williams 1974: pp. 89–95)), a kind of social contract theory of necessity. These are all significant differences; but on this view they are differences in tactics and detail – the overall strategy and project remain unchanged. No wonder Hacker thinks that Wittgenstein's claims to have made a break with the philosophical tradition are "over-inflated" and "exaggerated" (Hacker 1972: pp. 138–9).

I shall argue that this line of interpretation is deeply misguided. Far from adopting the Kantian problematic, he attacks it. In the first part of this chapter, I shall criticize the notion that Wittgenstein's piecemeal, non-systematic approach, though it gives a special flavor to his style of writing, represents a difference in tactics and detail but not in strategy and project. I shall argue that if this is correct, Wittgenstein's tactics are wholly inappropriate. Many of his most typical ways of arguing verge on being silly and ultimately irrelevant if this conception of his task is correct. His appeal to the diversity of language, his use of disproof by reminder (often rather homely reminders), his emphasis on the particular case, his use of satire, all seem childish compared with what Kant offers. Commentators who speak of Wittgenstein's "metaphysics of experience" or his transcendental idealism tend to forget just how trivial and commonplace are many of the examples and discussions in the later work. On the other side of the same coin is the importance of Kant's architectonics to this project. Just as there is some tendency to ignore much of the way in which Wittgenstein actually proceeds, so there is the temptation to treat Kant's commitment to system as something more properly scrutinized by the psychoanalyst than the philosopher. Wittgenstein's satiric asides and Kant's tables must not be taken as merely reflecting the personal idiosyncrasies of these men. On the contrary, I shall argue that the architectonics of Kant are essential to the task of locating the "scope and limits of knowledge." And in understanding this, we can better understand the significance of Wittgenstein's way of arguing; for Wittgenstein, like Kant, is trying to diagnose and cure certain philosophical illusions, but the most important is precisely the myth of a priori limitations to the scope of human knowledge and experience. In the *Investigations* and *On Certainty*, Wittgenstein is not attempting to map the limits of language but to argue that the philosophical search for limits is senseless.

After making the general point about method and argumentative strategy, I shall examine two substantive claims central to the Kantian interpretation. The first is that Wittgenstein's grammatical statements or "propositions that hold fast," as he expresses it in *On Certainty*, are the linguistic counterpart to Kant's synthetic a priori judgments. They provide, it is held, the unconditioned grounding necessary for ending any chain of justification or for making experience possible at all. I shall argue that they are not the ground that makes particular judgments possible, but that the array of particular judgments makes a place for them. The second claim is that forms of representation (paradigms, schemata, rules) are the linguistic counterpart to Kant's concepts. I shall show that they aren't concepts at all in Kant's sense. I shall conclude the chapter with a discussion of the problem of oscillation that so many see in Wittgenstein. If he is not doing transcendental philosophy or at least aiming at transcendental insights, then is he engaged in an empirical investigation of actual language usage, a task better left to linguists and anthropologists? Wittgenstein is unmistakable in his rejection of this:

> If the formation of concepts can be explained by facts of nature, should we not be interested, not in grammar, but rather in that in nature which is the basis of grammar?—Our interest certainly includes the correspondence between concepts and very general facts of nature....But our interest does not fall back upon these possible causes of the formation of concepts; we are not doing natural science...

> (PI II §xii)

2 The significance of the architectonic

So Wittgenstein, like Kant, is supposed to be searching for the scope and limits of possible human knowledge. But the idea of being able to draw a boundary around possible knowledge is really quite odd. In order for it to make sense as a project, one needs a particular conception of knowledge. The view of knowledge that most plausibly lends itself to the idea that such limits exist and can be located is what has been called the "two-component theory of knowledge" (Williams 1977). Knowledge, on this view, is constituted of two components or elements: the materials or building blocks of knowledge and the operations or principles whereby these materials are related or associated. If one could get a complete list of the kinds of available materials and operations, and show that it was complete, the limits of possible knowledge would be fixed. This is the project and strategy that Kant takes on in *The Critique of Pure Reason*. The intuitions of Sensibility and the categories of the Understanding are the two components in terms of which Kant can draw the boundary between possible knowledge and experience and transcendent metaphysics.

Thus, although Kant may take system-building to an extreme, architectonic considerations are built into the very nature of the project. Indeed, it is this necessity for system that gives point to the notion of a search for the limits of possible knowledge. A partial list or a list that could change or grow simply would not speak to the issue. Such a list would leave the question of what is possible and what is not still open, but the task envisaged is to answer that question once and for all. Thus, an exhaustive list is indispensable.

Yet this very idea, so integral to Kant's project, is precisely what Wittgenstein challenges when he asks:

> But how many kinds of sentence are there? Say assertion, question and command?—There are countless kinds: countless different kinds of what we call "symbols", "words", "sentences". And this multiplicity is not something fixed, given once for all; but new types of language, new language-games, as we may say, come into existence, and others become obsolete and get forgotten.
>
> (PI §23)

This theme of the diversity of language, so central to Wittgenstein's later philosophy, is radically inimical to Kant's goal of completeness, fixity, and system. Yet these goals are, as shown above, inherent in the project of locating limits. Wittgenstein's pluralism, thus, is not a variation in detail but a fundamental rejection of the Kantian project.

But through the lens of the Kantian interpretation, Wittgenstein's evident rejection of an architectonic approach is construed as a peculiar brand of transcendental philosophy. Instead of there being a single unified groundwork of all experience and knowledge, Wittgenstein is alleged to show us that the linguistic terrain is broken up into subdivisions each with its constitutive forms of representation (cf. Hacker 1972: Chs 5 and 6). Thus, Wittgenstein's appeal to the diversity of language is construed as the claim that there are numerous subdivisions to the linguistic terrain and not a single whole to be delimited. This makes the transcendental task more complicated but not impossible. As Hacker tells us, "nothing but superficial interpretation of Wittgenstein's philosophy shows the impossibility of architectonic endeavor" (Hacker 1972: p. 141). It is a superficial interpretation on Hacker's view because it presupposes that where there is diversity, there cannot be system, theory, or completeness; and this is obviously not so.

Yet Wittgenstein *does* maintain that his pluralism rules out having a theory of meaning or a *theory* of knowledge. What he challenges in this way is the philosophically significant idea that there are *privileged* modes of classification. When Wittgenstein says that there are countless kinds of sentence, he does not mean that there is no way in which they could be counted. As Robert Fogelin has pointed out, "given some method of classi- fication, it doesn't turn out that there are endlessly many kinds within the classification. Wittgenstein does, in fact, give an indication of the sort of classification he has in mind for he speaks of *assertions, questions and commands* (PI §23). Using this as our starting point, do we really find count- lessly many different kinds of sentence?...I doubt it" (Fogelin 1976: p. 151). This is true, but it is not Wittgenstein's point. Rather his point is that no one method of classifying is privileged epistemically nor is the diversity itself fixed – both evolve and change with the cultural and intellectual evolution of human society. One will not find what the epistemologist or logician have sought in language, namely, an ordered structure which grounds the apparent multiplicity:

> Our language can be seen as an ancient city: a maze of little streets and squares, of old and new houses, and of houses with additions from various periods; and this surrounded by a multitude of new boroughs with straight regular streets and uniform houses.
>
> (PI §18)

> It is interesting to compare the multiplicity of the tools in language and of the ways they are used, the multiplicity of kinds of word and sentence, with what logicians have said about the structure of language.
>
> (PI §23)

What we see here, then, is an application to the categories of language of Wittgenstein's general point about simplicity (cf. PI §47–8). There are no more natural primitives within language or thought than there are in the physical world.

Wittgenstein seeks to convince us that there is no underlying structure or order of language and knowledge that informs and warrants our ways of talking. There are only the ways of talking. Wittgenstein underscores this by reminding us of the different ways we talk and act, by pointing to the limitless diversity of possible lamguage games, by emphasizing the gap between the actual uses of language and the goals of the logician. But these are rather banal remarks in themselves: Language is used in lots of ways, you can count up kinds of sentences in different ways, what a sentence means can vary given the circumstances in which it is uttered;

more particularly, questions can be used to state facts, declarative sentences to give commands, imperatives to plead. All could agree to these remarks. So their philosophical significance cannot lie just in themselves. Their significance derives from the impact they ought to have on our philosophical biases. They have no intrinsic interest for us. For Wittgenstein, the difficulty is to understand what prevents us from taking commonplace facts *seriously* when doing philosophy and to overcome our resistance.

Hacker suggests that Wittgenstein's reminders are not the banal claims they seem to be. On the contrary, they are philosophical assertions that form part of Wittgenstein's brand of transcendental idealism (language is used in lots of ways), part of his theory of knowledge (you can count up kinds of sentence in different ways), part of his theory of meaning (what a sentence means can vary given the circumstances in which it is uttered). As Hacker tells us, "many aspects of Wittgenstein's critical philosophy can be systematically presented and readily reveal the thoroughness and comprehensiveness of his work. More importantly, it is far from obvious that his later views on semantics cannot be coherently represented and indeed formalized so as to yield what most philosophers would call a comprehensive theory of meaning" (Hacker 1972: p. 141).

But Wittgenstein's appeal, e.g., to the diversity of language, does not get its philosophical significance from being part of a philosophical theory. This otherwise trivial point takes on philosophical significance as part of the challenge to traditional accounts of meaning or knowledge, not as an alternative account within the tradition. It is part of a series of arguments, considerations, reminders that is intended to convince us of the bankruptcy of the traditional problems and the solutions to them.

There are two considerations that detract considerably from the view that Wittgenstein's rhetorical devices are actually employed in the service of theories of language, meaning, and knowledge. First, Wittgenstein's kind of argument simply seems inappropriate to the task of fixing the limits of knowledge or supporting a theory of meaning. When one is looking for the fixed and determinate boundaries of knowledge and human experience, demonstrative arguments on the grand scale seem called for. But Wittgenstein's strategy is to constantly chip away at attempts at philosophical theory-building. The very fact that he uses the piecemeal approach and that he offers a range of considerations speaks against interpreting him architectonically. To seek to give the argument or demonstration that shows once and for all that this theory is right or that theory is wrong is part of the tradition that says that human discourse is a structured whole. If one's target is this very idea, then one cannot use arguments and strategies appropriate to a commitment to this idea. It is no surprise, then, that Wittgenstein's congeries of points, persuasive devices, and reminders are what they are. Given this critical task, Wittgenstein's mode of arguing is just what is necessary.

Second, we can't but wonder why Wittgenstein doesn't proceed in a more systematic way and why he insists on metaphilosophical claims that deny that philosophy is systematic, offers theses, or has a method. This must be explained away as a kind of hubris, arising presumably out of his own quirks of personality. On my interpretation, a harmony is restored both between his philosophy and metaphilosophy, and between his goal and methods. Precisely because he is attacking the idea of there being limits of possible knowledge which can be specified once and for all, he doesn't attempt to give a demonstration, a transcendental deduction, or indeed any grand argument that settles the issue. Thus, he proceeds in a way that is intended to persuade rather than to demonstrate. His introduction of family resemblance and open texture, his appeal to diversity, his reminders and examples as well as satire and rhetorical questioning are all rallied to undermine the view that knowledge or language could have a priori determinable scope and limits. On the positive side, this "motley of argument" doesn't lend itself to supporting theories, nor does Wittgenstein intend it to. Philosophers are right when they feel frustrated when trying to tease a theory of universals out of the notion of family resemblance, a theory of meaning out of his claim that meaning is use, a theory of knowledge out of his use of language games. Yet for this rejection of attempts to make Wittgenstein's later philosophy conform to architectonic considerations, I need to make good the claim that Wittgenstein does not present forms of representation, grammatical truth, or propositions that hold fast as linguistic counterparts to Kant's categories of the Understanding constitutive of, and so necessary for, human experience and knowledge.

3 A priori synthetic judgments and propositions that hold fast

Kant takes great care to mark out precisely the proper domain of philosophical inquiry: philosophy uncovers synthetic a priori truths. These truths are not vacuous tautologies though they share absolute certainty with tautologies; neither are they discovered or established inductively though they are genuinely synthetic truths. They are not discovered at all, but are always known (implicitly) as soon as one knows anything. They are not justified or justifiable by experience. They can be shown to be justified only through transcendental philosophy, by showing that they are necessary for the possibility of knowledge. They make the justification of particular empirical claims possible without themselves directly justifying these claims. For Kant, in order to grasp, for example, any particular causal judgment, let alone offer evidence in favor of its truth, one must understand that it is a causal judgment; to understand this, one must be able to apply the concept of causation to the particular situation. To apply the concept, one must grasp the concept itself. In this way the particular judgment presupposes a rule of application (or synthesis) which in turn presupposes the concept which generates the rule of application.[3] Possible experience, thus, is fixed by the framework of concepts, which are themselves wholly independent of that experience. It is in virtue of this independence and the role of concepts in conditioning all experience that they *provide* positive limits to experience and knowledge.

What is important here is that the framework of a priori concepts is prior both epistemologically and semantically, as it were, to particular judgments. The conditions for understanding particular judgments, and so for the possibility of justifying those judgments, are provided by the framework concepts, which are themselves unconditioned. The key ideas, then, of transcendental philosophy are that: (1) there is that which *provides* the limits to what is possible, and these limits constitute a substantive boundary; (2) this unconditioned boundary, or ground, is independent of actual, particular experience; for Kant, it is the framework of pure concepts; and (3) this unconditioned ground, to be a ground, must be universal (or inherently representational) and not particular. I shall refer to these three features as, respectively, the thesis of a positive limit, the independence condition, and the universality condition. I shall show that Wittgenstein rejects each one. But first let me characterize more fully the claim that Wittgenstein is doing a kind of transcendental philosophy.

Wittgenstein's own brand of transcendental philosophy, it is argued, is to be found in his account of grammar and grammatical truths. These, it is maintained, constitute a special kind of conceptual truth – deeper and more profound than tautologies, yet not established by experience. All experience, knowledge, and action is conditioned by, and so presupposes, some such grammatical truths. Where Kant found only twelve synthetic a priori truths for all of human knowledge and experience, Wittgenstein locates innumerable such truths, as many as there are language games. Grammatical truths are descriptions of forms of representation which together provide a composite picture or "surview" of language. Limits are delineated – not for all of language but for areas of discourse, each dominated and controlled by its own proper form of representation.[4] As with Kant, these grammatical truths set the context of inquiry – their peculiarity lies in their epistemic role. They look like ordinary empirical descriptions of fact – every event has a cause, no one else can feel my pain, the earth has existed since long before my birth – but they are not. They fix the standards which make inquiry possible, it is claimed, as well as setting the scope of inquiry. In *On Certainty* Wittgenstein addresses the epistemic role of these truths or propositions explicitly. To use his metaphor, these propositions constitute the river-bed of knowledge (OC §97); they are not so much a part of the justification for a particular claim as the context which makes that justification possible. That the earth existed long before my birth isn't what justifies me in believing that Napoleon was exiled to Elba; though if the earth hadn't existed, it wouldn't make sense to ask whether Napoleon was exiled or not. An advocate of this interpretation has expressed the parallel as follows:

> some propositions, among them some universal propositions, do not seem to allow exceptions, do not seem to admit empirical confirmation or disconfirmation....That all human beings have parents (OC §240), that all objects may exist unperceived (OC §314), that nature is uniform (OC §315), are examples. These appear to be empirical propositions but they lack the contingency of empirical propositions....
>
> The relation of these propositions to experience is, as for Kant, problematic. They are fundamental not in the sense of being most richly confirmed but in the sense of being outside confirmation altogether....They are not only outside confirmation but their being true makes possible the process within which confirmation of empirical propositions occurs...
>
> (Morawetz 1974: p. 431)

As this passage suggests, it seems plausible to treat Wittgenstein's noncontingently certain propositions as a form of synthetic a priori judgment. Wittgenstein describes such propositions as those which "hold fast" (OC §144ff.). The question for us, then, is whether propositions that hold fast are fundamental in the way that synthetic a priori judgments are in Kant's system. I shall argue that they are not.

To show that Wittgenstein's account of the role played by propositions that hold fast is quite different from the Kantian account of a priori synthetic judgments, I shall take up the three key features of transcendental philosophy. First, although it is true that Wittgenstein's propositions that hold fast stand "outside confirmation altogether," they do not stand as the *epistemic* conditions which make "possible the process within which confirmation of empirical propositions occurs"; that is, they are not the epistemic grounding or presupposition of all particular chains of empirical justification. They do not describe limits in any positive way. And it is only a positive sense of limits as boundaries that makes the quest for the scope and limits of knowledge and experience intelligible. Second, the independence condition requires a grounding that is independent of the actual; for Kant these are the pure concepts of the Understanding. Yet Wittgenstein wholly rejects the theory of concepts that Kant works with, and indeed the idea that anything could be inherently meaningful independently of a context of use. Finally, I shall consider the significance of the fact that Wittgenstein claims that particular propositions are as certain and as "fundamental" as knowing that objects continue to exist even when unperceived. The status of particular propositions like "My name is M.W.," "I have never been to the moon," and "This is my hand" (in normal circumstances) is as certain as "Every event has a cause" and "The external world exists unperceived." This undercuts the universality condition.

Thesis of a positive limit

It is true that propositions that hold fast, especially those that Wittgenstein calls "methodological propositions" (OC §318) or "hinge" propositions (OC §341), propositions like "objects continue to exist unperceived," "the world has existed long before my birth," "nature is uniform," stand outside confirmation. They cannot be established empirically, and thus, insofar as they are known, are known a priori. Wittgenstein's point, however, is that strictly they are not known, but hold fast. Of Moore and his claim to know with certainty such things, Wittgenstein says that "Moore does not know what he asserts he knows, but it stands fast for him, as also for me; regarding it as absolutely solid is part of our method of doubt and enquiry" (OC §151). Such propositions are not claims to knowledge that have an absolutely certain warrant, but propositions that stand fast for us.

First, let me explore the negative claim. Far from being special pieces of knowledge in virtue of being a priori and certain, these peculiar propositions are not properly claims to knowledge at all. We do not know that the earth has existed long before our births, yet neither is it the case that we don't know this. Rather this proposition and others like it are outside the sphere of knowledge. According to Wittgenstein, knowledge is that for which there can be evidence, about which we can make mistakes or be in doubt. But these peculiar propositions that are of special interest to the epistemologist are those about which one can be in doubt or for which one seeks evidence only in the artificial context of philosophical discussion. It is philosophy, on Wittgenstein's view, that generates the worries about the limits of knowledge and the bases of all knowledge, not the nature of knowledge itself, by extending the paradigm of hypothesis and justification to a context in which this paradigm is inappropriate. Propositions "held in place" by all we say and do and propositions that are "principles of judgment" (OC §124) are treated as informational. But the function of such judgments is not captured by, indeed is distorted by, treating them as knowledge claims, whose certainty is held to derive from the peculiar or special warrant said to accrue to these claims.

Let me first take up Wittgenstein's judgments that are held in place, judgments that "stand fast." I take the phrase from OC §152, a very important passage:

> I do not explicitly learn the propositions that stand fast for me. I can discover them subsequently like the axis around which a body rotates. This axis is not fixed in the sense that anything holds it fast, but the movement around it determines its immobility.
>
> (OC §152)

We can best develop the character of knowledge and the relation of knowledge to these propositions that hold fast by examining a concrete instance. In *On Certainty*, Wittgenstein looks at historical knowledge, mathematical knowledge, and scientific knowledge. To highlight his characterization of propositions that hold fast, I shall focus on his treatment of historical knowledge.

An example that Wittgenstein uses of historical knowledge is the fact that Napoleon won the battle of Austerlitz (cf. OC §182–90). This is a claim about which we could be mistaken or in doubt about its truth. As a matter of fact, we are not, and that is because we have overwhelming evidence for its being true.[5] But this is not the case for the methodological proposition that the earth has existed long before my birth. This claim has a completely different status relative to historical inquiry. If it were open to doubt or if we could be mistaken about it, the very idea of history would be meaningless. Does this mean, then, that this proposition provides the epistemic condition for the possibility of doing history? If so, this is in accord with the Kantian interpretation. To say that this an *epistemic condition* for the possibility of history is to say that in order to be justified in conducting any historical investigations, one must know this proposition to be true – it is a *presupposition* of any historical research. I shall break this issue down into two questions. First, is this proposition an epistemic condition or presupposition of doing history? Second, how is it justified?

Clearly the truth of this methodological proposition (that the earth has existed long before my birth) is a causal condition for doing history and is logically assumed by historical inquiry. It is not, however, an epistemic condition. In other words, in order to do history and to be justified in one's findings, it is not necessary to establish or determine the truth of that proposition. It simply doesn't figure in the justification of an historical claim. It is true that an historian in a reflective mood might indulge in certain meta-historical speculations in which he might think that all the while he was doing his researches, he had presupposed that the earth had existed for some time (though this wouldn't properly be construed as meta-*historical* reflection). Wittgenstein's view is that although we can say these things (always after the fact, as it were), it is not the case that we were justified in our particular claims only to the extent that we were justified in this general one. It is very easy to slip from noticing certain causal conditions and/or logical relations to asserting corresponding epistemological connections. That the earth has existed for a long time simply isn't a part of the justification for any historical claim and so it is misleading to claim that all along the historian has *presupposed* the truth of this general claim. "Presupposition" implies epistemic priority; it implies covert reliance on an untested (and possibly false) belief; it implies that belief ought to be checked before we are justified in going on with our researches.

On the Kantian view, the relation between methodological propositions and particular knowledge claims is that of presupposition: Particular knowledge claims can be warranted to the extent that the underlying methodological propositions are. Thus, by making these latter explicit and showing their absolute epistemic certainty, we make the particular knowledge claims firmer. We save ourselves from scepticism.[6]

Wittgenstein holds the opposite view. In making the methodological "presupposition" explicit, in presenting it like a piece of knowledge to be evaluated and assessed for its warrant, one doesn't pin things down more firmly. Rather the very act of raising it for scrutiny carries with it questions about the validity of the so-called "presupposition" itself. This is only to be expected, for claims of knowledge are just those claims that are open to doubt, to mistake, to evidence. So rather than solving the question of what can be known, the scope of the question is artificially and incorrectly extended. Finding warrant for methodological propositions doesn't make them or any other claims firmer; if anything it has the opposite effect, assimilating incorrectly that which cannot be doubted, which stands fast, to that which can be doubted and so needs evidence.

Moreover, Wittgenstein denies that checking out the methodological propositions makes particular historical claims more certain or better warranted. On the contrary, making particular historical claims and justifying them is what makes the methodological proposition certain: "What we call historical evidence points to the existence of the earth a long time before my birth; – the opposite hypothesis has nothing on its side" (OC §190). The certainty of the general proposition "derives" from the particular judgments and claims and not the other way around.

From where does the certainty of the propositions held fast derive? Their justification is not empirical. One might try to argue, using the quotation just above, that the evidence is overwhelming in favor of the earth's having existed for a long time; in fact, it might be said, the evidence is far more extensive than the evidence for Napoleon's having won the battle of Austerlitz. It is far more extensive, for everything speaks for this claim and nothing against it. But what this shows is not that this is the most soundly supported claim, but that it is not subject to confirmation or disconfirmation at all. To say that everything speaks for it is to say that *we accept nothing* as counting against it.[7] It is not open to reasonable doubt, error, or support – it is not a claim to knowledge. The certainty that this claim has is not the surety that a well-confirmed empirical claim has (such as, Napoleon was exiled to Elba). So we return to our original questions, what kind of certainty is this and what is its origin?

The certainty of propositions that hold fast does not derive from their belonging to a transcendental structure which conditions all concrete empirical judgments; rather *their certainty derives from the concrete empirical judgments that we make*:

> Bit by bit there forms a system of what is believed, and in that system some things stand unshakeably fast and some are more or less liable to shift. What stands fast does so, not because it is intrinsically obvious or convincing; it is rather *held fast by what lies around it* (my italics).
>
> (OC §144)

> I do not explicitly learn the propositions that stand fast for me. I can discover them subsequently like the axis around which a body rotates. This axis is not fixed in the sense that anything holds it fast, but *the movement around it determines its immobility* (my italics).
>
> (OC §152)

> I have arrived at the rock bottom of my convictions. And one might almost say that *these foundation-walls are carried by the whole house* (my italics).
>
> (OC §248)

The italicized phrases in each passage give voice to Wittgenstein's central insight. What appear reflectively to be presuppositions supporting particular judgments and propositions are, on the contrary, held in place because of these very particular judgments and actions we engage in. Because we do history, because we make claims about the past, because we celebrate past events, because we hold grudges, because we give birthday parties, because we are sad when an anniversary is forgotten – because of all these concrete particular actions and many others, it is certain that the world has existed long before my birth. Our practices, our judgments, our actions don't leave room for anything else. And so we want to say, "Of course, there is a past" or "Of course, the world has existed long before my birth"; what could be more certain? But this shows that this claim is perhaps really a kind of nonsense. There is no way for it to be doubted, and so there is no reason for it ever to be said. Its certainty is not the transcendental certainty of necessary truths; its certainty is guaranteed by our actions and judgments.

Two central themes emerge. First, these propositions are not presupposed by particular empirical claims. They are not the epistemic conditions for the possibility of knowledge. It is true that in reflective moments one can point out that they are causal conditions for, say, doing history or going to the dry cleaners (e.g., that there is a past); or that they are logical conditions (one can't study the past unless there is a past). But to note that they are "presupposed" in these ways is not to show that they are epistemically presupposed in our justification of particular historical claims. These candidates for setting transcendental limits play no active normative role in our practices. But, interestingly, there are propositions that are standards for use; these are paradigmatic judgments like "Napoleon was exiled to Elba" or "That is red" pointing to a sentry box in England. Yet they are hardly appropriate candidates for setting transcendental limits. These normative judgments differ from the methodological judgments even though there is a kinship. In my discussion of the independence condition, I shall be considering these normative or paradigmatic judgments.

Second, the certainty of methodological propositions is a feature of the judgments we make, the practices we engage in, and the actions we perform. Though this is the origin of their certainty and the guarantor, as it were, of their certainty, these actions and judgments are not evidence in support of their truth. Rather these propositions are immanent in our practices. In being immanent in our practices, rather than the transcendental condition for those practices, propositions that hold fast cannot give us a positive limit to the possibility of experience, or as many commentators prefer to express it, a limit to what is intelligible. Wittgenstein does not offer us a way to draw a principled line or boundary around what is intelligible.

The independence condition

The second condition for making sense of the idea of a substantive boundary or limit to intelligibility calls for the independence of the constituents of that boundary from what actually occurs. For Kant, those independent elements are the pure concepts or categories of the Understanding, mental entities that are inherently representational. They are representations, not because they picture or copy anything (pace the Cartesian view), but because of the role or function they play in our experience and knowledge. They function to unify and so make intelligible what would otherwise be a "blind, buzzing, blooming confusion." To an extent, Wittgenstein's account of meaning is similar, for he emphasized, if anything, that a word has a symbolic function only given the role it plays in a larger context. However, this similarity pales against the fact that Wittgenstein simply hasn't got an idea of "concept" at all. The relevant notion of "concept" here is that of a mental entity or special kind of idea with a meaning or function that is fixed and unchanging. The concept, in order to be the concept that it is, is inherently representative or inherently has the meaning that it does. This idea that something inherently or necessarily has a certain function or meaning is alien to Wittgenstein's later philosophy. This can be brought out most clearly by considering his own account of how an individual object can be a linguistic sample or paradigm, that is, play a general representative role.[8]

An object can acquire a special linguistic and epistemic status by being given that status as a way of solving or dealing with a particular problem or set of issues. This special status is not due to any intrinsic features of the object but only to the respect accorded it by the community in adopting a certain practice. The status is achieved in virtue of the role. For Kant, the opposite is true: The role is possible only because of the special metaphysical status of the object. According to Wittgenstein, this is to confuse the *object as representation for the representation as object*.

Wittgenstein inverts the Kantian order of priority. On the Kantian view, our particular applications of a concept are derivative. They are the applications of the schematized concept itself. Thus, the concept as providing or generating the rule of use is prior to particular applications in practice. For Wittgenstein, this representative role is realized only in the context of an ongoing practice of use. Thus, the practice of use is prior to the concept or rule as representative or guiding; only in terms of a practice can the place be found for using the object as a paradigm. This way of putting it is somewhat misleading in that a practice, for Wittgenstein, involves the use of objects, processes, and/or judgments as representative paradigms. The main point here is that an object can play this role only within a practice. For example, the case of the standard meter in Paris is an instance of formally taking an object – a particular piece of metal – as the paradigm for what a meter is. For the sake of a particular task, an object can temporarily be given the privileged status of representative, as when we ask someone to bring all the flowers like this one, pointing to a random daisy. It may, of course, quickly fall and become one of the many gathered.

One of the important insights of *On Certainty* is that *judgments* can function as a standard or norm as well as objects like the standard meter bar, charts, schemata, formulae. Judging that Napoleon was exiled to Elba is constitutive of doing history, and so sets a standard for doing history. If a student refused to accept this, the student would be incompetent to do history, just as would a pupil who fails to put "1001" after "1000" in carrying out the natural number sequence. Coming to judge in these particular ways is part of coming to do history or mathematics. "Napoleon was exiled to Elba" has the form of an empirical proposition, but the way it functions within historical inquiry shows it to be normative. These propositions that hold fast are certain in a way that is different, though related, to the methodological propositions. While methodological propositions are immanent in our practices, and thus not independent grounds for these practices, normative judgments have the certainty that accrues to any standard or paradigm, without, however, being inherently privileged or inherently representational. What appears to be the specialness of the object, whether chart, meter stick, or judgment, is in fact the specialness of the way it is used in concrete instances of social practice. The notion of "concept" as the fixed locus of meaning, and so independent of particular applications, is eliminated. The rule of use is thus not prior to, nor independent of, the particular applications in concrete situations.

The universality condition

As we have already seen, there are different kinds of propositions that hold fast, and this very fact undermines further the Kantian interpretation, for there are many instances of such propositions that simply can't be interpreted to fit the Kantian model.[9] Wittgenstein introduces methodological propositions in his discussion of the nature of certainty, doubt, and error, but these are not the only propositions that stand fast for us. He also includes certain *particular* claims as being equally certain. Knowing one's own name (OC §569–76) or that one has never been to the moon (OC §110–17) or whether one has ever visited China (OC §333) are also certainties, propositions that hold fast, yet they are not even appropriate candidates for the Kantian interpretation. Unlike Kant, where the certainty of transcendental truths comes from their playing the same role in experience and knowledge, Wittgenstein allows that there are different kinds of certainties that play different roles. There is no uniform account for the certainty of these various propositions.

I shall look briefly at three examples. (1) My name is M.W. (2) I have never been to China. (3) Here is a hand (raising, in Moorean fashion, my hand). None stand in need of justification; none can reasonably be doubted; none can be the object of mistake. They are not knowledge claims. All of these categorical claims stand in need of some modification, though in different respects. (1) is a certainty in any society whereas (2) is culturally bounded in that any normal European or American knows whether he has ever been to China or not (unless there are some peculiar circumstances in the individual's life that make it doubtful). (3) is a certainty because there is no evidence that one could appeal to in support of this claim that is stronger than the claim itself (cf. OC §153).

When I say that none of these can be doubted, I do not mean this in a psychological sense. If I have amnesia, I may well doubt that "M.W." is my name or I may not know whether I have ever been to China. Also I can doubt that this is a hand – if I suffer from aphasia or schizophrenia. All these cases where doubt arises, or where I don't know, are cases of mental disturbance. If I suffer from amnesia, aphasia, schizophrenia, all of these things may not be certain. But their dubiousness arises from my deranged mental state not from the existence or discovery of countervailing evidence or a lack of evidence (cf. OC §71–4).

This meshes with the remarks about the character of the methodological propositions and their certainty. Their certainty was a reflection of our lives (understood in terms of the practices, actions, and judgments we make). To be in genuine doubt about them is to forfeit living and to fall into madness. The king who believes that the world began with his birth is the greatest of megalomaniacs. The person who believes that objects don't continue to exist when unperceived is psychotic. Whether we consider these general propositions that hold fast or particular propositions, doubt is a reflection of some kind of disorder, not the discovery of new evidence. It is, as Wittgenstein puts it, in the form of life that certainty is fixed.

4 The problem of oscillation

Once we acknowledge these profound differences between Wittgenstein's views and Kant's, what are the implications for the problem of oscillation so many commentators have seen in the *Investigations* and that Wittgenstein himself is aware of when he denies that he is doing natural science or natural history (PI II §vii), or when he warns that a proposition can shift from an empirical to a non-empirical use (PI §85; OC §321), or that there is no sharp boundary between an empirical and non-empirical proposition (OC §318–20), or when he argues that we can be misled by "something whose form makes it look like an empirical proposition, but which is really a grammatical one" (PI §251). Does Wittgenstein move from a transcendental perspective to a realistic one, from a transcendental interpretation of language to a realistic interpretation, from a Kantianized grammar to empirical linguistics?

The problem, roughly stated here, fails to disentangle two distinct questions, each of which addresses the issue of whether Wittgenstein, like Kant, seeks to describe a transcendental limit to language and so to delimit, once and for all, all that is actually and potentially intelligible. The first question concerns the status of propositions that hold fast: Are these propositions transcendental propositions or empirical? Do they make a transcendental claim or an empirical claim? The second question concerns the status of Wittgenstein's characterization of these propositions as propositions that hold fast: Is this an empirical description or a transcendental one? It seems that we are faced with the following alternatives: Either these propositions are transcendental and so the subject matter of a transcendental philosophy; or they are empirical and thus better pursued by the linguist or anthropologist. Wittgenstein's metaphilosophy seems strongly to support the idea that these are empirical matters, and that recognition of this brings philosophy to end. On the other hand, Wittgenstein's discussion of grammatical statements and of propositions that look like empirical propositions and yet are not argues against treating them as empirical prositions, thus making a transcendental interpretation plausible.

The dichotomy is a false one: Though Wittgenstein repudiates any attempt to find a positive limit to what is intelligible or possible, he does not hold that propositions that hold fast are thereby empirical, nor that philosophical inquiry is thereby a kind of non-systematic empirical study.

Let me first summarize where there are affinities betwen Wittgenstein and Kant and where there are differences. Wittgenstein holds with Kant that our practices and actions logically presuppose methodological propositions like "The earth has existed since long before my birth," and he shares with Kant a reaction against classical empiricism and transcendent metaphysics. But this is as far as the analogies go. Where Kant looks for transcendental boundaries, Wittgenstein locates certainties immanent in our practices. Where Kant views the independent concept as generating the rule of use (in the schematism), Wittgenstein sees the pattern of application as making room for the concept. Whereas Kant's holism is grounded in the conception of knowledge and experience having two elements (intuitions and concepts) brought together, Wittgenstein espouses a kind of contextualism in which there is no place for the picture of two elements brought together, for the very significance and status of concept as concept or experience as experience is to be found in the context of use. The components we need to make sense of the search for a transcendental limit to all possible experience are missing from Wittgenstein's thought.

The notion of a form of life and his use of language games as a basic philosophical tool highlight his reaction against the two-component view of knowledge and experience. Both "form of life" and "language game" involve ways of speaking within a context of activity. Indeed the speaking is part of the activity itself, and cannot be peeled away as an independent entity. Both language as a set of grammatical rules and language as expressed in Wittgenstein's grammatical statements are abstractions only from the concrete reality. They are not independent realities that come into play in concrete situations. As such, the elements necessary for a transcendental philosophy are missing: The boundary itself cannot be described positively and independently of the concrete situations in which judgments are made and actions engaged in.

Wittgenstein's contextualism is not the same as constructing a transcendental argument from within our practices. His contextualism does not lead to describing a substantive boundary. His view of language and grammar is not the linguistic counterpart to Kant's metaphysical psychology. There is no way to tell in advance of what we actually do what is possible for us to do or say. Wittgenstein's contextualism and what I call his doctrine of immanence (a later variety of the doctrine of showing) do not constitute a transcendental philosophy.

Yet, as I have already argued, propositions that hold fast have a status altogether different from that of empirical propositions although, even here, a sharp boundary cannot be drawn between empirical propositions and non-empirical propositions (OC §318). Such propositions have a normative function that is missing from empirical descriptions. Though the status of these propositions differs, which propositions are normative and which are empirical is not fixed once and for all. Changing circumstances can involve changing norms. "Napoleon was exiled to Elba" may cease to be a standard of historical judgment and become, in some distant future, the rediscovery of a forgotten episode in human history. What I have been calling "methodological propositions" also have a different status from empirical generalizations, for they are held in place by any activity or practice in which we engage; they are immanent in whatever we do without thereby constituting a transcendental limit to what we do. Thus, Wittgenstein replaces the contrast between "empirical" and "transcendental" with certainties that function differently in our lives, with a constrast between the empirical and the normative, that is, between empirical statement and norm. This addresses the first question, but what of the second?

As many commentators have noted, Wittgenstein is concerned with our overstepping the bounds of intelligibility. They construe this concern as a desire to describe positive boundaries. This is not the way to understand it.

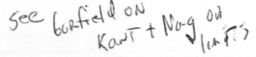

see barfield on Kant + Nag on [...]

It is interesting to note that questions of intelligibility arise for Wittgenstein in our seeking to make philosophical claims. And here Wittgenstein's strategy is not to draw a limit in advance but to develop and examine certain tempting lines of thought from various approaches, showing the bankruptcy of each. The strategy, in a sense, is negative, to show the futility of certain kinds of inquiry.

But if Wittgenstein is not engaged in transcendental metaphysics, just what is the status of his own remarks about grammar, propositions that hold fast, certainty, and the like? They are descriptions cited to a philosophical end. But how does this differ from saying that they are philosophical statements with a status wholly other than that of empirical descriptions? And if there are such philosophical statements, doesn't this come perilously close to a transcendental view, since they are intended to "describe" the outer limits of all of our practices? There is a difference between saying that they are descriptions used to a philosophical end and saying that they are transcendental statements. That difference can be seen by locating them within Wittgenstein's own philosophical method, a method that I argued earlier is not architectonic. They are empirical descriptions in that they do describe and characterize various uses of language; yet they are philosophical in point because they are brought in to combat and/or to provide alternatives to philosophical theses, alternatives that draw us back to the ordinary, back to the "rough ground." Their profundity lies in the place they hold in the philosophical journey, not in their intrinsic significance, and so they are simply not of interest to the anthropologist. Wittgenstein, in displaying various kinds of propositions that hold fast, is combating metaphysical theorizing, not offering his own variety of the metaphysics of experience.

4 Language learning and the representational theory of mind

In J. A. Fodor (Fodor 1975 and 1981) we have a new and very up-to-date champion of the representational theory of mind (RTM), the theory that an organism's cognitive relations to the world are mediated by a system of mental representations. According to Fodor, Descartes and other seventeenth- and eighteenth-century philosophers were essentially correct in their approach to understanding the mind; it was in the details of their mentalistic models and in their preoccupation with epistemological problems that they went wrong. Originally the RTM was adopted, not because of its plausibility as an explanatory theory in psychology but because it was able, *prima facie*, to meet the stringent demands of a foundationalist epistemology. On Fodor's view, however, the RTM can be disassociated from epistemology (Fodor 1975: pp. 44–5) – as convincingly as Kepler's laws can be separated from his fantastic views about the solar system. To salvage the laws in this way requires showing them to be part of a different and viable theory. In other words, Kepler's laws are not self-evidently acceptable but are acceptable only insofar as they are grounded in a viable theoretical framework. Kepler's mysticism about perfect geometric solids does not provide such a framework; Newtonian physics, on the other hand, does.

Likewise the RTM needs a new theoretical grounding. It has been argued, and Fodor seems to accept, that the foundationalist program has been discredited. (In any case, Fodor wants to turn his back on epistemological issues.)[1] With the loss of this original theoretical framework, the RTM must be newly grounded. This is achieved, according to Fodor, in the work of contemporary cognitive psychology. But how does work in cognitive psychology provide a new and viable theoretic grounding for the RTM, a theory so appropriate for answering the "scope and limits" problem of knowledge? Fodor's argument is simple and straightforward (Fodor 1975: p. 27):

1   The only psychological models of cognitive processes that seem even remotely plausible represent such processes as computational.

2   Computation presupposes a medium of computation: a representational system.

3   Remotely plausible theories are better than no theories at all.

4   We are thus provisionally committed to attributing a representational system to organisms.

Psychology is concerned with what beliefs are and how we come to have any, not with how we justify beliefs about the world. Philosophical questions concerning modes of justification give way and are replaced by psychological questions concerning the nature of cognitive processes. And these theories and models are computational.[2] We see, then, that it is the computational theory of cognitive processes (CT) that provides the new theoretical foundation for the RTM. Thus, whether, and to what extent, the RTM is acceptable depends on whether, and to what extent, the CT is defensible. What is crucial, then, is Fodor's defense of premise (1) that "the only remotely plausible" psychological theories are committed to the CT.

Fodor's strategy is to cite three important problem areas of common concern to psychology and philosophy, holding that only a computational model can adequately address them:

> My point will be that not only considered action, but also learning and perception, must surely be viewed as based upon computational processes; and, once again, no computation without representation.
>
> (Fodor 1975: p. 34)

So commitment to the CT, Fodor tells us, is our only hope of explaining deliberate action, learning (and concept learning in particular), and perception. To be able to explain these phenomena, so long resistant to philosophical or psychological solution, is a powerful inducement to accept the CT and so the RTM. (And with these Fodor's counterintuitive claims that the system of representations is a non-natural language and that all concepts are innate.) Tactically, Fodor supports the CT by arguing that there are no viable alternatives and that cognitive psychology gives us empirical support for the success of the CT.

What I intend to show is that what ultimately Fodor defends about the CT is not what induced us to take it seriously. The promise of answering the interesting philosophical and psychological questions dies, leaving a rather narrow and arid research program behind.

In a sense, my argument shall be narrower than this conclusion implies, for I shall focus solely on Fodor's treatment of learning, in particular concept learning. What I have to say about this will, I hope, be suggestive of similar difficulties with respect to computational accounts of perception or considered action. I begin, then, with Fodor's account of what language learning must consist in, which seems to permit nothing but the computational model.

1 Language learning

"Concept learning," Fodor asserts, "is one of those processes in which what the organism knows is altered as a consequence of its experiences; in particular, as a consequence of its interactions with the environment" (Fodor 1975: p. 34). From this starting point, Fodor intends to show that "concept learning is essentially inductive extrapolation" (Ibid.: p. 42); and inductive extrapolation is a computational process. But a good bit of filling in needs to be done, for there is a tremendous gap between the starting point and the conclusion.

Indeed, the starting point makes such a minimal claim that it is fully acceptable to the behaviorist, the cognitive psychologist,[3] or one who is sceptical of psychological processes. Disagreement arises when substantive content is given, for all the crucial terms stand as placeholders. For the behaviorist the process is one of operant conditioning whereby the emergent behavior of the organism is the causal result of a history of positive and/or aversive reinforcement. For the sceptic of inner mental processes, the process may be one of social acculturation and training which gives rise to rule-governed action. For Fodor, speaking on behalf of the cognitive psychologist, the process is a computational one in which what the organism knows is the causal result of the instantiation of a series of computational states. Thus, starting with the minimal statement, we get radically different accounts of what is learned (a piece of behavior, an action, or a bit of knowledge), the process of learning (operant conditioning, social training, or inductive extrapolation), the characterization of the experience the organism has (positive and/or aversive reinforcement, training in a practice, or the collection of data).

Of these theory-schemas concerning concept attainment, only one, Fodor maintains, provides a viable scientific explanation; that is the hypothesis, associated especially with the work of L.S. Vygotsky (Vygotsky 1965)[4] and J.S. Bruner *et al.* (Bruner *et al.* 1965),[5] that "concept learning is essentially a process of hypothesis formation and confirmation" (Fodor 1975: p. 35). Neither of the alternatives to the cognitive approach mentioned above conforms to the constraints of the hypothesis-formation model, and so neither is acceptable, according to Fodor. Behaviorism offers a genuinely explanatory account of concept learning – concept learning is the result of an appropriate schedule of reinforcements – but one that doesn't work. It offers a reasonable research program, but it turns out to lead nowhere. (Insofar as it seems to be successful, it is because it is really a camouflaged hypothesis-formation theory (Fodor 1975: pp. 35–6n).) On the skill model, concept acquisition is to be explained wholly in terms of social training without appeal to inner processes. For Fodor, such a view would be tantamount to rejecting any attempt to look for a genuine explanation of cognitive phenomena. It is the psychological nihilist's position – the position of one who denies that psychology gives a scientific account of the mechanism whereby a concept is acquired. Since to turn one's back on scientific explanation is not a viable alternative, the only plausible research program available to us is that offered by the hypothesis-formation model.

The substantive models of hypothesis formation developed by cognitive psychologists such as Bruner are models of inductive extrapolation. We need to examine the justification given for adopting inductivist models. (Fodor's justification for accepting it, tentatively, is that it is what empirically minded psychologists have developed.)

There are certain methodological constraints under which cognitive psychologists work that make something like an inductivist model, if not inevitable, highly promising. One is that, as J. S. Bruner *et al.* put it in *A Study of Thinking*, "in order to study a psychological process one must externalize it for observation" (Bruner *et al.* 1965: p. 51). Another is that the possibility of controlled experimentation requires that the "externalized" process be analyzable into fairly discrete steps and factors. (In saying that psychological processes are "externalized," Bruner is not stating a theoretical view, but making clear a heuristic principle.) These two methodological demands are necessary for a systematic experimental inquiry into hidden psychological processes. The hidden processes must be modelled on public processes if they are to become "observable." In order for these processes to be subject to systematic experimentation, the experimenter must be able to discriminate and so control for various discrete contributing factors to these processes.

Bruner describes how psychological processes can be appropriately externalized for observation as follows: The first step is to identify the phenomenon to be explained; in this case, it is the phenomenon of attaining a new concept, a process which often appears inexplicable. We often seem to move quickly from a state of confusion or uncertainty about what a term means to a state of clarity – the "aha! experience." At this level of description the change is a mystery. The task of the psychologist is to remove the mysterious gap by, in effect, telling a story in which one moves step by step in a coherent and rational manner from a state of confusion to one of clarity. A person could learn a new concept by offering a number of tentative suggestions as to what the concept means and then making decisions as to how to proceed given the response to his suggestions. In the story we can see the agent making a number of decisions as to how to carry on; comparative examination of a number of such stories will show that the decisions made are not random but form a pattern of regularity. By making the decisions explicit and overt, the psychologist is in a position to observe patterns of decision making, patterns which point to underlying strategies. The strategies which guide concept attainment are varieties of inductive extrapolation. In other words, the agent attempts to extrapolate generalizations about the extension of a concept or the criterial properties of a concept that determine its extension on the basis of the instances to which he is exposed. In short, one models the hidden processes of the "aha! experience" on public decision-making processes much as early atomic theories were modeled on the behavior of billiard balls.

A typical kind of experiment in concept acquisition is one in which the subject is asked to determine what the environmental conditions are for the correct application of a new concept. To use Fodor's example of a simple experiment of this kind (Fodor 1975: pp. 35–7), the subject is asked to determine which of an array of stimulus cards (cards with, say, one of three symbols in one of four colours) are bik, where "bik" is an artificial term denoting any card that has either a red or triangular symbol on it or both. What the subject must do is to extrapolate the hypothesis that all bik cards have red and/or triangular symbols on the basis of instances that do conform to this criterion. In order to do this the subject must begin by randomly identifying one of the cards as bik. If this is a correct identification, the subject will proceed according to one kind of strategy; if incorrect, he will proceed in another way. The decisions the subject makes at each stage point to his building up a confirmation matrix in which responses are correlated with the absence or presence of the criterial property. From this matrix the subject will be able to extrapolate a generalization about the criterial property of "bik." The experimental results, namely, the kinds of decisions subjects make in these learning situations, certainly seem to support the inductivist model of concept attainment.

But such support is illusory. At best, the inductivist model applies to certain rather specific situations. Yet this is not the intent. Though we explicitly use the inductivist strategies only in rather special circumstances, as a model it is meant to display the cognitive mechanisms of all (or at least most) concept attainment. But there are reasons for doubting that the inductivist model can offer a general account of concept learning.

First, it is simply not true that all concept attainment can be explained in terms of inductive extrapolation. This model works well for concrete classificatory concepts like "bik," but does not work for the attainment of, e.g., theoretical concepts without so attenuating the notion of observation as the justificatory basis for the extrapolation as to strip it of its explanatory value.

This point is similar to one of the standard objections brought against behaviorism.[6] The power of explanations couched in terms of stimulus–response associations turns on having a clear criterion for the proper way to individuate the stimulus and the response; both are to be identified and described in a neutral, non-intentionalist vocabulary. Yet in order to individuate the features of the environment and kinds of behavior that are associated in a regular way, the notions of stimulus and response are stretched in such a way that intentional structure is built into the characterization of the stimulus and the responses. Stimulus and response, instead of being independent variables, are identified in terms of each other. The apparently objective scientific explanation of behavior is disclosed as a scientistic cover for our ordinary intentionalist narratives.

This same difficulty threatens cognitive psychology if the model of concept attainment as inductive extrapolation is presented as fully general, rather than as applicable to a fairly restricted range of concepts. Inductive extrapolation as a means for generating hypotheses about the criterial properties for the correct application of a word makes the basis of justification for the hypotheses observational. Observation here, if it is to play its explanatory role, must be taken as ordinary perceptual observation, which explains by justifying and justifies because observation reports are just the things to be taken at face value. But observation cannot play the same role when we talk of acquiring theoretical concepts, and it cannot play this role because ordinary observation is not the justificatory basis for correct application of theoretical concepts. The subject claims that this particular card is bik because he sees that its symbol is red and triangular, and he has determined that being red and/or triangular is criterial by extrapolating these observed features from the observed positive instances of bik cards. But the subject who claims that this is an electron because he sees the tracks being formed in the Wilson cloud chamber is not justified in his claim by this observation per se. To oversimplify, the reason for this is that the theory sets the criteria of justification. The laboratory apparatus doesn't simply display the truth, for it was constructed in accordance with certain theoretical constraints and for particular theoretical purposes. One cannot acquire a theoretical concept by extrapolating the criterial properties from observed positive instances of the concept; one is only justified in claiming to have "observed" an instance when one has grasped the theory in terms of which an observation is possible. Whereas in ordinary experience and with ordinary concrete classificatory terms, observation is a sufficient justificatory basis, this is not true for theoretical terms. One is warranted in one's observations by the theory, and so ordinary direct observation cannot provide sufficient evidence or justification. The point is that though one may grasp the "bik" concept by a method of inductive extrapolation, one could not acquire the concept "electron" in this way. To force a fit by insisting that going to physics classes and learning to manipulate a Wilson cloud chamber and other sophisticated apparatus are forms of observation from which one extrapolates the concept "electron" so stretches the claim as to make it vacuous.

Second, not only can we question the full generality of this model of concept attainment, we can also raise doubts about its covering even the restricted range of ordinary classificatory concepts. Again a parallel with behaviorism is useful. It has been suggested that the principles of operant conditioning do not so much explain modified behavior as characterize the nature of the Skinner box (Chomsky 1959; Dennett 1978b). It is the highly controlled and restricted range of options that gives the appearance that modified behavior can be explained in terms of stimulus–response associations and schedules of reinforcement. It is because the environment has been impoverished that an intentionalist vocabulary seems unnecessary. It is important to note that the environment is impoverished in two ways: the number of options is radically reduced and the relationship between behavior and goal is rendered completely arbitrary. It is no wonder that the only way in which the subject can learn these relationships is through a schedule of reinforcements, and it is no wonder that the relationships so established can be described in a neutral non-intentionalist vocabulary. But a theory tailored to fit an environment deliberately constructed so as to undermine and negate ordinary circumstances and conditions can hardly be said to provide a model for understanding ordinary behavior (Dennett 1971: pp. 98–9).

Does the same difficulty arise with Bruner's testing of concept attainment? Does the model of inductive extrapolation show something more about the experimental situation than the experiment shows about concept attainment in general? There is good reason to suspect this. The very way in which the subject understands his task limits his options: he can either not cooperate at all or, if he cooperates, he can either make random guesses or use some method of inductive extrapolation. The very nature of the test situation determines that a cooperating subject must proceed inductively. It is the features of the card that are significant: Some subset of these will be criterial, hits will be identified as such, there will be no exceptions. Generalizing from this controlled environment to the ordinary social world is no more warranted than generalizing from the artificial world of the Skinner box to the natural world. The social world in which we actually acquire concepts does not guarantee that any properties or features will be necessary and sufficient for the application of a concept (if anything, the contrary is true); that all positive instances will be identified as such; that there will be no exceptions.[7] The background conditions necessary for the successful use of inductive extrapolation are missing. These inductive strategies, as Bruner calls them, are appropriate to the test situation because of the nature of the test situation. The most we are justified in claiming is that in controlled situations of a certain type, these strategies are appropriate.

Thus, we see that the inductivist interpretation of the hypothesis-confirmation theory, though a substantive theory suitable to the laboratory, is inadequate as a general account of concept acquisition or inapplicable to a very wide range of cases of concept attainment. Fodor's conclusion that "so far as anyone knows, concept learning is essentially inductive extrapolation" (p. 49) just is not substantiated, not even with the proviso. Fodor might respond that, despite the apparent endorsement of the inductivist model, it is really only a "useful illustration of our main thesis (cognitive processes are computation processes and hence presuppose a representational system)" (Fodor 1975: p. 34). As an illustration, it cannot constitute empirical support for the CT. So where does support for the CT (and so the RTM) come from? The answer is that the grounds are in fact a priori.

Fodor takes it as an obvious truth that language is learned and, moreover, that learning a language is a matter of concept learning. At first sight, these claims seem quite unexceptional. After all, children do learn a language and, in so doing, they learn to wield concepts. But Fodor presses the advantage with these commonplaces and tells us that "Concept learning is one of those processes in which what the organism knows is altered as a consequence of its experience" (Fodor 1975: p. 34). This is Fodor's version of the minimal starting point discussed at the beginning of this section. The significance of this version, which I deliberately overlooked earlier, is that it effectively puts the organism in "the logical space of reasons and justification," to use Sellars' apt phrase (Sellars 1963: p. 169). Clearly the behaviorist would totally eschew such a claim; and so could the sceptic for he might argue that although the organism's actions could only be understood in non-causal terms, it does not require attributing explicit knowledge (even if unconscious) to the organism itself. So Fodor is not starting with the obvious, non-controversial claim, but with one biased towards the CT.

What kind of process this is, or must be, is determined by considering what would count as genuine learning. Not every kind of alteration in what the organism knows would *count* as *learning*. Being hit on the head or taking a pill could result in a change of what the organism knows, but that change would not be a result of learning. Very roughly, learning must be the result of a process in which the relevant experiences[8] are logically or internally appropriate to what is learned. The only process that meets this restriction is that of hypothesis formation and confirmation, for this is just a way of saying that the subject's experiences stand as justification or evidence for the hypothesis submitted. But now it is patent what the source of Fodor's commitment to the CT is. It is not accepted on the empirical grounds that it is a well-tested and confirmed psychological theory (it is doubtful that such grounds exist), but on the a priori ground that the hypothesis-formation model is the only interpretation of a conceptual truth about learning, coupled with the *unargued assumption* that the hypothesis-formation model entails the CT. Fodor has moved from a conceptual truth about what counts as learning to an empirical claim about concept acquisition. There is no warrant for this. All that can be said with empirical warrant is that a first language is acquired, not that it is learned.

It now seems that Fodor's commitment to the computational theory has neither empirical nor a priori support. No substantive computational theory has been defended that is adequate to explain how a first language is acquired. Bruner's inductivist model was shown to be inadequate. A priori considerations about what constitutes genuine learning lead us only to recognize that we have no reason to suppose that a first language is learned. Finally, if Bruner's theory was intended only as an illustration by Fodor,[9] illustrations are not needed but substantive theories.

2 The language of thought

A plausible line of response to the argument of section 1 is that unless we construe acquiring a first language as involving some form of hypothesis formation and confirmation, language acquisition is left an inexplicable mystery. At least with the hypothesis-formation model we have a way of explaining this most significant cognitive achievement (or the promise of such a way). The hypothesis-formation model, it could be argued, has tremendous explanatory power. The price of this model in general, Fodor emphasizes, is commitment to a system of internal representations.[10] And the price of applying this model to language learning is commitment to a language of thought that is both innate and non-natural:

> one cannot learn a first language unless one already has a system capable of representing the predicates in that language and their extensions. And, on pain of circularity, that system cannot be the language that is being learned. But first languages are learned. Hence,

at least some cognitive operations are carried out in languages other than natural languages.

(Fodor 1975: p. 64)

My view is that you can't learn a language unless you already know one. It isn't that you can't learn a language unless you've already learned one ... the language of thought is known (e.g., is the medium for the computations underlying cognitive processes) but not learned. That is, it is innate.

(Ibid.: p. 65)

But what explanatory role does this innate and non-natural language of thought play? For it is defensible only insofar as the model of which it is a part is defensible; and the defense of that model turns on its alleged explanatory power.

Fodor takes it that Augustine, as characterized by Wittgenstein in the *Philosophical Investigations*, had the correct understanding of the need for such a language:

Wittgenstein, commenting upon some views of Augustine's, says: "Augustine describes the learning of human languages as if the child came into a strange country and did not understand the language of the country; that is, as if it already had a language, only not this one. Or again, as if the child could already think, only not yet speak. And 'think' would here mean something like talk to itself..."

Wittgenstein apparently takes it that such a view is transparently absurd. But the argument that I just sketched [viz. one cannot learn a language unless one knows a language] suggests, on the contrary, that Augustine was precisely and demonstrably right and that seeing that he was is prerequisite to any serious attempts to understand how first languages are learned.

(Fodor 1975: p. 64)

But about what was Augustine "precisely and demonstrably right?" On the Augustinian view, the language of thought is not only necessary in order to learn a first language, it explains how the subject learns it. He learns it in the way a foreigner learns a new language. He already has all the concepts and beliefs (background and immediate) for using them; he only has to discover the new words for these concepts. It is interesting to note that in his discussion of concept attainment, Bruner motivates his theory of hypothesis formation by telling a story of a foreigner trying to discover what the English word "influential" means. In both Bruner's motivating story and the Augustinian case, the learner is hypothesized as being fully competent, conceptually and epistemically, and it is only in virtue of these competencies that he is able to attain the new concept. Bruner's foreigner acquires the word "influential" by discovering the criterial properties associated with the use of this word, properties expressed and understood in his native tongue. As was pointed out above, if he is to make any headway at all, he must have considerable understanding of what sort of predicate this is; he must understand, for example, that this is a social relational predicate not a personal attributive one, that age, economic status, and religion matter rather than height, weight, or body temperature. Thus, our foreigner must possess a rather sophisticated understanding of contemporary society in order to acquire this predicate.

On the Augustinian model of language learning, the subject already has a network of beliefs, not just a system of "concepts." He has beliefs about the objective, how to identify the tentative criterial properties; methodological beliefs about what counts as good evidence and how to proceed; and background beliefs about medium-sized objects, the general character of social interaction, and so on. What can be studied and controlled for is how this mass of information and methodological tools can be marshalled and used in constructing the correct mappings from the foreign language onto the native. Insofar as this is done, how one can come to learn a new language has been explained. However, *it does not and cannot explain how one acquires these background and methodological beliefs*, for that competence is already part of the model. Ryle's charge of regress and Wittgenstein's charge of explanatory vacuousness are both directed against any attempt to construe the Augustinian model as an explanation schema for *these* competencies.

The strength of the Augustinian model is thus also its fatal weakness. It construes having a language of thought as having a complex system of beliefs, recognitional and judgmental capacities, and techniques. In other words, to have a language of thought is to be able to use it; and to use it requires taking many things to be true of the world and one's relation to it. This gives the appearance of explaining how one learns a natural language by reproducing what one wanted to explain about natural language competence in the first place. Thus, the "explanation" disintegrates under scrutiny, giving rise to the same set of questions one had about natural language competence in the first place.

Yet Fodor maintains that the Augustinian view is "precisely and demonstrably right." This is primarily a rhetorical flourish, but one that is misleading. Fodor does not accept the full-blown "theory," though his claim to do so suggests that the appeal to a language of thought will do far more explanatory work than in fact it can. Fodor maintains that to attribute a language of thought to an organism is not to attribute any beliefs to the organism about how to apply a concept in particular circumstances, about the general nature of the world or social interaction, about what constitutes good evidence for what nor any of the abilities that are arguably part of having such beliefs (Fodor 1975: pp. 60–3). Belief and action are separate from meaning. On Fodor's view, what the Augustinian model got right is that learning a first language requires having the concepts to be learned, but it mistakenly ties "having a concept" to epistemological requirements broadly speaking, i.e., to beliefs about the world and procedures for applying the concepts properly.

But the price for restricting the language of thought to a system of concepts is forfeiture of even the appearance of explaining how we learn a first language. If we restrict the domain of the innate to concepts, the issue of explaining active language use and language acquisition is as much an open question as before. Without a network of *beliefs* the hypothesis-formation model is inapplicable, and so we are no closer to understanding how language is acquired. In brief, Fodor is faced with a rather unpleasant dilemma: If the hypothesis-formation model is the only plausible explanation for language acquisition, *a fortiori* we are committed to a system of innate beliefs. Yet in hypothesizing the existence of a set of beliefs and cognitive abilities, we duplicate what we wanted to understand about cognitive development in the first place: The explanation is a pseudo-explanation. On the other hand, if we restrict the language of thought to a system of internal representations only (denying that there are any innate beliefs), then the hypothesis-formation model can't be used, for it requires attributing beliefs to the subject. A general consequence of this dilemma is that the grounds for accepting the RTM have been lost. One might say that the representational theory of mind is still a possibility, but this in itself provides no reason to accept it. Without a substantive hypothesis-formation model, there is no reason to accept that theory of the mind.

In effect, Fodor attempts to find a way out of this dilemma by attacking the second horn; he maintains that one can both restrict the innate language of thought to a system of representations and successfully use the hypothesis-formation model. Such a defense, I shall argue in the next section, succeeds only by turning over the interesting philosophical and developmental issues to others.

3 "Rationalist psychology"

In breaking out of the dilemma, Fodor once again moves to higher ground, away from defending any particular account of language learning to a characterization of what scientific psychology *must* look like. So in the end his defense of the CT as a way of explaining cognitive processes derives from his view that this is the only form that scientific psychology can take, not from its being a consequence of the only viable explanatory model for our most important cognitive abilities. Before moving directly to a discussion of his new defense of CT, I shall offer a reconstruction of the dynamics that take Fodor to this new defense. As I shall show, even the new defense is a way of trying to attack the second horn of the dilemma I have presented. I shall begin with Fodor's elaboration on what the mind is doing when it correlates English words (or the words of any natural language) with its innate representations. As we shall see, however, Fodor's account of this very quickly takes us to the higher ground I have alluded to, in which we are concerned with what the mind is doing when it is engaged in any cognitive performance, a much broader issue.

On Fodor's view, the meaning of a word is given by a truth rule. So what the subject learns when he acquires a new word is a truth rule of the following form: $\lceil Py \rceil$ is true (in English) if x is G, where "P" is a predicate in English and "G" a predicate in the language of thought (Fodor 1975: p. 59n). The importance of this account of meaning and of what is learned in acquiring a new word is that the epistemological issues concerning background beliefs and the like can, it seems, readily be divorced from questions of meaning. Truth rules can be stated entirely independently of any epistemological issues, for knowing a truth definition or truth rule is distinct both from being able to give a non-trivial statement of the truth rule and from knowing how to determine when the truth conditions obtain. To know that the truth condition for "This is a chair" is that this is a chair does not entail that one knows that, or has any way to find out whether, *this* particular object is a chair. On the contrary, learning a language proper, so far as the psychologist is concerned, has little, if anything, to do with the world; for one forms hypotheses, not about what things in the world are part of the extension of the new English word, but about which representation in the language of thought (a representation already known) is to be labeled, or associated, with the English term. The baby might well form the wrong hypothesis about "ball," perhaps accepting "This is a ball" is true (in English) iff this is a chair. Upon disconfirmation of this hypothesis, the baby would form a new hypothesis and so on until he got the correct one, namely, "This is a ball" is true (in English) iff this is a ball.

But how are these hypotheses supposed to be formed? How is a confirmation or disconfirmation to be understood as such? Epistemological issues (broadly speaking) seem to disappear because Fodor holds that the learner is forming hypotheses, not about objects in the world, such as balls and puppies, but about English words, "ball" and "puppy." But this does not eliminate the need for background beliefs, principles of evidence, and the like: it simply changes the beliefs needed. The mere presentation of numerous objects all of which are red, e.g., is not sufficient for the subject to extrapolate and confirm the hypothesis that "red" means red in the language of thought. There is nothing in the instances themselves that will trigger or announce which is the appropriate internal representation to be labeled by the English word "red," for with this database the child could just as well extrapolate that "red" means being a physical object or having shape or being three-dimensional and so on. As Wittgenstein put it, a place must be made for the concept, and that place can only be made within a network of beliefs.[11] Fodor must show how the formation of hypotheses in the language of thought differs from ordinary hypothesis formation such that the former presupposes no background and methodological beliefs.

This problem of background belief re-emphasizes the difficulty Fodor faces in eluding the dilemma posed at the end of the previous section. He needs a third way between admitting innate beliefs and giving up the hypothesis-formation model. He attempts to find one by recasting the hypothesis-formation model. Intuitively it is a model that appeals to epistemic links that explain in virtue of their content and the content of the beliefs to which they are directed. Fodor's proposal involves replacing evidential and methodological beliefs with a repertoire of innate operations that are applied solely in virtue of the *form* of the innate representations. In this way, neither the content of the "hypotheses" nor the content of the "epistemic" principles that select among the vying hypotheses are relevant to the psychological explanation. Thus, Fodor would agree that no database can in itself select for the relevant hypotheses, but "the way out of this puzzle," Fodor tells us, "is to assume that candidate extrapolations of the data receive an a priori ordering under a *simplicity metric*..." and "simplicity metrics must be sensitive to the *form* of the hypotheses that they apply to, i.e., to their syntax and vocabulary" (Fodor 1975: p. 39). In brief, as he develops this idea in a later article, "formal operations apply in terms of the, as it were, 'shapes' of the objects in their domain" (Fodor 1981: p. 310). This is the proper study of what he calls "Rationalist Psychology." This formal account quite deliberately and effectively eliminates all that is epistemic and contentful:

> The very assumption that defines their field – viz., that they study mental processes *qua* formal operations on symbols – guarantees that their studies won't answer the question how the symbols so manipulated are semantically interpreted.
>
> (Fodor 1981: p. 315)

So here is the way between the horns of the dilemma: The problem of background belief is solved by postulating formal computational operations that apply in virtue of the shapes rather than the content of the internal representations. But this solution is not without costs.

As has been claimed by Fodor on numerous occasions, the hypothesis-formation model seems to provide the most viable and promising model for important cognitive abilities. It is this model that seems to provide the support for the computational and representational theories of mind. Yet it is precisely the epistemic and contentful dimensions that are necessary to explain these psychological phenomena. The model explains concept learning, deliberate action, and perception precisely because it involves establishing evidential links, drawing inferences, assessing data, ranking competing hypothesis, and the like. After all, learning does require that the experiences of the learner are taken as evidence or support for a claim (otherwise, as we saw in section 1, it wouldn't be learning); deliberate action clearly involves the weighing of options; perception goes beyond the bare database of retinal stimulation. All of these phenomena cry out (or so it seems)[11] for an explanation in terms of an epistemic model, and that model is the hypothesis-formation model. It is the promise of achieving explanations of such phenomena that led us all to look so favorably upon the hypothesis-formation model. But the connection the computational theory apparently had with the hypothesis-formation model, the connection that gave us reason to support the computational theory, has been severed by deliberately eliminating all that is contentful from the computational theory.

In doing this, we have lost the only reason we had to find the computational theory plausible. The hypothesis-formation model was defended as the only plausible account of language learning on the ground that it involved evidential, i.e., contentful, relations between the database and the candidate hypotheses. Yet Rationalist Psychology, as Fodor characterizes it, has nothing to do with content. And so the grounds for accepting the computational theory have been lost. Fodor's Rationalist Psychology doesn't speak to the problem of background belief. Yet the hypothesis-formation model, for which this problem is a problem, provides the ground for the alleged plausibility of the computational theory. So in giving up pursuing contentful explanation, we give up any reason for pursuing formal explanation.

Yet, the computational theory, having been disassociated from the hypothesis-formation model and the problems it addressed, takes on a life of its own. The philosophical and psychological problems – language acquisition, deliberate action, perception – which initially led us to the computational theory remain as pressing and as unanswered as they were without the computational theory. By Fodor's own account, all the interesting developmental and cognitive questions, i.e., any that involve organism–environment interaction, are not part of Rationalist Psychology.

So what is the subject matter of Rationalist Psychology? It is the study of mental processes *qua* formal operations on the shapes of symbols: It is the psychology of "syntax." As Fodor puts it, there is a "drastic narrowing of the ordinary ontology of the mental" (Fodor 1981: p. 310). This "narrowing" results, as Fodor acknowledges, from the commitment to the formal interpretation of the computational theory. Though radically impoverished, attempts are made to reconstruct links with contentful psychological states:

> if the computational theory of the mind is true…it follows that content alone cannot distinguish thoughts. More exactly, the computational theory of mind requires that two thoughts can be distinct in content only if they can be identified with relations to formally distinct representations.
>
> More generally, fix the subject and the relation, and then mental states can be (type) distinct only if the representations which constitute their objects are formally distinct.
>
> (Fodor 1981: p. 310)

In short, where there is a difference in content, there must be a difference in shape. Of course, this connection must obtain only given a priori commitment to the formal CT. This commitment forces a fit between content and shape where there is no such "fit" naturally.

In ordinary English, there is no natural correspondence between the semantic and syntactic properties of words. First, there are the well-known cases of semantic ambiguity, where we do not have syntactically distinct objects for each semantic unit. Indeed the possibility of there being more than one interpretation of a word, phrase or sentence is virtually always available, though for the most part context and background belief remove any real possibility of confusion or ambiguity. Thus commitment to this formal CT commits one to the highly dubious claim that both meaning and syntactic object must be fixed and ambiguity-free in the strongest sense (i.e., not relative to a context or background) as well as to the claim that there is a unique shape for every semantic unit. Second and closely related to this first point, there are equally well-known cases of syntactic ambiguity. Both of these points are fully general, but there is also a third point that bears on Fodor's appeal to simplicity metrics in order to explain the acquisition of words.

This third point is that even if there are distinct formal objects correlated with distinct semantic entities (i.e., every possible symbol has a unique shape), this is not enough for a psychology of syntax. Even if there is a unique syntactic form for every semantic unit (and so in this way the language of thought differs markedly from ordinary language), simplicity of syntax does not mirror simplicity of content. Yet Fodor needs such mirroring if he is to reconstruct a link to the hypothesis-formation model and so to cognitive processes in general. To make this point, let us go back to Fodor's introduction of the simplicity metric as a means for answering the problem of background belief. The simplicity metric and other computational operations are sensitive only to the form or shape of hypotheses and confirmations that constitute the process of language acquisition (or perception or deliberate action). Keeping that in mind, consider why, in the early stages of development, hypotheses about ordinary medium-sized objects like blocks or mamas are favored over hypotheses about geometric cubes and Motherhood. We have a rough-and-ready explanation for this in terms of the baby's needs, what it is capable of physically handling, and the kind of theoretic and evidential support necessary to wield concepts like cube or Motherhood. Clearly this explanation is as far from a formal account as could be. Fodor's explanation must be couched solely in terms of the form of the internal representations and the relative simplicity of those forms; this is how the simplicity metric applies. Intuitively, blocks are simpler than cubes because blocks are objects that can be picked up, stacked and so on, activities within the grasp of the toddler. Cubes, on the other hand, are geometric shapes, consisting of six connecting plane sides all corners of which form right angles; these are theoretic features beyond the grasp of the toddler. (Similar things can be said about "mama" and "Motherhood.") Yet from a purely formal point of view, there is no guarantee that "block" will be simpler than "cube" in the language of thought. In considering the sentence strings of which they could each be a part, they seem to be equally simple. In considering their shapes, "cube" is simpler than "block " – it has one less element. The general point is that the criteria for simplicity vary depending on what is being so evaluated and for what purposes.

Thus, the retrenchment to a psychology of syntax seems to undercut the possibility for using the hypothesis-formation model of explanation. Fodor's reply – and indeed the only way to avoid this conclusion – is to claim that all epistemic relations are purely formal. That is, talk of belief, justification, evidential links just is talk of formal properties.[13] As Fodor puts it:

> to have the belief that P is to have the belief that P is warranted; and
> conversely, to have the belief that P is warranted is to have the belief

that P. And the upshot of this is just the formality condition all over again.

(Fodor 1981: p. 327)

But is there any good reason to suppose that all epistemic relations are purely formal? To make good on this claim would require, for example, that inductive reasoning proceeds in accordance with some purely formal inductive logic. Yet no attempt to develop such a logic has succeeded. The reason is not that formal inductive logics cannot be constructed, but that any inductive logic rests upon some non-formal starting point, e.g., axioms that assign some initial probabilities to the primitives, assignments that reflect antecedent beliefs about the world.[13]

Fodor's defense, presumably, would be the familiar one that there must be such a purely formal inductive logic, for this is what we have to accept if we are going to preserve Rationalist Psychology. Initially this line of defense for accepting the more unexpected and intuitively unacceptable consequences of cognitive models was a powerful tool in undermining the force of many objections. But surely such a defense wears thin if overused, and at some point, as the gains go down and the costs go up, the plausibility of this line of defense weakens considerably. I conclude that it is simply not sufficient as a way of defending Fodor's program, and so the second horn of the dilemma has not been successfully evaded.

4 Conclusion

I shall conclude this chapter by briefly summarizing the main line of argument. Having noted in my introductory remarks Fodor's contention that the "only remotely plausible" explanatory schema in psychology is the hypothesis-formation model and that this provides the theoretical grounding for the RTM, I went on to examine in the subsequent three sections three interpretations of that model and found each wanting. First, the inductivist model of concept learning, I argued, is at best adequate for a rather small range of concepts acquired by the competent language user under special circumstances. In section 2, I considered the move to higher ground with the defense of the Augustinian model. The Augustinian model, despite its defense as the only account that could explain this important cognitive achievement, leads nonetheless to an unfortunate dilemma: One can either accept the hypothesis-formation model and hypothesize innate beliefs along with innate concepts (assuming such a sharp distinction can be maintained), in which case it cannot be an explanation of how such competence is acquired; or one rejects the idea that beliefs could be innate and so gives up the hypothesis-formation model, in which case Fodor loses the only ground he cites for accepting the CT and the RTM. The attempt to find a third way leads Fodor to formulate and defend a formal interpretation of the hypothesis-formation model. Evidential and methodological beliefs are replaced by formal operations that apply to the shapes of the internal representations. In section 3, I entered two major reservations about this final line of defense. Fodor's advocacy of cognitivist models is rooted in their explanatory power, a power that derives from an intuitive understanding of what it is to form hypotheses, to select among competing ones on the basis of available evidence, and the like. Fodor begins with just such an understanding. My first reservation concerned whether the explanatory power of the hypothesis-formation model can be retained once Fodor has eliminated all that is contentful from Rationalist Psychology.

My second reservation concerned Fodor's attempt to replace evidential links and methodological beliefs as intuitively understood with purely formal operations, which commits him to holding that a purely formal inductive logic can be found. This is only a promissory note and a rather large one at that. There are grounds for being sceptical that it can be redeemed.

Since the defender of cognitivism finds himself, in the end, issuing such a large promissory note, he cannot really claim that his approach to psychology is the only viable one, as Fodor often does. Opponents of cognitivism, who emphasize skills and training in explaining action and cognitive abilities, are often reproached for the vagueness and indefiniteness of their explanations. This amounts to charging them with issuing promissory notes that they do not at present see how to redeem, but the cognitivist is in no better a position, and possibly a worse one.

Postscript to chapter 4

Fodor's thought has developed considerably since the publication of *The Language of Thought* (Fodor 1975), driven by problems arising from his commitment to the computational theory of mind and the language of thought hypothesis. Just as I argued that his fundamental commitment to these theses led to a retrenchment of the explanatory domain of scientific psychology, so problems concerning the holistic character of belief and the semantics of mental representations lead Fodor to solutions that further diminish the explanatory scope of cognitivism. In this Postscript I shall examine the ways in which Fodor addresses the problem of background belief and the problem of mental content. These two major problems lead to further retrenchments of the claims made on behalf of cognitivism. These are not viewed as retrenchments by Fodor, but as temporary setbacks awaiting further theoretical innovation.

In Chapter 4, I argued that the move from Intentionalist Psychology to Rationalist Psychology is the first retrenchment, from the identification of full-fledged perception, considered action, and language learning as the explananda to explanation in terms of the implementation of formal systems. Intentional states and actions are explained insofar as an isomorphism exists between the states of an intentional subject and the states of a computational system, but, as I argued above, there are serious doubts about the possibility of satisfying this condition. Now I shall show that the problem of belief holism and the problem of mental content lead to further retrenchments. At each stage, the domain of intentional states and actions is further removed from the explanatory scope of the computational theory. I hope to show that in addressing the problem of belief, Fodor gives up on showing how the computational theory can explain any of the ordinary intentional states we ascribe to persons; and in addressing the problem of mental content, he can provide at best a rationale for introducing proprietary notions of "representation" and "content" that cannot be extended to a general semantic theory. In brief, the three retrenchments can be characterized as the move from Intentional Psychology to Rationalist (Formalist) Psychology to abstract neurophysiology. Each step marks a growing scepticism about the possibility of explaining intentional states computationally.

1 The second retrenchment: the problem of background belief

In showing how beliefs and desires can be psychologically real causes, Fodor endorses the sentential theory of beliefs. This creates a deep internal tension between the hypothesis-formation model (H-F model) of psychological explanation and the sentential theory of the objects of the attitudes. Fodor, like Ptolemy, is forced to countenance a growing gap between his kinematics (his picture of the mind's structure or architecture) and his dynamics (his account of how the mind works). The computational kinematics was originally introduced and supported as the only empirically viable way to realize the dynamics of psychological activity. The hypothesis-formation model itself was defended as the only way to explain what Fodor comes to call our "central cognitive capacities" including learning (and especially language learning), acting and perceiving (Fodor 1983). It is important to note that the grounds for endorsing the H-F model are not empirical but conceptual. A modification or adaptation in behavior *would not count* as learning unless the relation between the data and the belief acquired on the basis of those data were an evidential relation. A deliberate action would not count as such unless it were the result of weighing the pros and cons of the available alternatives. The computational theory, on the other hand, is presented as an empirical hypothesis of how that epistemic assessment takes place. It looks promising, but what epicycles does Fodor introduce that clash with the hypothesis formation explanatory model of belief acquisition? Or, to express it in Rylean terms, how does the idea of the mind as a para-mechanical device conflict with the explanatory power of the Intellectualist Doctrine?

Fodor originally uses the H-F model to argue that there must be a language of thought in which the hypotheses are couched. Insofar as this argument is plausible, not only must there be some language in which hypotheses can be expressed, equally importantly there must be some set of substantive beliefs expressed or presupposed by the hypotheses themselves as well as what is accepted as confirmation or disconfirmation. If an adult sees something near a barn, then her perceptual problem, for which she offers hypotheses, is to identify what that object is. What constrains the hypotheses that are initially selected? Why would or should she favor hypotheses concerning farmyard animals rather than zoo animals or pets or factory machinery? In forming hypotheses she restricts herself to those that are appropriate given the circumstances. Of course, collateral information that this barn is now used to store factory machinery would significantly affect the range of hypotheses that would be generated. What would count as evidence for or against various hypotheses? How much information is sufficient to warrant acceptance? There is clearly an array of beliefs that are operative in the formation of various hypotheses. These include the roles played by collateral information, general background beliefs, and methodological and epistemological principles. Both first-order and second-order beliefs are involved. This would be equally true of a child just learning a language. The argument for innate mental representations as necessary for forming the young child's earliest hypotheses about the linguistic sounds she hears is equally an argument for an array of innate beliefs that provide the background and collateral information necessary for forming and testing the relevant hypotheses.

Merely citing these features of the H-F model does not yet show that there is any incompatibility between that model and the computational theory that draws on the sentential theory of the attitudes. It does show that the Fodorian view has the unwelcome consequence of committing the advocate to the existence of a large array of innate beliefs (or belief-analogs) as well as innate representations.[1] There are, however, other features of the H-F model that do conflict with the computational theory in a principled way. These are that the beliefs or belief-analogs of higher-level cognitive systems and their operations (like recognizing an object, making a decision, or learning a word) are *domain inspecific* in that they exploit different kinds of information (e.g., visual, tactile, auditory, syntactic) and *unencapsulated*, that is, they are penetrable by background beliefs, epistemic principles, contextual information, and the like (cf. Fodor 1983: Part IV). This epistemic and conceptual openness is incompatible with the closed character of a computational system. A system of belief is open and holistic in a way that a computational system cannot be.[2]

Fodor accepts the cogency of these Wittgensteinian-Quinean points, and this leads him to his second major retrenchment. The prospects for cognitive science are "gloomy," he tells us (Fodor 1983: p. 120), in that we do not currently have the theoretical resources for explaining any of the higher cognitive functions and competences. These are the competences that underwrite deliberate action, full-fledged perception, language use, and learning. The only systems currently amenable to scientific inquiry (i.e., computational modeling) are what he calls the "modular systems." These are the peripheral perceptual systems and a hypothesized sentence-recognition system. Modular systems are informationally encapsulated in that each is sensitive to a specific kind of sensory stimulation (visual or auditory or morpho-syntactic, for example) and is immune to inferential penetration from information of the higher cognitive systems. Because of encapsulation, "we can think of each input system as a computational mechanism which projects and confirms a certain class of hypotheses on the basis of a certain body of data" (Fodor 1983: p. 68).

The modular systems escape the difficulties that arise with the holistic character of belief but only at the cost of limiting computational modeling to modular mechanisms using very "shallow" levels of representation. The level of representation is shallow because it can virtually be "cashed in" in neurophysiological terms. As Fodor says, there is a "characteristic neural architecture associated with each of what I have been calling the input systems," for "neural hardwiring is pretty much what you would expect given the assumption that the key to modularity is informational encapsulation" (Fodor 1983: p. 98). On this construal of cognitive psychology, it is difficult to see the difference between doing scientific psychology and doing what Dennett calls "abstract neurophysiology" (Dennett 1987: p. 64). Saving the computational approach leaves cognitivism looking virtually indistinguishable from neurophysiology. All the rest rides on a promissory note that is to be redeemed at some time in the future in some theory or model other than the current computational models. As Fodor expresses it,

> the limits of modularity are also likely to be the limits of what we are going to be able to understand about the mind, given anything like the theoretical apparatus currently available.
>
> (Fodor 1983: p. 126)

Cognitivism no longer appears to have the theoretical resources to explain those achievements that Fodor himself targeted as requiring cognitivist (or at least mentalist) explanation, namely, perceptual constancy, the predictability of people's behavior, deliberate action, learning. The computational theory swings free of these matters. The real support thus stands free of the purported support. At this point, one might conclude that only much more modest claims can be made on behalf of the computational theory and that we might have to face the fact that only an explanatory pluralism about the mind is possible. This, however, is not the conclusion that Fodor draws. On the contrary, he remains as committed to the LOT hypothesis and computational theory as ever.

The only plausible explanation for the continued defense of this conception of mind is not the empirical evidence in favor of it nor the ubiquity of the H-F model in explaining cognitive achievements. Rather it reflects a philosophical commitment to a metaphysical realism about the world as "a connected causal order" (Fodor 1983: p. 105) and what he thinks this entails for our understanding of mind. In the context of Fodor's concern, this is a commitment to there being systematic and theoretically interesting connections between the causal order of the inanimate world and the causal order of our minds. It is a picture of the completion of the seventeenth-century scientific project in which the mind is incorporated into this "connected causal order." If the computational theory were to be true of the higher cognitive competences, this would show how psychological processes and structures fit, in a complementary way, into the larger causal nexus. In light of this metaphysical picture, redrawing the boundaries of the explanatory scope of the computational theory to include the peripheral systems and exclude the central cognitive systems is a serious setback.

As we can now see, Fodor's response to the problem of background belief leads to a further (de facto) narrowing of the explanatory scope of the computational theory, and with this narrowing comes a widening gap between scientific psychological theory (construed as computational modeling) and ordinary intentionalist explanation. The explananda of the two are not the same, and (as of *The Modularity of Mind*) there is no theoretic path from the computational operations of the modules to our believing, acting, and learning. But, given this restriction, what room is there for the idea that the operations of these peripheral systems involve contentful mental representations?

2 The third retrenchment: the problem of mental content

Fodor approaches the problem of accounting for mental content as a fully general requirement for his theory. Given his ideal of "the connected causal order," this is conceived as a reductionist problem, the need to naturalize the semantics of the language of thought, for

> [i]f the semantic and the intentional are real properties of things, it must be in virtue of their identity with (or maybe of their supervenience on?) properties that are themselves *neither* intentional *nor* semantic. If aboutness is real, it must be really something else.
>
> (Fodor 1988: p. 97)

Showing that "aboutness is…really something else" is, for Fodor, a matter of defending a causal theory of meaning. On Fodor's view, the object of belief is the content sentence to which the subject is related in the believing mode. The content of this sentence is a function of the reference of the constituent non-logical elements of the content sentence. So, a theory of mental content comes down to a theory of naturalized denotation, which can only be a causal theory of reference.[3] What Fodor takes as innovative in his account is the way in which he hopes to solve the problem of misrepresentation. The mark of a representation is its normativity, that is, that it can be applied correctly and incorrectly. It is the possibility of misrepresentation that distinguishes signs from other events in the causal chain. The central challenge Fodor sets for himself is to show how causal connections can ground this normative distinction.

Briefly, he accounts for the normative distinction as follows (Fodor 1988): The referential relation is a causal relation holding between, for example, horses and tokenings of the mental representation #horse#. The issue of the normativity of this causal relation arises because tokenings of #horse# can also be caused by objects other than horses, like cows under certain circumstances. There must be some naturalistic ground to distinguish and privilege tokens caused by horses from those caused by cows. To this end, Fodor introduces an asymmetry principle, according to which "misfirings" of the representation (i.e., tokens caused by the wrong sort of thing) are only possible in worlds where the primary (i.e., reference preserving) causal relation obtains. The value of this reductionist strategy is that it shows how representation is part of the "connected causal order."

There are numerous objections to the causal theory of reference in general and to Fodor's asymmetry principle in particular (cf. Baker 1989; Cummins 1989). Though I present a direct criticism of Fodor's purported solution to the problem of misrepresentation in the next chapter (see pp. 132–36), I am not interested here in attempts at such direct refutation. Rather I want to show how Fodor himself, in his articulation and defense of his account, is forced to a third retrenchment, one in which the language of "representation" and "content" is revealed as strictly proprietary, namely, as technical terms in neurophysiology that presuppose ordinary attributions of intentionality and so cannot explain intentionality. In other words, even when considerable charity is accorded Fodor's Causal Theory of denotation, the theory is squeezed into a very uncomfortable shape. What I hope to show now is that the internal difficulties force Fodor, first, to a proprietary understanding of the mental representations of the modular systems, one that is not fitted to provide a general account of intentionality or content; and, second, these difficulties, when directed to the central cognitive systems, force him to acknowledge the role of social convention in creating and sustaining normative structure in our lives. In short, where we find causal relations of the right sort for Fodor's project, there we find "shallow" representation, the proprietary kind used in the neural sciences. And where we find thick concepts in play in our lives, there we find "thin" causal laws and much social structuring. The point is that even if we allow that the asymmetry principle works (at least in some cases), and this is not a claim I would support, Fodor's Causal Theory cannot explain the content of thick representations. The real explanatory work is done, not by the computational theory, but by the neural sciences and appeal to social practices. Where the Causal Theory has a claim to success, mental representations are the shallow representations of the neural sciences. Where our concepts are too thick to be identified with such shallow representations, the notion of a causal relation, or nomic relation, is thinned, shifting the burden of explanation away from the alleged nomic relation to what sustains it. In brief, where causal relations explain the denotation of mental representations, we have the neurophysiology of our perceptual systems; and where we have higher cognitive representations, nomic relations cannot explain their use.

Let us begin with the first critical claim, that the Causal Theory of meaning can succeed only where the representations are so shallow that they can be cashed in in neurophysiological terms. Though Fodor illustrates his theory of content with the use of terms referring to ordinary middle-sized objects like horses and cows, he is very much aware that we haven't the resources to specify the precise nomic generalization in which veridical tokenings of #horse# covary with the presence of horses (cf. Fodor 1988: pp.111–13 and 116–17). As he says, "the viability of the Causal Theory depends on its being able to specify" the relevant set of circumstances under which tokenings of #horse# covary only with horses, that is,

> on its being able to specify (in naturalistic vocabulary, hence in nonsemantic and nonintentional vocabulary) circumstances such that (a) in those circumstances "horse"s covary with horses; i.e., instantiations of *horse* could cause "horse" to be tokened in my belief box…were the circumstances to obtain; and (b) "horse" expresses the property *horse*…in virtue of the truth of (a).
>
> (Fodor 1988: p. 118)

Fodor concedes that we cannot specify these circumstances in practice, for the range of conditions which constitute the presence of a horse is simply too great and variable. But, if this problem cannot be solved, at least in principle, then "…*we have no idea at all* what a naturalized semantics would be like for the nonlogical vocabulary of Mentalese" (Fodor 1988: p. 122). At the very least, a naturalized semantics requires that it be possible to specify the physical properties that covary with the tokening of a mental representation.

Although we are in no position to do this with respect to ordinary objects such as horses, Fodor maintains that we are in a position to specify such physical conditions for *primitive* mental representations of properties like looking red or hearing C-sharp. The reason that phenomenal representations like #red# are candidates for a naturalised semantics is because "tokenings of those symbols are connected to instantiations of the properties they express *by psychophysical law*" (Fodor 1988: p. 113). What Fodor means by this is that

> there are circumstances such that red instantiations control 'red' tokenings whenever those circumstances obtain;...*and the circumstances are nonsemantically, nonteleologically, and nonintentionally specifiable.*
> In fact, they're *psychophysically specifiable.*
>   (Fodor 1988: p. 112; emphases in the original)

In other words, neuropsychology is the only place where we can actually specify the causal chains that allegedly support word–world semantic relations. These psychophysical laws will be expressed in "the vocabulary of wavelengths, candlepowers, retinal irradiation, and the like" (Fodor 1988: p. 113). The laws will express correlations between certain physical properties in the world under certain conditions and certain neurophysiological states of the subject. Presumably they will look something like this: "Light waves of such-and-such a length under such-and-such circumstances cause #red here# to occur," where "#red here#" can be specified neurophysiologically.

How does the representation "red" function in these psychophysical laws? It is certainly introduced in order to keep track of which phenomenal color the scientist is tracking in the elaboration of the causal path from light waves reflected from the surface of an object to localized stimulations within the brain. "Red" is used to track the environment–brain causal chain under investigation. Insofar as "red" is used to individuate a particular kind of neural state in order to express a causal law, it can be cashed in in terms of a purely physiological description. This is using "red" as a shallow representation. Such shallow representations are necessary to express those psychophysical laws required by Fodor's Causal Theory. These shallow representations are to be understood in a proprietary way, as used within neural science. This is a perfectly legitimate use of the notion of representation, but it cannot be interpreted as "the 'red there'" that Fodor claims "gets stuffed into your belief box *willy-nilly*" (Fodor 1988: p. 112). Unlike the "#red there#" that is automatically tokened when the appropriate neurophysiological conditions are met, the *belief* that red is there is part of a network of beliefs, a network that can only be characterized in logical, epistemic, and normative terms. It is an assertion about the world or the subject's experience, not the mere occurrence of a neural event. Nor can the shallow representation, as used in the neural sciences, be identified with the phenomenal experience of red, at least not without a great deal of argumentation for the identity of neural state and phenomenal state. Neither the phenomenal experience of red nor the notion of representation as introduced in neural theory has any implications for a language of thought. So, the psychophysical laws that Fodor hypothesizes, laws which express the covariance of light waves of a certain length n with language of thought #red there# tokenings, are inferred from the covariances between light waves n with neural representation "red" which flags the connection with the phenomenal experience of red. The case for the psychophysical basis for "the content of an organism's belief box" turns on the failure of keeping these three uses of "red" distinct.[4] These three uses, once again, are: (1) a LOT representation #red# which is subject to rules of syntax and logic; (2) the phenomenal experience of red; and (3) the proprietary neural scientific notion of "red" that can be cashed in in neurophysiological terms. The point that I am making now is that the legitimate but proprietary use of representation-talk in the neural sciences does not provide a general theory of reference, a naturalized semantics for mental content. What is offered as a general philosophical theory of meaning turns out, at best, to apply only to the shallow representations involved in modeling the peripheral or modular systems.

In sum, the strongest cases for Fodor's Causal Theory of meaning, physical property–neural state causal relations, involve the weakest notion of representation, namely, the shallow representations of the neural sciences, talk that can be cashed in for neurophysiological descriptions. The illusion of getting more than this from these nomic generalizations is a function of eliding the distinctions among three ways of using the expression "red."

To provide a general theory, Fodor recognizes that not only must he provide some kind of "phenomenalist" analysis of #horse# in terms of #horsey looks#, he must also accommodate the *robustness* of representations, the fact that they are tokened correctly in all manner of ways and not just in perceptual situations. Correct tokenings of #horse# are not always caused by the actual presence of a horse; indeed many such tokenings are only rarely so caused. They can be caused by reading *Black Beauty*, considering a philosophical example, deciding to take riding lessons, and so on. So, if the asymmetry principle is to remain the primary device for explaining the normativity of reference relations, it cannot be part of a theory of reference that requires all correct uses to be caused in perceptually optimal situations. Semantic theory must be freed from an account of how the association between sign and referent is effected.

This is just what Fodor does. In a striking reassessment of Skinner, Fodor maintains that the Skinnerian approach to semantic theory is the correct one: "[t]he basic idea of Skinnerian semantics is that *all* that matters for meaning is 'functional' relations (relations of nomic covariance) between symbols and their denotations" (Fodor 1990: p. 56). The challenge for Fodor is to show how Skinnerian semantics can be rescued from Chomsky's early critique of Skinner's account of language use (Chomsky 1959). Fodor attempts this salvaging task by maintaining that Chomsky's arguments against Skinner were not directed against his semantic theory (the nomic covariance of horses and "horse"s) but against the behaviorist theory of learning and the allied claim that responses are non-intentionally describable behaviors (Fodor 1990: pp. 53–7). We need first to remind ourselves of Chomsky's criticism of Skinner's theory of language and then to assess Fodor's attempt to save Skinnerian semantics by distinguishing semantic theory from accounts of *how* the nomic relation between sign and referent is effected and maintained.

Chomsky's argument that is relevant to this issue focuses on the view that the denotational or referential relation is the covariation between a property in the world (the "controlling stimulus") and a verbal response. The objection is that the claim that there is a lawlike relation between stimulus and response has no explanatory weight. "We can," Chomsky says, "in the face of presently available evidence, continue to maintain the lawfulness of the relation between stimulus and response only by depriving them of their objective character," i.e., of their being describable in neutral physical terms (Chomsky 1959: p. 31). We do this by identifying the controlling stimulus with whatever property the response designates.

> If we look at a red chair and say *red*, the response is under the control of the stimulus "redness"; if we say *chair*, it is under the control of the collection of properties "chairness", and similarly for any other response. This device is as simple as it is empty... properties are free for the asking.
>
> (Chomsky 1959: p. 31)

Chomsky's conclusion is that the concept of stimulus has lost all objectivity since the stimulus is identified precisely by reference to the response. It is only the content of the response that enables us to identify the property that is the "controlling stimulus." Is there any difference in Fodor's claim that there is a causal connection between instantiations of the property of being a horse and occurrences of the mental representation #horse#? It is the horsey look of the cow that causes the mistaken tokenings of #horse# as well as the horsey look of horses. Here, too, it is tempting to say that the device is as simple as it is empty. The only reason it looks explanatory is because it relies on our understanding of the non-naturalistic relation between horses and the English word "horse." If we were to replace the "horse–#horse#" device for identifying a covariation with something like "light waves of such and such a length; etc. covary with neural functioning B" or some arbitrarily chosen expressions like "property 32 – ##," there would be no temptation to accept this as a general account of reference. The only place we can come close to identifying the causal relation objectively concerns the hypothesized shallow representations of the peripheral systems, but these representations are insufficiently robust to provide an account of meaning in general. Moreover, their use is dependent on fully phenomenal-intentionalist descriptions of sensory experience in order to track the relevant causal paths.

Chomsky's argument just given is part of a larger strategy to discredit behaviorism by showing, in different contexts, that intentional descriptions and so-called neutral descriptions (i.e., descriptions in physical terms) are not extensionally equivalent. This forces a dilemma on the behaviorist: Either behaviorism is false as a general account of behavior or it fails to eliminate essential use of intentional structure. Interestingly, Fodor himself argues similarly in his early defense of mentalism. He argues, for example, that the phenomenon of perceptual constancy cannot be explained in behaviorist or any other purely physicalist terms. It requires appeal to intentional content. Cases of perceptual constancy are

> cases in which normal perception involves radical and uniform departure from the informational content of the physical input. It has been recognized since Helmholtz that such cases provide the best argument for unconscious mental operations, for there appears to be no alternative to invoking such operations if we are to explain the disparity between input and output.
>
> (Fodor 1968: p. 85)

The concepts involved are more abstract than can be realized by purely physical descriptions. Physical features and intentionally characterized categories simply cross-classify. There is no set of physical properties that all instances of "Lillibullero" have in common. Yet behaviorist semantics requires precisely that kind of correlation in order to get lawlike generalization relating stimuli and responses. Equally, Fodor's causal semantics requires the existence of correlations between specifiable physical attributes and mental representations describable in non-intentional terms. If these arguments of Chomsky and Fodor against behaviorism are correct, then the appeal to intentional or semantic terms is ineliminable and so a naturalized semantics is not possible.

Fodor seeks to finesse these problems by distinguishing between the semantic relation and the mechanism which mediates that relation:

> semantics depends on a "functional relation" – a relation of nomic dependence – between symbols and their denotata. How this relation is mediated – e.g., that it is neurologically mediated, or for that matter, psychologically mediated – isn't part of the *semantical* story.
>
> (Fodor 1990: p. 99)

This distinction allows Fodor to preserve a version of his semantic theory, but only by eliminating from the semantic theory the substantive and explanatory matters concerning how such nomic dependence is sustained. "Nomic dependence" is a very thin notion of causal connection since it is fully compatible with the mediating mechanism being neurological, psychological, or sociological. In other words, defending Skinnerian semantics, on Fodor's account, does not require defending the claim that the mechanism of mediation can be described in non-intentional, non-semantic terms. Indeed, Fodor acknowledges that the robustness of our concepts is to be explained by "appeal to asymmetric dependences among *linguistic practices.* And linguistic practices depend on linguistic *policies*" (Fodor 1990: p. 98). His project for a naturalized semantics is preserved, he hopes, by the claim that "[l]inguistic policies don't make semantic relations; but maybe they make *causal* relations, and maybe causal relations make semantic relations" (Fodor 1990: p. 99).

Suppose that there was a tribe living in a region where once both pelicans and loons lived in abundant numbers. In their heyday, pelicans were out and about during the daylight hours whereas the loons came out from hiding only in the twilight hours and at night. The tribespeople had a word for the pelicans that was embedded in a great deal of folklore about pelicans and their activities. Occasionally a member of the tribe would mistakenly take a loon for a pelican. Let us agree that Fodor's asymmetry principle holds in this case. There is a nomic relation between the tokening of the representation (or word) "pelican" and being a pelican. Also, a causal relation holds between tokenings of "pelican" and loons under certain conditions. This causal relation only holds, however, in virtue of the primary causal relation. So, the tribe never would have had a word "pelican" without the nomic relation between tokenings of that word and pelicans. This holds by stipulation. So, "pelican" means pelicans. Nonetheless, loons can cause tokenings of "pelican."

With the passage of time, let us suppose that the pelicans die out but the linguistic practice and policies associated with talk of pelicans does not. And indeed over time the misrepresentations of loons as pelicans are accepted as correct identifications. Pelicans are difficult to spot and one can usually do so only at dusk or in the moonlight. One can imagine superstitions growing up around them – that they bring good luck or bad luck, that their cry at night is a sign of a death to come and so on. Clearly a complex and successful linguistic practice, resting upon what Fodor would call the systematic misidentification of loons, is quite imaginable. The point is that even if we grant that the word "pelican" really means pelicans, its use with respect to loons is nonetheless intelligible and causally grounded. The semantic theory is of little relevance to the linguistic practice of the tribe. Moreover, without a full discussion of the practices and policies of the tribe, the role of the expression "pelican" – or its robustness to use a favored adjective – cannot be understood. The semantic theory does not account for the robustness of the expression's role in a linguistic practice. From the point of view of the practice, there is no way to distinguish between systematically "mistaken" uses of an expression and correct usage. The "true" meaning of the expression "pelican" is irrelevant to this issue.

So, in all consistency, Fodor should accept the third retrenchment. A naturalized semantics for mental representations may be possible for the proprietary terms introduced in connection with accounts of the modular peripheral systems. This should not be confused with a fully general semantic theory for all systems of representation. It may have a limited, though nonetheless useful, role to play in the accounts of the peripheral systems. What Fodor has not succeeded in defending is his full philosophical theory of mind and meaning. The naturalist project Fodor promotes holds, at best, for abstract neurophysiology combined with a large promissory note that somehow it will be extended to all the rest of our mental and cognitive activities, although we do not currently understand how that note can be redeemed in computational terms nor how the principled objections are to be addressed.

5 Social norms and narrow content

Individualism with respect to the individuation and ontology of mental states and processes remains a dominant feature of current theories of mind. Minimally, individualism is the doctrine of supervenience, according to which "an individual's intentional states and events (type and token) could not be different from what they are, given the individual's physical, chemical, neural, and functional histories" (Burge 1986b: p. 4). But many think that a stronger form of individualism is required: "An individual's being in any given intentional state (or being the subject of such an event) can be explicated by reference to states and events of the individual that are specifiable without using intentional vocabulary and without presupposing anything about the individual's social or physical environment" (Burge 1986b: p. 4). Both are part of the larger naturalist project for locating the human mind in the causal nexus, but the stronger form has implications for how to understand the content of our thoughts and beliefs. Mental content must be internal to the individual, must be in the head of the individual. Tyler Burge, for one, has argued strenuously against an individualist conception of mental states. In this essay, I shall support Burge's conclusions. The distinctive approach he uses, however, is limited in showing why internalism and individualism are mistaken. So, though I shall use the thought-experiment approach as a way into the problem of individuating mental content, my target is to show why individualism goes wrong.

Burge's basic methodological tool is that of the thought experiment. In each paper, he invites his reader to consider a real world case and a counterfactual world case in which the individual protagonists of each story can be described identically in terms of what goes on from the surface of the skin inwardly. Yet the content of their psychological lives differs, and that difference, Burge maintains, can only be accounted for in terms of environmental differences, sometimes a difference in the physical environment and sometimes a difference in the social context.

Though Burge's conclusions have been met with hostile criticism, I will argue that Burge is correct in his attacks on individualism. The mistake he makes is in assigning too much weight to our intuitive readings of his thought experiments. His thought experiments are readily susceptible to more than one reading; and so they invite the introduction of a more sophisticated version of individualism, one that rests on distinguishing narrow mental content from wide content. What is most important about Burge's work are the *theoretical* explanations he suggests (without full development) for *why* individualism fails. If Burge is right, what sets the standards for the correct use of concepts that figure in the individuation of beliefs or other intentional states are "archetypical applications" and "norms of understanding" which are operative within a social context. As I shall show in this chapter, the ways in which theories of narrow mental content fail tie in with the social explanations of the formation and use of standards that Burge suggests. Mental content does involve the natural and social environments of the individual as both are necessary to the ways in which standards and norms inform content.

In section 1, I characterize Burge's three most interesting thought experiments, showing the distinctive contribution of each. The limitations of this approach are examined in section 2, where I develop the two arguments that figure most prominently in the idea that there must be individualistic narrow mental content. These arguments support two distinct theories of narrow content, one of which focuses on individualism as a principle of individuation (narrow content as conceptual role) and the other of which focuses on individualism as the ontological thesis of supervenience (narrow content as anchored). I argue in section 3 that both theories of narrow content fail, which calls for a new look at the way in which social practices in particular figure in the individuation and reality of intentional states (see section 4).

1 Individualism and the thought experiment

The thought experiments

Burge's cases split into two kinds. Those that are held to show that the physical environment is involved in mental content (by way of reference) and those that are held to show that the social environment is involved (by way of social norms of understanding). Burge appeals to Putnam's original twin-earth thought experiment about water on earth and its counterpart on twin earth to show the role played by nature in fixing mental content (Burge 1982). Briefly, Oscar lives on earth where he drinks water, bathes in it, cooks with it and so on. $Oscar_2$, on the other hand, lives on twin earth where everything, including his own internal states, is exactly as it is on earth except for the liquid called 'water'. On twin earth, this liquid has a chemical composition XYZ that differs from that of our water, namely, H_2O. Though Oscar and Oscar$_2$ drink, bathe, and cook simultaneously in identical ways, they do so with different liquids. Burge endorses Putnam's conclusion that the contents of thoughts about water and water$_2$ cannot be the same because the referents differ in the two cases, and the referent of each concept is part of the content of that concept. Having thoughts about water requires being related to water (that very stuff) in the right sort of way. If Putnam and Burge are correct about this, then the contents of natural kind terms cannot be individuated by appeal solely to features internal to the individual. The subject's total ignorance of the true constitution of water is irrelevant to whether or not he is referring to water, thus revealing the slack between how the term "water" applies to the world and what the subject knows or need know.

The second two thought experiments concern the role of society, rather than nature, in fixing mental content. The first of these concerns the role that expertise plays in fixing the content of our specialized vocabularies (Burge 1979). Burge identifies it as a case of incomplete understanding. The subject Oscar on earth believes that he has arthritis in his thigh. This belief derives from a misunderstanding of what arthritis is. As the medical experts will tell Oscar, arthritis is an inflammation of the joints and so cannot occur in a muscle. What "arthritis" picks out is determined by the medical experts of our society whereas what "water" or "tiger" pick out is determined by water and tigers. But this is not yet a case that supports radical anti-individualism. This is because it looks as though the experts stand in the same relation to arthritis as the layman does to water. The experts use "arthritis" to pick out a particular type of disease. If arthritis were discovered to be caused by a particular virus or bacillus, then arthritis (if "arthritis" is treated as a rigid designator by the experts) could be discovered to occur in muscles as well as joints, provided the right kind of virus were discovered to be the cause of the thigh pain. But Burge does not want to talk about the case in this way; he wants a case in which the role of experts is salient in fixing the content of a term, and I shall follow him in this emphasis as far as possible. To complete the thought experiment we must introduce Oscar$_2$ who lives on twin earth where the medical experts agree that arthritis$_2$ is an inflammation of both joint and muscle. Thus, though Oscar and Oscar$_2$ engage in the very same lines of thought and inference in their use of the expression 'arthritis', the contents of their thoughts are quite distinct: What Oscar believes is false whereas what Oscar$_2$ believes is true.

The last thought experiment attempts to establish the more radical claim that a social element is constitutive of content itself. Accordingly, it does not involve dependence on experts. In this case, Burge hopes to show that a perfectly ordinary concept can be shown to implicate what he calls, the "norms of understanding" of the society (Burge 1986a). The concept he chooses is that of sofa. In this case, Oscar entertains rather odd and certainly deviant beliefs about sofas. Sofas are, he believes, really religious artefacts, not pieces of furniture. Burge's contention is that Oscar can believe this of sofas only if indeed these objects are sofas. And whether they are sofas or not is not up to him but up to the community of which he is a part. He attempts to show that by contrasting Oscar with Oscar$_2$ who holds the very same beliefs (it would seem) about elongated chair-like objects existing on twin earth. The only difference between the world of Oscar and the world of Oscar$_2$ is that on twin earth these objects really are religious artefacts; only Oscar$_2$ doesn't know that everybody in his linguistic community knows this. He, like Oscar, believes that the members of his community think that the objects designated by "sofa" are pieces of furniture. This single difference in social convention between earth and twin earth is enough to show, Burge holds, that the contents of "sofa"-thoughts on earth and the contents of "sofa$_2$"-thoughts on twin earth are distinct. After all, earth "sofas" are indeed sofas whereas twin-earth "sofas$_2$" are sacred safos. One must not mistake a sacred relic for a trinket. Just so, one must not mistake a safo for a sofa.

This third case differs from the first two in a significant way. Oscar does not suffer from a failure of knowing what any competent speaker within the linguistic community knows; it is not that he is ignorant or has only a partial understanding of what sofas are.[1] It was this lack in Oscar in the first two cases that led Burge to conclude that nature and society took up the slack. But in this third case, Oscar has full understanding of what anyone in his community would take to be true of sofas; he just thinks that they are all wrong. He has formed an alternative and deviant hypothesis about sofas. The concept of sofa has a different "cognitive value" for Oscar than it has for the rest of his community. This slack between the way "sofa" applies to the world (by way of conventional meaning) and what Oscar believes to be true about sofas is not due to his "beliefs" falling short of the world, but due to his forming a different conception of these objects. Burge's point here, though he does not put it this way, must be that the idiosyncratic cognitive value sofas have for Oscar presupposes the smooth functioning of our ordinary linguistic practices in the use of "sofa."

These thought experiments certainly seem to be powerful devices for disclosing elements external to and independent of the subject in the iden-tification of the contents of the subject's intentional states. But even if it is true that the individuation of particular mental states requires adverting to environmental factors, does this show that contentful mental states aren't in the subject's head? Critics read these cases as showing that we must distinguish between narrow mental content and wide content, thus replacing a crude Cartesianism, which draws upon such rough-and-ready distinctions as that between my beliefs about water and the stuff that is really out there, my (limited) understanding of diseases and the experts' (full) understanding, my perspective and valuation of commonplace objects and the community perspective, for a more sophisticated version.

Narrow content vs. wide content

Just what is the distinction between the narrow and wide content of mental states? As one advocate of individualism has put it, narrow content is what is left over after we "chop off" the referring and socially bounded arms that reach out to the world (cf. Block 1986). Narrow content is what is left over when all objects, persons, and institutions external to the individual are taken away. What we want to know in this chapter is, what is this left-over part? Two strategies are available to those defending a place for narrow content: Narrow content is to be identified with functional role within a complex internal causal system (conceptual role semantics); or narrow content is to be identified with the internal effect of certain environmental causes (causal theory of representation). I shall show in section 3 that both strategies fail. For both, narrow content becomes attenuated to the point of spontaneous elimination, the former through uncontrollable expansion and the latter through a shrinking to the point of invisibility. But before witnessing the demise of narrow content, we need to consider more carefully the case for the distinction.

Putnam's original twin-earth case brings out some of the complexity (Putnam 1975a). The meanings of the expressions that enter into the specification of intentional states are irreducibly multi-faceted. Factors external to the individual enter into the determination of the content itself. For natural kind terms like "water," the determinant of its extension is the similarity of stuff in the world to *this* very stuff called "water" right here. Nothing in the individual's head can play the normative role that this stuff in the world plays in fixing the extension of the term. This multi-faceted view of content threatens the integrity of the Cartesian subject. The traditional Cartesian subject is autonomous (the contents of intentional states are in the head) and self-aware (the contents of her intentional states are latently if not actually available to the subject). If part of the content of the subject's mind is external to the subject and is such that the subject could be wholly ignorant of its nature, then the Cartesian subject has been lost, and with it the claim of internalism.

The twin-earth argument thus creates a serious problem for the crude Cartesian picture, but at the same time it appears to provide the resources for solving the problem. The solution lies, of course, in distinguishing narrow content from wide content. Wide content is the full multi-faceted content, which includes both internal and external determinants of meaning. Narrow content is what is left over after severing the subject's connection to the external determinants of meaning. That portion of content, it is maintained, is in the head of the subject and known by the subject. Following Putnam, we can say that the stereotype (itself a norm in that it sets criteria for correct use) – the assemblage of properties commonly used to pick out paradigm examples – and the indexical component of meaning are in the head, but the sample picked out by the indexical and which sets *the* standard for membership in the extension of the term clearly is not in the individual's head. This certainly seems a neat solution.

What could Burge object to here? How can Burge use the very same thought experiment and yet draw such a different, and incompatible, conclusion? According to Burge,

> Putnam interprets the difference between Earth and Twin-Earth uses of "water" purely as a difference in extension. And he states that the relevant Earthian and Twin-Earthian are "exact duplicates in…feelings, thoughts, interior monologue etc." On our version of the argument the two are in no sense exact duplicates in their thoughts. This shows up in oblique occurrences in true attributions of propositional attitudes.
>
> (Burge 1982: pp. 102–3)

It is crucial for Burge's attack on internalism that the semantic role played by the environmental contributors to mental content not be lost when their referring terms occur in oblique contexts. In other words, Burge needs to block the move that some find natural from the occurrence of a term in an oblique context to the term's being literally in the head.[2] Far from this being an entailment of the claim that a term occurs obliquely, it can only be an explanation for its occurrence in the oblique context. The argument must go something like this: Consider the propositional attitude sentence, "Oscar believes that water is refreshing." The content of the that-clause identifies the particular belief that Oscar has. In so identifying this particular belief, each term embedded in the oblique context must occur opaquely, that is, co-referring expressions are not permissible substitutions. None of this carries with it the idea that the content sentence of the belief sentence must be in the head of the individual. That move comes with an explanation of the opacity of the terms. The reason, it might be held, that one cannot substitute co-referring expressions for obliquely occurring expressions is that opacity results from these expressions being the very ones that the individual uses, in her head as it were, in forming her particular belief. But this strong psychological explanation for opacity is not required: All that is required is that belief content is sensitive to how something is described. And Burge holds that the description by which the content of a belief is expressed retains its semantic relations to the world. The oblique context does not sever semantic relations to the world. So whatever the argument is for narrow content, it cannot be that what occurs in oblique contexts must be "in the head" contents. Opacity is not internality.

But does opacity rule out internality? Of course not. After all, Putnam, like Burge, maintains that opaque terms do not lose their semantic relations to the world just in virtue of being opaque. Indeed the point of the thought experiment, for Putnam, is the opposite. So what is the difference in the way that Burge and Putnam interpret this twin-earth thought experiment?

The difference comes, according to Burge, in the way that they each explain the semantic bond itself between the referring term and its referent (Burge 1982).[3] Putnam holds that the referring link itself is created and sustained because natural kind concepts like "water" have an indexical component, and it is this indexical component that relates thought to the world. So Oscar and his twin, in virtue of being indexically related to different liquids, have beliefs with different extensions even though, in virtue of a shared stereotype, they have beliefs with the same intension. In this way the indexicality of natural kind terms explains both the difference and sameness of the twins' respective beliefs about water and water$_2$.

Burge objects to this way of explaining the semantic relation that obtains between "water" and its extension. If extensions are fixed in virtue of natural kind terms having an indexical component, this would make their extensions subject to contextual constraints, depending upon where the individual happens to be. But this cannot be correct. The correct explanation, according to Burge, is that natural kind terms are rigid designators. They are originally fixed by the use of genuinely indexical expressions, but they are not indexicals themselves nor do they have an indexical component. If we accept this, then we can see that the opaque occurrence of the term "water" in specifying the content of Oscar's (or his twin's) belief does not abnegate Oscar's semantic relation to the originating sample of H_2O. As Burge puts it, "water" is a context-free term

(Burge 1982: p. 107). I agree with this but for one very important qualification: "Water" is context free *so far as any individual is concerned*. This is quite unlike genuine indexicals which are always used contextually and individualistically. That "water" is a rigid designator means that the actual liquid out there in the world is implicated (1) in the opaque occurrence of "water" in oblique belief contexts, but (2) independently of the particular location of the individual. It is important for Burge's account that the individual need not be nor have been in any physical proximity to the liquid H_2O in order to have beliefs about water. Being a rigid designator (rather than an indexical term) allows for the environment playing an indispensable semantic role and for Oscar and his twin being identical "molecule-for-molecule."[4] This is just what Burge needs. There is a gap clearly between the individual, and everything that goes on in the individual, and the extension of the term; and yet the term guarantees that there is a semantic relation between the individual and the extension of the term. The semantic properties of the term accrue to the term independently of anything the individual does or fails to do.

What is crucial for Burge's interpretation of the thought experiment is that natural kind terms are treated as rigid designators. If the meanings of natural kind terms were fixed by stereotypes, then, it might be held, meanings could be in the head. If they were fixed, in part, by an indexical component, then content could be narrow and wide. If meanings were fixed by what the individual happened to know or where the individual happened to be, then meaning would be context bound. But Burge argues for a "context-free interpretation" of natural kind terms. For a term to be a rigid designator is for it to be context free. This is where Burge goes wrong. As I shall argue later, rigid designators are not context free in an absolute sense; rather they are *individual-context-free*. There is an indispensable role played by the community in fixing and sustaining the extension of rigid designators that cannot be performed by the individual alone. What is correct in Burge's explanation is that any given individual need not herself have or have had contact with the liquid H_2O. The individual is detachable from that part of the environment that contributes to determining meaning, but the content of her thought is not.

There is also a second and distinct sense in which natural kind terms are context free. It is possible for everyone on earth to have attitudes towards water without any of them knowing what water is, without, that is, realizing what its true microstructure is. Though the stereotype must be known to the subject, the real essence of water need not be known to the subject (or anyone else). Still what "water" picks out in virtue of its referring relation must be water and nothing else. It is the great weight given to the referring relation that secures "water" to water and not another thing, no matter what anyone knows or believes to be the case. Once the refer-ring relation is in place, it is unbreakable. So the argument goes. This, of course, is a purely metaphysical point. So long as we hold this view of reference, then referring expressions are necessarily tied to the objects they pick out. But this is an overly inflated view of what reference can do. Our beliefs about water can be (and have been, before around 1700) *theory-context free*. That is, we need not have any theoretical beliefs, or any accurate theoretical beliefs, about the microstructure of water in order to refer to it successfully. So the moral of the thought experiment holds. Any time a referring expression forms part of the content of a mental state as expressed by the embedded that-clause of an attitude statement, the indi-vidual subject is semantically tied to the referent no matter what the subject, *or anyone else*, may or may not know about the true constitution of the referent provided we, that is, our linguistic community, use the refer-ring expression rigidly. Then rigid designators occurring in oblique contexts preserve the semantic relation to their referents.

Does the same explanation work for Burge's other two cases, the "arthritis" case and the "sofa" case? Structurally, the "arthritis" case seems to mirror the "water" case. Just as the full or wide meaning of "water" depended upon the existence of an actual liquid in the world, so the full meaning of "arthritis" depends upon the judgment of a group of experts. Just as the baptismal sample of water determines the extension of "water," so the judgment of experts determines the extension of "arthritis." There is an important difference, however, between the two cases. For each, some initial referring act determines extension, but with "water," a sample of the extension itself fixes membership in the kind (whatever is like *this* stuff) whereas with "arthritis," the judgment of the experts fixes the stereotype for the rest of society. It must be this way; otherwise, we could simply forego appeal to the experts and treat "arthritis" in exactly the same way as we treat "water." But Burge wants to show that in this case there is a social dimension to meaning that cannot be treated equivalently to the simple referring relation.

With terms of art or expertise, like "arthritis," someone must know the stereotype, for the expression is tied to the stereotype as authorized by experts. This is quite unlike the "water" case where no one's specialized knowledge or expertise is required for successful use of the term. This is part of the value of rigid designators. Thus, insofar as Burge's argument against internalism turns on the rigidity of referring expressions, it has limited scope. Our question becomes: Does this kind of rigidity belong to "arthritis" as well? It would seem not. Though the subject in his use of "arthritis" is thereby constrained by the experts, it certainly is not because "arthritis" refers to the experts. Rather it is because a certain authority is accorded the experts. Unlike "water," were the experts to revise their judgment, the meaning of "arthritis" would thereby be altered. This cannot happen with "water" unless we are changing concepts altogether, and merely using homophonic expressions for the two concepts. Oscar's belief that he has arthritis in his thigh involves an oblique occurrence of "arthritis." What is the character of the semantic relation of "arthritis" to the group of experts? One might think that they are accorded authority because they know what "arthritis" refers to. But then what would matter is the referring relation, and the authorities would only come into it in a secondary way, not a primary way. The thought experiment sheds no light on this, but merely draws attention to the fact that the only difference between earth and twin earth is a social difference, and so the explanation of the meaning of "arthritis" must implicate this social difference. But how?

Here what is needed is not a Kripkean account, but something more akin to a Gricean account. Oscar supports his use of "arthritis" by certain second-order intentions, the most important of which are his intention to use the term in accord with the judgment of the experts and his willingness to allow his use to be overruled by their judgment. These "deference" intentions concern the status of his use of the term itself, and are indispensable to Oscar's using the expression at all.[5] This just is what the linguistic division of labor is about. Any attempt to eliminate the role of the expert in Oscar's use of "arthritis" by eliminating these second-order epistemic beliefs renders his use of "arthritis" so highly idiosyncratic that any similarity to our concept of arthritis is accidental. If Oscar protests that he does mean the same by "arthritis" as we do, then *perforce* he acknowledges as his own the second-order epistemic intentions that link his use of "arthritis" to the experts.

In these two cases, it is a contingent fact that Oscar lives in the world that he does, but once living in the world he does, the contents of his mental life are fixed in part by items in that world whether or not he knows what they are and whether or not he comes into contact with those items. In both cases the key term has an essential semantic link to an item in Oscar's environment. The item is essential because of the *normative role* it plays. The item actually sets the standard for correct application of the term in question. For "water," that link is guaranteed by the term's being a rigid designator. For "arthritis," that link is guaranteed by the term's being a medical term of art. But what of Burge's third case, the one concerning a completely ordinary concept, namely, that of a sofa?

Here there is no hidden but natural essence; nor is expertise required. Here a gap is created between the individual and the world he lives in by attributing a deviant belief to our Oscar. He believes that sofas are not pieces of furniture, but religious artefacts irreverently misused. It is important to Oscar's belief that he is talking about *sofas* and that he believes sofas are religious artefacts. What counts as a sofa is what any competent speaker of the language would pick out as a sofa. As a competent speaker himself, Oscar can pick out sofas as well as any one else in the community. In order to create the dissonance required by these thought experiments, the concept of sofa is held to have a different "cognitive value" for Oscar, where cognitive value is explicitly individualistic. The cognitive value of the concept of sofa is set over and against, though presumably dependent upon, the conventional meaning of "sofa" which is fixed by community practice.

Unless we have an account of the dependence of cognitive value upon conventional meaning, the distinction invites the response that content can be both wide and narrow. Cognitive value is narrow content, it might be argued. Since "sofa" is not a rigid designator nor a term of art, just why does the oblique occurrence of "sofa" carry with it a semantic tie to those pieces of furniture? Burge's claim must be that, whatever this tie is, the thought experiment shows that it must exist, for our intuitions are that there is a difference in the contents of Oscar's thoughts and Oscar$_2$'s thoughts, and the only differences between the worlds are social differences. So the thought experiment, as Burge wants to use it, must carry the full weight of the argument for anti-internalism in a way that it does not for "water" or even "arthritis." But it simply cannot carry that philosophical weight. We need an explanation of why cognitive value is dependent upon conventional meaning.

2 Defense of internalism

So, do we have to look at the thought experiments from Burge's recommended perspective? If we cease to take that God's eye point of view, and look at the matter from the perspectives of our individual subjects, then it seems equally intuitive to say that there is something the same in what the twins believe about water, arthritis, and sofas.[6] Call that "cognitive value" or "narrow content," but the intuition is the same. It is what the individual thinks is going on, or how she conceives it, that matters both in individuating the contents of her beliefs and in explaining her behavior.

Advocates of internalism have looked for some way of making the classical semantic relations between terms and the world irrelevant to specifying narrow content, without, however, eliminating *all* normative properties of narrow content, and thus forfeiting the claim that narrow content is indeed content. The point of attack has not been, as one might have expected, Burge's argument that the semantic ties of terms occurring in oblique contexts are not broken within such contexts. Rather critics grant that Burge's thought experiments do show that the natural and social environments are part of the oblique content that individuates particular beliefs, but object to his identifying this content with mental or psychological content (cf. Loar 1988; Bach 1986).

That-clause Ccontent vs. psychological content

Individuating beliefs by appeal to the embedded that-clause is not as straightforward as Burge makes it seem. Looking at the thought experiment from a different perspective or looking at more complicated cases can leave one certain that there must be something like narrow content. For example, if Oscar and his arthritic$_2$ twin could be instantaneously switched at the moment of their entering the doctors' waiting rooms, each would pursue his alternate's path, although the descriptions used to characterize their beliefs and desires would become extremely baroque if we were strict in maintaining Burgean principles of individuation. In fact, we would begin to lose a grip on just what Oscar really does believe. After all, Oscar's belief that he has an arthritic thigh pain is confirmed by the doctor$_2$; at the dinner table, he and his family$_2$ discuss his arthritic thigh pain; his friends$_2$ commiserate. We know that the doctor$_2$ was wrong in thinking that Oscar has an arthritic thigh-pain, though he was quite correct in diagnosing an arthritic$_2$ thigh pain. What does Oscar believe? After much discussion with family$_2$ and friends$_2$ of the nature of his complaint, does Oscar continue to believe that he has arthritis or does he come to form new beliefs (undetectable by himself) that he suffers from arthritis$_2$? When he remembers the first time he felt his arthritic pain, what is he remembering? The "false" memory that he had an arthritic pain; or the true "memory" that he had an arthritic$_2$ pain? Could both be involved? Just such confusion about how to individuate and count beliefs is exploited by critics of Burge, who want to make room for a notion of narrow content.

When confusion arises over how to individuate beliefs by appealing to the external component of their content (H_2O or XYZ; our doctors or their doctors), it is tempting to look for a different criterion for counting. The candidate cannot be the de facto semantic links to environmental items, for that is precisely what has been brought into question by switching Oscar and Oscar$_2$. Historic community and contemporary community push in opposite directions, and so render Oscar's beliefs confused and obscure to us, although Oscar himself suffers no disability from his confusion. But perhaps that shows that the criteria that matter in individuating Oscar's beliefs are not the semantic links to the world, but

something else. The most plausible candidate is the cognitive role the belief
state plays in the utterances and behavior of our Oscar. Individuation by
cognitive role and individuation by referent need not be the same. And so
it looks as though we need to distinguish what Brian Loar calls the "social
content" or "that-clause" content from the "psychological content" of a
belief state (Loar 1988).[7]

The case Loar uses is that of puzzling Pierre (cf. Kripke 1979).[8] Pierre,
while still in France, is told "Londres est jolie" and believes what he is told.
Later he moves to London, not realizing that London is his "jolie
Londres," and settles in Kensington. He comes to believe that London is a
beautiful city. Let us agree that "London" and "Londres" are both rigid
designators, picking out the same city. This is Burge's strongest case for
explaining the semantic tie between term and world. Does Pierre have one
belief or two? On Burgean principles of individuation, Pierre has one
belief, and the place occupied by "Londres" and "London" in his network
of beliefs and other attitudes is quite irrelevant. And yet Pierre has a strong
desire to visit Londres which is only checked by his pleasure of living in
London. When away from his home in London, he experiences a deep
melancholy whenever he thinks of London; to distract himself, he sometimes tries thinking about Londres instead. In such a situation, the only
reasonable response is that Pierre has distinct beliefs about London and
Londres. And in accepting this reading, we must conclude that social
content and psychological content are distinct. This way of making space
for psychological, or narrow, content is compatible with Burge's claim that
"London" and "Londres" each occur obliquely in the beliefs we ascribe to
Pierre as well as being the very terms Pierre uses himself when expressing
his beliefs. Pierre picks out the city London in both cases, and so everything he believes about Londres is believed to be about the city itself, just
as all his beliefs about water are beliefs about H_2O, even though he is ignorant of the chemical composition of water.

So the defender of internalism is ready with a reply to Burge. Burge
goes wrong, according to his critics, in identifying that-clause content with
psychological content. This may be due to a failure to distinguish between
the first-person perspective and the third-person perspective (cf. Forbes
1987; Loar 1987); or it may be dramatically shown in various thought
experiments in which the complexity of the subject's beliefs outstrips the
relative simplicity of the that-clause description (cf. Loar 1988; Bach
1986). The gap that emerges, it could be argued, is not between "the relevant environmental facts and relations to the environment, on the one
hand, and what the individual knows and can discriminate, on the other,"
as Burge says (Burge 1986a), but a gap between the simplicity of ordinary
belief ascriptions and the complexity of properly refined descriptions of

the subject's mental state. The crudity, as it were, of ordinary attributions must be replaced by the refinement of in-depth attributions. This allows the defender of narrow content to grant Burge his point that social content retains semantic connections to the world. But these semantic ties are not essential to the identity of the underlying psychologically real mental content. Thus, whether or not it is correct to hold that when "water" occurs in oblique contexts, it retains its semantic tie to water itself, we can readily "chop off" the individual's relation to the real stuff without affecting how he thinks about that stuff. Indeed, it could be argued, this was part of the thought experiment. The defender of narrow content is merely exploiting the subject's ignorance. With respect to the "sofa" case, here too the defender of internalism can exploit features of the thought experiment itself, namely, the introduction of cognitive value. Individual cognitive values may or may not conform to the conventional meanings of the community, but it is the former that are required to individuate the deviant beliefs of our subject. So the defender of individualism seems able to "chop off" the referent at one end of the continuum of cases (the "water" case) and endorse the individualistic component at the other end (the "sofa" case).

What about Burge's case of "arthritis"? The defender of internalism cannot straightforwardly "cut off" the expert, for the focus is on the special role that the expert plays *for* the subject. Nor can the defender endorse the cognitive value in a straightforward way because the subject places authority for his beliefs outside himself. This is what is important about linguistic division of labor. In his own use of "arthritis," the subject tacitly appeals to the authority of the expert. So here it might be said that because the subject is "borrowing" a concept, as it were, the oblique occurrence of the expression "arthritis" is semantically tied to the group of experts. But here too this argument for the oblique occurrence of "arthritis" opens the way for the defender's simply "chopping off" the experts as he "chopped off" the referent. There still seems to be left over what is known or is available to the subject even if it isn't much. In this way the "chopping off" of the semantic links to the external world disparages, in a way, the importance of the referring and deferring relations of terms to items or persons in the world.

What is emphasized is the place of expressions within the subject's individual ecology of beliefs, desires, and behaviors. Assessing cognitive value locates the role played by the expression within this complex structure. Defenders of individualism who take this tack support a conceptual role semantics, and hold that conceptual role can be specified internalistically and individualistically. The weakness of the thought experiment, thus, is that it only shows that (some) concepts *are* public and social, not that they must be.

What advocates of narrow content want to preserve is, as I would like to put it, the normativity of mental content. The classical semantic properties of reference and truth conditions require the relation of terms to the world, but the normativity of mental life, that concepts are rule-governed, can be individualistic and internalist. They are guided by logical principles, epistemic principles, rationality constraints, and other normative principles. Because they are normatively characterized, we can misrepresent items, draw fallacious conclusions, ignore relevant evidence, defy rationality. The important question here is, can the individual provide what is necessary to make these kinds of mistakes as well as being guided in the proper fashion? If narrow content fails to display these normative features, whatever happens to be picked out can hardly be described as "content." So sophisticated advocates of narrow content find themselves defending the following three claims: (1) That-clause content has semantic ties to the natural and/or social world (the semantic condition). (2) Psychological content is literally in the head of the individual (the internal reality condition). (3) For anything to count as "content," it must be subject to standards for correctness (the normativity condition).

The first two conditions are apparently reconciled by distinguishing between *that-clause content* namely, the proposition that is specified by the that-clause, and *psychological content*, namely, the inferential place of the item within the network of beliefs and desires of the subject. Psychological content differs from that-clause content in that relational semantic ties to the actual world are irrelevant to its identity. However, in order to count as content, psychological content must have some normative property, such that correct usage can be distinguished from incorrect usage. Moreover, though it is arguable that social content and psychological content are distinct, still there must be some interesting and non-accidental relation between them. So this first reply to Burge's arguments leaves us with two new problems that need answering: First, if narrow content is this psychological content, how does psychological content set its own internal standards for correct vs incorrect usage? Second, how is this psychological content related to social content?

But why should we believe that these are distinct? Clearly there is a tension between two criteria for identifying content, namely, the appeal to the referent and the appeal to a system of beliefs within which the content is embedded. But does this show that we have two kinds of content? Why doesn't it show only that under abnormal circumstances, the two criteria don't dovetail as they normally do? This, it is arguable, is a mark of the strangeness of the circumstances, but not a sign of the existence of two kinds of content. What is needed for defending the stronger ontological thesis is the rationale for mental content. This, it seems to me, is provided by the argument from causation.

This argument can be seen as a defense of a fourth condition on psychological content: (4) States with psychological content have causal properties (the causal condition). Narrow content is required if there is to be *mental* causation. But, prima facie, this conflicts with condition (3) that psychological content must be normative if it is to count as content at all. So the fundamental rationale for the *internal* reality of mental states makes their being contentful suspect, as both semantic and normative properties seem to be incompatible with mental states' being causes.

The argument from causation

The argument from causation is simple and direct, and for that reason quite powerful. It can be characterized as consisting of two stages, each reflecting a prior metaphysical commitment. First, a commitment to psychological realism, that is, to the idea that mental states, like belief and the other propositional attitudes, are discrete and causally efficacious; and second, a commitment to physicalism, which is the thesis that everything is explicable ultimately in terms of physical matter.[9] The first stage of the argument goes like this. There is no action at a distance, and so the mental causes of behavior must *perforce* be local. If mental states have causal powers, then they must be states internal to the individual. And if these causal states are mental, then they must have content. If they cause in virtue of the content they have, then that content must likewise be internal to the individual. It clearly follows from this that if content is not internal to the individual, then mental states do not have the causal powers they do (if any) in virtue of their content. So it seems we must choose between the following: Either content is not in the head, in which case we must reject the idea that mental states are causally efficacious; or the causal efficacy of mental states is obviously correct, in which case content must be in the head.

The second stage is a defense of supervenience. At the very least, a commitment to physicalism requires that intentional states supervene upon physical states. As J.A. Fodor sums it up, "if mind/brain supervenience goes, the intelligibility of mental causation goes with it" (Fodor 1988: p. 42). Thus, for Fodor and other advocates of psychological realism, Burge's arguments purporting to show that mental content involves social norms must be wrong. Fodor's central argument against Burge's anti-individualism is a "diagnosis" of how Burge goes wrong.

Burge's error, according to Fodor, is to conflate methodological individualism and methodological solipsism.[10] Methodological individualism, Fodor maintains, is a fully general methodological constraint on any science. That constraint is that any scientific taxonomy must be a taxonomy by causal powers. It is the causal power of objects that is relevant to scientific inquiry, including psychology. Just insofar as the referents and social norms that help individuate oblique content do not affect the causal power of the mental state itself, they are irrelevant to the formation of laws of psychological causation. But this, Fodor insists, is not tantamount to eliminating all relational properties from the individuation of appropriate taxonomic groups, for some relational properties can be relevant to the causal powers of members of the taxonomic group. Burge confuses this methodological principle, according to Fodor, with a substantive empirical thesis, viz., methodological solipsism. Methodological solipsism is the empirical hypothesis that mental states "are computational, hence syntactic" (Fodor 1988). Burge, thus, is alleged to take a methodological constraint on taxonomy formation for a substantive empirical hypothesis about psychological entities, namely, that they are (non-relationally individuated) formal entities. The difference between the two is as follows: If semantic (or other relational) properties can be shown to effect or bear upon the causal powers of the mental state, then they would be respectable candidates for constructing a scientific taxonomy. Methodological individualism allows for relational individuation. Methodological solipsism, on the other hand, explicitly rejects the relevance of any relational property to the individuation of psychological states. So the fact that relational properties may be useful or even required to construct a scientific taxonomy does not support the conclusion that an internalist and individualistic psychology is mistaken. And arguments against the empirical hypothesis that mental states are formal entities do not thereby entail that internalism or individualism has been discredited.

Is this what Burge has done? Has he (mis)construed arguments against methodological solipsism as arguments against methodological individualism? What are the relational properties that Burge argues individuate mental content? As we have seen, they are of two types: The referents of natural kind terms ("water") and social conventions as fixed by the community as a whole ("sofa") or by an expert sub-community ("arthritis"). Fodor's position can accommodate these, for he himself develops a causal theory of meaning which calls for items in the environment to trigger appropriate mental representations, so that these representations can get on with their causal work in the production of other mental states and behavior. What Fodor finds unacceptable is Burge's idea that items of the environment figure in the individuation of mental states *whether or not* the individual has causally interacted with these items.

This is the real source of disagreement, and it has nothing to do with conflating methodological solipsism and methodological individualism.[11]

Indeed, the confusion Fodor attributes to Burge is the same confusion Burge attributes, by another name, to critics making use of the argument from causation, the very argument Fodor constructs. Burge is attacking methodological individualism on the ground that it "conflat[es] causation with individuation" (Burge 1986b: p. 16). How we individuate the content of our mental states need not be restricted to what has causal impact on our bodies. This presumably is the lesson of the thought experiments. This lesson is supplemented with examples from other sciences in which individuation and attribution of causal powers diverge. Continent shift is explained by appeal to peripheral impacts and chemically constituted events and objects, while we individuate continents themselves in part by their relations to other land masses. Similarly, intentional states and processes are identified by their propositional content, a content which adverts to social conventions and natural kinds. So there is a profound disagreement about the nature of mental content that can only be resolved by looking at the theories of content developed by each. It certainly cannot be resolved in favor of Fodor's position by the "diagnosis" offered, as that diagnosis misfires.[12]

Fodor's second objection to Burge's anti-individualism is that insofar as Burge's view is correct, it isn't very interesting (Fodor 1988: p. 44). The thought experiments only draw our attention to "a difference between the way psychology individuates behaviors and mental states and the way common sense does," and this kind of cross-cutting of taxonomies, Fodor reminds us, is a commonplace in science. So "mind/brain supervenience" need not extend to all ways of individuating mental content, only to the causally efficacious elements. But there is a hidden danger here for Fodor. More is at work than merely citing a truism of scientific practice. If the cross-cutting of taxonomies goes too far, few mental states will survive the cuts, leaving little for psychology to theorize about. As Fodor acknowledges, what might turn this banal observation about scientific taxonomies into an ominous looking cloud hanging over intentionalist psychology is that psychology might cross-cut commonsense notions of mental content in a way that eliminates a place for intentionalist psychology.[13] The underside to the charge of banality against Burge is the charge of impoverishment of domain against Fodor. This strategy for undermining Burge's attack on individualism can be seen to cloak very serious concessions concerning what survives the cut, hence what counts as psychologically real.

3 Two theories of narrow mental content

In sum, these two objections to Burge's anti-internalist conclusions were: First, social content and psychological content need not be identical, and so the semantic ties to the environment that characterize that-clause content need not belong to psychological content. Second, mental causation requires internal mental content. Separating that-clause content and psychological content results in an uneasy relation between the semantic condition and the internal reality condition by eliminating the relevance of that-clause content to psychological explanation. But this carries in its wake the problems of characterizing the relation between these two contents and of offering an account of *internal* normative standards. The argument from causation generates a conflict between the normativity condition and the causal condition. How can causal principles provide the normative standards by which to judge a causal occurrence as correct or incorrect? Both conflicts make providing an account of internal individualist norms crucial. Focusing on one or another of these conflicts has given rise to two prominent theories of narrow content: Giving pre-eminence to the first conflict, that between the semantic condition and the internal reality condition, gives us conceptual role semantics (cf. Loar 1981; Block 1986); and giving pre-eminence to the second conflict between the normativity condition and the causal condition gives us causal theories of mental representation (cf. Stampe 1977; Fodor 1988).

"Anchored" content: the problem of misrepresentation

Fodor's response to the arguments based on the original twin-earth case (the "water" case) is to grant that this case does show that intension by itself cannot determine extension while denying that this shows that the connection between intension and extension has been broken. On the contrary, Fodor argues that the twin-earth thought experiment does not show that there are two factors of meaning but that content determines extension *only relative to a context*. Narrow content must be "anchored." Meaning is univocal: It is the denotation of the representation. Thus, to "chop off" the referent is to eliminate content. There is no such thing as substantive narrow content to which extension can be added, thereby giving us full wide content. Narrow content can only be captured indirectly as "a function from contexts and thoughts onto truth conditions" (Fodor 1988: p. 47). It is itself inexpressible.

So Fodor rejects the idea that that-clause content and psychological content differ. The cost of honoring the semantic condition, however, is the *nominal* satisfaction only of the internal reality condition. Fodor calls the internal function "narrow content." It is the advocate of a conceptual role semantics who wants a substantial notion of internal content and who, thus, insists upon the importance of this contrast. For Fodor, such a contrast is the beginning of the end for an intentionalist psychology (and he may well be correct once we acknowledge what is involved in specifying the full functional role of a belief). What remains for him is the conflict between the causal condition and the normativity condition. This, he attempts to resolve by arguing that normativity can be captured in purely causal terms.

To reconstruct his argument, we need to understand the two determinants of narrow content, viz., what it is to be "anchored" in a context and what thought is. Thoughts presumably can only be the sentence-like entities that are individuated syntactically. The context is the world of H_2O and other such physical stuffs. Mental content is the function that maps syntactic structures (thoughts) and local physical contexts onto truth conditions (Fodor 1988: p. 48). But how do we know which mapping is the correct one, i.e., is the one which maps syntactic structures onto the correct set of truth conditions? Fodor attempts to find the solution in certain causal relations between mental representations and the local environment of the subject: "a symbol expresses a property if it's nomologically necessary that all and only instances of the property cause tokenings of the symbol" (Fodor 1988: p. 100). In brief, "horse" means horse in virtue of the fact that horses and only horses always cause tokenings of "horse" in mentalese.

Clearly, this won't do as it stands: First, because not all horses have caused tokenings of "horse" in anyone's mind; and second, because sometimes other creatures, such as cows, can cause tokenings of "horse." However, when something other than a horse causes a tokening of "horse," this tokening is a mistake. But how can a causal theory of meaning account for error and misrepresentation? This is the problem of normativity. Fodor calls it the "disjunction" problem in order to highlight the fact that tokens of an effect can result from more than one kind of cause. So if cows can on occasion cause the tokening of "horse," why, on the causal theory of meaning, doesn't "horse" mean horse or cow? Fodor interprets this as a challenge to provide a criterion for distinguishing the *relevant cause* of tokenings of "horse" from irrelevant causes.[14] This distinction, however, must be drawn in wholly naturalistic terms. To use semantic or intentional terms would be begging the question, as Fodor is seeking to ground such properties in causal relations. So, it can't be that cow-causes are ruled out because only horses are relevant to the meaning of "horse." The causal relations that obtain between tokenings of "horse" and objects in the world must show that only horse-causes are relevant to the tokening of "horse."

Fodor quickly rejects one possible solution that has its origin in Dennis Stampe's important paper defending the causal theory of representation. The solution involves what I call a "natural teleological" account of normativity. This solution focuses on the background circumstances within which the object causes its representation. It involves the notion of a system's functioning as it is supposed to do so, where "well-functioning" and "function" are identified in terms of natural selection. The fallacy embodied in this approach to the problem, according to Fodor, is that this naturalism is only skin deep. Smuggled into the notion of "well-functioning" or "fidelity conditions" or "optimal circumstances" is a normative standard; yet the point of going to a causal theory of representation was to ground the normative in the non-intentional and non-normative, namely, in the physical. Appeal to fidelity conditions assumes that there must be a fit between truth and well-functioning. Break that connection between truth and optimality, and the allure of the appeal to optimal conditions vanishes. "For the sake of" arguments, even of this biological sort, cannot explain mental representation without tacitly bringing in semantic notions. Fodor wants a strictly non-intentionalist criterion for distinguishing "relevant cause." He seeks to ground normativity in straight causal talk.

Fodor hopes to distinguish the relevantly (i.e., correctly) caused tokenings of "horse" by providing a criterion for identifying mistaken, or wild, tokenings of the symbol. His claim is that wild tokenings of "horse" presuppose veridical tokenings of "horse" whereas veridical tokenings do not depend upon the wild tokenings (if any). This asymmetrical dependence can be expressed, without appeal to "wildness" and veridicality, in terms of the counterfactual properties of the symbol: "If B-caused 'A' tokenings are wild – if they falsely represent B's as A's – then there would be a causal route from A's to 'A' even if there were no causal route from B's to 'A's; but there would be no causal route from B's to 'A's if there were no causal route from A's to 'A's" (Fodor 1988: p. 108). In other words, in nearby possible worlds where there are horses but no cows, there will be tokenings of "horse." But in other nearby possible worlds where there are cows but no horses, there will be no tokenings of "horse." In worlds, such as our own, where there are both cows and horses, there will be tokenings of "horse" as effects of both horses and cows. Thus, an asymmetry is revealed in the counterfactual properties of symbols that is strong enough to support the normative distinction between correct representation and misrepresentation.

The first question to ask is: are these counterfactual properties sufficient to make this distinction? In the nearby world where there are no horses but there are cows, if "horse" in our world is tokened by cows under certain conditions, namely, those abnormal conditions in which cows look like horses, then why wouldn't "horse" be tokened on that cow-world provided the cow is in the right circumstances? After all, there are tokenings of "horse" in the presence of cows in certain circumstances. As this is a purely causal connection, why wouldn't it obtain on cow-world? Fodor might say that in order to mistake a cow for a horse, one must have the concept of both cows and horses. No one would disagree with this; it is a truism that in order to take something for an F, one must have the concept of an F. What we want to know is why the cows on cow-world don't cause tokenings of "horse" when the cows are in the right circumstances, namely, *those abnormal ones* in which cows look like horses? To take care of this, Fodor has only two options: (1) He can simply *stipulate* that these counter-factuals obtain in nearby possible worlds. Such stipulation in no way connects with the causal explanation that Fodor gives. There is no causal explanation for why cows in nearby possible worlds fail to cause tokenings of "horse" when they are in the "right" abnormal circumstances. Perhaps in these nearby possible worlds, cows could cause tokenings of "horse" just as, in our actual world, sea cows prompted mariners to token "mermaid." Either this stipulation is ad hoc and arbitrary, which is unacceptable; or it is introduced in virtue of some independent consideration. That independent characterization can only be that the asymmetric dependence must respect semantic distinctions. But then the asymmetric dependence presupposes the semantic distinctions it is intended to ground.

(2) The second option available to Fodor is to hold that the only way one can get the concept of "horse" is by experiencing horses. In other words, the concept "horse" must come from actual horses and no where else. This makes the asymmetric dependence a causal dependence. But, why should we believe this? Why can't the citizens of cow-world make up horses just as we have made up griffins and centaurs? Also if the meaning relation between horses and "horse" is in fact causal, then presumably it is the horsey look of the horse that causes tokenings of "horse." And if it is the horsey look that matters causally to the tokening of "horse," then cows, in those abnormal circumstances in which they look horsey, cannot but cause tokenings of "horse."

So either the asymmetrical dependence presupposes the semantic distinction it was intended to explain (option 1); or it in effect self-destructs, as there is no (causally) principled reason why the horsey looks of cows cannot cause tokenings of "horse" even in worlds where there are no horses. In sum, the semantic properties of "horse" cannot be explained solely by appeal to its causal relations to horses.

Fodor virtually admits this (Fodor 1988: pp. 111–12). This simple causal theory cannot work for any complex concepts, not even of the sort like "horse" (Fodor 1988: p. 116). If it can work anywhere, it is with concepts of phenomenal experiences, like the experience of red. This is because, according to Fodor, the circumstances in which red instantiations cause "red" tokenings are *"nonsemantically, nonteleologically, and nonintentionally specifiable.* In fact, they're *psychophysically* specifiable" (Fodor 1988: p. 112). Complex concepts can then be seen as constructions out of this base of experiential tokenings. From the tokenings or representations like "red" to the fixing of beliefs like "red there," horsey looks can be constructed that warrant the tokening of "horse." All this, of course, sounds remarkably familiar. It is the reintroduction of phenomenalism; and it carries with it all the difficulties traditional phenomenalism faced. Most importantly, there are principled difficulties with the idea of phenomenalistic constructions and there are principled difficulties with the phenomenal base as well. With Fodor we have a strong case for psychology recapitulating epistemology. And psychology is in no better shape than epistemology in sustaining such a picture of concepts and thought.

"Indexed" content: the problem of interpretation

If the attempt to find a place for narrow content within a denotational semantics fails, perhaps it can be found in a conceptual role semantics, a fully internalist semantics. Advocates of this position explicitly adopt a two-factor theory of meaning, according to which the meaning or content of a symbol can be split into (at least) two components: The internal conceptual role played by the symbol and the external referential connection the symbol has to some state of affairs in the world. Fodor's denotational theory of meaning made the external referential connection basic and in doing so ran afoul of the problem of misrepresentation as there is no way that a purely causal theory of denotation can account for the normative dimension of representation. Not only does Fodor's denotational theory fail to accommodate the normativity condition, it also results in the atrophy of narrow content, reducing it to an inexpressible function from thought to the world. This only nominally satisfies the internal reality condition. Conceptual role semantics (CRS), on the other hand, promises to satisfy all four conditions and to provide a fully adequate account of narrow content: Narrow content is something like Fodor's thought without regard to its referring relation to the world. It's what is left of Fodor's account when the inexpressible function is left out of consideration.

Thought is construed broadly to include thinking, believing, intending, wanting, and all the other propositional attitudes. What CRS exploits is the idea that meaning is given in the uses to which an expression is put, and not given by object(s) in the world (if any) to which it refers. What matters is the conceptual role played by the expression, and that can be specified fully in terms of the expression's characteristic roles in a system of expressions regulated by rules of logic, evidence, and rationality. With this emphasis on the complex logical network rather than the referents of particular representations, the fundamental unit of psychological reality cannot be the isolated mental representation but the thoughts in which the representation plays a role. As Ned Block, an advocate of CRS, puts it:

> the exact nature of the external factor does not matter....The internal factor, the conceptual role, is a matter of the causal role of the expression in reasoning and deliberation and, in general, in the way the expression combines and interacts with other expressions so as to mediate between sensory inputs and behavioral outputs. A crucial component of a sentence's conceptual role is a matter of how it participates in inductive and deductive inferences. A word's conceptual role is a matter of its contribution to the role of sentences.
>
> (Block 1986: p. 628)

It is also important to this view that the rules that govern the expressions need not be explicit; on the contrary, their operation is shown through the ways in which the expressions are, or can be, manipulated. I shall, for convenience's sake, call this system "the logical system."

As the quote from Block shows, internalist[15] CRS is tied to a functionalist theory of mind. Mental state types are individuated by their causal role in a larger system, a system consisting of perceptual inputs (really, proximal stimuli), behavioral outputs (motor commands), and other mental states and processes. The key to CRS is the idea that the logical system is *isomorphic* to this causal system. Thus, there is held to be, for any given expression, an isomorphism between the conceptual and logical roles played by that expression (its role within a rule-governed, or normative, system) and its causal role in mediating sensory inputs, behavioral outputs, and other internal processes.

CRS seems to be in a very strong position for accommodating all four conditions discussed above while resolving the apparent conflicts between the semantic condition and the internal reality condition and between the normativity condition and the causal condition. The semantic properties of that-clause content can be excised, leaving that which is wholly internal to the individual, namely, "the causal role of the expression in reasoning and deliberation." In this way, the advocate of CRS wholly endorses the distinction between that-clause content and psychological content, holding that psychological content is given by the conceptual roles expressions play (the narrow content) whereas that-clause content is to be identified in terms of the referent and/or truth conditions of the expression (the wide content). CRS also seems to resolve the conflict between the normativity condition and the causal condition. In severing connections to referents, truth conditions, and social conventions, the logical system is understood to be a closed system within which the expressions or symbols of the system are fully governed by the (implicitly) determinate rules of the system. The functionalist theory of mind also posits a system whose elements can only be individuated within the system itself. Although the logical system is a normative system (though not a semantic system, strictly) and the functional system is a causal system, the idea of narrow content is nonetheless preserved because the causal connections of the functional system mirror the logical and inferential connections of the normative system. It is in virtue of this mirroring relation, and only in virtue of it, that the causal system – a neural system after all – can be said to be contentful – subject, that is, to the normative constraints of rules. For the advocate of narrow content, this isomorphism *must* obtain. If it doesn't, there is no hope for an internalist psychology. This isomorphism, then, between the logical system and the causal system requires close examination.

We need to look both at the relata and at the relationship itself. One suggestion is that there is a de facto correlation between words or sentences of natural language and expressions of mentalese and between the logical relations among the former and the causal relations among the latter. This is a curious idea. The alleged correlation is not empirically grounded. As a matter of fact, actual *tokens* of natural language sentences are simply not produced for the most part, and so are not available for correlating empirically natural language tokens with tokens of sentences in mentalese. The point here is not that we have no independent way of individuating tokens of mentalese – though that is true also – but that no such actual contingent correlations exist. When I pick up my umbrella upon noticing the dark clouds in the sky, I do not typically (if ever) utter the sentences "There are dark clouds in the sky" and "Dark clouds mean rain." So the isomorphism is not one that obtains between the actual tokenings of natural language sentences and tokenings of corresponding sentences in mentalese.

The natural language sentences can only be part of something like rational reconstructions of inferences, such that behavior can be interpreted as something like the conclusion of an Aristotelian practical syllogism. So the correlations must obtain between appropriate interpretive redescriptions of the aetiology of behavior, descriptions expressed in natural language sentences, and tokenings of sentences in mentalese. But because these natural language sentences are themselves part of a theory of behavior that looks very much like the theory in which sentences in mentalese are postulated, it is difficult to see how we have discovered *contingent* correlations. For this approach to work, it is necessary to assume that the natural language reconstruction is the same as the mentalese pattern of inference and deduction. The correlations that matter most for CRS must be found to hold between explicitly displayed inferential systems and neural systems. This is typically the way in which examples are constructed in order to persuade the reader of the intuitive plausibility of CRS (e.g., Block 1986: p. 628). A simple form of deductive reasoning, such as modus ponens, could be mirrored, it is suggested, by neural activity in the brain. So for the reconstructed inference that is alleged to explain my picking up my umbrella, there is a corresponding causal path instantiated in my brain. That inferential pattern looks something like this:

> There are dark clouds in the sky.
> If (or nearly always when) there are dark clouds in the sky, there is rain.
> Therefore, there [will be] rain.
> Rain gets unprotected bodies wet.
> Therefore, if my body is an unprotected body, my body [will get] wet.
> My body will not get wet.
> Therefore, it is not the case that my body is unprotected.

The final conclusion of this enthymeme is held to be a behavior (such as my picking up an umbrella) or a motor command (issued to the relevant set of muscles). The fully articulated inference, even in a simple case like this, is extremely lengthy, of course, but the point of such illustrations is clear: The inference consists of repeated applications of simple logical argument forms like modus ponens and modus tolens. Provided we can associate each sentence type, and/or each element type of the sentences, with a neural type, we can mirror the inferential connections that obtain among the sentences and their elements with causal connections that obtain among the neural states. The inferential patterns go through whether or not the sentences are interpreted or have any semantic properties at all. In this way, we seem justified in saying, with Block, that "[c]onceptual role is *total causal role*, abstractly described."

Despite the apparent plausibility of this picture, closer examination shows serious strains within CRS. Theoretical problems arise for both relata of the isomorphism. Neither the logical system nor the causal system can provide what is necessary to make CRS plausible. The logical system itself must be such that each of the lengthy enthymemes implicated in a decision or an action or a perception or a whim is fully explicit and fully determinate with respect to both its elements and its inferences. It must be fully explicit in that each step of the pattern of reasoning must be statable; and it must be fully determinate in that each premise and each element within each premise must be formed precisely correctly. The simple enthymeme above clearly fails to honor both of these requirements. The premises themselves are conclusions from other inferences. *Ceteris paribus* clauses are understood to hold, but have not been made explicit. The shapes of the elements in each line of the enthymeme must be fixed precisely. So although, in the rough-and-ready way in which this was presented as an illustration, it didn't matter whether a proposition type was inscripted as "there is rain" or "there will be rain," for the purposes of CRS there can be no such laxity.

Each of these problems is familiar. The first gives rise to the frame problem that so plagues artificial intelligence research. The second gives rise to the problem of specifying the class of formal or syntactic items that can be substituted for each other without disrupting the inferential pattern. Though in this illustration, the first premise was given as the sentence "There are dark clouds in the sky," intuitively it ought not to make any difference to the explanation of behavior if we substitute "Dark clouds are in the sky" or "Dark clouds are overhead" or "The sky is full of clouds that are dark" and so on and so on. They belong together because they mean the same thing and so these slight variations in sentence structure shouldn't matter. Yet on this view of mental activity, such differences can make all the difference. From the point of view of the resources available to CRS, there is no reason why they should belong together. Such groupings can only be seen as ad hoc and coincidental. Moreover, if we were to substitute for any of the members of this group, such as "The sky is full of clouds that are dark," the enthymeme would fail to go through, and I would leave the house without my umbrella. For "The sky is full of clouds that are dark" and "If there are dark clouds in the sky, there is rain" don't match properly to derive the sentence "Therefore, there will be rain."

The second problem area concerns the causal system. Semantic properties and constraints, provided by reference or truth conditions, are, by design, irrelevant to CRS. This means that other kinds of normative constraints are crucial to the intelligibility of this position. We may not be able to assign truth values to any of the sentences of mentalese nor appeal to the referents of any of its terms, but nonetheless the terms and sentences of mentalese are normatively guided and evaluable. There can be correct or incorrect use of terms; valid or invalid patterns of reasoning; efficient or inefficient use of data; and so on. Yet no causal system can deliver normative principles. The normativity of the causal system can only be derivative, depending upon its instantiating valid or correct or efficient patterns of reasoning. Suppose that upon seeing the dark clouds, I take off my coat as I leave the house. Have I made a mistake? Or have I engaged in a different pattern of reasoning? Or is there no connection at all between my perception and my action? The causal system cannot distinguish among fallacious reasoning and novel interpretation of premises and different rules. Only in the context of the logical system do we get a handle on these normative notions, so "conceptual role" cannot be identified with "total causal role" simpliciter, for what is relevant is not the de facto total causal role, but only that aspect of the causal role that is isomorphic to the logical system. And this means that the criterion of causal relevance is given by the normative rules. So CRS, construed as requiring a correlation between two independently characterizable systems, fails.

The difficulties with this direct approach to the isomorphism, namely, that there must be a correlation between the elements and patterns of inference within the logical system expressed in natural language sentences and neural states and patterns of neural activity within the causal system, suggest that CRS might be better defended by an indirect approach. This is the strategy developed by Brian Loar (1981). The relata are persons and propositions; and the relation is not one of the subject's "having" a proposition but one of the proposition's indexing the underlying functional state.

Propositions, Loar tells us, are "sets of possible worlds" individuated in a fine-grained way (Loar 1981: p. 58). The function of belief ascriptions is to "index underlying states with propositions which...encode counterfactuals about that state" (Loar 1981: p. 62). The counterfactual relations that obtain among the underlying states mirror the logical relations among propositions. So "[b]y virtue of its unique place in the logical network a proposition can index a belief's unique functional role" (Loar 1981: p. 62). Can this isomorphic relation between underlying mental states and abstract logical systems save the notion of narrow content?

I need to preface the discussion of indexing by pointing out two important features of propositions. First, though beliefs are relations to propositions, this does not require that propositions be something that actually exist. They are not to be construed as abstract entities existing in some platonic realm (cf. Loar 1981: p. 142). Propositions are to be construed as sets of possible worlds.[16] The only way to do this, it seems to me, is, in effect, to treat beliefs as expressing sets of dispositions to behave in certain ways under certain conditions.

The second important feature of propositions is their relative flexibility compared with sentences. They can be tailored to fit exactly the psychological or mental content of the subject's belief. This is what Loar means in holding that fine-grained propositions are to be associated with fine-grained functional roles for beliefs (Loar 1981: p. 58). Even though mental content can be more fine grained than the typically crude specification of oblique content, there is no one particular sentence that must be identified as specifying *the* content of the particular belief. In this way, it avoids one of the difficulties that arises in searching for a correlation between sentences and functional roles. Thus, Pierre's beliefs about London and Londres can be distinguished without having to specify the particular sentences that capture the exact contents of the two beliefs.

By identifying propositions as the objects of belief, Loar can accommodate the distinction between that-clause content and psychological content while avoiding the impossible task of trying to identify the very sentence that captures the precise psychological contents of Pierre's beliefs. Psychological content is given by the propositional index, which encodes the full functional role of the underlying state. That-clause content is given by our commonsense psychological specifications and explanations that "are so generally shot through with social and causal presuppositions that narrow content cannot in general be captured thus" (Loar 1988: p. 14). This alleged distinction, however, is harder to draw than it appears. Loar argues that there are two kinds of content. In distinguishing these two kinds of content, two criteria operate, neither of which draws the distinction in the way that Loar wants. The first identifies that-clause content with wide content, namely, content identified by its semantic properties, especially its socio- and referential-causal relations to the world. This distinction can apply both to our that-clause content and our psychological content. The second criterion also blurs the alleged distinction between two kinds of content, for it seems to turn on a consideration of the *degree of crudeness* or refinement in the specification of the propositional content. "London is beautiful" and "Londres is beautiful" are crude propositional indices of Pierre's beliefs, retaining their semantic properties, whereas something more fine grained like "London, the city to which I moved in 1988, is beautiful" and "Londres, the city I have never visited, is beautiful" capture more fully the actual psychological content of Pierre's beliefs and show the way in which they diverge. It is very difficult to say whether our commonsense belief ascriptions posit a wholly different kind of content or are simply crude. What is wanted, of course, are appropriately refined propositional specifications of content, stripped of referring or truth conditional relations to the natural and/or social world. What is most important in substituting propositions for sentences as the objects of belief is that Loar has thereby substituted sets of possible worlds for referents in the actual world as semantically more important, and has thus freed the individual mind from more than accidental constraint by this actual world. The success of this strategy turns on the work being done by "indexing."

What is this indexing relation that associates propositions to underlying states? As the name indicates, they are a special kind of "label" for identifying psychological states. They individuate the psychological state they index without describing that state. The psychological state itself, e.g., the belief, is a functional state, meaning that the particular belief's "possible states are counterfactually related to each other, input and output thus and so" (Loar 1981: p. 44). Thus, indexing is another way of characterizing the "standard association" between the causal structures that are literally in the head, and their counterfactual properties, and the abstract logical and inferential structures that characterize the propositional system. In brief, the proposition indexes a distinct functional role.

There are two ways of interpreting this relation, neither of which is very satisfactory for the advocate of narrow content. It could be treated as a name which labels a set of states (cf. Loar 1981: pp. 59–60). This is a very unhappy solution, as the logical interconnections that obtain among propositions in virtue of their logical form are lost. So, from "Sam believes that Sally plays the piano very well," we cannot directly infer the truth of "Sam believes that Sally plays the piano." The latter is a distinct name or label that must be discovered to apply to another set of Sam's underlying states. This is clearly an unsatisfactory tack to take. But if indexing is not a naming relation, what is it?

Loar's view is that propositional indices are a special kind of label for psychological states. "Labels" of this sort, it seems to me, can be characterized in terms of the following three features: (1) These "labels" are introduced for the benefit of the theorist about mental states. They are introduced as part of a theory about the underlying states that cause behavior, especially verbal behavior. As such, they are *convenient fictions*, abbreviations for the full specification of the underlying state. (2) But they are not ordinary labels, as the indexing proposition, in all its internal logical complexity, is indispensable for the individuation of the underlying state and all its counterfactual properties. It is this internal logical complexity that enables the proposition to encode all the counterfactual properties of the underlying state. The proposition provides the *individuation conditions* on psychological states. (3) Finally, a proposition P is the correct label for an underlying state M if and only if the causal properties of M track the logico-inferential properties of P. Contingent counterfactual relations among the underlying states *mirror* necessary logical relations among propositions.

It seems to me that propositions are being asked to function both as names for states (convenient fictions), such that their logical structure is irrelevant, and as interpretations of the underlying states, such that what they mean and what logical structure they have are indispensable. Loar's naturalism demands that propositions be eliminable and his desire to explain mental content requires that they be essential. So the tension that exists in satisfying the causal condition and the normativity condition is masked in part by describing propositions as indices. At the very least, to describe them as convenient fictions is misleading, and for two reasons. First, as "fictions" it is suggested that the full specification of all that is abbreviated by their use is both possible and, if done, explanatory. Both claims are dubious. Second, as "fictions" it is suggested that they were never necessary to the theory of mental states, but only used for pragmatic reasons. Yet this is false on Loar's own account of how such a theory appealing to propositional indices could have developed.

The first objection. If these fictions are eliminable, with what are they to be replaced? According to Loar, they are to be replaced with grotesquely complicated constructions which consist of hugely long conjunctions of all the instantiations of all the conditions of all nominalized belief-desire sentences. As Loar says himself, "To each sentence 'x believes that p', there corresponds a preposterously unmanageable sentence that does not quantify over propositions and is equivalent to 'x believes that p' apart from the latter's reference to a proposition" (Loar 1981: p. 144). The equivalence between the individuation of the belief by appeal to its propositional index and this grotesquely large sentence lies in the alleged fact that "[t]hey agree exactly on x's functional state" (Ibid.: p. 144). This alleged agreement is a fiction. This entire approach assumes that all possible conditions in which x believes that p can be specified in advance; that the notoriously troublesome "ceteris paribus" clauses that are always associated with specifying conditions and behaviors can be unpacked in a full and perspicuous manner. No such analyses have ever succeeded; and there is no reason to believe that they will succeed in this case.[17] Moreover, one of the seeming advantages of taking propositions rather than sentences as the objects of belief is lost. Difficulties with specifying the very sentence that captures the exact content of belief that arose for a sentential CRS now arise for Loar's propositional CRS.

In addition, no such sentential replacement is at all explanatory. Loar is right in his observation that "[t]he unwieldy theory, with indices eliminated, seems to have no claim to express intentionality apart from its relation to the theory with indices" (Loar 1981: pp. 126–7). This is not just a pragmatic matter. The propositions we use in individuating the underlying states determine what is relevant. In eliminating the proposition we would eliminate our criterion for sorting out the relevant causal connections from the irrelevant ones. So the appeal to indices does provide a way of determining which causal connections are relevant to being a particular belief. This leads directly to the second objection.

Loar's own story of how we could have come to develop the belief-desire theory makes propositions theoretically indispensable. The idea is that our early theorists of the mind hypothesized underlying functional states as the normal cause of utterances of *s*. This supports a classical dispositionalist account of beliefs as dispositions to assert *s* under appropriate conditions. "But that causal relation," Loar tells us, "may itself be then *reconstructed within the theory*; we come to say that *x* uttered *s* because *x* had certain communicative purposes and beliefs, where these are referred to via the more abstract indexing system" (Loar 1981: p. 124). However, the very idea of such a reconstruction requires the use of propositions as theoretically essential, as providing the "defining properties" of belief. This hypothesized reconstruction is only possible given appeal to propositions; it would not be possible using the long sentences as replacements for the propositions.

My final objection concerns the "mirroring" condition: Causal properties of the functional state must track the logical properties of the proposition. This idea is the real motor behind all versions of CRS. Equally all versions of CRS face the same difficulty. The causal interrelations of the functional state are contingent. That these interactions track logical relations is contingent. Logical relationships, however, are necessary. Suppose some functional state of a living organism has successfully tracked the logical relations of some proposition. Suppose further that at some time in the life of the organism the causal relationships diverge from the logical relations of the proposition. Has the organism made a mistake? Have the causal relationships been tracking a different proposition than the one used to describe and explain the organism's behavior? Or has that causal pathway nothing to do with tracking at all? Nothing within CRS provides a way of distinguishing among these different possibilities. *How* the functional state is interpreted or indexed is crucial to determining what went wrong. But nothing in the causal nexus of the functional state can resolve this normative problem.

Loar acknowledges this anti-internalist argument that no internal properties of an individual can determine how a thought represents something (Loar 1987). But he argues that the anti-internalist conclusion that takes the representational properties of thoughts to be essential to psychological explanation is mistaken. It is mistaken, he maintains, because "representational properties that are essential to psychological explanation need be representational or intentional only from a subject/projective perspective" (Ibid.: p. 114). What he means by this is that our "primitive notion of aboutness is subjective, and this is the foundation of the semantic" (Ibid.: p. 116) where "subjective intentionality is the disposition of thoughts to reveal themselves 'as intentional' upon reflection" (Ibid.: p. 102). Reflection reveals that "my thoughts appear *self interpreting*" (Loar 1981: p. 99).

Intentionality thus is an artefact of reflection, for which there may be explanation, but it is not essential theoretically to the explanation of behavior. That is given by the causal/functional roles of neural states within the neurophysiological system of the organism. The conflict between the normativity condition and the causal condition is thus resolved by arguing that the normativity, or intentionality, of psychological states is irrelevant to psychological explanation. Intentional states, namely, self-interpreting states, are nomological danglers.

But even if we hold that intentionality is epiphenomenal, there are still two difficulties for Loar: What makes the study of these functional systems an inquiry into *psychological* processes? This position looks like a form of eliminativism in favor of the neural sciences. The second problem is that this account of intentionality doesn't really answer to the normativity condition. That condition required that psychological representations and states be rule-governed, where specification of the rules reveals what is a correct or incorrect representation. A purely causal account cannot mark this normative distinction. So it would seem that the subjective intentionality revealed by reflection provides the criterion for distinguishing relevant from irrelevant features of the total causal system. The selectivity, then, of psychological states is revealed through primitive subjective reflection. This makes the *sui generis* self-evidence of psychological states indispensable. It also shows why Loar picks self-interpretation as the product of primitive reflection (rather than say incorrigibility of primitive mental states), for he is looking for a way to ground rule-governed content. Loar, thus, comes to identify narrow content with the self-interpreting inner state. The naturalism that first motivated hypothesizing a CRS has collapsed.

In conclusion, both Fodor and Loar come to agree that no naturalistic account can be given for intentionality, representationality, or normativity. Because both are committed to internalism and individualism, both revive previously discredited accounts of the mental, Fodor in terms of incorrigible phenomenal experiences and Loar in terms of self-interpreting private inner states. It is my view that none of these three features of mental life can be understood from the perspective of this strong internalism. Content must be rooted in the public and social domain.

4 Norms and social practice

What Burge draws our attention to is the importance of social practices and the linguistic division of labor in understanding individual mental life. No purely internalist and/or individualist account of mental content can explain or ground the normativity of our practices or the intentionality of our mental states. Both Fodor's denotational theory and Loar's conceptual role theory fail to solve the problem of normativity. As shown above, for Fodor, this becomes the problem of specifying the relevant cause of the tokening of a neural state that endows that state with representational content; for Loar, the problem of normativity becomes the problem of how to characterize the "standard association" between a logical network of propositions and a functionally described physical system. Neither anchoring nor indexing can solve the problem of normativity without presupposing the very standards of correctness anchoring or indexing was to explain. As I suggest above, recognition of this failure is shown, it seems to me, by the return of both Fodor and Loar to phenomenal experience and subjective intentionality respectively as the *sui generis* source of intentionality. This is the only recourse open so long as internalism and individualism are held to be unrevisable givens in our understanding of the mind.

Social theory of normativity

But if these individualist positions cannot account for the intentionality of mental content, how can a social theory? The key to understanding the social theory of mental content turns on seeing that normativity is basic to *human* intentionality. Human intentionality (unlike animal intentionality) is marked by its sensitivity to norms and standards. Thus, the problem of normativity is the problem of understanding how standards are set that fix meaning and provide the guide and/or justification for subsequent use. The normativity of intentional states, that is, their being accurate or inaccurate, correct or incorrect, is dependent upon their relation to socially fixed standards, what Burge calls "norms of understanding." Neither anchoring nor indexing can perform this role. Both presuppose the very normative standards they are supposed to ground. The setting of standards is thus simply not within the provenance of the radically isolated individual.

As already indicated in the discussion above, each of Burge's three thought experiments highlights different roles played by the community in fixing the standards for use of a term. With natural kind terms like "water," being a rigid designator explains why even in oblique contexts the expression "water" retains its semantic connection to H_2O. Yet rigid designation obtains only within a social structure. This is so for two reasons: First, the original baptism that fixes the relation between term and object or person requires a setting that is rich enough to make room for naming. This is the Wittgensteinian point that a certain stage setting is required in order to name, as naming is not the mere association of a word with a place, person, or object. What is to be named has to be made salient against a background myriad of simultaneously occurring properties and aspects that could be named. At this point, I shall simply make the claim that a social practice is necessary for setting the stage. I shall return to this point shortly. Second, once an object or person has been named, the causal chain that preserves the connection between name and referent is a socially sustained chain, one in which the members have an interest (even if unarticulated) in maintaining the relation between name and referent, an interest which is expressed in the continuation of the appropriate causal chain. The appropriate causal chain is, of course, the one that originates in the baptismal object. In normative terms, the baptismal object sets the standard for correct and incorrect future use of the naming expression. That future usage and the baptismal object are related by a *social* chain is obvious. What may seem less obvious is that the originating baptismal act itself requires a social practice.

With the concept of arthritis, however, its relation to the experts is not explained by the term "arthritis" being a rigid designator; likewise with "sofa." So what is the relation of the individual's use of "arthritis" to the experts'? There must be a more Gricean explanation. When I use terms of art or expertise, I use them intending to use them as the experts do and intending my audience to so understand my usage.[18] Satisfying this "deference condition" is part of the layman's successful use of terms of expertise. The experts are accorded a special epistemic status because of their specialized knowledge; and it is for this reason that their judgment provides the standard for correct usage of the term by the layman. An important part of what this means is that I am aware of my limitations, and so knowingly open myself to correction by the experts. In sum, the layman's use of terms of expertise must satisfy a deference condition. This condition consists of two parts: First, expert judgment provides the standard of correct usage for the layman; and second, the layman acknowledges his own limitation in this matter. The very way in which the layman's use of terms of art is related to the experts shows that these cases do not reveal anything basic about the social dimension of normativity. They concern a limited range of cases, all dependent upon our ordinary linguistic competence.

It is to be hoped that Burge's "sofa" case, on the other hand, will shed light on this basic competence, and for this reason it requires close examination. For "sofa," there is a third explanation for how environmental factors, this time the linguistic community, are involved in fixing and sustaining norms. The explanation is not that "sofa" is a rigid designator, so come what may, when Oscar uses "sofa" he thereby refers to sofas. Nor is this a matter of his use being parasitic upon community use in the way that his use of "arthritis" is parasitic upon the judgment of the doctors.

Oscar doesn't intend to use "sofa" as those in the know do. This is because Oscar is just as much "in the know" as anyone else. So neither does he take himself to be open to criticism and correction by other competent speakers. He *is* a competent speaker. Neither feature of the deference condition characterizes his use of "sofa." So if "sofa" does not rigidly designate what a particular linguistic community says (any more than "arthritis" designates what a group of experts say) and if the subject is not self-consciously dependent upon those in the know, what is the relation of the individual in his use of ordinary terms to the community?

The relation is two-fold: First, in the process of learning language, the child is clearly dependent upon the adult in a way that is similar to the relation of the layman to the expert. It is similar but not the same. The deference condition that marks adult use of terms of expertise does not govern the child's early uses of language. The child is not a small adult using words with the intention of using them in accord with expert judgment. This intention of the adult is too sophisticated for a child to have. This intention presupposes a general mastery and competence against which the importation of the exotic, the unknown, and the theoretical is intelligible, and so it cannot ground such competence.[19] The young child, in using ordinary words of ordinary discourse, is not using them against such a background of knowledge and linguistic competence. Her dependence upon the adult world is much more thoroughgoing than that of the layman on the expert. Her use is sustained, not by her own background competence, but by the competence of the adult world. In first acquiring language, she does not intend to use words as adults do; she just uses them, increasingly in the right contexts. The child is not open to correction because she knowingly places herself in that position; the child just is corrected. In these ways, the young child's relation to language is external. It is, then, a misdescription of the child's relation to the adult to characterize it as one of deference.[20]

The second relation that the individual's use of such ordinary notions of "sofa" has to the linguistic community is more important for the purposes of this chapter. It concerns the normativity of linguistic usage more directly. In representing a part of the world we thereby open ourselves to misrepresenting it. We can use our words correctly or incorrectly. The account of this normative dimension of language use involves the community but not in the obvious and direct way in which a rigid designator is related to its referent nor in the way in which lay uses of terms of art are parasitic upon expert judgment. The subject does not open herself to correction from the community; if she does make an error, she is as much able, from a linguistic stance, to correct it as anyone else. So if a person mistakenly takes a cow for a horse, given the surrounding circumstances, her linguistic competence is not impugned, but the difficult circumstances are. The problem here is to account for the fact that words are normative, that they can be used correctly or incorrectly. We know why the experts are given the authority they are. Because they know about the obscure or exotic phenomenon, experts are accorded a special epistemic status because of their specialized knowledge. But the community is not accorded a special epistemic status; and so the way in which the community grounds the normativity of ordinary linguistic practices cannot be in the way in which the experts do. The community does not have a special authority, which is why individual community practices can be challenged even by a competent individual. The point is that the activity of members of the community, as expressed in the de facto harmony and agreement of their judgments, grounds the fundamental contrast between correct and incorrect.

It is no accident that Burge's third case involving an ordinary concept is a case of deviant belief, not of error as with "arthritis." In this case, it is important that Oscar is not making a mistake similar to that of wrongly believing that arthritic pain can occur in muscles or similar to mistaking a cow for horse. He hasn't mistaken a sofa for a religious artefact in the way that one might, for instance, mistake a bead necklace for a rosary. Nor does he intend to use "sofa" as the furniture experts do, willingly reforming his own usage if it conflicts with that of the experts. He is not in poor or abnormal conditions for recognizing these perfectly familiar objects. He, like any other competent speaker, can identify sofas without help. But it is only in virtue of his membership within the linguistic community that he is able to form deviant individualistic conceptions of ordinary objects. Community judgment as expressed in the actual uses of ordinary terms in context just *is* the norm or standard of correct usage. The authority of the community derives from the fact that it is only within a community that the primitive distinction between correct and incorrect can get a hold. The most primitive form that a norm takes is expressed in the conformity of the individual's behavior to the community of which she is a part.[21] There are three features of this conformity that are of special interest. In order of importance, the first is that this basic or primitive conformity is necessary for human intentionality and genuine individualism; the second is the non-theoretical and non-reflective character of our engagement in various language games; and the third is the importance of exemplars as norms or standards. In order of explication, however, I shall begin with the role of exemplars.

The point at which language most obviously connects with items in the world is with the use of ostensive definitions, archetypical applications, indexicals, and rigid designators. As we have already seen, the two most promising alternatives to the social theory of content, namely, the causal theory of reference and conceptual role semantics, fail, in distinct but complementary ways, to account for ostensive definitions (and their kin). The causal theory cannot account for the stage setting needed to isolate the baptismal object and sustain an appropriate causal chain; and conceptual role semantics cannot get from functional roles to referents without independent interpretation of the functional roles. Both failures have to do with the background network necessary for the activities of naming, referring, and ostending. Neither a logical system nor a complex causal nexus can provide the right kind of background. But social practice can, for the community provides the stage setting within which any of these world-referring activities occur.

No object *in itself* can stand as paradigm for a class or kind of object nor can the usage of an expression in itself count as an archetypical application, as Burge expresses it. For a pool of water to count as a standard-setting sample, that pool must be accorded a special status. That status is manifested by its place within the behavioral and verbal activity of a socially structured group. The arguments for meaning holism and attitude holism, that a concept or belief is only what it is within a network, support such a view. But rather than looking for an explicit list of propositions and their logical and evidential relations, one looks for the ways in which a community uses language in their practices, the usage thereby displaying (rather than describing) the normative role assigned certain objects.

This assigning of normative roles need not be understood as an actual ritual occurring at some definite time (though it may be this); rather the assignment is shown in the actions of the community. The point to be emphasized here is that the background network is not something that occurs in the head. Social practice provides the needed context, and that just consists in the patterned and harmonious ways of acting and judging that exist among the members of the community. The beliefs, desires, and other attitudes of the individual are embedded within this natural and social environment. They are best understood as dispositions, the analysis of which would appeal both to kinds of behavior and kinds of contexts. This is not a recommendation to revive a strongly reductionist account of these dispositions. But it is a recommendation to see beliefs and other such states as acquired dispositions, the exercise of which involves both patterns of behavior and structured circumstances. This enables us to account both for the way in which society can contribute to the content of a belief or thought without directly causally affecting the individual and for the sense in which it is true that beliefs are psychologically real states.

Since the individual's personal experiences do not themselves fix the meaning of terms, though the socially constrained actions of the members of the community do, it is possible for an individual to use a word meaningfully without ever having come in contact with a member of the class of objects referred to. This is clearly the case with both natural kind terms and terms of expertise. The use of such terms is individual-context-free; that is, a substance like water need never have been in the local environment of the individual who successfully uses the term "water" and forms appropriate beliefs about the liquid. These beliefs are psychologically real, not in the sense that there are literally contentful states internal to the individual, but that there are real patterns of action within the social and natural world that are the exercise of the water beliefs. In emphasizing patterns of action, I intend to press against the idea that where there are dispositions, there must be the categorical bases of the dispositions, bases *whose properties explain the disposition* itself. In the case of psychological states, there is no reason to expect to find such underlying bases. Indeed much suggests the contrary. Even advocates of an intentionalist psychology acknowledge that ordinary psychological concepts may cross-classify scientific psychological concepts; and, of course, the cross-classification diverges even more and more strikingly between neurological-level descriptions and ordinary descriptions. There may well be no interesting and systematic correlations between neural patterning and ordinary dispositional patterning. This gap does not warrant, however, the conclusion that ordinary descriptions are to be eliminated on the ground that they constitute a bad theory of human behavior. This is because they are not part of a theory in rivalry with neurophysiology.

This takes us to the final feature of ordinary linguistic competence. Not only does ordinary competence involve the use of objects as normal samples by our community practices, ordinary competence also is non-theoretical and non-reflective. Part of what this means is that the attempt to model such basic competence upon the basis of theory construction and use is going to distort the character of this competence. Theory construction is a more sophisticated cognitive enterprise, one that presupposes basic competence, and so cannot be used to explain that competence.[22] This basic competence, which embodies both understanding of the world one lives in and understanding of language, is not a way of interpreting the world but a way of acting and judging non-reflectively in accord with others. This marks another great difference between the use of ordinary expressions like "sofa" and expressions of expertise like "arthritis." Expert terms are embedded within theories whereas ordinary terms are not. As I expressed it earlier in this chapter, ordinary terms, whether of natural kinds or not, are theory-context-free unlike terms of expertise. They do require a context of use, but that context is not a theory. We can now understand why it is important that Oscar's deviant belief is a *hypothesis* about the value and proper use of these objects. Like any hypothesis or theory, it presupposes a stable background of linguistic practice against which the hypothesis may be formed and evaluated.[23] But, as I have been emphasizing, this background itself is not a system of hypotheses.

Conclusion

What I have tried to show in this chapter is that the notion of narrow mental content is in serious trouble, and that trouble derives from stresses and tensions within the two most promising theories of narrow content. The causal theory of representation and conceptual role semantics, though bedeviled by different problems, end up in curiously similar positions. Both theories treat the referential function of narrow content as an inexpressible function from what goes on within to something external; both theories are forced to broadly dispositionalist accounts of psychological attitudes by way of possible worlds; and both save internalist intentionality by appeal to a given subjective experience.

The most plausible alternative to these internalist and individualist theories is a social theory of normativity. This requires giving up homogeneous conceptions of belief and learning. In particular and most importantly, the models of belief as hypothesis, of learning as hypothesis formation, and of norms as algorithmic rules cannot serve as *general* models for all cases of belief, belief fixation, and normative practice. This is because these practices of hypothesis formation and testing *presuppose* a mastery of rule-governed competence. This basic cognitive competence is possible only against a background of dynamic social practices in which primitive normativity is grounded in social conformity, belief in complex dispositions to behave verbally and otherwise, and explicit norms in objects accorded the status of exemplars.

Part II

A new direction

6 Rules, community, and the individual

In this chapter, I shall show both that, some recent critics notwithstanding, Wittgenstein does hold a community view of rules, the view that the objectivity of rule-following is essentially social, and that that view is quite plausible. Indeed I think it is correct. By the "objectivity of rule-following," I mean the fact that rules distinguish between correct and incorrect applications (what I shall call the "normativity of rules") and that they impose a constraint on the behavior of the individual that is independent of his mere say-so ("the necessity of rules"). The community view is strikingly at odds with our traditional understanding of language, for which the number of people speaking is irrelevant to accounts of the objectivity of meaning and rule-following. This individualistic assumption is so deeply rooted as to make the community view of rules, to many philosophers, obviously wrong. I shall argue that it is only through a community view of rule-following that space can be made for the basic normative distinction between correct and incorrect action and for the power of rules to constrain the individual's behavior.

1 The Classical View of rule-governed practice: objectified meaning

There are two dimensions to rule-governed practices and actions: the *practical, or psychological, dimension*, the way in which the behavior or judgment of the individual is in fact guided or determined; and the *justificatory, or epistemic, dimension*, the way in which the action or judgment is assessed for correctness.

What I am calling the Classical View gives a clear and initially plausible account of both. On this view, a rule serves both as a guide to the individual in determining what he does or says, and as a basis for justifying or assessing what he does or says. We are naturally led to the idea of the epistemic primacy of the rule as a standard for assessing correctness or appropriateness. The normative character of the applications, the fact that they can be evaluated at all, seems to imply a standard of correctness that is independent of the applications. Moreover, we need a more than accidental or coincidental connection between our actions and how we justify them. Unless there is a convergence of our justification and our guide to action, we are left with an unsettling gulf between why we ought to act as we do and why in fact we do so act. So it is important that the rule appealed to in justifying the action actually play some role in the production of the action.

In the central passages of the *Philosophical Investigations*, Wittgenstein successfully challenges this Classical View. The remarks I shall focus on are those that are directed against the idea that a rule determines its applications and guides the individual.[1] The central concerns of §§139–242 are to display the multiplicity of interpretations available to any rule and action alike and to undermine the idea that "understanding" and its allied concepts (grasping a rule, following a rule, and the like) designate a state or process (whether mental, neural, or environmentally causal). These two concerns reflect the epistemic and practical dimensions of rule-governed behavior, respectively.

Wittgenstein begins his discussion of rule-following with a difficulty for his idea that meaning is "the *use* we make of the word" (PI §138):

> But we *understand* the meaning of a word when we hear or say it; we grasp it in a flash, and what we grasp in this way is surely something different from the "use" which is extended in time!

Wittgenstein's task for the succeeding passages is to show that the idea that there must be something different from the use is illusory. There is no something that can perform the role assigned, namely, to determine and fix all the possible applications of the word and yet be grasped in a flash. And so he opens his discussion of understanding and rules by drawing the reader's attention to the difference between a picture of a cube, which might be thought to be the meaning of the word "cube," and the method of projection for using this picture. This serves to highlight the fact that any picture, chart, schema (i.e., any *isolable* representational object) is susceptible to more than one interpretation, to more than one use. "What is essential," Wittgenstein tells us, "is to see that the same thing can come before our minds when we hear the word and the application still be different" (PI §140). It is important to note that the multiplicity of interpretations is an observation; it is *not* itself an argument, but it does set the stage for the entire discussion.[2] It needs to be shown why our ability to think up alternative methods of application, if sufficiently imaginative, creates a problem. On the face of it, nothing in our imagining bizarre and convoluted alternative projections to our usual projections thereby undermines the correctness of our usual projections. It is only against the background of certain assumptions that this imaginative capacity of ours can be seen to threaten our epistemic preferences. What assumptions enable us to take a projection of "cube" that picks out triangles as a *rival* to the usual projection that picks out cubes?

The picture that lies in the background and informs our use of the multiplicity of interpretations is the following. We are looking for something that (1) can come before the mind and be grasped "in a flash," in other words, something isolable, but which (2) can serve as a guide for certain future actions, and also (3) can set a standard for the correctness of those actions. It is a picture of meaning that, itself, paradoxically results in the collapse of the distinction between correct and incorrect uses that the picture was thought to explain. It is only in the context of this picture of meaning that *imagined* possibilities can function as objections. This picture of meaning is that of objectified, or reified, meaning. The meaning of an expression is something which places constraints upon the use of the expression, constraints that are independent in principle of our actual practices and judgments.

To develop Wittgenstein's attack on this picture of meaning, I am going to separate two arguments that are often treated as the same. The first is a variant of the Infinite Regress Argument and the second is the Paradox of Interpretation so emphasized by Kripke.[3] The Regress Argument shows that nothing could meet (1) and yet perform the task set out in (2). And the Paradox shows that nothing meeting (1) could fulfill the role set out in (3). The Regress, I shall argue, shows that in the end meaning must be something other than an act of interpretation or that which requires interpretation. The Paradox builds on this to establish a more radical conclusion, namely, that the very distinction between correct and incorrect collapses from within the Classical View: We have no standard for correctness at all.

There are two passages in which Wittgenstein explicitly introduces the regress problem, PI §141 and PI §198. PI §141 focuses on our taking a picture as giving the meaning of a word and PI §198 focuses on our appeal to a rule as determining its applications. The same problem arises for both. Having already observed, through simple illustration, that the same picture can have different applications, Wittgenstein considers the response that "not merely the picture of the cube, but also the method of projection comes before our mind" (PI §141). "But," Wittgenstein asks, "does this really get me any further? Can't I now imagine different applications of this schema too?" If there is a problem of multiple interpretations for the picture, the same problem arises for the method of projection; treated as something that "comes before the mind," it too is subject to more than one interpretation. Wittgenstein alludes to the same threat of a regress in PI §198 where he holds that "any interpretation [of a rule] still hangs in the air along with what it interprets, and cannot give it any support. Interpretations do not determine meaning." The regress is generated, not by the multiplicity of interpretations per se, but by the assumption that that which guides is something that can come before the mind, isolable from any context and history of use. In other words, if our picture of being guided by a rule requires interpretation because the rule as something that can come before the mind and be grasped in a flash – an isolable entity – is subject to multiple interpretations, then *for the same reason* our interpretation requires interpretation, and so on.

The Paradox of Interpretation builds on the Regress Argument but shows something distinct and more radical. The very picture that was alleged to give the best account for normativity eliminates all space for normativity:

> This was our paradox: no course of action could be determined by a rule, because every course of action can be made out to accord with the rule. The answer was: if everything can be made out to accord with the rule, then it can also be made out to conflict with it. And so there would be neither accord nor conflict here.
>
> (PI §201)

This is a distinctively Wittgensteinian argument, unlike the Regress Argument. Here Wittgenstein attempts to show that the very assumptions that make the realist picture of rules appealing undermine the coherence of that picture. Given the fact of multiple interpretations, for any action, that action can be characterized both in a way that accords with a given rule and conflicts with it – even if the interpretation of the rule itself were transparent. This is the source of the paradox: Even if the application of a rule is correct, the action could be made out to conflict with it. Nothing in the application of objectified meaning guarantees what the particular actual action really is. This renders the notion of accord or conflict, hence of rule-governedness itself, meaningless. It is not just that we cannot see what makes one interpretation preferable to another (the point of the Regress Argument), but that we cannot make sense of the very distinction between correct and incorrect action, even if the rule in the subject's mind were transparent, i.e., were self-interpreting. Even a transparent rule carries no constraint on *what* action is performed, as any action can be characterized to accord with that rule or not. So the idea that the rule imposes constraints on what we do is empty. The rule doesn't "hook up" with action in any substantive way. The defender of objectified meaning may be led to say, at this point, that he can feel that it was his rule that was successfully applied and so accounts for the action. But this defense takes us away from the rule and back to a feeling of being guided by the rule or a feeling of certainty. Arguments raised earlier in the rule-following discussions already show the vacuity of this strategy: I may well have all the feelings associated with following a rule and yet not be following it. So what one feels is neither here nor there in determining what action one actually performed.[4] Interpreted rules were introduced precisely to get away from such phenomenological markers. To reintroduce them as the way to save objectified meaning from the Paradox can hardly make them better candidates for explicating rule-following.

To complete these two arguments, what is needed is to refute attempts to find some interpretation that is self-interpreting or some state or process which is itself privileged in being inherently unambiguous and for this reason capable of grounding the rule. For the Regress could be stopped if a unique interpretation or method of interpretation were self-selecting, and the Paradox dissolved if that privileged role or interpretation could be shown to constrain action. Wittgenstein considers a familiar array of such candidates – intuition, what was meant, decision, formula, machine-as-symbol – and finds all wanting.[5] None of these candidates for privileging an interpretation and constraining action is successful, and so the conclusions of the Regress Argument and the Paradox stand. The Regress Argument shows that the view of objectified meaning as embodied in decision, formula, or any other candidate for the role cannot account for the *necessity of rules*, for the fact that rules constrain the behavior of the agent. The Paradox shows that the view cannot account for the *normativity of rules*, for the fact that there is a substantive distinction between correct and incorrect. There is nothing in the mind of the agent or in the behavior of the agent that shows what rule he is following, so long as we think of rules as embodying objectified meaning. In sum, there is no explanatory role (via the Paradox) nor epistemic role (via the Regress) for objectified meaning to play.

2 Two alternatives: scepticism or autonomy?

What moral are we to draw from this? Wittgenstein's critique shows the futility of trying to locate an unrealizable ideal in something actual. The Classical View, with its commitment to objectified meaning, attempted just this. Kripke takes these arguments to establish a sceptical conclusion, namely, that there is no way rationally to ground how we distinguish correct from incorrect judgments, moves, continuations, or actions. The justificatory dimension of understanding and rule-governed behavior is illusory; we can only replace the rational grounding with a psychosocial grounding in community consensus. The psychological swallows up the epistemic dimension. Baker and Hacker, on the other hand, attribute to our rules an autonomy that is obvious (Baker and Hacker 1984). On this view, Wittgenstein's critique only shows the pointlessness of engaging in the philosophical debate at all. The justificatory overlays the psychological. Both positions take it that without the sceptical problem, the community view has no support. Though each position reveals something of importance to the community view of rule-following, neither response is adequate.

Hybrid scepticism

Kripke[6] interprets Wittgenstein as holding that an individual cannot follow a rule or engage in a practice except as a member of a community of rule-followers. Rule-following, and the understanding implied by it, just are the regular use of signs by a group of human beings. With this broad statement, I am in complete agreement. What I want to examine in this section is Kripke's account of how the community is implicated in the meaningful actions and utterances of the individual. This will enable me to contrast the unmasking Humean solution he offers with my understanding of the role of the community in grounding the normative contrast btween correct and incorrect. As I hope to bring out, the difference between these two versions of the community view turns on the difference between power and authority in sustaining the contrast between correct and incorrect actions.

On Kripke's account, Wittgenstein has successfully launched a new sceptical problem, a problem that shows that "the entire idea of meaning vanishes into thin air" (Kripke 1982: p. 22). Kripke takes the Paradox of Interpretation to establish a sceptical conclusion about meaning in general. He aligns the various elements in Wittgenstein's arguments to reflect this understanding of the problem. He argues that there is no isolable fact about me or my past that determines what I mean in using an expression. And so, with each assertion, I make an "unjustified stab in the dark" (Kripke 1982: p. 17).

For the purposes of this chapter, I am more interested in the "sceptical solution," which Kripke develops in three stages. In the first stage, Wittgenstein is held to concede to the sceptic his conclusion that there is no fact about the individual that determines what he means. Nothing about the individual gives the truth conditions for the statement that he means one thing rather than another. However, "ordinary practice is justified because it does not require the justification the sceptic has shown to be untenable" (Kripke 1982: p. 66). Instead:

> All that is needed to legitimize assertions that someone means something is that there be specifiable circumstances under which they are legitimately assertable, and that the game of asserting them under such circumstances has a role in our lives.
>
> (Kripke 1982: pp. 77–8)

Assertability conditions (namely, the ordinary ways in which we accept or reject sentences), not truth conditions, license our utterances.

The second stage of the "sceptical solution" is to apply this general theory of meaning to our meaning assertions. In what circumstances, then, is the individual licensed to say "I mean such-and-such by..."? The assertability condition that licenses the individual is "that he does what he is inclined to do" or his "feeling of confidence" that what he does is correct (Kripke 1982: p. 88). But, in the final stage, Kripke argues that this cannot be the whole story, for our usual concept of following a rule enables us to distinguish between an individual who thinks he is following a rule even though he is not and an individual who is correctly following the rule. And it is this normativity of rule-following that takes us to the role played by the community. Let me elaborate a bit.

Kripke puts enormous weight on PI §202:

> And hence also "obeying a rule" is a practice. And to *think* one is obeying a rule is not to obey a rule. Hence it is not possible to obey a rule "privately": otherwise thinking one was obeying a rule would be the same thing as obeying it.

PI §202, as Kripke takes it, draws the conclusion of the Paradox of Interpretation. If we pay attention to the individual's justification conditions alone, all we can say is that he is licensed to follow the rule as it strikes him. But "to think one is obeying the rule is not to obey the rule. Hence it is not possible to obey the rule 'privately'." Only public checkability of the individual's assertions as to whether they conform to community practice can provide the solution to the sceptical challenge: "The solution turns on the idea that each person who claims to be following a rule can be checked by others" (Kripke 1982: p. 101). And the community's shared judgment is a *brute fact* about the community. Judgments as to correct or incorrect behaviors mask judgments of conformity or failure to conform.

What we have here is a hybrid scepticism. Kripke has retained the idea found so clearly in the Classical View that applications of a rule must be guided and justified by something. The failure to find a guarantee for correct application leads him to cite a lesser warrant than truth conditions, namely, in terms of assertability conditions. I may not be certain as to what I mean, but I am justified just insofar as I do what I am inclined to do when I reach bedrock and what I am inclined to do conforms with what everyone else does. This does look like a sceptical solution, for where we thought that the source that would bind together all our particular applications would also justify our binding them together, we find no rational justification. Instead the source is to be found in how the matter strikes me and everyone else in my community. We stand in a mutual policing relation to each other.

This hybrid scepticism reflects, in both its elements, a continued allegiance to the ideal expressed in the Classical View. It involves both an attempt to identify a ground for our particular judgments and actions (the assertability conditions) and our disappointment in failing to find any such ground (the brute fact of our agreement). Since Kripke takes the Paradox of Interpretation to give rise to a genuine sceptical problem, he of course gives the sceptical solution an epistemological slant. Yet it is precisely the locating of the "solution" in the domain of knowledge that distorts Wittgenstein's account, even if we look only for justificatory conditions and not truth conditions. As I shall argue later, Wittgenstein does not replace truth conditions with justification conditions. Nor does he move from subjective checkability to public checkability. Wittgenstein's alternative is not a sceptical solution at all, for the point of the Paradox of Interpretation and related arguments is to show the bankruptcy of a certain philosophical picture, the very picture that makes the sceptical problem possible.[7] Wittgenstein's alternative is just that; it describes rule-following and understanding in a way that is quite foreign to the ideal captured by the Classical View.

The autonomy of grammar

Baker and Hacker are unmistakable in their rejection of Kripke's entire approach to the Paradox of Interpretation and its "solution." On their view, with which I am sympathetic, what Wittgenstein shows is that rule-following is a form of action, not of thought (Baker and Hacker 1984: p. 20). He is neither raising a problem about meaning in general nor is he appealing to a community of practitioners. What Baker and Hacker emphasize is that a certain behavior just is, e.g., adding or decorating if done in the right surroundings; and that being an instance of adding is not justified by appeal to what everyone would say, nor is anything made an instance of adding in virtue of everyone saying so. The relation between a rule and the instances of its application is, as they repeatedly assert, an internal relation. Minimally, this means that a rule and its applications cannot be treated as two independent things: "to grasp a rule is to be able to say what accords with it. There are not two separate operations of understanding, only one – an ability to judge that *this* and *this* and *this* accord with the rule that..." (Baker and Hacker 1984: p. 96). The central objection these authors raise against the community view is that "[i]n place of that internal relation the community view only as interpreted substitutes the notion of community *agreement*, which is not an *internal property* of the rule" (Baker and Hacker 1984: p. 75). This is a cogent objection to the community view as part of the sceptical solution in which what one ought to do is replaced with what most people in fact do. An empirical generalization about what most people do is not the same as a norm standing for what people ought to do. What Baker and Hacker are looking for is a way of characterizing norms that is distinct from the Classical View and yet is not an unmasking thesis. Their way to an alternative is via this notion of the "internal properties" of a rule.

Baker and Hacker attribute three internal relations to rules: (1) "to understand a rule *is* to know what acts count as correct applications and what acts as incorrect ones" (Baker and Hacker 1984: pp. 100–1); (2) there is an internal "relation between an intentional act and a rule which is described by saying that in acting thus the agent *followed* this rule" (Ibid.: p. 101); and (3) "acting in certain ways (what is called 'acting in conformity with the rule') are *criteria* for understanding a rule" (Ibid.: p. 103). The italicized words all express the internal relations that are severed in developing the sceptical argument and only externally reconnected, according to Baker and Hacker, by the community view.

Though the crucial terms are italicized, we still don't know what an internal relation is. Each such relation is explicated by contrasting it with its corresponding external relation: (1′) grasp of a rule can be separated from knowledge of how to apply it; (2′) the relation between the intentional act and the rule "is described by saying that this event is *explained* by this hypothesis....within the framework of hypothetico-deductive explanation" (Baker and Hacker 1984: p. 101); and (3′) "an individual's behaviour is merely inductive or quasi-inductive evidence for his understanding a rule-formulation" (Baker and Hacker 1984: p. 103). In short, to externalize relations is to treat rules or interpretation of rules as empirical generalizations or hypotheses for which behavior is either evidence for their truth or instances of their operation. To externalize is to treat as empirical what is grammatical. "Internal relations," they tell us, "are the product of grammar, of linguistic convention" (Baker and Hacker 1984: p. 124). And

> [g]rammar is autonomous. Hence sceptical doubt about whether what is laid down in grammar as grounds for a proposition are really adequate grounds is not merely unjustified, it is literally senseless. For a denial that such-and-such is a ground disrupts an internal relation...
>
> (Baker and Hacker 1984: p. 99)

So internal relations are "the product of grammar" and "what is laid down in grammar" are internal relations. We seem to be going round a rather tight circle. It is not clear how the appeal to grammar gets us any further than traditional appeals to acts of meaning, which in some mysterious way encompass their objects. Unless the notion of grammar is spelled out, it threatens to become another candidate for a "philosophical superlative," the quest for which Wittgenstein seeks to undermine:

> You have no model of this superlative fact [grasping meaning in a flash], but you are seduced into using a super-expression. (It might be called a philosophical superlative.)
>
> (PI §192)

Baker and Hacker do, however, give two hints as to how to think of grammar. First, they suggest most strongly, though not exclusively,[8] a kind of transcendental reading of grammar. This is captured in the idea that grammar is autonomous and so sets the limits of sense, independently of the characterization of any actual community and actual uses of language (Baker and Hacker 1984: p. 99). But we haven't even the mentalistic apparatus of Kant to explain this transcendental standing.

Second, content is given the notion of grammar by contrasting it with the empirical. Rules are not statistical generalizations. They are not explanatory hypotheses. Our actions and judgments are not instances of such generalizations, nor do the former provide inductive evidence for the latter. But these negative claims don't exclude all that may be correctly described as empirical, let alone add up to the transcendental vision of grammar as that which sets a priori limits to sense. It seems that Baker and Hacker take an abstract characterization of grammar to be basic as the only way of accounting for the fact that a particular isolated behavior could embody or instance a grammatical structure independently of any social structure. What we have here is the mystification of grammar, captured in the phrase "the autonomy of grammar." Grammar is autonomous just because it is, not because of the structure of human society or because of any mental apparatus.

3 Normativity of rule-following

If Wittgenstein is providing an alternative that retains an account of the necessity and normativity of rules (*pace* scepticism) and yet rejects any form of objectified meaning (*pace* autonomous grammar), just what is it?

PI §198 is a pivotal passage in the *Investigations*. There Wittgenstein suggests a fresh start to the problem by asking a different question. The question we have been asking about rules "But how can a rule show me what I have to do at this point?" is the question that has misled us into looking for a privileged interpretation or special act of the mind or something of that sort to constrain our actions. We have been looking for something suitable to guide us and justify us in our actions. Wittgenstein wants us to look at the matter from a different perspective:

> Let me ask this: what has the expression of a rule—say a sign-post— got to do with my actions? What sort of connexion is there here?—Well, perhaps this one: I have been trained to react to this sign in a particular way, and now I do so react to it.

This suggestion is followed immediately by the objection:

> But that is only to give a causal connexion; to tell how it has come about that we now go by the sign; not what this going-by-the-sign really consists in.

But this objection misses a crucial feature of the reply, and that is that the connection is between my reaction and a sign-post, not a piece of wood poking out of the ground. The sign-post is a sign-post only insofar as there is a regular social use:

> On the contrary; I have further indicated that a person goes by a sign-post only insofar as there exists a regular use of sign-posts, a custom.

In this passage all the key elements of Wittgenstein's alternative have been introduced. First, we need to change our way of looking at the problem, to ask different questions, for the very way we have posed our problem has directed us towards an intellectualist solution, namely, a solution in terms of some interpretive act or decision or the like. Second, training into a custom or social practice is the way in which we come to follow rules. The process of learning is crucial to our understanding of understanding. Third, meaning is a social phenomenon and so the individual cannot be radically isolated from the community. And finally, in being so trained, the individual has come to master a technique: "and now I do so react to it" (PI §199).

At the heart of his alternative, then, are the social character of meaning and the importance of the process of training. Each introduces a new approach, respectively, to what I have been calling the epistemic and practical dimensions of rule-following. Under this new approach, these two dimensions change to that of the normativity and necessity of rule-following. Together they provide an account of the objectivity of rule-following. Each avoids positing an isolable state of mind or formula or interpretation as the objectified, and so constraining, meaning. Each develops a dynamic rather than static account of rule-governed practice. This is just what would be expected in developing the idea that meaning is use.

The way out of the difficulties raised by the Regress Argument and the Paradox of Interpretation is, according to Wittgenstein, to recognize that "there is a way of grasping a rule which is *not* an *interpretation*, but which is exhibited in what we call "obeying the rule" and "going against it" in actual cases" (PI §201). In short, there is a way of engaging in rule-following that is not *following* a rule nor *justifying* by appeal to a rule nor adverting in any way to a rule conceived as having an objectified content, that is, a content that is independent of our engagements in our practices. This is the point of Wittgenstein's remarks that "my reasons will soon give out. And then I shall act without reasons" (PI §211); and "[i]f I have exhausted the justifications I have reached bedrock, and my spade is turned. Then I am inclined to say: 'This is simply what I do'" (PI §217). And what I do "when I obey a rule, I do not choose. I obey the rule *blindly*" (§219). Wittgenstein's appeal to the metaphor of blind obedience is his way of emphasizing that bedrock rule-following is normative without being justificatory and necessary, or constraining, without being independent of human practice. Though causal factors are relevant to our understanding of rule-following, a fully causal account cannot make space for the basic normative distinction, that between correct and incorrect actions. The problem is to determine what it is for me or anyone else to go on in the same way, where it is not up to me simply to decide or say what is the same, that is, what is correct. There are constraints on behavior that cannot derive from the objectified meaning of the Classical View, and yet they are not purely causal.

Wittgenstein gives us a new way to think about the normativity and necessity of "rule-governed" practices. Both features involve the community. The normativity of rules is grounded in community agreement over time; and the constraint or necessity of rules is grounded in forming a second nature, which is achieved through a process of acculturation. From the epistemic perspective, to follow a rule blindly is to reach that bedrock in the chain of justification where "one's spade is turned." It is to act, in the now famous phrase, with right but without justification (PI §289). The chain of justification terminates with what has become our second nature. That which is self-evident is precisely what we accept without justification. The very logic of actions, of obeying a rule, presupposes a context of structure, and that is provided by the actual harmonious interactions of a group of people. The focus of Wittgenstein's critique of the Classical View has been to show that the mind of the individual cannot provide that structure. Nor can the attempt to find a Platonic structure, whether in the idea of an abstract formula or in an autonomous grammar, succeed. That structure is a social structure, that is, the dynamic interactions of a group of people in sustaining certain regularities, customs, and patterns of action over time.

Manifestation: use over time

On the sceptical reading, regularities over time do not support or fail to support the subject's understanding or meaning something. No matter how long a regularity has been in existence, the regularity in itself shows nothing about what the subject means nor is such a temporal regularity part of the sceptical solution. What matters is that what the subject does conforms and can be seen to conform to judgments of others. The autonomous grammar interpretation, on the other hand, requires that understanding be displayed in regularities of behavior over time. These regularities over time, whether displayed by an individual or a community, just are certain kinds of action. So the debate between these two positions becomes a debate between public checkability and public regularity. Is, then, multiple application of a rule over time (and not necessarily across individuals at a time) required?

It is incontestable that Wittgenstein maintained that regular use over time is required. In PI §199 and PI §204, Wittgenstein explicitly rejects as incoherent the idea that there could be a single occasion of using or following a rule:

> Is what we call "obeying a rule" something that it would be possible for only *one* man to do, and to do only *once* in his life?…
>
> It is not possible that there should have been only one occasion on which someone obeyed a rule.[9]
>
> (§199)

Baker and Hacker, along with others, argue that these passages only support the idea of a practice as a regularity *over time*, not as a social regularity.[10] What we want to know here is why it is impossible for there to "have been only one occasion on which someone obeyed a rule."

Colin McGinn, for one, has argued against this Multiple Application Thesis, as he calls it.[11] He starts his argument by noting that Wittgenstein's position does allow for certain exceptions, namely, it does not require that *all* rules must actually be followed more than once in order to be rules. Rather Wittgenstein's point, on McGinn's reading, is that at least some rules must be multiply applied; and against this background, we can make sense of the notion of having grasped some other rules that have never been applied. For example, it is possible for a person to know the rules of chess, including of course the rule that permits pawns to move two spaces forward on their initial move without that person ever having applied that particular rule.[12] McGinn asks us to accept the possibility of such a person, namely, a person understanding a set of rules some of which he has never applied. We begin then to subtract rules, one by one, from this individual's set of active rules to his set of potentially active rules. In doing this, we will eventually reach the point where the subject has only one rule that he has actually acted upon. And then McGinn asks, "why should not the final stage of the subtraction go as smoothly as the rest, leaving us with a *totally* idle set of grasped rules?" (McGinn 1984: p. 131). Surely it is such a small step to the bottom of this slippery slope that nothing can be said for holding back so close to the finish. And if that is so, why withhold the attribution of grasped rules to one who does not ever apply any of them?

The answer, in short, is because such rules are the pretence of rules only. McGinn's slippery slope argument cannot work against Wittgenstein's position because Wittgenstein would never allow him so far down the slope in the first place. McGinn mistakenly holds that "Wittgenstein thinks that all the rules can be supposed preserved while subtracting their application save that we have to leave at least one that is applied more than once" (McGinn 1984: p. 131). This characterization of the Wittgensteinian position suggests that it is allowable that a person could have grasped all the rules of our complex practices provided that he had, on more than one occasion, moved a pawn forward one or two places on a checkered board. On this reading of the Multiple Application Thesis, it is of course absurd to suppose that acting on the rule that governs the movement of pawns makes all the difference.

But this reading ignores Wittgenstein's commitment to the holistic and contextualist features of language mastery and use, the stage setting. Moving a piece on a checkered board only counts as the movement of a pawn – indeed only *is* the movement of a pawn – within the practice of chess. So for McGinn's objection to work, if the subject can correctly be said to have moved a pawn, we must be able to identify the "grasped but unapplied rules" that constitute the whole practice of chess. But this means that McGinn's "subtraction argument" against the Multiple Application Thesis begs the question by presupposing, in the first premise, that grasping rules is independent of using rules – but that is what was to be established by the argument.

The question for McGinn is, in what does understanding a rule consist? Yet McGinn has accepted Wittgenstein's negative arguments that no formula is self-interpreting, that no inner act of mind can fix meaning. He takes these arguments to support the claim that only in use can rules be made manifest, and so provide the ground for ascribing understanding. And this motivation for the Multiple Application Thesis, namely, that actual use is the only warrant for attributing understanding, McGinn finds completely unconvincing. If the issue is what grounds we have for ascribing grasp of a rule, why, then, McGinn asks, shouldn't one instance of rule-following be sufficient, why require two?

The argument as it stands is perfectly correct. Often one can ascribe understanding on the basis of witnessing only one instance of the subject's following the rule in question; whether this is so depends upon the context. Where McGinn goes wrong here is with the antecedent. The main point of the Multiple Application Thesis is not to solve the episte-mological problem of *telling* when a person has followed a rule or grasped a rule. Rather the point is metaphysical. In what some have called Wittgenstein's "manifestation argument,"[13] Wittgenstein's position is that to understand an expression is to know how to use it, where such "know-how" is the having of a practical skill or skills, the having of which lies in the actual exercise of that "know-how." In brief, unless understanding displays itself in practice, the attribution of understanding, whether from a first-person or a third-person perspective, is empty. And it is empty because the understanding does not exist, even if the potential to acquire that skill does.

The combination of these two features of multiple application is quite revealing about the nature of understanding. The two are that rule-following is context bound ("the stage-setting" point) and that understanding is the patterned activity of the individual within the appropriate context ("the manifestation" point).[14] Understanding is thus highly structured and public.

On McGinn's view, the subtraction argument supports the conclusion that understanding is something that is independent of all uses: "there *is* something left when actual use is subtracted, namely that state which is the causal basis of use" (McGinn 1984: p. 130).[15] But this conclusion is not warranted by the substraction argument. It must be supplemented with an additional philosophical commitment, viz., that there is an internal state that grounds uses while being distinct from those uses. This fundamental philosophical commitment McGinn shares with advocates of the Classical View, but where they posited a privileged mental state, McGinn posits a cause. But whether mental state or underlying physical cause, neither can account for the normativity of rule-following.

Normativity: use as social

The crux of the matter turns on whether an isolated individual can engage in behavior that is normatively guided, that goes against a rule or not. In considering such a case, it is important to note that we are concerned with a *radically* isolated individual, that is, someone who has never been in contact with a community. There is no problem for the community view in allowing for individuals who have left society and yet continue to engage in rule-following and indeed invent new practices for themselves. The challenge comes from the idea that the behavior of the radically isolated individual could display and be of a normative character. Baker and Hacker, who champion a regularity interpretation of rule-governed activity, see no problem in this, for "it is his behavior, including his corrective behavior, which shows both that he is following a rule, and what he counts as following a rule" (Baker and Hacker 1984: p. 39). What is needed for solitary rule-followers are "regularities of action of sufficient complexity to yield normativity" (Baker and Hacker 1984: p. 42). According to these authors, the communal or social aspect of meaning, the conformity or agreement in judgment among members of the practice, is not an essential aspect of meaningfulness. "It is quite wrong," they say, "to suppose that distinctions between appearance and reality are inapplicable to an individual in isolation, or are ones which that individual cannot employ" (Baker and Hacker 1984: p. 39). In holding this, they are maintaining that the distinction between thinking one was following a rule and really following a rule can be displayed in the complex regularities of behavior of the individual, behavior that would include corrective behavior. The textual defense for the regularity view focuses on their interpretation of Wittgenstein's use of "practice." This use, they maintain, has nothing to do with its being a social practice; rather the significance of the term is to show that rule-governed activity is a form of action, not a form of thought. In other words, rule-following must be public, but not necessarily social.

But will this account of practices as "regularities of action" do? Let me ask the obvious first question. How do we recognize these regularities of sufficient complexity that Baker and Hacker appeal to? What kind of complexity is required? After all, we know that insects and animals can and do display behavior of remarkable intricacy and complexity without our attributing a normative character to their behavior. Clearly, the kind of complexity Baker and Hacker are looking for is corrective behavior. But how is corrective behavior to be identified as such? Baker and Hacker's example (derived from Wittgenstein's RFM VI.41) of a Robinson Crusoe using a decorative pattern is intended to answer this. We are told that "he might use the pattern − − · · · − − · · · as a rule or pattern to follow in decorating the walls of his house; when he notices four dots in a sequence he manifests annoyance with himself. He goes back and rubs one out, and perhaps checks carefully adjacent marks, comparing them with his 'master-pattern' " (Baker and Hacker 1984: p. 39). Our Robinson Crusoe acts as we would act if we were following a master-pattern. Insofar as our isolated individual's behavior counts as being corrective, it is only in virtue of his behavior being like our own, of assimilating his behavior to our corrective practices. The only standard available for what counts as corrective behavior, and so *is* corrective behavior, are the paradigms of correcting that inform our practices. Behavior wildly different from our own, bearing no discernible similarity to our practices of correcting, is simply not corrective behavior. This underscores both the objectivity and the publicness of rule-following, features Baker and Hacker endorse. Yet they seek to explain the objective character of rule-following in terms of the relation of that behavior, whether of Crusoe or of ourselves, to an autonomous grammar. It is the attempt once again to find an objectified meaning to stand as the measure of what we do or Robinson Crusoe does; but a Platonized or Kantian version of objectified meaning is no better than the mentalistic candidates already rejected. It is only in virtue of Robinson Crusoe's *notional* membership in our own community that he can be said to follow rules at all. The normativity of Robinson Crusoe's behavior is derivable not from the mere complexity or publicness of his behavior, but from the assimilation of that behavior to the complex practices of what we do, practices that distinguish among correcting, modifying, and terminating an activity. The individuation and identity of Crusoe's practice requires assimilation to our practices. It is only in this way that the requisite background for distinguishing among alternative actions (correcting, rebelling, modifying, etc.) can be provided. The community provides the logical space for an array of alternatives in terms of which the caveman's behavior can be understood. A consequence of this is that solitary rule-following is only intelligible as the exception. Not all membership in a community could be notional.

Yet even in assimilating his behavior to our practices of decorating and correcting, given the impoverished world that Robinson Crusoe inhabits, there is no way that we can distinguish corrective behavior from a modification of the rules or from the termination of one game for another or from the introduction of an exception permitted by the rule. Perhaps the "and so on" implicit in the master-pattern warrants systematically altering the pattern inscribed, so that the four dots Crusoe put down initially were the correct continuation, and Crusoe's gesture that we took as a sign of annoyance was rather a sign of rebelling, his examination of the master-pattern and his subsequent behavior a rejection of that master-pattern for another. Other stories could be told that change the interpretation of his behavior and the rule he is purported to follow. That his behavior is seen as corrective depends upon how *we*, as a matter of course, would take the master-pattern. The resources for drawing these distinctions derive from the complexity of our own practices that admit of ways of differentiating among these various alternatives.

But what about Robinson Crusoe himself? Would he count his behavior as corrective, that is, as constrained by something other than his own whim or amusement in drawing the pattern of dots and dashes? From his point of view, he engages in a repetitive behavior derived from a series of dots and dashes initially drawn on the wall, "derived" in the sense that he reproduces the same series of dots and dashes as produced in the original sequence. Nothing more can be said of his behavior and its relations to the so-called "master-pattern" without reintroducing the notion of his engaging in an act of interpreting the pattern, and that, of course, has already been rejected as an account of rule-following. Wittgenstein holds that our caveman Crusoe is doing something that is akin to following a rule, but falls short of that:

> There might be a cave-man who produced regular sequences of marks for himself. He amused himself, e.g., by drawing on the wall of the cave:
>
> $- \cdot - - \cdot - - \cdot - - \cdot$
>
> or $- \cdot - \cdot \cdot - \cdot \cdot \cdot - \cdot \cdot \cdot \cdot -$
>
> But he is not following the general expression of a rule.
>
> (RFM VI.41)

This is because it is "only in the practice of a language" that a word can have meaning (RFM VI.41). And "the phenomenon of language is based on regularity, on agreement in action" (RFM VI.39). Baker and Hacker's Crusoe and Wittgenstein's caveman differ in one important respect. Baker and Hacker's Crusoe has a master-pattern and Wittgenstein's caveman does not. What makes this difference significant is that rule-governed regularity is objective, that is, is constrained by something other than the individual's whim or disposition. For Baker and Hacker, that something is the master-pattern; for Wittgenstein, it is the practice of a language or agreement in action in relation to which a sequence of marks functions as a master-pattern. As we have already seen, the intelligibility of our isolated rule-follower requires that we grant him notional membership in our own community. The introduction of the master-pattern looks like it provides the standard whereby Crusoe's behavior is the "following of the general expression of a rule," but in fact it is the vehicle by which we connect the behavior of Crusoe to the rule-following behavior of our community. It provides the public item in relation to which we can see Crusoe's behavior as corrective.

Wittgenstein's point is that a rule or master-pattern is such only from within a practice that is itself a kind of complex regularity, namely, community regularity as expressed in agreement in action and judgment. The objectivity of rules, then, derives from the harmony in actions and judgments of a community of agents, a harmony that constrains the actions and judgments of the individual. It does not derive from an objectified meaning, i.e., meaning that is independent of the judgments and actions we engage in.

The central point is that the very idea of normativity, and so the structure within which the distinction between correct and incorrect can be drawn, cannot get a foothold unless the practice is a social one.[16] As a first approximation, the normativity of our bedrock judgments and actions lies in the defeasibility of these judgments, in that one can go wrong. And, as we have already seen, this normativity cannot be found in rules isolated from a structure of use. An object can only function as rule, exemplar, or representation in virtue of the way in which it is used. Wittgenstein's point is that only a social structure can provide the context within which objects can be used as standards and representations. For the defeasibility of our judgments, that is, that judgment can be incorrect, can only get a hold in our being able to contrast the actions of the individual with the actions of the community. It is the very conformity of action and judgment that allows for the possibility of deviation and so incorrect behavior. It is only in conformity and failure to conform that a significant contrast between correct and incorrect actions emerges. And these bedrock practices are rooted in "the common behaviour of mankind" (PI §206). What Wittgenstein is really emphasizing is not even defeasibility so much as our *agreement* as human beings. The very emphasis that commentators have placed on *corrective* behavior is out of place. Error and correction are very much the exception. Checking, whether by others or oneself, simply doesn't feature prominently in the exercise of a practice, except in the case of the learner. What our agreement expresses is that *this* is obeying an order and *this* is telling a story and *this* is being afraid and *this* is being in pain. What we have is agreement in paradigms.

It is in this sense that community agreement is constitutive of practices,[17] and that agreement must be displayed in action. There are two important features about this account that need to be highlighted. First, it is the *social* practice that provides the structure within which individual understanding can obtain or individual judgment be made. Central to Wittgenstein's thought is the claim, repeatedly argued for, that no isolated event or behavior can correctly be described as naming or obeying or understanding. The rule as formula, the standard as chart, or the paradigm as an instance have no normative or representational status in their own right. They have this status only in virtue of the way the formula or the chart or the instance is used. It is the use that creates the structured context within which sign-posts point, series can be continued, orders obeyed and paradigms be exemplary. Only then can we see a particular action as embodying or instancing a grammatical structure. In short, the mandatory stage setting is social practice.

Second, community agreement does not constitute a justification for particular judgments. What is indispensable for correct, or appropriate, judgment and action is that there *is* concord, *not* that each individual justifies his (or anyone else's) judgment and action by appeal to its harmony with the judgment of others. Baker and Hacker's criticism of the community view, that it makes the internal relation between actions and rules external, fails to recognize the importance of this point. What we mean is not explained by an appeal to generalizations about what most people say. But that we mean what we do is because of what most people say and do. In light of this, consider the three kinds of reasons given for continuing as we do when we reach bedrock judgments: (1) That just *is* rule-following, or a chair, or the continuation of the natural number sequence. This is the appeal to the exemplary status of the object, action, or judgment. Here justification gives way to explanation, and explanation to description. (2) "I know English." This is a metalinguistic way of appealing to the community, to what we all say. (3) "This is what I do." This is a most interesting reason, for here I appeal to myself as a representative member of the community. The normative dimension is implicit in my appeal to what I am inclined to do; it is a way of saying that I am qualified to judge or act. All three bedrock reasons function *not* to justify the judgment in question but to bring the requests for justification to an end.

What all three of these bedrock groundings have in common is that the action or judgment is grounded by situating it within a *structured* context that provides the stage setting. We have standards only *in virtue* of group harmony and *against the background* of group harmony, but the standards themselves do not refer to, nor are described in terms of, group harmony. It is important to see that whatever is meant by "following a rule," it cannot be captured by a description of actual practice. The community view does not provide a schema for analyzing normative expressions in terms of what most people do or are disposed to do. The meaning of statements like "S understands addition" is given by an explanation of the sentence. Though it would be wrong to say that what we *mean* by "S adds" is that most people do such-and-such, nevertheless that S is adding holds only *in virtue* of most people performing and having performed certain manipulations with the sign "+". In short, the community view is not a reductionist thoery; it is not a theory about the analysis of certain expressions.

Grammar, then, for Wittgenstein, is *immanent* in our practices, not the transcendental condition for our practices. It is not independent of our lived practices. These practices just are de facto agreement in action and judgment. The community is not required in order to police the actions and judgments of all members, but in order to sustain the articulated structure within which understanding and judging can occur and against which error and mistake can be discerned. And, finally, understanding is a disposition of the individual, namely, the ability to act in appropriate ways under appropriate circumstances. And that ability, precisely because its content is normative, can only be exercised within a social context, where the social context is the de facto harmony in the actions and utterances of a group of people.[18] The origin of normativity, then, lies in the agreement that creates the place for standards and in the possiblity of deviation from the actions of the community that hold the standard in place.

4 Necessity of rule-following

This notion of blind obedience takes us to the second element of Wittgenstein's account of rule-following behavior. To "follow" rules is a matter of establishing a second nature. The power of the rule to guide (that is, to go on in a rule-patterned way) just is the power of that which is obvious, inevitable, natural: "The rule can only seem to me to produce all its consequences in advance if I draw them as a *matter of course* " (PI §238). And what is obvious, inevitable, and a matter of course is what we all do without thought, blindly, and more importantly (in this context) what I do myself blindly and without thought. It is the sort of thing, in other words, with respect to which scruples can only be artificial:

When someone whom I am afraid of orders me to continue the series, I act quickly, with perfect certainty, and the lack of reasons does not trouble me.

(PI §212)

Just try—in a real case—to doubt someone else's fear or pain.

(PI §303)

But how, then, does one come to see things as a matter of course? Or, as Wittgenstein also puts it, how is it that I or another come to see that *matters must* be like that:

But he does not say: I realised that *this* happens. Rather: that it must be like that. This "must" shews what kind of lesson he has drawn from the scene...

(RFM VI.7)

This *must* shews that he has adopted a concept.

(RFM VI.8)

Blind obedience to a rule expresses seeing how matters must be. It is this lived mustness that constitutes the form of life against which error and mistake, truth and falsity can be discerned. These communal regularities thus have the status and rigidity of what is necessary. How does this "must" form part of our lives?

Two domains: the novice and the master

Learning, for Wittgenstein, is pivotal. For the process of learning is such that the activity of, say, writing down the natural number sequence (i.e., the actual training of the novice) becomes transformed: The continuation of the sequence, putting "6" down after "5," is seen as revealing how things must be. The novice now sees that "this outcome has been defined as essential to this process" (RFM VI.7). In seeing this, he has taken responsibility for sustaining the process. He is not convinced of a psychological fact or an empirical fact: " 'I realised that it must be like that' – that is his report" (RFM VI.7).

The process of learning is a matter of being trained in a technique, and it is the technique of application that lies in the background and gives content to the formula as rule. But saying that the technique lies in the background can only mean that there are those who are masters of the technique; otherwise, one runs the risk of reifying technique. This is why

Wittgenstein holds that in the end to explain a rule showing how it determines its applications is to describe how the rule is learned:

> It may now be said: "The way the formula is meant determines which steps are to be taken". What is the criterion for the way the formula is meant? It is, for example, the kind of way we always use it, the way we are taught to use it.
>
> (PI §190)

A consequence of this view is that how we are trained, how we learn, is constitutive of what we mean. The process of learning, or training as Wittgenstein puts it, cannot be dissociated from an understanding of meaning. In other words, the search for a rule which guides the individual is replaced by looking to the process of training whereby the individual comes to master a technique for using signs. The connection between a rule and an action is to be explicated in terms of the kind of training a person has into a social custom. This requires distinguishing between the *master* of a practice (the adult or teacher) and the *novice* who is being trained (the child or pupil).

To understand Wittgenstein, we must look at these two domains and their interrelations. Metaphysically, the social context is required for both master and novice, though in different ways. For the master, the social context is what makes his actions and judgments what they are:

> A coronation is the picture of pomp and dignity. Cut one minute of this proceeding out of its surroundings: the crown is being placed on the head of the king in his coronation robes. – But in different surroundings gold is the cheapest of metals, its gleam is thought vulgar. There the fabric of the robe is cheap to produce. A crown is a parody of a respectable hat. And so on.
>
> (PI §584)

It is obvious that an event like a coronation requires a particular social setting. It is less clear that non-institutional actions and events, like counting, reading, going for a walk, require a social setting in order to be the actions they are. But the community view applies even to such apparently non-institutional, solitary activities. The point emphasized here is that the actions of the master presuppose both a certain history and a certain setting.

For the novice, on the other hand, as part of the process of training itself, an indispensable courtesy is extended to his behavior and utterances. They are accorded the status of actions and judgments before they really are such. This makes the novice doubly dependent upon the community. Like the master, his action is what it is only against the background of its historical and social setting; but unlike the master, this status is not ensured by his own competency but by that of the master. This second kind of dependency upon the adult community has a further consequence. For many performances of a novice, there simply is no fact of the matter as to whether he understands correctly or not. This is because it is not enough to go on correctly; the correct performances must be the exercise of the right kind of disposition. Acting from one's own competency, understanding, and acting correctly all go hand-in-hand.

The second significant point is that those practices characterized as "bedrock" do not involve knowledge claims; that is, they are not claims that stand in need of justification. The question of justification arises neither for the novice nor for the master in the process of learning bedrock practices. The pupil learning the natural number sequence does not need to justify his claim that "6" follows "5"; he only needs to get it right. Getting it right does not involve having a justification, that is, an independent proof of correctness or evidence for its acceptability. It is equally a mistake to think that the master provides the justification. The master's judgment of how to carry on is the standard for correctness, but it is not the justification. Nor need the master have any justification independently of his own judgment in the situation. The master, no more than the novice, has a proof or a justification for why "6" follows "5," or why enjoying something just is a good reason for doing it, or why setting the table for two shows that you expect another to dinner. The answer in every case to "why?" is "because it just is," which is another way of saying that there is no reason or justification or proof. The point of learning bedrock practices is to come to share the same sense of the obvious.

Though the issue of knowledge and justification does not arise for the novice, the question of legitimation is foremost. There is a concern with checking what the novice does against the training given by the master; indeed, one can correctly say, with the intentions of the master. The actions and judgments of the novice are checked and subject to correction. But this correction is not a matter of justifying the judgments or actions of the novice. It is to bring the novice into conformity with what the masters do. Such blind obedience is distinctive of the relation between novice and master. What Wittgenstein is arguing is that the child's submission to authority is both what happens in fact and what is required to constitute a form of life, and thus provide the context in which knowledge proper can be pursued. Questions of knowledge and justification can only arise against the background of that which is fully taken for granted. That is provided by the bedrock practices, practices that constitute our form of life.

Issues of legitimation do not pertain to the master. There is no question of licensing the master or checking up on him. The relation among peers is altogether different from the relation between master and novice. Each master speaks with an authoritative and representative voice. Failure of understanding in the master does not indicate the need for correction (or if it does, the master himself is able to make the correction), but some kind of physical or mental disorder. For understanding is shown in continuing correctly as a matter of course. In acting with right, he is not under the scrutiny of others. So it is no accident that when Wittgenstein turns to those passages in which he develops the community view (PI §196–239), he speaks of what *I* do as a full-fledged master of language. The "we" is dropped. In being acculturated into this community, this form of life, I am enabled to speak for the community without justification for what I do and without being checked by others in the community. The master is autonomous and yet his autonomy is grounded in a dependence upon the community, both for his actions to be what they are and for his accultura-tion into the practice since the *way* one learns provides the paradigm for what is learned.

There is the objection that although it may well be true that we do come to acquire language through a process of acculturation, this process of learning is not part of what is learned and so is dispensable from a philosophical discussion of rule-following. It makes no difference whether we learn language through a process of training or through taking a pill or through some kind of spontaneous awakening. The necessity of rule-following is a matter of having the right sort of dispositions no matter how acquired. Such an objection overlooks two features of understanding and rule-following. First, understanding and rule-following have been assimilated to the exercise of skills, to know-how, rather than to proposi-tional knowledge. Skills and techniques of use are closely tied to their manner of acquisition; skill dispositions are distinguished in large part from other dispositions (such as reflex or conditioned dispositions) by their genesis. Second, the techniques of use which are mastered in acquiring a skill cannot themselves be rendered as a statable set of instructions. So we have no way of understanding how a skill could be acquired or realized by an individual except through a process of training. To appeal to such suppositions as a skill-pill or a spontaneous "awakening" underscores the fact that instantaneous acquisition of a skill-disposition is utterly myste-rious. Moreover, no matter how acquired, skill requires public exercise in order to warrant the attribution of such a disposition to an individual and in order for the individual to have the skill, as understanding is the patterned activity of the individual within the appropriate context.[19] So at best such spontaneous awakening can only be seen as the realization of skill retrospectively. It is as fictional as the group of people who convened to usher in the ur-social contract and with it political society; and it is subject to the same objections. The most telling objection to social contract theory as an historical reality is that this ur-political act presupposes the existence of some kind of social contract to provide the framework within which such an event could occur. This same objection applies to the idea that understanding could occur instantaneously. Having a skill is acting in the right ways under the appropriate circumstances. A skill cannot be acquired spontaneously precisely because to attribute understanding at a time presupposes prior duration in time.

Since skill and its manner of acquisition are interwoven, the explication of skill-dispositions requires that we consider both the domain of the master and the domain of the novice. In interpreting many of Wittgenstein's remarks, it is thus important to be clear about whom Wittgenstein is talking. Kripke takes the situation of the novice as exemplary and extrapolates from there to the situation of the master. The child, in his ignorance and immaturity, highlights the active role of the community. The behavior and utterances of the child cannot be sustained without the active support of the adult in two crucial ways. First, the understanding attributed to the initiate and the characterization of his behavior as actions is sustained by the community of adults until the child has mastered the practice himself. Second, the novice's ignorance, inexperience, and immaturity open his actions and judgments to checking and correction. If one takes the novice as the exemplar for rule-governed behavior, then it is only natural, in extrapolating from the situation of the novice to that of the master, to see correction and the need for correction as central to an account of understanding. But this is to incorporate the ignorance of the novice into full mastery of language. In this way, the authority of the master is lost, replaced by arbitrary peer agreement, achieved by mutual checkings for conformity. This is to read the child into the adult, and to replace power for authority. This is indeed a sceptical "solution," and one that misconstrues the nature of the community view.

Baker and Hacker, on the other hand, focus on the master's situation, emphasizing the autonomy and authority of the individual, and so fail to see the significance of the community and the process of acculturation itself (cf. Baker and Hacker 1984). The structured context within which the judgments and actions of the individual have their significance thus becomes that object of spontaneous intuition "autonomous grammar." But the master's actions and judgments too depend upon a community. The very normativity of any rule-governed actions (that they are correct or incorrect) and the necessity of such actions (that they are required by a rule or standard) are to be explained by appeal to social factors. Both the normativity and necessity of rule-governed action are to be explained in terms of blind obedience.

Blind obedience: the primacy of action

Our bedrock judgments and actions are blind, first in the sense that no recognition of a rule or standard is required of the individual in order to carry out the applications. Indeed "sighted" rule-following, that is, actions that result from explicit application of a rule, presuppose the mastery of a technique which displays the correct continuation in its *actual* applications. This is what I call the *primacy of action*. What is correct is shown in what we do. The applications create the space for the rule; they are not derived from the rule. Our actions are blind in a second sense as well. As novices, we act blindly in the sense that we follow the example and instruction of the master as a matter of course. This is because the novice does not have the resources for constructing or entertaining alternatives to what is presented as a matter of course by the masters of a practice. As masters, we also act blindly, but in a different way. Though a community is required to created the structured context within which we name, decorate walls, obey rules, and the like, we, once we have mastered language, are blind to the community in that we act and judge without checking with others. The individual thus has an autonomy that is not subject to community check; she is as able to recognize error as anyone else. What is common to both the novice and master, though in different ways, is that their rule-following does not carry with it any live alternatives to what they are doing. This is completely unlike the Classical View, for which any given interpretation of a rule or action is offered against a background of alternative interpretations (or intuitions or decisions). This feature of blind obedience, I shall call being *alternative-blind*. Both the primacy of action and being alternative-blind are true of the actions of the novice and the master, though in different ways.

Just what does place normative constraint on the individual? To this question, the three most plausible accounts are: (1) The individual is related to some *objectified, or reified, meaning*, which provides the standard for correct moves and the constraint on the individual's behavior; in other words, some version of the Classical View. (2) The individual is related to the natural environment, such that she must adapt her behavior in order to survive. A kind of *natural teleology* is at work to constrain the individual's array of behaviors. (3) Finally, the rule-following behavior of the individual is *conventionally normative*, and so is to be explained by her relation to social practices. As discussed above, the potential discrepancy between the behaviors of the individual and those of the community creates the logical space for the distinction between correct and incorrect action. In this section, I shall bring out the way in which both the primacy of action and being alternative-blind bear upon Wittgenstein's account of the way in which rules constrain the behavior of the individual. The fact that action can be correct or incorrect shows that people can, as a matter of fact, act differently, but their blindness to these alternative ways of acting shows, in their action, what they take to be obvious and that no different action could count as correct.

The attack on the first option, that of objectified meaning, has already been discussed in section 1. What I want to show here is that Wittgenstein's appeal to blind obedience as the way to address the problems of the Regress and Paradox is not part of a sceptical conclusion. A Humean or projectivist solution seems to be the only option available once one has granted the impossibility of finding a privileged interpretation of a rule.[20] On a Humean interpretation, there are no norms or rules though we do have an explanation, the true causal explanation, of that superlative fact that we "follow rules." It may seem on my account that each individual is conditioned by the others to act in certain ways, the success of which creates secondary dispositions. This causal basis of our behavior is hidden by our projecting upon one another an illusory dignity or a special status, a projection achieved by describing ourselves as following rules. On this reading, the community view looks like a thinly disguised variant of Skinnerian behaviorism.[21] Broadly speaking, rule-following is replaced or explained naturalistically by one or more of the natural sciences, neurophysiology, conditioning theory, or evolutionary theory being the prime candidates. Why isn't the blind obedience of the novice or the habitual natural actions of the master just such a projectivist account?

The explanation for why it is not requires a closer look at the Regress Argument and the Paradox of Interpretation. The plausibility of the Humean reading turns in part on having treated these two arguments as being the same. The Regress Argument focuses on the interpretation that is (allegedly) required by the individual in order to apply the rule, and concludes that the interpretation is in no better condition than the rule itself. If the meaning of a rule, that is, how it is to be applied, requires an interpretation, then, for the same reason, the interpretation requires an interpretation, and so on. This argument has been, of course, put in the service of a general sceptical problem, for it raises questions about what fact can ground the application or interpretation of a rule. The conclusion that Wittgenstein reaches in *The Blue Book* concerning the Regress Argument is that "adopt whatever model or scheme you may [of saying and meaning something], it will have a bottom level, and there will be no such thing as an interpretation of that" (BB 1958: p. 34). Clearly, blind obedience, that is, simply acting in accord with the rule, is a response to the Regress. It provides a "bottom level" that is not an interpretation.

The Paradox of Interpretation differs from the Regress in that it does not focus on the interpretation, but on the action itself and the fact that *it* can be multiply interpreted. It is important to see that the interpretations themselves could be transparent (and so would not generate a regress) and yet the action could be made out to accord or conflict with the given interpretation. For example, any finite numerical sequence can be made out to conform to more than one mathematical formula. It is because of this that the very distinction between correct and incorrect collapses. What Wittgenstein tries to show is that the very philosophical model or picture of meaning and rule-following that seems so compelling is, paradoxically, precisely what ushers in the collapse of the basic normative distinction, that between correct and incorrect. Wittgenstein's target is a compelling, but deeply misguided, picture of rule-following, namely, that the individual is constrained and guided by an interpreted rule, a rule available to him as an individual. Wittgenstein's answer to the Paradox is not a *sceptical* throwing up of hands with "But this is what I or we do," but an appeal to the social embeddedness of rules. What provides the background structure within which rules can "guide" the individual is social practice. Through the practice of the community, constraints are imposed upon the individual through the process of learning, and space is made for distinguishing correct and incorrect behavior of the individual.

What happens if you slide the two arguments together is that there is a natural move from the fact that we can't find an interpretation to stop the regress to the claim that the very distinction between correct and incorrect has collapsed, and that the solution to both is to be found in something that stands outside the practice that will tell us which interpretation is *the right one*. Combine this realist project with treating the community as a large individual, and the sceptical conclusion is irresistible. In rejecting an intellectualist solution to the problem of the objectivity of rules, Wittgenstein does not thereby endorse a sceptical conclusion or a sceptical solution in the form of a kind of conditioning theory.

But are we forced to a social explanation of normativity? Even if we reject the intellectualist idea of rule-following as interpreting, can't we have a private actor whose actions are not social but are rule-governed? Here what would shape the behavior of the individual and provide the background against which the actions of the individual could be correct or incorrect is the individual's relation to his natural environment. An action is correct insofar as it contributes to the satisfaction of the individual's needs, all of which are related to her survival. If an action fails to contribute to the individual's well-being or survival, that action is incorrect. This "natural teleology" does not require that the individual understand that what she does is correct nor does it require that she entertain hypotheses about what is most conducive to her survival. What matters is that some behaviors are adaptive and others are not; and our private actor is one who changes her behavior when it fails to contribute to her survival or well-being. This sort of behavior human beings share with animals.

However important adaptive behavior is, it cannot provide a full account of rule-governed behavior. It does not account for clearly conventional cases of rule-following (like that of our cave decorator discussed above), nor more importantly does it provide an account for the self-corrective behavior of the radically isolated actor. There is a distinction between adaptive or teleological behavior and conventional or rule-governed behavior, a distinction that can be blurred by the use of "law" or "rule" to describe both cases. The difference is the familiar Kantian distinction between acting in accord with a generalization (which is true of teleological behavior) and acting from a conception of the rule. What is suggested by the teleological conception of normativity is that normative rules or laws be recast as, or seen as covers for, descriptive generalizations about self-interested behavior. This makes the natural teleology view a variant of a projectivist position. But to make this redescription stick, we must stretch the notions of "adaptation" and "survival" far beyond their legitimate use. The cave-dweller who "corrects" his design on the wall of his cave must be seen as adapting his behavior in a way that de facto enhances his chances for survival much as the deer avoids drinking from the lake when the moon is full.

But, it could be objected, doesn't the Wittgensteinian appeal to blind obedience make a similar mistake? After all, bedrock human behavior does not issue from a *conception* of the rule, but rather is that which we do unthinkingly just as the deer keeps still in the shadows. Wasn't the whole point of the Wittgensteinian alternative to reject this view of the individual agent? There is this affinity with animal behavior, but this does not exhaust human behavior even at the bedrock level. What we do unthinkingly has a conventional and self-reflective element, which is ineliminable and cannot be derived solely from attempts to satisfy our basic animal needs. What we can do unthinkingly, and yet is rule-governed, can only derive from our relationship to the community. The adaptive behavior of the animal does not give it the resources to correct itself or to distinguish between corrective behavior and merely different behavior. It is only in relation to the structured social practice of the community that the individual can engage in normative activity. The individual alone, as "thinker" or "actor," hasn't the resources for creating the context within which actions can be correct or incorrect.

7 The philosophical significance of learning in the later Wittgenstein

"When a child learns this..." "What is 'learning a rule'? – *This*." Anyone familiar with Wittgenstein's later philosophy recognizes these phrases as wholly typical of that philosophy. The appeals to the way in which a child learns, to learning in general, and to the italicized use of the indexical – all are familiar themes. In the *Philosophical Investigations*, Wittgenstein develops his position on three crucial philosophical issues by beginning with the way in which a child learns. First, his critique of referential theories of meaning: "An important part of the training will consist in the teacher's pointing to the objects, directing the child's attention to them, and at the same time uttering a word" (PI §6). Second, his attack on essentialist theories of understanding: "How does [the pupil] get to understand this notation? – First of all the series of numbers will be written down for him and he will be required to copy them....And here there is a normal and an abnormal learner's reaction" (PI §143). And finally, his attack on the Cartesian model of consciousness: "A child has hurt himself and he cries; and then adults talk to him and teach him exclamations and, later, sentences" (PI §244). These three critiques are the cornerstones for his later philosophy, and at the beginning of each he appeals to how children learn. Moreover, Wittgenstein's subsequent writings show an increase in the explicit appeal to learning and to a child's learning. In *On Certainty*, Wittgenstein's final work, virtually every page involves appeal to learning. In spite of this, most commentators treat the appeal as incidental.

When commentators have discussed Wittgenstein's use of learning cases at all, they have been drawn to one of two closely related interpretations. The first interpretation construes the appeal to learning as an *expository device* (cf. Malcolm 1966). Appeal to a child's learning is useful in elucidating the grammar of certain key notions, most especially, the distinction between criterion and symptom. What counts as part of the criterion for the application of a term is what one would appeal to in explaining or teaching the word to a child. Appeal to these facts, however, is completely dispensable. Thus, such appeal can be seen primarily as a literary device in that it provides a more colorful, more concrete display of the conceptual contours of such notions as "meaning," "understanding," and "sensation." It belongs, in short, to the style of the *Investigations* rather than the content. How in fact we learn these concepts is strictly irrelevant to grasping or elucidating their grammar.

The second interpretation sees the appeal to children learning more as a *heuristic device* for making perspicuous what is obscured in complex adult language (cf. Hardwick 1971; Bloor 1983). This interpretation emphasizes the connection Wittgenstein makes between the artificial language games he introduces and children's learning. The natural case is simply an available alternative to the invented case, but it plays the same role, viz. a simple version of complex adult language. If you want to understand "the nature of language," it is best to understand the simple forms out of which it is built.

Both interpretations distort and diminish the significance of the appeal to learning in Wittgenstein's later philosophy, and both are rooted in drawing a strong distinction between the empirical and the conceptual (or grammatical). By contrast, the interpretation I want to explore sees the process of training as pivotal in creating the logical space for the very distinction between the grammatical and the empirical. As Wittgenstein expresses it in the *Remarks on the Foundations of Mathematics*, appeal to initiate training is a crucial part of the "radical explanation" for how we "harden the empirical proposition into a rule" (RFM VI.22). Discussions of learning, of how we typically are trained, occur in contexts in which the issue is the problem of normativity, of how to make or sustain a substantive contrast between correct and incorrect uses of words. The contention of this chapter is that understanding the role learning plays sheds light on the nature of normativity itself.[1]

I shall proceed by discussing three roles learning plays in the acquisition and determination of concepts and rules, beginning with the least problematic and ending with one that runs strongly counter to certain of our philosophical intuitions. The first, and least controversial, is a *causally grounding role* in fixing meaning for the initiate learner. Wittgenstein appeals to a process of ostensive teaching in which objects are taken as exemplary in the use of a word. Here the central problem is to distinguish ostensive teaching from ostensive definition and operant conditioning. Second, learning plays a *methodological role* in disclosing the source of normativity by distinguishing the context of the novice, or initiate learner, from that of the master of a practice. The key problem here is a "bootstrapping" problem: How does the novice become a rule-follower? How does the linguistically incompetent person become the competent language user?

Finally, I shall argue that learning plays a *constitutive role* in that how we learn (bedrock) concepts is constitutive of what we learn. This view runs counter to the idea that the relation between learning and its product cannot but be contingent, and so a matter of "mere history." How we acquire beliefs – whether from explicit instruction, taking some appropriate pill, by "osmosis," or by accident – is irrelevant to the content of these beliefs. There may be many paths to belief but the content is the same. If how we learn is constitutive of what we learn, then the intuitive appeal of this objection must be countered.

1 Causally grounding role: ostensive teaching

Let me begin with what is apparently the least controversial claim about the learning period, and that is that being taught causally grounds the initiate learner's use of the words of a natural language. In brief, teaching fixes the meanings of natural language words for the novice.[2] Stated neutrally, this claim would be accepted by virtually everyone, from the classical behaviorist (Watson 1930; Skinner 1957) assimilating verbal behavior to chained reflexes to the cognitivist endorsing a hypothesis-formation model of language learning (Fodor 1975). The differences emerge in the particular account given of the process of learning and the nature of language itself. The two are tied intimately together. *How* learning (or adaptation to particular environments) occurs determines the behaviorist's conception of language. For the cognitivist, on the other hand, *what* language is determines the account of how learning occurs. Wittgenstein exploits this connection in his opening critique of a familiar and powerful conception of language and meaning. On that conception, the meaningfulness of language is a function of the meanings of its individual words and the meanings of the words are the objects they denote. Wittgenstein attacks this denotational theory of meaning by undermining a companion picture of how language is acquired (PI §1–38). The object of the attack is the meaning-conferring relation alleged to exist between an object and its name, a relation secured by ostensive definition.

The companion picture of language acquisition is a simple one: Adults point to individual objects in the immediate environment of the child and name them. The child, as a result of this demonstration, associates the name with that particular object and subsequent to making this association uses the same name for any other object belonging to the class of which the first originating object was a member. The understanding that the child has of the words she has learned is essentially the same as that of the adult. The problems with this picture of language learning emerge with the examination of (1) the initial association between name and object and

(2) the subsequent identification of objects belonging to the same class as the originating, or baptismal, object. How can the utterance of a word by one person while standing close to an object effect an association in the mind of a second person such that the second person can subsequently identify the same objects as the first person? On the classical view Wittgenstein is examining, the key to solving this puzzle lies with the fact that the relation between the utterance and the object is not one of simple association or close physical proximity, but one of ostensive definition. The effectiveness of the ostensive definition lies with the intellectual or cognitive capacities of the pupil, in particular, the capacity to grasp that the baptismal object is the exemplar that functions as the standard for correct application of the term uttered. Wittgenstein's concern is whether this picture of language and language learning is adequate to explain the normativity of language or even to recognize the extent to which language is normatively informed. And if it is inadequate, what sort of error has been made that nonetheless leads to the illusion that a genuine explanation has been offered?

Wittgenstein's well-known attack on ostensive definition undermines the initial plausibility that appeal to ostensive definition had in explaining initiate learning. The most serious objection is that explanation of initiate learning by appeal to ostensive definition leads to an explanatory regress. Teaching by ostensive definition cannot explain how the pupil comes to identify correctly members of a class of objects or properties precisely because it presupposes that the pupil already understands the notion of class membership, can take the baptismal object as the paradigm by which other members of a class can be so recognized (that is, identified as the same), and realizes that the teacher is not only uttering a word, but a name which functions to designate a class. The conclusion that Wittgenstein draws is that naming cannot fix meaning, but is itself a semantically sophisticated act that presupposes a great deal of cognitive stage setting and language use: "only someone who already knows how to do something with it can significantly ask a name" (PI §31).

In disclosing these profound philosophical problems confronting ostensive definition as the primary vehicle for concept acquisition and language learning, two very important features of language and language learning are revealed. First, Wittgenstein never gives up the idea – central to the classic conception of language under attack – that the word–object relation is central to language. Ordinary objects *are* used as exemplars in the life of any natural language. Second, the classificatory work of language cannot take place without stage setting, without the right kind of context. One can't name an object or property without providing the logical space for individuating that which is to be named. So, in a sense, naming is the last linguistic act performed, not first in the development of linguistic ability. What this clearly points to, of course, is that a Wittgensteinian understanding of both the exemplar and the stage setting that is involved in naming must be recast.

While many agree with the Wittgensteinian rejection of ostensive definition as the vehicle for language learning, not all agree that the grounds for rejection are that it leads to an explanatory regress by explaining linguistic mastery in terms of linguistic mastery. The revival of "rationalist psychology" in the work of Chomsky and Fodor quite centrally involves the rejection of the implicit charge of explanatory vacuity. Both hold that language learning can be explained in terms of an innate and unconscious cognitive structure consisting of rules and representations, an innate grammar, or an innate language of thought. What this hypothesis requires, of course, is that the object of explanation must shift. The acquisition of linguistic competence is not explained by the process of language learning, for competence is not learned at all. Only the acquisition of words in a natural language is to be explained; and for that some form of hypothesis formation and testing is the most promising explanation.[3] But on Wittgenstein's view, the cognitive mastery (both linguistic and epistemic) required for both naming and generating hypotheses is precisely what the initiate learner lacks and not just overtly.

Wittgenstein speaks of "stage setting." But just what is the stage, and where is it located, since it cannot be within the initiate learner's mind? To answer this, we need to examine Wittgenstein's notion of ostensive training and the way in which it contrasts with ostensive definition (PI §6). Ostensive training or teaching, for Wittgenstein, has affinities with the behaviorist notion of conditioning. Learning the use of a word in connection with an object is better understood as a conditioned association that results from training rather than, say, the confirmation of a hypothesis about the translation of a natural language word into the language of thought. The learner, however, is not a *tabula rasa*. Ostensive teaching does require the learner to have certain behavioral and perceptual capacities; otherwise the training will fail. This much is conceded to the nativist. However, these capacities are not identical to the distinctively linguistic competencies acquired in mastering a first language. The objection to ostensive definition was that the learner had to have mastery of *semantic* and *epistemic* competencies. Therefore, in order to avoid the regress, one must find a way to describe learning such that the cognitive and behavioral capacities the learner starts with are significantly less sophisticated than those that are to be acquired. Capacities akin to those hypothesized by behaviorists are of the right order of cognitive sophistication to attribute to the initiate learner. The learner must be able to discriminate behaviorally objects within her environment, but this does not require that the learner use standards, norms or exemplars, or the semantic notion of naming. Ostensive training, unlike ostensive definition classically conceived, does not impute *higher* cognitive competencies to the novice in order to explain low-level forms of behavior. What the child is learning is to adapt her behavior to norms, for which language mastery is the indispensable means.

To make this claim more forceful, I want to distinguish normativity from biological purposiveness, or natural teleology. "Normativity," as I shall use it throughout this chapter, is restricted to performances, non-verbal as well as verbal, that can be judged to be correct or incorrect. Such performances can be individuated only by reference to some norm, standard, exemplar, or rule. This is because both the objects used as norms (whether formula as rule, post as signpost, or rose as exemplar) and the actions themselves (writing down a particular number, taking the left fork in a road, or gathering more of the same) are devoid of any intrinsic biological significance or utility and are open to multiple interpretations if considered in isolation from their historical and contemporary contexts.

This openness or flexibility makes room for normativity and distinguishes normatively guided behavior from instinctual and biologically determined behavior. This latter kind of behavior does have direction, and can, in an attenuated sense, be described as correct or incorrect. Such behavior serves to meet (or fails to meet) certain biological needs and drives of the organism, or to use the preferred locution, satisfy some biologically proper function (Millikan 1984; also see Dretske 1988; Papineau 1987), and when such behavior misfires in some way, it can be said to be "incorrect." But the "correctness" of such behavior has to do only with its being biologically successful. It is not incorrect relative to a standard or norm of correctness.

Ostensive training builds on capacities and competencies that display the purposiveness of natural teleology. Without such capacities, learning to master normative practices simply could not take place. But when, earlier, I said that Wittgenstein's critique of ostensive definition shows the indispensability of stage setting for naming, the "stage" is not this purposive or biological competence. The stage must be normative competence as displayed in a rule-governed practice. The initiate learner does not have that competence. Only the teacher or the master of the practice (the one who is training the learner) has this. What is distinctive, then, about the learning situation is that the learner does not have the necessary background competencies that make what she does naming (when the child calls out "ball" in the presence of a ball) or counting or identifying a pain. That background structure can only be provided by the social environment personified in the actions of the teacher. The significance of this is that the "judgments" of the child and the judgments of the adult cannot have the same status or mean the same things to the two agents. The status of the naive learner's utterances (that, for example, they are taken as judgments or requests) is a function of the status extended to those utterances by masters of that practice. In other words, the initiate learner speaks, makes judgments, requests, and the like only by virtue of a courtesy extended to the learner by those who have already mastered the practice. What this position underscores is the linguistic and cognitive dependence that the initiate learner has on the teacher, and by extension the social environment.

Wittgenstein's notion of ostensive teaching indicates how these various elements are dynamically united within the learning context. The competence presupposed by the meaningfulness of a given utterance or other linguistic action is the competence of the adult or teacher who thereby structures the situation within which the child learns. The medium for learning itself is the training whereby the child learns to associate word with object. There is a temptation to identify this process of association with behaviorist conditioning. This is a mistake. What makes this kind of training importantly different from conditioning is that the association is structured by a practice, which for Wittgenstein is rule-governed, that is, normative. Thus, the training is not in the mere reinforced association of word and object, but an association that is effective in enabling the novice to realize her more basic desires by shaping her behavior to conform to, or perhaps better, mimic the activities licensed by the practice or custom. Successful training is training that results in the initiate learner becoming a skilled and so autonomous practitioner.

Creating a normative practitioner whose actions are guided by rules requires regularizing the novice's behavior. Without regularity, the notion of "the same" is empty; and judging for sameness is essential to being guided by rules or other norms. But there are at least three different forms of regularity which must be kept distinct, for they characterize different ways in which behavior is related to a rule or abstract pattern. There are behaviors that conform to rules, behaviors that are pattern-governed, and actions that are rule-obeying.[4]

Rule-conforming behavior is behavior that, as a matter of fact, conforms to some rule or complex pattern but does not conform in virtue of the rule or pattern; it just happens to follow the rule or to realize part of a complex pattern. The behavior of a dog walking beside a road with the flow of traffic conforms to our right-hand drive convention, but does not do so in virtue of that convention. A chicken that happens to stretch its neck and wings in accord with the mating ritual of the wandering albatross is not stretching its neck in virtue of this mating pattern although the albatross is. Rule-obeying behavior, on the other hand, is behaving with the intention of realizing a system of moves or with the intention of following the rules or pattern. Such behavior involves both a game (the moves that are being made) and a metagame (the game in which the rules are situated). This distinction is an old one, drawn most forcefully by Kant when he distinguishes those actions that merely conform to the moral law and those actions that are done from a conception of the law. But Kant's distinction conceals a third kind of regularity, namely, pattern-governed behavior. This is behavior that exemplifies an abstract pattern or a part of that pattern. The wing-stretching behavior of the albatross is a part of its mating ritual; or, to use the example favored by Sellars, the movements of a bee when it returns to the hive after locating a clover field are part of a complex dance, not accidentally, but essentially – they are performed because they are part of the dance though not from a conception of the dance. The explanation for, and individuation of, the particular move is given by its relation to the complex patterned whole. As Sellars puts it,

> It is open to us to give an evolutionary account of the phenomena of the dance, and hence to interpret the statement that this wiggle occurred because of the complex dance to which it belongs – which appears…to attribute causal force to an abstraction, and hence tempts us to draw upon the mentalistic language of intention and purpose – in terms of the survival value to groups of bees of these forms of behavior.
>
> (Sellars 1963: p. 326)

These distinctions provide a good way to understand Wittgenstein's account of ostensive teaching and its contrast with ostensive definition. What the initiate learner is being trained into are pattern-governed behaviors; in other words, behaviors that are performed because they conform to, or contribute to, a complex social pattern but not because the agent recognizes and follows a set of rules that may provide an abstract description of the pattern. The initiate learner shifts from behavior that merely conforms a pattern but whose cause is independent of that pattern to behavior that conforms in virtue of being a part of the pattern. The difference between us and the bees is that our patterns are social and socially transmitted whereas the bees' patterns are hard-wired and to be explained in evolutionary terms.[5] Yet there is an interesting similarity between the bees and the newly trained novices, and that is that neither engage in their patterned behavior "on purpose," that is, as a result of intending to follow rules or apply norms.

Let me summarize the two major contentions of this section that support the thesis that language learning requires cognitive stage setting that cannot be provided by the initiate learner herself. The first is that what motivates much of Wittgenstein's thinking about these matters is his long-standing concern to identify and avoid any threat of regress. It might be objected that Wittgenstein's way of avoiding a regress is in fact a way that only postpones its re-emergence. The regress was alleged to be that one cannot explain the acquisition of publicly demonstrated linguistic ability by attributing to the person an "inner" linguistic ability. Insofar as there is a question about the former, there is a question about the latter. Wittgenstein's alternative suggestion is that the child is trainable in a socially structured environment in which the ability or competence to be taught is already mastered by the teacher. But don't we now get a different kind of regress, namely, how does the teacher, and by extension the society or community, acquire this competence? This regress is illusory. For each individual, there is the story of his or her becoming a language user, in which the explanans is not simply a duplication of the explanandum within the individual. So the focus of attention must shift to society itself and the question of how humanoid creatures became language-using social creatures. Presumably anthropologists and evolutionary theorists will be able to provide an account of this. But this sort of account is not one that issues in an explanatory regress.

The second contention is that when learning occurs, it involves norms and stage setting. There is no satisfactory way to explain normative learning individualistically without running afoul of the regress problem. Thus, insofar as the utterances of the novice are linguistic utterances, and not simply noises associated with objects, this is because they are so treated by those who, in making similar utterances, genuinely have the background cognitive competence to speak. The structuring provided by the adult is a necessary support both logically and physically for the novice's linguistic actions. It is logically necessary for it provides the system of background beliefs, actions, and competencies, the complex pattern necessary for the token-utterance to have significance and so to be an utterance. It is physically necessary for it provides the actual training and disciplining of the novice without which the novice simply would not, as a matter of fact, be able to continue. Ostensive training is the causal ground for the development of the cognitive competencies constitutive of language mastery and the mastery of any genuinely normative practice.

2 The methodological role: the normativity of rules

One might well object at this point that whether or not we learn by a process of ostensive training is an empirical matter and that one cannot rule out of hand the possibility that learning might in fact be quite a different sort of process from that sketched above. It is obvious that children don't start out life speaking a natural language, and most philosophers now accept the Wittgensteinian critique of ostensive definition. But why should we accept the claim that initiate learning is public social training rather than an individualist process of hypothesis formation and testing of the sort proposed by Chomsky or Fodor? Or a matter of operant conditioning in which the individual's behavior adapts as a result of his interaction with the public (but not necessarily) social environment?

The cognitivist strategy of Chomsky and Fodor seeks to avoid the charge of vicious regress by distinguishing between an innate repertoire of unconscious rules and representations and an acquired use of a natural language; so consciously following norms is to be explained in terms of unconsciously doing so. As we have already noted, this strategy requires recasting the explanans: Chomsky and Fodor don't seek to explain becoming linguistically competent in the sense of becoming able to follow rules and use representations; rather they seek to explain how we acquire the rules and representations of a particular natural language. The target of Wittgenstein's critique is directed to the former, for he is after an account of representation and rule-following. If the Chomsky/Fodor thesis is correct, then we don't *become* competent to follow rules and use representations; we just are so. Their problem becomes one of finding an adequate account of representation and rule (cf. Fodor 1988).[6] The behaviorist strategy, on the other hand, denies that there is any such thing as following rules and using representations in a normatively guided sense. Patterns of behavior are reinforced in connection with features of the environment. Though it is difficult now to take operant conditioning theories of language mastery seriously, there is the related view that the regularities of behavior necessary for the manifestation of linguistic competence, or the display of rule-following, can be accounted for in terms of an individual's ongoing relation to his natural environment. These are variants of the view that "natural teleology," as I have called it, is at the core of normatively guided behavior. Stage-setting, it could be argued, is provided by the biological capacities of the organism in its relation to the environment and its evolutionary history.

The point of this section is to build on the argument of the first section by showing that there are positive reasons for thinking that the stage setting

NORMATIVITY provided by social practice

required for initiate learning must be public *and social*. It is Wittgenstein's
social characterization of meaning that does the work here. An important
consequence of this is the *indispensability* of initiate training. That meaning
is social and learning is indispensable are two sides of the same coin. If
meaning is inherently social, then the individualist hypotheses of the
cognitivist and the natural teleologist cannot explain what they purport to
explain, the former because it misappropriates the concepts of rule and
representation and the latter because it cannot generate normativity from
its limited resources.

Where there are right and wrong ways of going about matters, there
must be standards of correctness. And, in the end, there are only three
sources for such standards of correctness: They can originate in objectified
meanings derived from the intellectual powers of the mind, in objectified
meanings as Platonic or Fregean objects, or in the role of words within
public social practice.

Considering only the passages on rule-following (PI §139–242), what
Kripke (Kripke 1982) has designated Wittgenstein's "sceptical problem of
meaning" is in fact Wittgenstein's attack on various forms of objectified
meaning. The two most important conceptions he attacks are the idea of
the formula as containing its own applications and the idea of an interpretation uniquely specifying applications. The only view of norms that ends
neither in mystery-mongering nor in a regress is the view that standards
are embedded within socially constituted bedrock practices. These practices, according to Wittgenstein, are not deliberately chosen conventions,
but are constituted by the harmonious "blind" agreement in words and
deeds of a group of people over a period of time. Such agreement is
"blind" only in the sense that it does not result from the self-conscious or
explicit application of rules; it does not mean that people are unconscious
automata "blindly obeying" rules. Drawing on the distinction introduced
above, "bedrock" social practices are pattern-governed behaviors, rather
than rule-obeying behaviors. Another way to express this is to say that the
normative dimension of language is supervenient upon community agreement (that is, harmony) in word and deed. Normativity supervenes on
community agreement in virtue of the fact that an object can only acquire
the status of exemplar or norm or standard if it is used as such. That is, if
it is accorded a role in adjudicating disputes and (most importantly) *in
teaching or otherwise acculturating the initiates.*

Given, then, the social dimension of normative practices, no individual,
in radical isolation from all social practice, can follow rules or engage in
actions that are correct or incorrect. Such an individual may engage in
behavior that enhances her survival chances but she cannot be guided by
norms. Initiate learning is the indispensable device for linking individual

and society. Because norms and normatively characterized behavior must be public, the content of what is learned (or perhaps otherwise acquired) must be made manifest in public. A training period is therefore also a testing period. I want to develop this claim and its significance by way of two arguments, the first to the effect that understanding requires public manifestation of mastery of the practice and the second to the effect that the practice must be social.[7]

Let's take the "manifestation argument" first (cf. Wright 1986: Introduction; McGinn). Why doesn't it make sense to suppose that a person might well understand something, even though that person has never revealed her understanding? Couldn't the person nonetheless understand, say, chess or how to add? There seem to be two ways to make sense of this supposition. Either there is something in her mind in virtue of which she understands chess or addition; or some counterfactual statement is true of her to the effect that if she were asked to play a game or describe the rules of chess or some such thing, she would respond appropriately. The burden of this argument is to show that the first alternative is empty, and the second is really a refinement upon the requirement that understanding be public.

Most of Wittgenstein's efforts are directed towards showing that the first alternative is empty. His arguments turn repeatedly on the fact that the mere tokening of a formula, sentence, or feeling does not and cannot determine how that formula, sentence, or feeling is to be interpreted and so guide judgment and behavior. Neither can any interpretation be privileged as the final or self-evident interpretation of the tokened sentence or formula or feeling. The failure of any state of mind or interpretation to do the work assigned it is what makes plausible, prima facie, the idea that the mind must have some mysterious powers in virtue of which the formula, feeling or interpretation is endowed with a self-evident application. But appeal to the mysteriousness of mind is the mark of having failed to find an adequate solution to the problem. So Wittgenstein concludes nothing found in the mind of the individual could be identified with the understanding of the rules for chess or for addition or anything else.[8] Understanding must be displayed in what the subject does, even for the subject herself. In giving up the idea that a thought could be self-interpreting, we thereby give up the idea that the subject has an epistemologically privileged access to the contents of her own thoughts. In seeing how rules "guide" we must look to the public domain of action.

This line of argument is supplemented by a second. Both in the *Investigations* and in the *Remarks on the Foundations of Mathematics*, Wittgenstein asserts that it makes no sense to suppose a rule could be followed only once: "In order to describe the phenomenon of language, one must describe a practice, not something that happens once, *no matter of what kind*" (RFM VI.34; cf. PI §199 and RFM VI.21). Rule-following requires regularity over time. We need to establish patterns such that individual behaviors occur *because* they are part of the pattern. A single instance of following a rule could not be distinguished from an action that superficially resembles the rule-governed one, but is not a move in a game or practice. Someone idly picks up a small wooden marker and sets it down again on a checkered board, as it happens one square closer to the middle. Clearly such an action is not that of moving a pawn one space forward. The history and context of the action are all wrong. To make this clear, let me extend Sellars' example of the pattern-governed dances of the bee. A bee wiggles because a drop of acid touched its body. Though physically like the wiggle that, in the context of a dance, indicates the direction in which the flowers are to be found, this wiggle does not indicate that. It is only a physical reaction to the irritation of its body's surface; it is not done because it is a *part* of a dance. We come again to Wittgenstein's emphasis on stage setting. The point is not a psychological one. The logic of the move requires a certain setting and history. This is what he means by stage setting. So the manifestation argument can be seen to be of two parts, the first to show that the mind cannot in some special way provide what ordinary objects and actions cannot and the second to show that the logic of individual moves requires a structured setting in the public domain, where that structure is provided, in part at least, by our unthinking pattern-governed responses.

If understanding (in order to be understanding) requires public participation within a practice, then we need to know what a Wittgensteinian practice is. A practice sets the stage for particular actions to be moves within the game or practice. Moreover, the indispensability of practices points once more to the indispensability of learning. For Wittgenstein, we must alter our way of looking at the relation between a sign (or rule) and action (cf. PI §198). Instead of seeing actions as flowing from the sign, we need to see the mutually supporting interconnections between sign and ways of acting. How we act fixes the rule. The rule is made a guide, or standard, for action *by* our acting towards it in ways that are fixed by our training. So the limitations and constraints on our behavior that understanding a game or a rule always entails cannot be characterized but in terms of the interconnection between behavior and an object used as sign.

To repeat, a Wittgensteinian conception of practice is one in which an object becomes a standard or norm in virtue of the ways in which that object is used. The attitudes, judgments, and actions of the participants in the practice hold the object in place as a standard. This is true whether the object is explicitly and self-consciously chosen to function as a standard (as with the platinum bar adopted as the standard meter stick (cf. PI §50)) or whether an object is used without such explicit stipulation (as with the teaching and explaining of most ordinary concepts). Standards (of whatever kind) must be embedded within practice, that is, within actual ways of behaving, both verbally and non-verbally, that are regular and sustained over a period of time and are independent of *any* individual's say-so.

The manifestation argument can be seen to reject the idea that such embedding might be notional only. In other words, Wittgenstein rejects the idea that a rule or the understanding of a rule might be captured by a set of counterfactual statements only. Such counterfactuals specify the practice within which a rule must be embedded. To this extent, the idea of notional embedding conforms to the Wittgensteinian conception. And though it is intelligible to suppose that some rules have only been conceived by way of counterfactuals without ever having been acted upon, it is not intelligible to suppose that all or most of our rules have only been or could have been so conceived. The thrust of the manifestation argument is to show that the understanding of rules or standards of any sort requires that the agent actually act in accordance with them. The reality of rules requires that they be part of actual practices. Rules that have never been acted upon can only be the exception, and their intelligibility turns on assimilating them to rules that are part of actual practices.

The upshot of the manifestation argument is that understanding a norm requires actually behaving in appropriate ways. This is the force of saying that normative practices must be public. But a Wittgensteinian practice is not only public, it is social.[9] Accordingly, learning is the only way to become a practitioner.

The force of "social" here is to be found in its contrast with "individual" rather than "solitary." There are some practices which are social in the strong sense that they are "team" practices. There is a division of labor or play, such that these practices can only be enacted by more than one individual. Factory production, baseball games, weddings, teaching, and the like cannot be carried out by a solitary individual. In this, they are unlike going for a walk, doing mathematics, composing music, and many other such activities. But even solitary practices are cultural practices and so have a social dimension since the context of regularity and agreement in judgment (in what is said) must be provided by a community, that is, by a group of people reacting, judging, and behaving in harmony. They owe their identity to this social background even though they may be carried out by one individual at a time. Without conformity to a group at bedrock level, normativity is impossible.

Two caveats must be entered. First, this agreement that Wittgenstein variously describes as an "agreement in judgments" (PI §242; cf. RFM VI.39), as an "agreement in form of life" (PI §241), as that which "all or the majority of us agree in certain things" (RFM VI.39), and so on concerns "the agreement of *humans*." This kind of agreement is part of our human natural history, as Wittgenstein puts it. It is agreement in our reactions to pointing or judgments of sameness or reactions to pain. Second, though we must share a sense of the obvious, this is not to say that what we *mean* when we make a judgment of sameness is that the majority, if not all, of the people will judge that way:

> And does this mean e.g. that the definition of "same" would be this: same is what all or most human beings with one voice take for the same?—Of course not.
>
> For of course I don't make use of the agreement of human beings to affirm identity. What criterion do you use, then? None at all.
>
> (RFM VII.40)

Though I certainly don't mean, when I assert that $2 + 2 = 4$, that the majority answers "4" when asked "what is $2 + 2$?," nonetheless without this agreement "$2 + 2 = 4$" would cease to be meaningful. The very contrast between a correct and incorrect way of proceeding or judging requires conformity to a common way of continuing as a matter of course. That which decides the normative contrast, at the bedrock level, is a way of acting that is captured in the description "the obvious thing to do." What is obvious is what we all do as a matter of course. This is what Wittgenstein describes as the "blind obedience" to rules, with which any threatened regress of rules or interpretation of rules ends (cf. PI §198–219). It is not a matter of a privileged interpretation nor of mystical insight nor of arbitrary decision, but of our "peaceful agreement" in how to go on:

> It is of the greatest importance that a dispute hardly ever arises between people about whether the colour of this object is the same as the colour of that…, etc. This peaceful agreement is the characteristic surrounding the use of the word "same".
>
> (RFM VI.21)

Bedrock practices express our common sense of the obvious. The role the obvious plays in grounding normative practices is indispensable. To support this claim, consider the way in which Wittgenstein characterizes our sense of the obvious at the beginning of his discussion of rule-following and again at the end of his discussion of rule-following. When Wittgenstein first raises the difficulties in trying to explain how a standard or rule guides behavior, he seems to dismiss our natural response in applying a picture of a cube as a rule: "For we might also be inclined to express ourselves like this: We are at most under a psychological, not a logical, compulsion" (PI §140). By the end of his discussion of rule-following, he summarizes his solution to the paradox of interpretation as follows: "The rule can only seem to me to produce all its consequences in advance if I draw them as a *matter of course*" (PI §238). In §140, what comes naturally to us as we respond to a standard is apparently dismissed as a mere "psychological compulsion." In §238, the alternative to finding a privileged interpretation of a standard is to identify the way in which we respond, as a matter of course, to that standard. Wittgenstein's point is that it is only under the influence of the interpretation theory of rule-following that acting as a matter of course is seen as a mere psychological compulsion, and so essentially extraneous to the logic of rule-following. Once disabused of that theory, we can come to see that the so-called psychological compulsion is really part of the logic, or as Wittgenstein would say, the grammar of following a rule.

If peaceful agreement about what is the same is to do the work that, traditionally, was thought to require a criterion or privileged interpretation for "the same," then how are we to explain what counts as the same or as agreement for someone who does not already play the game? Wittgenstein's answer at every point is that "one learns the meaning of 'agreement' by learning to follow a rule" (RFM VII.39), "but how can I explain [the rule] to anyone? I can give him this training" (RFM VII.40).[10] With respect to our bedrock practices, to be rule-governed the individual must judge in agreement with others. Training is what links the individual to the community. Given the social foundation of norms, acquiring an understanding of rules and other norms requires assimilation into community practices. The point is not just that there is a de facto causal link between the training of a novice and assimilation into a practice though this is obviously true. The point is rather that there is no other way to explain the acquisition of *normative* competencies. Moreover, in the absence of some actual social practice, there is no fact of the matter as to what the novice or the radically isolated individual understands or even is doing. Suppose a child who has not learned any arithmetic says "4" when the question "what is 2 + 2?" is directed to him. Given the child's history and abilities, we simply cannot say what the child meant (if anything) in saying this, not even that he had numbers in mind when he uttered that sound nor that he was responding to a question nor that he was ignorant. There is no fact of the matter.

This approach to language learning clearly raises a "bootstrapping" problem. How does the cognitively incompetent novice *become* the competent master of a practice? Let us consider Wittgenstein's example of the pupil learning the natural number sequence (PI §143–55, 179–81), the case he uses to focus his discussion of rule-following. Wittgenstein clearly differentiates the roles of the two participants, and it is this that I want to highlight. The teacher is one whose judgment is autonomous precisely because she has mastered the practice herself, and so how she judges sets the standard for what is correct so far as the pupil is concerned. The novice does not have and is not required to have the skills or knowledge that are necessary for the successful participation in a practice. As I pointed out above, this differentiation of role enables the adult to extend a courtesy to the child's performances which is indispensable to learning. The stage setting of the background necessary for judgment is within the domain of the master of the practice whereas the "judgment" itself is the utterance of the novice. In this way, the background structure and cognitive competence necessary for language use or rule-following to occur at all is provided by those who have been acculturated into the practice, while the initiate learner's behavior is shaped and made intelligible by this background. The cognitive skills of the teacher provide the "bootstrap" for the novice.

It might be objected that this reply isn't adequate. After all, the problem arises because we discern the need to bridge the gap between the competencies of the novice before and after training. Aren't we still forced to the idea that training and the development of skills through training can only be of secondary importance in the explanation? That what is of primary importance is the nature of the change *within* the novice herself? In particular, isn't it the internalization of the rule or standard for sameness that matters? Something must happen to the novice that effects an internal change so that her utterances after training no longer require "courtesy" support but express the autonomous judgment of a full-fledged language user. The behavior of the novice must change from merely conforming to the rules to occurring because of the rules. The traditional way in which this change has been described is as a shift from rule-conforming behavior to rule-obeying behavior. And rule-obeying behavior is acting with an intention to follow the rule, where this involves a recognition of the rule. This way of characterizing the change in the novice leads inevitably to one of two inner process stories. Either the training is the causal trigger for certain innate cognitive competencies and rules; or the training provides the evidential feedback to the novice necessary for inductively extrapolating the rule, in which case the novice has all the requisite cognitive abilities and background knowledge necessary to construct the set of rules used by the teacher. The internalist story thus needs to pry rules free from their embedding in social practices. Yet the argument that leads

Wittgenstein to training or learning as the final explanation of what it is to continue in the same way (and so follow a rule) shows that we can't make sense of a rule independently of the matter of course reactions that we share with others. So the change in the novice is the change from an unskilled participant in the practice to a skilled actor. Obeying rules and internalizing rules can only be a secondary formation, as rule-obeying is dependent upon becoming skilled in judging sameness.

Moreover, the internalist stories are allied to the idea that the bootstrapping in question is justificatory as well as causally efficacious. Yet, for Wittgenstein, the issue of justifying what is to be learned does not arise either for the teacher or for the novice. Rather, whether the novice continues correctly or not is the central issue. The behavior of the novice is correctable by the teacher in that the teacher accepts or rejects the moves made by the novice, and perhaps even literally guides her hand in her formation of numbers. That 3 follows 2 is no more subject to justification in this context than that "3" is formed by two connected semicircles. The teacher is the final authority on what is correct in that how she judges, how she goes on as a matter of course is the determinant or "standard" of what is correct and incorrect. This use of "standard" needs to be put in scare-quotes because what she is inclined to say is not a justificatory standard, that is, it does not provide a justification or reason for why 3 follows 2. But it shares certain features with a justification, namely, it is the arbiter of what is correct. That it can serve this role is due to the fact that the teacher's own inclinations are in harmony with the inclinations and judgments of the community of which she is a part. Her judgments have authority because they are representative of the judgments of the community. They carry weight for the pupil, however, independently of whether they are properly authoritative. Her judgments determine a normative practice for the pupil just in virtue of the learning relation that obtains. The success of the instruction is gauged by how well it results in producing agreement in the judgments and actions of the novice. This agreement, as we have seen, is essential to rule-governed activity. It "is a presupposition of logic" (RFM VI.49), and so a necessary condition for the possibility of justifying practices. In other words, what we take as the obvious way to proceed in the use of rules, paradigms, or standards must be shared skills. Otherwise nothing can function as a rule or paradigm or standard. This is not to say, however, that *what* is learned can be expressed in terms of doing what the teacher does. This is what Wittgenstein is getting at when he says that

[t]his seems to abolish logic, but does not do so. It is one thing to describe methods of measurement, and another to obtain and state

results of measurement. But what we call "measuring" is partly determined by a certain constancy in results of measurement.

(PI §242)

Training into a practice is the means whereby the individual is brought into conformity with a community. Such training is as much a matter of testing as it is teaching. The two are not radically distinct episodes in the process of initiate learning. This is because in the absence of some *actual* process of testing the effects of teaching, there is no fact of the matter as to what is learned. This is as much so for the novice as it is for others. The novice herself cannot know what she has mastered independently of what she can go on to do, especially with respect to bedrock practices where there is no criterion of use and no justification independent of what practitioners find obvious. These judgments that are constitutive of our form of life are not rule-obeying behaviors at all, but pattern-governed behaviors, which is why Wittgenstein must resort to pointing – *This* is counting by 2s – in order to explain what he means. Training into the patterns is the only way to become a practitioner, and so capable of engaging in full-fledged rule-obeying behavior.

In sum, given that meaning is social, individuals must be acculturated into the community in a probationary period of learning. Learning thus is indispensable in becoming a rule-follower. It might still be objected that the history of mastering a concept or practice is nonetheless "mere history" on the grounds that the character of that training is irrelevant to the product of learning provided that the novice "passes" the public, socially accredited testing. It would still leave appeals to learning as an expository device in exploring the content of a rule or concept. But Wittgenstein is saying something stronger than this, namely, that descriptions of training are the best (perhaps the only) explanations for how we judge at bedrock and this is because how we are trained is constitutive of what is learned.

3 The constitutive role: the adoption of a concept

How can the process of learning be constitutive of the content of what is learned? The key is the shared sense of the obvious that provides the background necessary for any meaningful use of language or rule-following. It is this shared sense of the obvious that is acquired paradigmatically in initiate learning, in grasping concepts through the acquisition of skills. It is that against which judgments can be made, rules cited, concepts applied. This background itself cannot be described or captured in a set of rules without distorting the very way it functions as a background.[11] It can, in short, only be shown. It is the indispensability of the background combined with the fact that it can only be shown that links the process of learning to the content of what is learned. This idea is most fully explored by Wittgenstein in Part VI of the *Remarks on the Foundations of Mathematics*. Wittgenstein discusses these matters in connection with mathematical proofs and concepts. However, his discussion here, as with his discussion of continuing the natural number series in the *Investigations*, is completely general.[12] It is just that the elements of the account are more clearly distinguished in the mathematical case.

RFM VI.8 is pivotal for the argument that learning is constitutive of the content of what is learned as it introduces the key features of Wittgenstein's explanation of "the determination of a concept":

[The pupil] tells us: "I saw that it must be like that."…
This *must* shews that he has adopted a concept.
This *must* signifies that he has gone in a circle.
He has read off from the process, not a proposition of natural science but, instead of that, the determination of a concept.
Let concept here mean method. In contrast to the application of the method.

Wittgenstein uses two metaphors in this passage that help organize the argument of Part VI. The first is that of adopting a concept. Wittgenstein associates "the determination of a concept" with "the adoption of a concept." In fact, he almost uses these expressions interchangeably. This might suggest that he endorses a picture of language in which the logical (or grammatical) is reduced to the psychological, a variant on the Humean idea that necessity is psychological compulsion. But this would be a mistake. For Wittgenstein, the psychological is grounded in the grammatical. The second metaphor is that of traveling in a circle. That he uses this metaphor helps locate the problem that he is addressing. In the background is the threat of a regress of justification. The circle traveled by the pupil is part of what Wittgenstein describes as a "radical explanation" for the proof or procedure that leads the pupil to the view that "it *must* be like that" (RFM VI.14). This explanation is part of Wittgenstein's attempt to distinguish between "a proposition of natural science" and "the determination of a concept." This distinction is at the core of his account of rule-following and language.

The circle concerns how the novice comes to see a result obtained from a proof as necessary, as what must be the answer and not merely the result that happens to be obtained on a particular occasion: "he does not say: I realized that this happens. Rather: that it must be like that" (RFM VI.7).

What Wittgenstein is interested in, and what he calls "the adoption of a concept," is how certain ways of looking at things come to seem necessary. It is the fact that they come to seem necessary that then makes the process of how one learned or acquired the skill or attitude in question seem only accidentally connected to what is learned. In other words, the sense that *how* one learns is irrelevant to *what* is learned is an artifact of what is learned, namely, of coming to see that things must be this way. The necessity of the conclusion suggests that there is no alternative to this way of seeing things, so that no matter what, we would have to arrive at just this point. But this is an illusion. As we know, Wittgenstein argues repeatedly in his later works that nothing is intrinsically necessary or normative or representational. Rather an object acquires this function or status in virtue of its role within a practice or custom, and this agreement in reaction and judgment of necessity *are* essential to the language games of which they are a part. The life of mathematics turns on *our* coming to see, as Wittgenstein puts it, "that it must be like that."

Just how is it best to unpack the metaphor that, when the pupil draws the moral that a certain result must follow, that " 'must' shews that he has gone in a circle" that will enable us to track the connections among necessity, rules, and learning? Wittgenstein opens the discussion with a characterization of mathematical proofs as that which "give propositions an order. They organize them" (RFM VI.1). He spells this out in a Kantian manner: "The concept of a formal test presupposes the concept of a transformation rule, and hence of a technique" (RFM VI.2). A proof, for Wittgenstein, is a pattern of propositions; it is a way of "organizing propositions." But no such organized set of propositions can be grasped as a proof, or indeed be a proof (and Wittgenstein puts the point in both the cognitive and ontological ways), unless it is understood "*as* a transformation according to such-and-such rules" (RFM VI.2). This is another instance of the familiar Wittgensteinian claim that no object or event carries within it some intrinsic evaluative or normative properties. No particular pattern of propositions, considered in isolation from rules showing how the propositions are related to one another, can be a mathematical proof. This, however, threatens to start a regress. For, if a proof presupposes transformation rules in order to be a proof, the transformations rules themselves, in order to be rules, must presupposes rules of application.[13] Wittgenstein rejects any attempt to stop this regress of rules by appeal to a rule that is self-interpreting or in some other way carries its application within itself. Instead Wittgenstein seeks to stop the threatened regress by embedding the transformation rules within a practice of application and use. This is what Wittgenstein here calls a "technique." It is a skilled activity, not a further set of rules.

There are two important features of this notion of a technique. The first is that "the technique is external to the pattern of proof" (RFM VI.2). There are no propositions that are part of the pattern that describe the technique for applying the transformation rules without which the pattern is not a proof. The second is that "only through a technique can we *grasp* a regularity" (RFM VI.2). This introduces Wittgenstein's concern with how we identify the conditions for sameness. Here his point is that we cannot recognize a regularity unless we have some way of applying or implementing a rule. These two features lead Wittgenstein to say that "it is only within a technique of transformation that the proof is a formal test" (RFM VI.2). Testing can be distinguished from the pattern of propositions (of the sort one might find in a mathematics text book) that is the proof. The test is the actual carrying out of the operations of the transformation rules and, as such, requires mastery of a technique.

Mastery of a technique is marked by our taking certain ways of going on as obvious such that we must get the results that we do. "This must," Wittgenstein tells us, "signifies that [the pupil] has gone in a circle" (RFM VI.8). This is the learning circle. It is temporally bounded. That which starts and ends the circle is, for example, the mundane activity of testing, of getting a mathematical result or even of continuing the natural number sequence. "$8 \times 9 = 72$" can be both the start and end of the learning circle. Nothing is different in the expression of the mathematical proposition. What differs is the normative status of that proposition for the pupil. The vehicle for that change in status is the mastery of a cognitive skill through training. The activity of testing, at the outset of the training, is what Wittgenstein calls "experimental" (RFM VI.2; cf.). It is performed without a sense of what the answer must be and without a sense of the way in which one must continue. It is the position of the initiate learner. It is important to note that the acquisition of this kind of basic skill cannot be achieved through a process of hypothesis formation and confirmation or a process of inductive extrapolation. These are much more sophisticated cognitive means for extending our knowledge that presuppose (and so cannot explain) the cognitive skills of initiate learning.

Techniques, as Wittgenstein is interested in them, are the regularities that create the space for going on in the same way. These regularities are not specified in propositional form (for then the problems identified in the regress above re-emerge), but are acted out in our reactions and actions that have been shaped by our initiate training. These regularities create the obvious ways to go on or continue in virtue of which judgments of sameness are made possible, and so rules thereby show what results must obtain. Through training in the use of the technique for continuing or proceeding correctly, the novice comes to see the activity as rule-guided which means he sees a certain outcome as necessary. Without judgments of sameness, judgments of necessity are impossible. Wittgenstein's radical conception of our judgments of sameness is that they are grounded in our shared sense of the obvious or the obvious way to go on. Initiate learning is a matter of learning what is obvious, not as expressed in explicit propositional form but as expressed in the learner's trained reactions. Mastery of the technique of going on or applying the rule is the vehicle for coming to see things as obvious. And coming to see things as obvious is the creation of the regularities necessary for judgments of similarity or sameness without which language or any rule-governed enterprise is impossible:

> For only through a technique can we *grasp* a regularity.
>
> (RFM VI.2)

> the phenomenon of language is based on regularity, on agreement in action.
>
> (RFM VI.39)

In the learning situation, regularity is guaranteed because no alternative way of responding is permitted. Through training in the use of the technique for continuing or proceeding correctly (that is, in the same way), the novice comes to see the activity as rule-governed. This means that a certain outcome is essential to using this rule. The activity of testing itself is transformed into one in which getting a particular outcome is essential to the process:

> "It must be so" means that this outcome has been defined to be essential to this process.
>
> (RFM VI.7)

> the result of the operation is defined to be the criterion that this operation has been carried out.
>
> (RFM VI.16)

In sum, the learning circle moves from the experimental activity of testing in which the pupil's reactions are shaped by the teacher, creating the sense of the obvious, to the activity of testing in which the result is seen as necessary, as what must be.

There is a sense in which the circle can be seen as Aristotelian: From the performance of particular actions, habits or dispositions of a higher order are formed the exercise of which is the performance of the same kind of actions. An important difference in the carrying out of these actions is that the actions that are the exercise of the disposition have a greater degree of autonomy than do the actions of the novice. This autonomy Wittgenstein expresses as coming to see that things must be like that. So, autonomous action and constraints or limitations go hand in hand. The function of training is thus to limit the array of behaviors available to the agent. In this way, the primary circle, the one that provides the radical explanation of the etiology of obviousness for an individual, moves from, and back to, the activity of testing itself, the difference being the autonomy with which the pupil carries out the test. This change involves a transformation in the status of the test from experiment to proof, or from what looks empirical to what is normative. This cannot be described in purely psychological terms, for it involves the transformation of the status of the test from experiment to proof. The description and explanation of the psychological change cannot be divorced from this conceptual change. It is this that makes the psychological change interesting and important, for

> It is as if we had hardened the empirical proposition into a rule. And now we have, not an hypothesis that gets tested by experience, but a paradigm with which experience is compared and judged. And so a new kind of judgment.
>
> (RFM VI.22)

Effecting this kind of change is the result of the learning circle.

Wittgenstein's discussion of what is involved in adopting a concept reveals a strong link between the process of learning and what is learned. The "must" that is part of grasping a concept comes from the training that the individual receives. This is training in a technique. I can now say in what sense the training itself is constitutive of the concept acquired. A concept like addition, for example, cannot be identified with the pattern of propositions that constitutes a proof or exemplar of addition, for it is a proof only against the background of a technique for applying the transformation rules which make it a proof. So to adopt the concept is to acquire the technique. As we have seen, technique is not something which can be captured in a set of rules itself. The technique can only be shown. Hence, Wittgenstein's repeated appeal to the italicized use of the indexical to show what is meant. What training is about is the mastery of technique. It is in virtue of this feature of technique that we can say that the process of learning (the training into a technique) is constitutive of what is learned (a concept). We do not have a concept without the technique of application, and we cannot display a technique of application except through the activity we call training. This also explains why, for Wittgenstein, "the adoption of a concept" and "the determination of a concept" are virtually interchangeable. The training we get is thus a part of what we learn.

Despite these arguments, it might nonetheless be pointed out that concepts can be acquired by different routes and that even if we do need to be trained as a matter of fact in the use of concepts, it doesn't seem impossible to acquire a concept by radically different means, by, for example, taking a pill or being struck on the head or just spontaneously knowing. Here it is suggested that whatever route of acquisition was in fact followed, the content of the belief would be no different and so the training actually received is still only history. How can this last suspicion be removed?

Let us suppose that we have a mathematics pill. Take this pill and you know addition, subtraction, multiplication, and division. No tedious hours of memorizing and drilling are required. The thought experiment is remarkably easy to entertain. A child, knowing none of these operations, is given a pill before going to bed and the next morning he awakens fully knowledgeable in these basic arithmetical operations. Q.E.D. The description of what goes on is misleading. It is asserted that the child knows these arithmetical operations in the morning. This sudden transformation in the child's competences is akin to the "aha!" experience, to the sudden realization that one now understands. Wittgenstein's discussion of rule-following in the *Investigations* opens with just this phenomenon. So what he says there should shed light on this thought experiment. In the "aha!" experience, the exclamation itself is not a report on an inner state of mind. It is rather expressive of confidence that one can go on in a certain way. Whether or not one really understands depends solely upon whether, in fact, one can go on in the correct way. What this underscores is that our concept of understanding applies to pattern-governed behavior (as well as to the more sophisticated rule-obeying behavior). What matters, from the point of view of the attribution of understanding, is whether the particular behaviors (the actual writing down of numbers) conform to the correct application of the arithmetic operators to such an extent that, given the history of training and the current context, the writing down of these particular numerals occurs because of their place in the pattern called "addition" or "multiplication" and so on.

Similarly for the child. Whether the child does know these operations and rules depends solely on what the child can go on to do. In other words, showing understanding and understanding go hand-in-hand, and in showing understanding, the child is in the situation of the learner. If, after taking the pill, the child looks blankly at a set of addition problems or writes numbers down in a seemingly random manner, then the child does not understand. Only if the child proceeds in a way that satisfies the teacher does the child understand. Checking for understanding in a child who has taken the pill is, in fact, training the child in the mastery of the skill. What the pill thought experiment leaves out is the dynamic character of the background technique, the correct way of actually manipulating symbols. Looking to training shows what that way is by seeing it displayed over time in the structuring and modifying of the behavior of the learner. That structuring is never fully eliminated though it is rightfully obscured from view in the behavior and judgments of those who have mastered a practice. The pill experiment gives rise to the illusion that the content of belief could be successfully disassociated from the background technique. Insofar then as these thought experiments are successful in suggesting that the manner of acquisition is irrelevant to the content of what is acquired, we see that the difference between initiate learner and master is narrowed. But we can also see that insofar as these thought experiments require separating the content of belief from a technique of use, they fail.

Wittgenstein makes this argument from a different direction. He asks:

> But couldn't we imagine that someone without any training should see a sum that was set to do, and straightway find himself in the mental state that in the normal course of things is only produced by training and practice? So that he knew he could calculate although he had never calculated. (One might, then, it seems, say; The training would be history, and merely as a matter of empirical fact would it be necessary for the production of knowledge.) . . . The training may of course be overlooked as mere history, if he now *always* calculates right. But that he *can* calculate he shows, to himself as well as to others only by this, that he *calculates* correctly.
>
> (RFM VI.33)

Wittgenstein's target is the idea that knowledge how to calculate is to be identified with, or in some other way closely associated with, a distinctive mental state. His objection is that the occurrence of this state is irrelevant to whether or not the subject knows how to calculate. What matters, of course, is what the subject goes on to do. Whether he can calculate is shown only by what he does. This line of argument is by now quite familiar to us. What I want to emphasize is Wittgenstein's characterization of the circumstances under which "[t]he training may of course be overlooked as mere history," namely, "if he now *always* calculates right" (RFM VI.33). The reason that the subject's behavior must be error-free, if training is to be "overlooked as mere history," is that the occurrence of error calls for correction of just the same sort that is involved in training itself. Once correction is required, training can no longer be overlooked.

That training is irrelevant, is "mere history," is an illusion fostered by imagining the error-free practice of one never trained in calculation. Yet even if a subject were error-free "that he *can* calculate he shews, to himself as well as to others only by this, that he *calculates* correctly" (RFM VI.33). As for the justification of the calculation itself, that can only be given in terms of the training and its usual results:

> the justification for the proposition $25 \times 25 = 625$ is, naturally, that if anyone has been trained in such-and-such a way, then under normal circumstances he gets 625 as the result of multiplying 25 by 25.
>
> (RFM VI.23)

In other words, the error-free agent must be assimilated to the trained agent as the only way to provide the background for assessing the correctness of the agent's calculations. But, as Wittgenstein immediately adds:

> But the arithmetical proposition does not assert *that*. It is so to speak an empirical proposition hardened into a rule. It stipulates that the rule has been followed only when that is the result of the multiplication. It is thus withdrawn from being checked by experience, but now serves as a paradigm for judging experience.
>
> (RFM VI.23)

It is because the proposition does not assert that one has been trained in the normal way that it looks possible to sever the connection between what is learned and the training involved in learning it. The idea of a mathematics pill exploits this, but even here it is not possible to effect the complete severance that is desired.

Conclusion

I have argued in an admittedly preliminary way for the following conclusions:

1   Training of the initiate learner is training into pattern-governed practices which display a regularity for reasons quite distinct from the reasons that rule-conforming behaviour and rule-obeying behaviour display regularity. Pattern-governed behaviours occur because of their place within a pattern.
2   Initiate training in language requires that the background context be structured and sustained by the adults who extend a "courtesy" to the

utterances of the child, treating them as genuine judgments, requests, questions, and the like.

3   Genuinely normative practices, that is, practices that are not causally necessitated but are structured by, and admit of evaluation by reference to, a standard, norm, or rule, are social. Thus, no individual in radical isolation from all social practices can engage in actions that are correct or incorrect. A period of training or learning is required to become a practitioner.

4   All concept use presupposes a background technique by which a concept is used, and that technique cannot itself be expressed as a set of rules or concepts without engendering a regress.

5   Training in techniques creates the regularities of behaviour necessary for any judgment of sameness, and it is for this reason that one can say the process of learning is constitutive of what is learned. Moreover, this explains why the psychological sense of the obvious is grounded in the grammatical, not the other way around.

In this chapter, I hope that I have been able to show that by taking seriously those many passages in Wittgenstein's later philosophy that concern initiate learning we gain additional insight into Wittgenstein's conception of language, concept mastery, and his contrast between the grammatical and the empirical.

8 The etiology of the obvious
Wittgenstein and the elimination of indeterminacy

Much of the discussion of Wittgenstein's later philosophy focuses on one or other of three arguments drawn from the *Philosophical Investigations*. The critique of denotational theories of meaning, the "paradox of interpretation" with respect to rule-following, and the private language argument. My aim in this chapter is to identify a deep underlying issue that is common to all three (though I will consider only the first two). That is what I will call "the problem of normative similarity." This concerns the normative role played by our basic judgments of sameness or identity with respect to categorization and rule-following. The arguments Wittgenstein develops against ostensive definition and rules, as the primitive or basic devices for fixing the normative standards of language use, show that both are indeterminate in their application and so cannot account for the normativity of language. Successful ostension and rule-following presuppose a background of what is obviously the same to the participants. And, according to Wittgenstein, that background consists in the mastery of techniques of application that are acquired in the process of learning. The process of learning techniques is in this way *constitutive* of what is learned, namely, of what is the same as what or what it is to go on in the same way. In learning techniques for using words, one is acquiring concepts and so learning how things must be. The normativity of our practices involves non-causal necessity, that is, logical or grammatical necessity. The aim of this chapter is to better understand Wittgenstein's treatment of necessity.

In developing this line of argument in Wittgenstein, I will contrast Wittgenstein's indeterminacy arguments with Quine's indeterminacy arguments with respect to translation and reference. Precisely because there are important affinities between their views, the comparison highlights more strikingly just where Wittgenstein and Quine diverge in their respective conceptions of language. The most important of these differences concerns the place of theorizing in language use and acquisition. For Quine, the import of the indeterminacy argument and the rejection of the analytic–synthetic distinction is that the web of belief is a web of empirical hypotheses. Theorizing is essential to all language use. For Wittgenstein, there is a complexity to our language games that requires both a substantive distinction between grammatical (or conceptual) propositions and empirical propositions and a place for judgments of the obvious, judgments that are not subject to indeterminacy. Not all language use can involve theorizing.

1 The problem of normative similarity

Wittgenstein objects to certain traditional philosophical pictures of categorization and rule-following. In both cases, part of his concern is to show that no object is inherently representational or normative.[1] An object, whether a commonplace everyday object like an apple or a post in the road, or something less substantial like a mental image, has representational and normative properties only within a context of actual use and against a background of cognitive skills. Fundamental to skills of application are those for judging sameness, sameness of kind and sameness of action.

For Wittgenstein an investigation into our judgments of sameness implicates how we learn to make these judgments. So, in his early examination of the denotational theory of meaning, Wittgenstein attacks this theory by undermining its companion picture of how language is acquired. The picture of language acquisition is a simple one. Adults point to an object in the child's immediate environment and name it. The child then associates the name with the object and henceforth uses that name for all similar objects. The effectiveness of the ostensive definition presupposes the pupil's capacity to grasp that the baptismal object is an exemplar that functions as the standard for correct application of the term uttered. Wittgenstein challenges the adequacy of this picture to explain what he is after, namely, the normativity of language itself. Naming cannot in general fix meaning because it is itself a semantically sophisticated act that presupposes conceptual stage setting and language mastery: "only someone who already knows how to do something with it can significantly ask a name" (PI §31). If that background understanding is eliminated, then ostensive definition cannot succeed, for it is always indeterminate in itself. There is no such thing as absolute similarity, only similarity relative to some description or aspect. Thus, the success of ostensive definition depends upon the recipient already having that background and conceptual competence that is required. For ostension to play a role in acquisition of language, it cannot be that of ostensive definition. There must be a way of categorizing that is not a matter of naming.[2]

A related, and equally radical, point is made in connection with rules. A rule qua formula (like the formula "+1" of PI §185) is indeterminate unless combined with a method of application. Some have held that the method of application can be supplied by an interpretation of the rule. But Wittgenstein objects that interpretations of rules "hang in the air along with what [they] interpret, and cannot give any support" to how the rule is applied (PI §198). Interpretations must be grounded in a kind of rule-following that is not informed by interpretation, but which provides a non-interpretive method of application against which interpretations can be made. Without this, interpretation collapses and with it any normative constraint. The "paradox of interpretation" is that our traditional device for determining correct usage (namely, interpretation of the rule) results in the collapse of the very distinction between correct and incorrect.

Use of interpretation and ostensive definition both presuppose the mastery of normative practices. Being intrinsically indeterminate, both need "stage setting," a background in virtue of which category judgments can be made, rules cited, concepts applied, derivations completed, and actions performed. The background itself cannot be more of the same – it cannot be more rules, interpretations, or bare pointings. If it were, it would be subject to the same kind of indeterminacy that affects ostensive definition and interpretation when these are seen as fixing meaning (that is, providing the identity conditions for the reapplication of a term). Rather the background is that against which we interpret, name, and justify by appeal to rules. Wittgenstein's task is to provide an account of our background normative practices that eliminates the indeterminacy that affects ostensive definition and interpretation while retaining the normativity of our practices. This is his response to the problem of normative similarity.

There are important affinities between Wittgenstein's two arguments and Quine's arguments for the indeterminacy of translation and the inscrutability of reference. Wittgenstein argues that ostensive definition, in itself, cannot fix reference; and that interpretation, if the only method for using rules, results in the collapse of the very distinction between correct and incorrect. Referring and interpreting both require background stage setting. Quine argues that different, and incompatible, translation schemes, because they involve different kinds of apparatus of individuation, are fully compatible with all the evidence available to the field linguist and so reference is inscrutable. There is an ineliminable indeterminacy in what we are referring to, precisely because reference can only be established by way of a background theory. These look like arguments that should lead to similar views of language, reference, and meaning. Nevertheless, the conclusions each draws from his arguments are quite different. This difference in the morals they draw for language is striking for a further reason: Both find language learning philosophically significant, agreeing in important respects in their characterizations of language learning. Both take the holophrastic sentence of early language learning as basic, not the word as a single referring expression; and both reject nativist accounts of language learning in favor of conditioning accounts (broadly conceived). Yet Wittgenstein seeks to show that it is the traditional philosophical theories of meaning and language that are the source of the indeterminacies, not ordinary language itself, whereas Quine endorses indeterminacy as part and parcel of our "home language" even as we "acquiesce in its use." This difference is rooted in their very different pictures of language and the methodologies employed to support these pictures.

Quine's approach to the problem of meaning is to begin with the situation of a field linguist trying to provide a translation of a radically alien language, a language of which the linguist knows nothing. His only resources for translating this language are the verbal and other behaviors of the natives, the environment in which they act, and his own language and sensory experience. These constraints on the evidential and theoretical resources of the linguist are revelatory, on Quine's view, of language and meaning in general. Wherever Quine discusses this situation of radical translation, he also draws parallels between the linguist and the child acquiring its first language. For both linguist and child, observation sentences, namely, those sentences "that are directly and firmly associated with our stimulations" provide "the entering wedge," as Quine puts it, for learning language and translating a language (Quine 1990: pp. 3–4). What Quine sees as common to the linguist and the child is the meager evidential basis each has for constructing a complex language. What supports this description of both the linguist and the child is Quine's fundamental commitment to a scientific naturalism that accords the sciences the prerogative in determining truth. The sciences of behavior, for Quine, are the neural sciences, especially the study of the psychophysiology of the sensory systems and scientific behaviorism, each of which identifies the stimulation of our sensory organs as the interface between ourselves and the world. In consequence of adopting this claim, both linguist and child can only acquire an understanding of the language to which they are exposed using the stimulations to their sensory receptors as their evidentiary starting point.

The only method available to the linguist is to form hypotheses about which of the native's utterances report (or at least correspond to) the presence of publicly salient phenomena. His example is the now famous hypothesis that the native utterance "Gavagai!" means "Rabbit!" (or "Lo, a rabbit!") in English. The only way the linguist can test this hypothesis is by actively questioning the native to see whether he assents to the question

"Gavagai?" when he has been sensorily stimulated by rabbits and dissents when he has not been so stimulated. The success of this hypothesis testing requires that the linguist can correctly identify assent and dissent in the native language and that he can empathetically identify the sensory stimulations of the native. The entire approach takes similarity of sensory stimulations, both for a single individual at different times and between individuals, as the only empirical evidence for constructing translation manuals or acquiring language. Quine's approach to language learning (whether that of the field linguist or the child) takes both the natural similarity of sensory stimulations and their logical interconnections with a growing web of belief for granted.[3] By contrast, Wittgenstein's problem of normative similarity extends precisely to what we can take for granted with respect to similarity in our observations as well as in our inferences.

Wittgenstein's response to his own indeterminacy arguments reflects a very different approach to language. Its central idea is that of the language game, which he characterizes in three ways: As a methodological tool in examining philosophical theories, as akin to the way in which children learn, and as an explanatory device describing language use in relation to other forms of acting (PI §5). Wittgenstein uses language games in all three ways to explore the stage setting or background involved in ostensive definition and interpretation. The background concerns our capacity for taking a range of objects or properties to be of the same kind and our actions and judgments to be going on in the same way – without their being reducible to sensory stimulation and without our doing so by applying principles of identity or interpretations of rules or hypotheses of use. In other words, for Wittgenstein the problem of normative similarity arises precisely because neither of the resources that Quine draws upon (sensory stimulations and hypothesis formation) characterize our capacity for judging sameness. This can be seen early in the *Investigations* where Wittgenstein discusses the role of ostension both in learning and in fixing the meaning of words (PI §1–38). Wittgenstein contrasts ostensive definition, which uses an object as an exemplar to fix the meaning of a word, and ostensive teaching, which effects an association between a word and an object (PI §6). Ostensive teaching does not fix meaning, even if it is an important part (as both Wittgenstein and Quine believe) of initiate language learning. This distinction is one that Quine completely overlooks, and it is for this reason that he misunderstands, and so underestimates, Wittgenstein's critique of ostensive definition.

Quine takes Wittgenstein's argument to be that ostensive definition requires the use of a kind term or sortal (Quine 1969b: p. 31). This he rejects on the ground that our innate sensory capabilities are such that we can be conditioned to respond to a particular property, say, a color like red, without the explicit use of the sortal expression "color." Indeed, for Quine, such basic conditioned associations between natural properties and words are the basis for all subsequent language acquisition. It provides the foundation from which we bootstrap ourselves up to higher levels of linguistic competence. There are passages in Wittgenstein that support a similar picture, but with the following important difference. Ostensive teaching is not simply a kind of stimulus–response conditioning. Rather it effects an association in a *normatively* structured setting. Or, as Wittgenstein puts it,

> Don't you understand the call "Slab!" if you act upon it in such-and-such a way?—Doubtless the ostensive teaching helped to bring this about, but only together with a particular training. With different training the same ostensive teaching of these words would have effected a quite different understanding.
>
> (PI §6)

By the use of the word "training," Wittgenstein means to draw attention to the practice within which ostensive teaching occurs. Different training involving the same association of a word and object would effect a "quite different understanding." It is not that Quine ignores the importance of the social setting within which conditioning occurs, but that he seems not to accept the significance that Wittgenstein attributes to this. Where Wittgenstein and Quine agree is that we are endowed with an array of natural reactions to certain kinds of situations and training. Quine seeks to identify these in terms of stimulations to our sensory receptors while Wittgenstein identifies them in terms of our behaviors in response to certain situations.

The normativity of the ostensive training of the novice is provided by society in the form of the teacher. Such training does not fix the meaning of the words (for their meaning determines the nature of the training), but it does endow the novice with the skills for using the words appropriately. Such training could occur, as Quine maintains, without the explicit use of sortals in the teaching itself.[4] Ostensive definition, on the other hand, does fix meaning in the sense that it supplies an exemplar or paradigm. But to know *how* to take the exemplar on the basis of its presentation does require a sortal to differentiate which property is the relevant one. This kind of explanation requires that the recipient be a competent language user and that a sortal be used if the definition is to succeed. So, Quine's quick dismissal of Wittgenstein's view of ostensive definition misses the point by conflating ostensive teaching and ostensive definition. Training draws on our natural reactions which are tied to the forms of sensory experience to which we are sensitive, but these natural reactions are not based upon the sensory stimulations to our perceptual organs in the way that Quine maintains. Ostensive training does not provide meager evidence, not even meager evidence presented in an orderly fashion by the teacher, nor does it fix meaning. It is not a matter of evidence at all but of exploiting the natural reactions of the novice in initiating that person into a practice or language game.

Parallel to this contrast between ostensive training and ostensive definition, but developed much more fully, is Wittgenstein's contrast between the role of interpretation or hypothesis in understanding a rule and what he calls our "blindly obeying" a custom in which we act as a matter of course (cf. PI §219) – that is, as we were trained to do. A mark of that blind obedience within a practice is the harmonious agreement and certainty among practitioners concerning what is the same, whether this concerns categorization or rule-governed action. It is a shared sense of the obvious that is acquired paradigmatically in initiate learning, in the grasping of rules and concepts through the acquisition and exercise of skills and techniques. And this shared, unquestioned, and certain sense of the obvious is normative. It can be objected that characterizing blind obedience as normative is to conflate automatic individual behavior and normative collective practice. It suggests that the normativity of our language games is a function of individually acquired automatic behavior.

But this would be to misunderstand Wittgenstein's point in appealing to our blindly obeying a rule as a response to the indeterminacy arguments raised in connection with rule-following. It is a misunderstanding because it presupposes an oversimplified conception of normativity. Just as ostensive teaching is a means that we humans have in associating word and object without that association fixing the meaning of the word, so blind obedience is that automatic and unthinking judgment distinctive of judgments of the obvious without that automatic response constituting the standard, as it were, of sameness. Both ostensive teaching and blind obedience occur within a language game, that is, within a social temporally extended practice. As the discussion of ostensive definition leads to an examination of the philosophical notion of reference, so the discussion of blind obedience within a practice leads to an investigation into the nature of logical necessity, of ways of judging and thinking that are implicit in what we do. We cannot understand the normativity of our practices without understanding how necessity, broadly considered, is an integral part of all normative practices. Our bedrock "blind" judgments and actions concerning normative similarity are part of that background without which rule-following, interpretation, and theorizing are impossible. So, to understand our "blind" judgments and actions is to understand how normativity enters and infuses human life. Wittgenstein's task thus can be seen as providing an account of the normative dimension of human life that eliminates indeterminacy. To do this requires showing the place of non-causal necessity in our practices.

2 Normative similarity and background technique

The notion of a background against which, or in virtue of which, the foreground is made salient or possible is familiar. It is now (virtually) the conventional wisdom of philosophy. We can distinguish several such notions. Knowledge and theoretical claims presuppose background theory and methodology. Beliefs, perceptual and otherwise, are embedded within a network of beliefs and other intentional states. Perceptual saliency presupposes a perceptual background. Words have meaning only in the context of a sentence. Insofar as meaning is use, the use of words must occur in the context of ongoing practices. So, appeal to a background is closely associated with holistic approaches to knowledge, mind, and language – or, if not holistic, at least anti-atomistic theories. This is certainly true of both Wittgenstein and Quine.

As a first step in better understanding Wittgenstein's characterization of the background, which includes the obvious, I shall look to Part VI of the *Remarks on the Foundations of Mathematics*.[5] Part VI concerns the acquisition (or adoption, as Wittgenstein puts it) of concepts, and in particular mathematical concepts. He thinks that how we learn these has profound implications for our philosophical understanding of the special justificatory status of proof and its grounding in our background judgments of what is obviously the same. He proposes providing what he calls "radical explanations" for the justificatory status of proofs by appeal to how we are trained in the mastery of mathematical techniques. The effect of such training is to see the hardness of the logical "must" as a "lesson...drawn from the scene."

Wittgenstein opens Part VI with a characterization of mathematical proofs as that which "give propositions an order. They organize them" (RFM VI.1). He spells this out in a Kantian manner: "The concept of a formal test presupposes the concept of a transformation-rule, and hence of a technique" (RFM VI.2). A proof is a pattern of propositions, a way of "organizing propositions." Any such organized set of propositions – if it is to be understood as a proof and indeed is a proof – is subject to transformation rules. The point is clear. No particular pattern of propositions, considered in isolation from rules showing how the propositions are related to one another, can be a mathematical proof. There must be rules of transformation. The point here is much the same as the point he makes with respect to ostensive definition and rules in general. Just as ostensive definition presupposes stage setting and rules require methods of application, so proofs presuppose a background of transformation rules. Appealing to transformation rules, however, threatens to start a regress. For, if a proof presupposes transformation rules in order to be a proof, the transformation rules themselves, in order to be rules, must presuppose rules of application. Wittgenstein rejects any attempt to stop this regress of rules by appeal to a rule that is self-interpreting or in some other way carries its application within itself. Instead Wittgenstein stops the threatened regress by embedding the transformation rules within a practice of application, which provides the background against which the proof can be constructed. This is what Wittgenstein here calls a "technique." It is a skilled activity, not a further set of rules. Implicit in that activity is much that stands fast for the practitioner in the exercise of that skill. Indispensable to Wittgenstein's understanding of what stands fast for us is the idea that such implicit commitments are not reflectively open to full articulation. Techniques can be shown in how we are trained.

To make these general remarks more concrete, let us take as an example of a proof and its relation to transformation rules Euclid's proof for the infinity of prime numbers.[6] This proof justifies the proposition that the prime numbers are infinite. Here it is:[7]

Let a, b, c,…k be any prime numbers
  Take the product *abc…k* and add unity.
  Then $(abc…k+1)$ is either a prime number or not a prime number.
  (1) If it *is*, we have added another prime number to those given.
  (2) If it is *not*, it must be measured by some prime number, say *p*.
  Now *p* cannot be identical with any of the prime numbers *a*, *b*, *c*,…*k*.
  For, if it is, it will divide *abc…k*.
Therefore, since it divides $(abc…k+1)$ also, it will measure the difference, or unity: which is impossible.
  Therefore in any case we have obtained one fresh prime number.
  And the process can be carried on to any extent.

(Euclid 1956: p. 143)

To offer this proof as a formal test for the infinity of prime numbers requires the ordered use of transformation rules such that for any finite set of prime numbers, a new prime number can be constructed. The transformation rules include certain rules of logic (like modus ponens and assumption introduction) and rules of calculation (add 1 to the product of the prime numbers).[8]

Using this proof as our blueprint or set of instructions for how to order our use of transformation rules, "we have," as one commentator on the proof says, "obtained one fresh prime number. And the process can be carried on to any extent" (Euclid 1956: p. 413). To construct this proof requires that we can use transformation rules of logic and of calculation. These transformation rules themselves presuppose techniques of inference and calculation. Using modus ponens or assumption introduction involves techniques for identifying premises, drawing conclusions, and constraining options. Adding, multiplying, dividing involve techniques for manipulating numerals to maintain equivalencies. The proof itself is a recipe for using these techniques in an ordered fashion to create the desired result as stated by the mathematical proposition that the number of primes is infinite. The meaning of that mathematical proposition is given by its proof. It is not a metaphysical proof concerning the totality of prime numbers. Rather it expresses the fact that for any finite set of prime numbers, it is always possible to construct another, and this process is indefinitely repeatable.

Wittgenstein explicates the close relation among mathematical proposition, proof, and transformation rules as a conceptual or grammatical connection. That there is such a close relation is not a matter of empirical hypothesis. Euclid's proof for the infinity of primes is an organized pattern of propositions that provides a "picture" of the proposition that the number of primes is infinite. But the background techniques involved in calculating or drawing inferences are activities, ways of applying the rules in the actual construction of a formal test. The foundational questions concern issues of application and so the production of regularities. For Wittgenstein, issues concerning application can only be explained in terms of the techniques of rule use. Mastery of techniques, as developed and judged in training contexts, just constitutes what it is to go on in the same way.

There are two important features of Wittgenstein's notion of a technique:

> only through a technique can we *grasp* a regularity....The technique is external to the pattern of the proof. One might have a perfectly accurate view of the proof, yet not understand it as a transformation according to such-and-such rules.
>
> (RFM VI.2)

His first point is that we cannot recognize a regularity unless we have some way of applying or implementing a rule. In other words, we can recognize regularities in nature, in society, in mathematics only to the extent that we can regularize our own behavior.[9] Using a technique is engaging in self-regulating behavior in certain contexts. The regularities (and so similarities) of nature are not forced upon us by some kind of natural resemblance or causal necessity alone; nor are they available to us by way of some principle or ideal of identity. This self-regulating behavior that marks the mastery of technique is the basis for what counts as the same. Judgments of sameness are a function of our own repetitive regulated behavior in virtue of which we can grasp other regularities. Self-regulated behavior is constrained behavior, not in virtue of being an instance of a physical law but in virtue of the subject being trained in techniques. Constraint, repetitive regular behavior, and normative judgment of sameness go together.[10]

The second feature of technique states that: "the technique is external to the pattern of proof" (RFM VI.2). There are no propositions that are part of the pattern that describe the techniques for applying the transformation rules without which the pattern is not a proof.[11] So one might see the proof written out and yet not be able to "understand it as a transformation according to such-and-such rules" (RFM VI.2). This is the situation of one who has not studied mathematics or logic and sees a proof or derivation written down, but does not understand how or why the successive lines of the proof or derivation are introduced. That individual cannot see a proof in the pattern of propositions, for he does not see it as an organized pattern in which the conclusion must be what it is. The pattern which is there cannot be recognized as such until the subject has mastered the techniques for using the rules through the actual repetition of constrained behavior. It is against the mastery of the background techniques that a proof is differentiated from a mere series of sentences.[12] We mark that difference syntactically. A proof is stated non-temporally whereas the activity of proving a mathematical proposition is temporally bounded.[13] Wittgenstein is interested in precisely this move we make from taking the activity of testing to be "so to speak, experimental" to taking it as a proof for a mathematical proposition. The distinction that Wittgenstein is drawing can perhaps be made more intuitively appealing by relating it to the everyday contrast we draw between rote learning and understanding concepts. In rote learning, the pupil can produce the formulae or propositions but cannot use them to do anything. With understanding, the pupil can use the proof as a recipe for generating new prime numbers from any given finite set of primes. A list of sentences is no more a proof than a list of objects is a description of a state of affairs.[14] Structure or organization must be added to both. Normative similarity judgments, involving the mastery of techniques, are part of that structuring.

We can draw a contrast, then, between the idea of a network of beliefs (and other intentional states) and the idea of the background techniques or know-how. This contrast brings out an important difference between Wittgenstein's two indeterminacy arguments. The stage setting that Wittgenstein argues successful ostensive definition requires is a network of beliefs that prepares the place for introducing the new term. The paradox of interpretation argument, on the other hand, shows the need for something other than more of the same (that is, more beliefs or propositions or rules). It shows the need for background technique. Because background technique cannot be captured in any description or set of rules, it can only be shown in the context of a language game. The place where it is best shown is the place where it is acquired – in the context of the initiate learner. How we learn these techniques is constitutive of what we learn precisely because what we learn cannot be separated from the context of use. What this also shows is that, echoing Plato, denotational theories of meaning are twice removed from linguistic reality. Ostension, as explaining meaning, presupposes a system of beliefs which in turn presupposes background techniques of sign use.

So, techniques of use are the source of our bedrock judgments of sameness. Linguistic competence consists, in large part, in the mastery of such techniques. Wittgenstein's very method itself of investigating theories of language by using language games of a familiar sort undermines the point of trying to separate language from language use. The kind of holism that Wittgenstein is endorsing here is *heterogeneous*, involving, as we have seen, not only the idea of a network of beliefs but also the idea of a background of techniques acquired over time in first language learning. As these techniques can only be demonstrated, their justification (or "radical explanation," as Wittgenstein puts it in RFM VI.14 and 23) lies with an appeal to how we learn, that is, to how we come to see that "matters must be like that." This is the topic of the next section, but first I need to bring out how Quine's position differs on these matters.

An intimate connection between what language is and how we acquire it is also found in Quine's writings. But, as we know, his account is governed by a very different method of inquiry into language, namely, that of the field linguist trying to translate the radically alien language of an unknown people. Part of what supports this approach is Quine's sense of a deep affinity between the position of the radical translator and the child. Both must develop complex theories using sensory experience as their sole, but meager, evidential base. As a result of assimilating first language acquisition and any act of communication to radical translation in this way, Quine concludes that the indeterminacy of reference revealed by his thought experiment is an ineliminable feature of all language use:

On deeper reflection, radical translation begins at home....Our usual domestic rule of translation is indeed the homophonic one, which simply carries each string of phonemes into itself.

(Quine 1969a: p. 46)

So, in the end, our similarity judgments derive from a limited natural resemblance (similarity within the quality space of each sensory system) and indeterminate theorizing, indeterminate precisely because natural similarity in perceptual quality space (such as, a rabbity pattern of retinal stimulation) is compatible with rival ontological theories. The holism that Quine draws upon to support this is a *homogeneous* holism. All is assimilated into the network of beliefs, which for Quine is a network of interconnected sentences, a network which includes even the laws of logic and rules of inference. The only background, in the sense in which I have been contrasting network and background, is the physiology of our various sensory systems.

A second way in which the views of Wittgenstein and Quine diverge in how they construe their respective indeterminacy arguments concerns the derivative semantic status of words, and so reference. Both agree that reference cannot be semantically basic. This can look like their both agreeing (minimally) with Frege's context principle that the meaning of the individual word is a function of its role in a sentence (especially, an assertoric sentence). While this is true of Quine's view, it can only distort Wittgenstein's position. For Quine, the holophrastic observation sentence used by the radical interpreter and the child is the entering wedge into language. But, for Wittgenstein, the entering wedge for the child is participation in a primitive language game just as the entering wedge, methodologically, for understanding what language is, is the primitive language game, the paradigm of which is Wittgenstein's builders game. When, after a period of gathering evidence, Quine's linguist hears a native say "Gavagai!," he hears "Lo, a rabbit!" When Wittgenstein's builder, who is trained in the building game, hears "Slab!," he hears a call to action.[15] This difference reflects Quine's conception of language as an interconnected set of theories and Wittgenstein's conception of language as ongoing regulated activities involving the coordination and cooperation of the participants.

A final point of contrast will take us to the next stage of the argument. Quine's indeterminacy arguments are part of his ongoing attack on the analytic–synthetic distinction and the idea of non-causal necessity. The language of necessity, for Quine, belongs to the realm of pragmatic considerations, indicating our reluctance to revise or give up certain claims. For Wittgenstein, however, the indeterminacy arguments show the inadequacies or incoherence of certain philosophical theories of language and meaning. Wittgenstein retains the contrast between the conceptual and the empirical, and with that distinction, a place for necessity. What must be is not just what we are loathe to give up, but what stands fast for us as obvious or implicit in what is obvious. Indeed, what Wittgenstein is arguing is that unless something stands fast for us, we can't even be in the position to be loathe to give anything up.

3 Normativity and "psychologized" necessity

As I noted above, Wittgenstein takes the non-temporal expression of a mathematical proposition as a syntactic mark of the normative role played by the proposition and its proof.[16] Mathematical propositions, like "The number of primes is infinite" or even "2 + 2 = 4" are themselves norms, not statements of metaphysical truths. Abstract objects, like numbers, are not metaphysical entities, but abstractions from our actual mathematical practices for which the techniques of use set the standards for reidentification. Returning again to the proposition that the number of primes is infinite, Wittgenstein holds that it is a rule and its proof is "a *blue-print* for the employment of a rule" (RFM VI.3). As such, it "stands behind the rule as a picture that justifies the rule" (RFM VI.3). So, a proof justifies a rule not by deducing certain eternal features of numbers which the metaphysical proposition describes. Nor does it provide inductively based evidence for extrapolating a mathematical generalization from the behavior of objects under manipulation by us. Rather the proof justifies the rule by showing how the rule is to be used. Euclid's proof for the infinity of primes is a blueprint or recipe for constructing a new prime number for any given finite number of primes. As Wittgenstein says, it "teaches us a technique of finding a prime number between p and $p! + 1$. And we become convinced that this technique must always lead to a prime number $> p$. Or that we have miscalculated if it doesn't" (RFM VI.6). The proof, then, as a picture that justifies the rule, is not a representation, that is, it does not show how things are, but how to produce what must be. Wittgenstein expresses this by saying that "mathematics as such is always measure, not thing measured" (RFM III.75). In other words, the elements of the picture are not isomorphic to some possible state of affairs, but are instructions for creating an isomorphism between a (normative) proposition and what actually occurs:

A proof leads me to say: this *must* be like this....What does "it *must* be like this" mean here in contrast with "it is like this"?...

I want to say that the *must* corresponds to a track which I lay down in language.

(RFM VI. 30)

If we grant Wittgenstein his thesis that "mathematics as such" is special because its propositions are normative rather than metaphysical, we need to better understand normativity and the necessity it imposes. This requires rethinking the modalities of necessity, contingency, and possibility in terms of normativity rather than metaphysical reality. Broadly this is a conventionalist account, but not one that appeals to either our intentions or our decisions. Moreover, his account of necessity is not restricted to the case of mathematical propositions. It applies much more broadly, with the mathematical case providing the prototype for his account of the necessity of the grammatical propositions of the *Investigations*,[17] the propositions that hold fast of *On Certainty*,[18] and the adoption of concepts. As such, it can be seen as an account of "conceptual truth," though that is a misnomer for Wittgenstein. Not because there is no such thing for him as propositions that are *conceptually* constraining but because there is no such thing as conceptual *truths*. Grammatical propositions and propositions that hold fast are no more truths (whether metaphysical truths or truths by virtue of meaning) than is the mathematical proposition that the number of primes is infinite. Like that mathematical proposition, they are not truths at all, but norms. As we know, in all three of his major critiques, Wittgenstein argues for two claims: First, that no object is inherently normative; and second that the individual mind cannot be the source of those norms (without generating regress or paradox). So, Wittgenstein is looking for a way of characterizing normativity, one that does not attempt to explain "the determination of a concept," as he puts it in the *Remarks*, in terms of either the powers of the individual mind or the object denoted by a concept. We can see that this revival of a contrast between conceptual (or grammatical) propositions and empirical propositions runs directly counter to Quine's central thesis that no such distinction can be made. However, Wittgenstein's way of drawing the distinction does not run afoul of Quine's objections, as it is not a distinction between kinds of truths but between norms of a game and moves within the game.

The expression "the determination of a concept" can be explicated in terms of two dimensions that are closely related to each other. The first concerns the logical space of concepts and the second the prescriptive role of concepts. These are dimensions of any norm. The first concerns what should be done (the normative content of a concept) and the second prescribes doing it (the prescriptive content). Wittgenstein does not develop a theory of concepts, though he speaks in terms of concepts in connection with ostensive definition, family resemblance, and mastery of techniques for using words or propositions. The logical space of a concept is created by the background techniques of application, whether these concern the use of words or inferential moves among claims, requests, commands and the like. In a typical Wittgensteinian reversal, logical space is seen as a function of the actual application of words within a language game, rather than the other way around. The logical space of a concept is realized in the normatively shaped behavior of the participants in the language game. To become a participant is to master the relevant techniques through a process of training. Participants, through a process of training, come to see that things "must be like that" (RFM VI.7). The justification that proofs afford their rules is due to the normative role played by the proof as a blueprint or recipe for getting the desired result. It shows how to obtain the results one ought to get if one has grasped the concept or rule. It does not, however, predict what will happen. If I don't follow the proof or I get distracted in the middle of things or if I think "who cares?," or if any other of an indefinite range of contingencies occur, I won't construct a prime number. This underscores the fact that "what I derive from the picture is only a rule. And this rule does not stand to the picture as an empirical proposition stands to reality. – The picture does not shew that such-and-such happens. It only shews that what does happen can be taken in this way" (RFM VI.5), namely, as following the rule correctly or not. The range of possibilities, the range of possible uses, is thus a matter of how in fact we make judgments and draw inferences. What we find obvious and what we find must be the case gives us the differentiation required for the creation of the logical space of possibilities.

In short, the actual use of an expression creates the space for the concept. That we share judgments about what is obvious and what must be the case creates the logical space of the concept. Wittgenstein approaches this same issue from another direction as well, by looking at the special way in which a proof justifies a rule. A proof justifies its rule by showing the order in which various techniques are to be used to produce the *predetermined* outcome (as specified by the rule). The series of prime numbers must be infinite. The answer to 9 times 8 must be 72. The "must" expresses a normative necessity that is not captured by the classical characterization of necessity in terms of truth, whether in terms of metaphysical reality or the law of non-contradiction. On Wittgenstein's view, the law of non-contradiction is simply too thin to support any substantive judgment of contradiction in a particular case. Rather our understanding of the law comes from our recognition of concrete cases of contradiction. This criticism of the law of non-contradiction is akin to a familiar criticism of Kant's Categorical Imperative. The Categorical Imperative, it is argued, is too thin and abstract to inform concrete moral judgment or behavior. It is compatible with any behavior provided the description of that behavior is appropriately gerrymandered. So, the abstract law of non-contradiction does not enable us to identify particular contradictions. Rather the result one gets in the particular instance of going by the rule "is, so to speak, *overdetermined*. Overdetermined by the fact that the result of the operation is defined to be the criterion that this operation has been carried out" (RFM VI.16). " 'It must be so' means that this outcome has been defined to be essential to this process" (RFM VI.7). If one does not get 72 when multiplying 8 and 9, then one has not multiplied correctly, not because we see that the law of non-contradiction has been violated but because getting 72 is "defined" as the result of multiplying these two numbers. Some commentators have preferred to express this as stating that the relation between a rule and its correct application is internal.[19] Their point is to emphasize that these propositions cannot be empirical propositions, subject to substantiation by experience. The rule is a way of judging what is done, not describing what is done. Getting that particular result is itself a criterion for having followed the rule (cf. RFM VII.61, esp. pp. 424–5).

Clearly this contrasts with Quine's insistence that the result one gets in going by the rule is underdetermined, if not indeterminate. For Quine, the very features that make room for normativity – that neither natural causation nor rational interpretation determines techniques of use – provide the grounds for claiming the indeterminacy of our concepts. How can Wittgenstein then see in these same features of rule-following practices an *over*determination of acceptable results? For Quine, propositions like "the number of primes is infinite" (or a Wittgensteinian example like "every human being has two human parents") are embedded in a network of sentences like any other sentence, such as "roses don't flourish in Illinois summers." The only difference is in how extensively the sentences are connected to other sentences in the web. They express empirical propositions and as such are underdetermined by the evidence available to us and indeterminate as to their reference. That is not to say that we won't believe them with certainty, but that certainty is not derived from the epistemic warrant that is available. The certainty, it seems, is psychological and to be justified, if at all, pragmatically. How can Wittgenstein, who would agree that the inductively available evidence for these claims is meager and certainly is not what underwrites our believing mathematical propositions, maintain that getting these results is nonetheless overdetermined by the rule? This explanation comes in connection with how we learn these rules.

This introduces the second element in the determination of a concept, the prescriptive role of concepts and rules. This is a function of how we acquire the relevant background techniques and their associated world pictures through initiate training. It is through the acquisition of such bedrock practices that we grasp the obvious and the necessary. Initiate learning is marked by the same blind acceptance of ways of going on that Wittgenstein appeals to in his response to the Paradox of Interpretation. Quine's failure to eliminate indeterminacy is explained by his misunderstanding of the conditions that must be met for language use, namely, the mastery of bedrock practices that provide the background of shared judgments of the obvious, of normative similarity. This leads to his mistaken assimilation of language learning to the situation of radical translation. But, for Wittgenstein, grasping a normative necessity is to be explained in terms of "signif[ying] that the learner has gone in a circle," not in terms of the learner's having rationally intuited the number system or tested various hypotheses concerning the use of words. So, to understand Wittgenstein's account of grasping a necessity, which is to engage in normative rule-following, we need to identify the learning circle to which Wittgenstein appeals.

The learning circle is temporally bounded. It is the actual process of teaching a pupil how to multiply, for example. The pupil begins and ends with the same mundane activity of getting a mathematical result. Something as simple as the activity of multiplying 8 by 9 to get 72 can be both the start and the end of the learning circle. Nothing is different in the expression of the arithmetic proposition. At the beginning of learning and at the end of learning (when the pupil sees that 8 times 9 must result in getting 72), the same expression is inscribed "$8 \times 9 = 72$." What differs is the normative status of that proposition for the pupil. The vehicle for that change in status is the mastery of a cognitive skill or technique through training. These skills are modes of behavioral self-regulation that create the space for going on in the same way by constituting a set of regularities (mathematics) or by revealing certain natural regularities (categorization). These techniques, as we have seen, cannot be fully specified in propositional form (for then the threatened regress re-emerges), but are acted out in our natural reactions and actions that have been shaped by our initiate training.[20] It is in virtue of the fact that these techniques cannot be specified propositionally that Quine sees indeterminacy in our acts of referring. But, for Wittgenstein, these techniques constitute the obvious ways to go on or continue in virtue of which judgments of sameness are made possible. The notion of what is obvious is normative.

Judgments of sameness, then, are not grounded solely in natural resemblances in the world to which our sensory systems are sensitive, but in our shared sense of the obvious or the obvious way to go on. An isomorphism is created between the techniques we have acquired through training and certain natural regularities. But it is the set of techniques (in part) that determine what natural regularities are salient for us (color, shape, size). Nor could Quinean hypothesis formation replace or do the work that training in techniques does. Neither simple conditioning nor rational interpretation determines techniques. It is precisely this that makes room for the normative dimension of rules and concepts. What overcomes the abstract problem of indeterminacy of ostension and interpretation is that we can be, and are, trained in certain ways. Quine mistakes the possibility of alternative principles of individuation for the indeterminacy of our actual judgments because he holds that both background theory and background individuating apparatus are presupposed, must be involved, in our actual judgments of the obvious. But Wittgenstein's point is that the background required is that of mastery of techniques, not the application of principles of individuation or theory.

Developing techniques of use creates the regularities necessary for judgments of similarity or sameness without which language or any rule-governed enterprise is impossible. As Wittgenstein puts this point in the *Remarks*, "the phenomenon of language is based on regularity, on agreement in action" (RFM VI.39). In the learning situation, regularity is guaranteed because no alternative way of responding is permitted. The role of the teacher is crucial here, for the resources available to the pupil are not simply his sensory stimulations but an environment shaped by the teacher. The learning circle moves from the experimental activity of testing in which the pupil's reactions are shaped by the teacher, creating the sense of the obvious, to the activity of testing in which the result is seen as necessary, as what must be:

> It is as if we had hardened the empirical proposition into a rule. And now we have, not an hypothesis that gets tested by experience, but a paradigm with which experience is compared and judged. And so a new kind of judgment.
>
> (RFM VI.22)

Effecting this kind of change is the result of the learning circle. What is involved in adopting a concept reveals a strong link between the process of learning and what is learned, for the training itself is constitutive of the concept acquired. To adopt the concept is to acquire the technique, and technique can only be shown and practiced. The training we get is a part of what we learn.

Explaining necessity in terms of the normative role that rules and concepts play after appropriate training looks in some ways like a revival of psychologism, the thesis that norms describe our de facto psychology. On this view, mathematical principles and laws of logic, insofar as they are laws at all, are empirical generalizations about how we think (or associate ideas) as a matter of fact.[21] In this way, logical or conceptual necessity is reduced to the psychological, a variant on the Humean idea that necessity is psychological compulsion. Logical or metaphysical necessity is thus a projection of how we are psychologically determined to think. But Wittgenstein does not revive this crude version of psychologism or the projectivism to which it naturally leads. He does indeed hold that our use of language, concepts, and rules is grounded in our shared natural history. He emphasizes that if certain general facts of nature were different, then our concepts and language games would be different.[22] To this extent, he agrees with the empiricist that our "necessary truths" are contingent, and so he rejects the rationalist idea that necessity goes all the way down, as it were, to metaphysical necessity. Yet he is not reductionist in his account of the relation between language and any of these general facts of nature. The philosophical problems involved are not to be solved by engaging in an empirical investigation:

> If the formation of concepts can be explained by facts of nature, should we not be interested, not in grammar, but rather in that in nature which is the basis of grammar?—Our interest certainly includes the correspondence between concepts and very general facts of nature....But our interest does not fall back upon these possible causes of the formation of concepts; we are not doing natural science.
>
> (PI II.xii)

The necessity expressed in mathematical propositions or grammatical propositions in general is not the causal necessity expressed by laws of nature or laws of psychology. This is the mistake of classical psychologism, which takes mathematical and grammatical propositions to be empirical propositions. Wittgenstein argues that these propositions look like they are fact-stating. This is what has led philosophers to treat them as either meta-physical truths or empirical generalizations. They are neither. Their necessity resides in the fact that they are normative propositions. Their normative functioning lies in the background techniques and world pictures which create the logical space for our judgments and actions concerning what is obviously the same and what must be so. These techniques are socially engendered and sustained.

So Wittgenstein's "psychologism," if it can be called that, arises in a way that differs from classical psychologism.[23] First, though these propositions are necessary in virtue of the normative role they play in our practices, it is a contingent fact that such practices exist and that we can engage in them. To underscore this point, Wittgenstein asks us to consider changes in certain general facts of nature:

> if anyone believes that certain concepts are absolutely the correct ones, and that having different ones would mean not realizing something that we realize – then let him imagine certain very general facts of nature to be different from what we are used to, and the formation of concepts different from the usual ones will become intelligible to him.

> (PI II.xii)

Second, the prescriptive role in our lives of mathematical, logical, and grammatical propositions is a function of the acquisition of the relevant background techniques and their associated world pictures through initiate training. It is through the acquisition of such bedrock practices that we grasp the obvious and necessary. Only by taking an object, not as the particular object or inscription that it is, but as a standard by which behavior is shaped can the pupil come to the view that things must be a certain way, and only by coming to hold that things must be this way can a pupil acquire concepts or the use of rules at all.

It is tempting at this point to say that Wittgenstein's account of necessity and possibility requires distinguishing between what is internal to a practice and what is external to that practice. For he seems to be saying that rules that are constitutive of a practice create necessities within that practice, but external to the practice the rules are contingent and so could be replaced by alternative practices or language games. This idea of what is external and internal to a practice has been endorsed by philosophers as diverse as Carnap and Foucault.[24] Wittgenstein himself struggled with this problem in the *Tractatus* in his attempt to find the limits of what can be thought. And it is tempting to interpret his notion of language games as involving such an idea. However, to apply this distinction straightforwardly either to his use of language games or to his account of necessity and rules in his later writings is a mistake.

It is a mistake, I think, for two important reasons. The first is that it suggests that there are alternatives to the necessities that inform our actual bedrock practices. This is a mistake for Wittgenstein because the very notion of alternative possibilities can only be made with respect to available concepts. The logical space for alternative possibilities requires some practice which constitutes the bedrock of certainty against which possibility is defined. Yet these practices and their constitutive judgments exist contingently both as practices and insofar as any individual participates.

They are contingent without realizing a pre-existent possibility. Possibilities, like simplicity, can be judged only relative to a normative practice. There is no way to make sense of the idea of possibilities independently of the contrasts that we can draw and their embeddedness in our shared judgments of what is obviously the same.[25] Wittgenstein's account of initiate learning concerns what it is for an individual's behavior to become normatively guided. That is by the adoption of concepts which involves taking certain results as necessary.

The second reason that applying the Carnapian picture of internal and external issues to Wittgensteinian bedrock practices is that these constitute our human form of life. There is no perspective outside of this. For ordinary games, like chess or football, there is no difficulty in applying the Carnapian picture. One can change the rules of a game in virtue of considerations that are external to the game. In football the goal posts were moved from the 0-yard line to the back of the end-zone. This was done for external reasons, to make kicking a field goal more difficult. Though Wittgenstein uses the game of chess to introduce his notion of a language game, our bedrock practices are unlike chess in certain crucial respects. Where chess may or may not be played in a society, naming objects, following rules, experiencing pains, anticipating the future are not optional practices that may or may not be played. Wittgenstein is concerned with those aspects of our form of life that are not optional, that we cannot imagine doing without or changing for reasons external to these practices. The logical connective tissue of our system of beliefs, our interactions with ordinary objects and other people, our memories of the past and hopes for the future all implicate propositions that hold fast and ways of going on that cannot be jeopardized without inducing madness. This is not a transcendental argument for the necessity of our form of life. It is rather an argument, or perhaps observation, that we cannot but start in medias res.

The only "justification" we have for what is obviously the same is a description of how we were trained in the acquisition of concepts and rules. That training itself occurs in the context of a way of living, a custom (cf. RFM VI.34) – a context in which "we talk and act. That is already presupposed in everything that I am saying" (RFM VI.17). On Wittgenstein's view, we have no better or deeper explanation of sameness than that we are trained to judge in conformity with others. No philosophical theory of identity, no physical or physiological account of natural similarity, and no psychological theory of certainty is sufficient to ground these judgments. Justification for these bedrock judgments of sameness is provided by radical explanations in terms of the social training the initiate learner undergoes. The sense of the obvious is mastered by the initiate learner who unquestioningly (this is redundant since the initiate learner is precisely the one without the resources for questioning or knowing) acquires – through training – a second "linguistic" nature, that is, dispositions for using words in connection with objects and as part of actions. Without a bedrock of the obvious, there could be no practices, no norms, no rules.

We can see that Wittgenstein is not opting for the elimination of (non-causal) necessity but for a different understanding of necessity, one that makes the contrast between necessary propositions and empirical propositions fundamental rather than that between necessary truths and contingent truths. Pace Quine, meaning and reference cannot be radically indeterminate while language nonetheless flourishes.[26]

4 Conclusion: indeterminacy of meaning or blind obedience?

Broadly speaking, both Wittgenstein and Quine develop indeterminacy arguments from which the problem of normative similarity arises. Both Wittgenstein and Quine reject the transparency of reference and with it denotational and atomistic theories of meaning. Yet despite this apparent overlap in arguments and philosophical views, there are striking dissimilarities. In particular, Quine holds that indeterminacy is an ineliminable aspect of language use whereas for Wittgenstein the bedrock similarity judgments we make blindly or as a matter of course are determinate. That this is a hand is as obvious as that "5" must follow "4" when we are counting. The certainty of these judgments is immune to Quine's scruples about reference and meaning, but Quine's scruples are not immune to Wittgenstein's arguments.

Quine's picture of language is such that the only point of contact with the world is the observation sentence and the sensory stimulation that is the sentence's stimulus meaning. The acquisition of language as well as any revisions to the interconnected network of sentences that constitutes our web of belief turns on this single point of contact with reality. This is his scientific naturalism at work. It prepares the ground for the universality of the indeterminacy argument, but, if indeterminacy is genuinely universal, it undermines Quine's own account of belief formation and change. Crucial to Quine's conception of revising the web of belief is the idea of recalcitrant experience that is at odds with existing beliefs and that forces changes within the network of accepted sentences. Recalcitrant experience is recurrent sensory stimulation that elicits assent to the corresponding occasion sentence even if that forces change elsewhere in the web of belief. The problem of normative similarity applies to the role that

Quine assigns the recalcitrant experience. If all is indeterminate, there can be no notion of recalcitrance. The idea of a recalcitrant experience carries with it both the idea of the violation of some expectation and the idea of some kind of necessary connection among beliefs. We must have expectations about what is the same recalcitrant experience and we must use some necessary inferential connections. Quine insists that nothing in the web of belief is immune to revision. He also holds that in the face of recalcitrant experience, the web or total theory must be revised. The notion of revising our total theory requires that we have some way of understanding in what the inferential connections among sentences consist. This is the point at which difficulties arise. Dummett has made the argument quite forcefully:

> Quine's thesis involves...that the principles governing deductive connections themselves form part of the total theory which, as a whole, confronts experience....we must recognize the total theory as comprising rules of inference as well as logical laws...But in that case, there is nothing for the inferential links between sentences to consist in.
>
> (Dummett 1973: p. 596)

Quine's picture of language is thus subject to the problem of normative similarity both with respect to categorization and rule-following and hasn't the resources for avoiding it. How can we have a recalcitrant experience unless we have expectations about what would be the same experience and about how the sentences of our total language are interconnected? Quine's picture of language as a total theory resting on a slight foundation of sensory stimulations collapses if indeed all is indeterminate.

Wittgenstein, on the other hand, rejects both Quine's picture of language and his interpretation of the child's socialization into the linguistic community. For Wittgenstein, the proper picture of language is that of the language game in which words and actions in context cannot be isolated from one another. An important feature of a language game is the lack of hesitancy or disagreement among the participants. What strikes Wittgenstein is not the meager point of contact between participants at the level of sensory stimulations but the considerable commonality in the judgments and reactions of the participants. These judgments and reactions are made as a matter of course and are justified, if at all, by appeal to the training in which the relevant techniques were acquired. Indeterminacy is eliminated, or rather simply does not occur, through the acquisition of techniques of application. What is so learned are not metaphysical truths or analytic truths but normative rules which fix what is the same and so what is necessary.

9 Wittgenstein's rejection of scientific psychology

Cognitivism is currently the most influential trend in the philosophy of psychology. Very broadly, cognitivism is the view that the organization of behavior is to be explained by an inner mental structure. It holds the promise of offering purely causal explanations within psychology while at the same time preserving the contentful and/or logical features distinctive of our descriptions and explanations of human beings.

Against the promise of such a powerful scientific psychology, Ludwig Wittgenstein concludes his *Philosophical Investigations* with the remark that "in psychology there are experimental methods and *conceptual confusions*....The existence of the experimental method makes us think that we have the means of solving the problems which trouble us; though problem and method pass one another by" (PI II §xiv). Most advocates of cognitivism would take Wittgenstein to have attacked an introspectionist, consciousness-oriented psychology, which no one takes seriously any more. They feel that contemporary cognitivism has been purified of all irrelevant and outmoded philosophical accretions. If true, this would make Wittgenstein's criticisms of psychology of antiquarian interest only. But my view is that it is not true.

First, I shall briefy characterize Wittgenstein's arguments against the possibility of a scientific psychology.[1] Second, I shall show the surprising extent to which advocates of cognitivism have come gradually to accept Wittgensteinian considerations though not to endorse Wittgenstein's nihilistic conclusions. Finally, I shall explore two attempts to accommodate Wittgensteinian strictures while drawing quite different morals: J.A. Fodor's "rationalist psychology" and Stephen Stich's "syntactic theory of mind."[2] I shall argue that Fodor and Stich impoverish psychology to such an extent that, contrary to their intentions, Wittgenstein's pessimistic view is fundamentally conceded.

1 Wittgenstein on psychology

Although Wittgenstein is concerned with states of consciousness as well as cognitive capacities, in this chapter I shall only be concerned with the latter. What he rejects is the idea that cognitive abilities or capacities (such as recognition, memory, problem solving, and the like) consist in, or can be explained by reference to inner psychological processes or structures. His two principal objections that are most pertinent to the cognitivist program would be that (1) causal stories are irrelevant to our understanding of cognitive abilities; and (2) believing, recognizing, remembering, etc. are not mental processes. Here Wittgenstein is objecting to all theorists who think of mental states as states of the individual considered in isolation from the social environment.[3]

Wittgenstein's first objection clarifies the meaning of the provocative remarks quoted above. According to Wittgenstein, the kinds of questions most often raised by psychologists and philosophers in their attempts to understand human beings are simply not causal questions at all, though mistakenly taken for such. The most interesting psychological questions, Wittgenstein argues, are conceptual. There are two aspects to this claim: (1) the criterial aspect in which we are concerned with what counts as meaning or intending or believing; and (2) the genetic aspect in which we are concerned with how an individual comes to be a believer or an intender. For Wittgenstein, both aspects are to be explicated in terms of social practices and ultimately our human form of life. What counts as anger or belief is constituted by our form of life; to become a believer is to become a member of and participant in that form of life. Thus, for Wittgenstein, the explication of an intentional notion is a conceptual matter, not in the sense of being a metaphysically sanctioned necessity, but in the sense of being constituted by our form of life. Though causal questions can be raised (e.g., how much adrenaline is released when a person gets angry?; what is the time lag between presentation of a visual stimulus and a perceptual report?), it makes no sense to ask what dreams are made of; or how anger or belief cause behavior; or where beliefs are stored.

The first objection raises questions about construing psychological states as causes of particular behaviors. The second is directed against the idea that recognition, memory, language use, and the like are to be identified with inner processes. Contemporary cognitive theorists generally explain these processes in terms of the storing of representations that can play different functional roles. They may differ over how representations are to be conceived. But Wittgenstein's reason for asserting "the barrenness of psychology" is that believing, meaning etc. are not inner processes at all, no matter how such a process is characterized and no matter how the representation is construed (e.g., as sentence-like or as imagistic).[4]

The standard interpretation of Wittgenstein is that he denies that there are inner processes on roughly behaviorist and verificationist grounds. This is a mistake. His point is that if one could freeze an individual at a given moment and give a full and complete description of everything going on in an individual at that moment, one would not thereby be able to individuate the beliefs, desires, or intentions of that person. As Wittgenstein puts it, not even God, looking into the mind of the individual at a given moment, could discern these important features of a person: "If God had looked into our minds he would not have been able to see there whom we were speaking of" (PI II §xi, p. 217). And this is not because beliefs are private to the subject or are unconscious; rather there is no occurrent feature or state of the person that constitutes meaning or believing.

According to Wittgenstein, understanding, belief, and meaning are states of a person *only within* a practice over time. Without the practice, there is no understanding or belief, no matter what may be going on in the person's head. It is this central idea that threatens current cognitive psychology for, prima facie, cognitivist models share the basic view that meaning, belief, and the rest must be inner, for the most part unconscious, states of that person. But holistic and social conditions for belief and other propositional attitudes are incompatible with scientific theory-building, or so Wittgenstein concludes. For if these considerations are correct, the individuation of particular propositional attitudes essentially involves environmental and social features. To see cognitive capacities as inner mental structures, independent of the social and natural environment, is an informing idea of cognitivism. Commitment to this strong autonomy of cognitive capacities cannot be given up without forfeiting the hope of developing a cognitivist research program. And this, of course, is precisely what Wittgenstein wants to forfeit.

Primarily for these two considerations, Wittgenstein rejects the possibility of a scientific psychology; that is, any theory that purports to explain behavior in terms of inner mental causes. If Wittgenstein is right, Fodor is wrong when he claims that "the structure of behavior stands to mental structure as an effect stands to its cause" (Fodor 1983). Causal questions can, of course, be raised, but these are not inquiries into the psychological causes of behavior but into the physiological and/or neurophysiological causes of behavior. In other words, on a Wittgensteinian view, there are the brain sciences but not the cognitive sciences. The brain sciences, however, are not a replacement for the cognitive sciences. There is no science of human action and intentionality.[5]

2 The problem of explanatory scope

I shall argue that both Stich's and Fodor's final substantive views about the scope and content of cognitive science virtually coincide with Wittgenstein's views. Where we have science we have the neurophysiology of perception and sentence recognition; and where we have cognitive capacities and processes, we are dealing with matters not amenable to the kind of systematic theoretical treatment that is the aim of cognitive psychology. Whereas Fodor gradually and reluctantly comes to this conclusion, Stich enthusiastically embraces a substantively similar view, seeing it as a brave new beginning for cognitive science rather than a forced retrenchment. Both advocates of cognitivism, needless to say, resist drawing these conclusions explicitly.

True, Fodor holds that there is a distinction between the "modular systems" of sensory perception and sentence recognition and the "central systems" that constitute the rest of cognition. But this is as far as the parallel with Wittgenstein goes. First, Fodor's modular systems, though "associated with fixed neural architecture" (Fodor 1983), remain cognitive systems, and as such they are to be understood on the model of systems that form and confirm hypotheses. But, even more significantly, Fodor continues to hold that the hypothesis-formation model applies in principle even to the central systems; though he concedes that, at present, we have no idea how. This is why he sees *gloomy* prospects for cognitive science. He sees us as (in all likelihood) doomed to *ignorance* of the inner structure and processes that constitute believing and desiring. For Wittgenstein, by contrast, there is no such structure to be ignorant of. Stich's tone is far removed from that of theoretical despair. His voice is that of the crusader. Stich, from the outset, is much more impressed with Wittgensteinian considerations concerning meaning, assigning content to propositional attitudes, and individuating propositional attitude states. But rather than drawing Wittgenstein's conclusion that there can be no scientific psychology he is much more tempted to conclude so much the worse for belief, desire, and the whole array of our ordinary intentionalist modes of psychological explanation and description: "folk psychology" as he calls it. The semantic or contentful aspect of folk psychology is simply not a part of scientific psychology. Scientific psychology is concerned solely with formal or syntactic features of mental states and processes. If the contentful states of our ordinary psychological descriptions correspond to the syntactically characterized states of science, that is a coincidence and one that perhaps explains why folk psychology fared so well for so long.[6] But there is no reason to expect that there will be such a happy coincidence, and so we cannot expect folk psychology to be saved "by courtesy," as it were. This sense of struggle and of overcoming deepseated superstition and resistance to scientific progress lends a tone of optimism and high adventure to Stich's work.

But how do Fodor and Stich come to their views concerning the scope of psychological theorizing? And why do they see their shared conclusion that mental states and processes are syntactic states and operations in such radically different lights? For Stich, the syntactic exhausts the scope of scientific inquiry, and for Fodor the syntactic mirrors the contentful though current scientific inquiry is limited to modular systems. And, finally, given the substantive conclusions they do draw, why don't they draw Wittgenstein's nihilistic moral for psychology?

The longer story is Fodor's, and so I shall begin there. Increasingly, Fodor has come to accept Wittgensteinian arguments against the possibility of a scientific psychology. This has not led him, as I have said, to give up the project but to truncate radically its domain of inquiry and explanation. Under pressure from internal difficulties, cognitive science, on Fodor's view,[7] has shrunk from providing an explanation (potentially) of deliberate action, learning, and perception (*The Language of Thought*) to a "rationalist" psychology that countenances only formal items and operations as part of the causal apparatus ("Methodological Solipsism") to a modularity hypothesis that further restricts the domain of psychology to perceptual and sentence-recognition systems (*Modularity of Mind*).[8] To see how this retrenchment has been effected, I turn to Wittgenstein's first objection.

To this first objection, namely, that the relation between belief and action is not that of cause to effect, Fodor offers a very powerful response (Fodor 1975: pp. 6–9). He argues that the Wittgensteinian conclusion (though he addresses this objection to Ryle) – that there are no interesting cognitive causal questions to be asked – is simply fallacious. Questions of the form "What makes x F?" (what makes Wheaties the breakfast of champions?, to use Fodor's example; or what makes a pratfall witty?; or what makes a belief the reason for an action?) can be construed both conceptually (what counts as being an F – to be the breakfast of champions, a cereal (trivially) must be eaten by champions; to be a witty pratfall is to occur unexpectedly and spectacularly) and causally (what is it about this cereal that makes those who eat it champions?; how does the clown deliberately make his action appear suddenly and unexpectedly?).[9] So what about the question: What is it to understand something (e.g., how to continue the natural number series)? Construing the question conceptually, something like the Wittgensteinian account of what is involved in going on in the right way (i.e., the way sanctioned by the teacher) may well be appropriate. But, Fodor maintains, the question can also be construed causally – what change in the individual explains (i.e. causally accounts for) his appropriate behavior? Thus, there is no principled ground for objecting to a causal theory of the mind.

That the mind can be construed as the arena of causal episodes that explain how the person acts as he does is not sufficient for a general defense of cognitivism. Cognitivism also involves essentially commitment to a data-inference model of the mind. As Fodor argues in his *The Language of Thought*, all cognitive processes are processes of hypothesis formation and confirmation, and as such "not only considered actions, but also learning and perception, must surely be based upon computational processes" (Fodor 1975: p. 34). This model is unabashedly epistemological, and so involves fully contentful representations and operations. Beliefs, for example, are individuated by their content and are related by inferential connections of both a logical and epistemic character to other beliefs, desires, and the like.

Intuitively, assigning content to propositional attitudes, like tracing the way individuals come to acquire particular propositional attitudes, involves reference to objects, events, and people in the world. Yet Fodor argues that there can be no science of organism/environment relations. His reason for this is that such a science would require specifying a causal connection between a thought and the object of that thought under descriptions that are law instantiating, which for Fodor means under physical descriptions (cf. Stich 1983: pp. 160–4). To obtain these law-instantiating descriptions, we must await the completion of science, for "the theory which character-izes the objects of thought is the theory of everything; it's all of science" (Fodor 1981: p. 248; cf. pp. 247–50). So, Fodor concludes, the science of psychology must deal with the individual in isolation from this natural and cultural environment. Cognitive psychology is committed to a strong prin-ciple of autonomy. Psychology is the study of the individual's capacities and behaviors from the point of view of what goes on within the indi-vidual. Fodor and Stich are agreed in this (Fodor 1981; Stich 1978).

Yet the study of the individual in such radical isolation conflicts with the appeal to content as essential to cognitivist explanations of behavior. Truth, reference, and meaning cannot be located in an individual's head, but involve the relations the individual has to the environment, both natural and cultural. This is Wittgenstein's second objection to scientific psychology. However, the response of both Fodor and Stich is not to give up on a scientific psychology, but to revise our understanding of the theo-retical vocabulary of that science and so of the mental structure that underlies and explains behavior. Both hold that only the formal features of representations and operations upon them can be relevant to the hypothe-sized cognitive processes. Fodor is led to this "formality condition" by his commitment to the computational model of mind:

The point is that, so long as we are thinking of mental processes as purely computational, the bearing of the environmental information upon such processes is exhausted by the formal character of whatever the oracles write on the tape....I'm saying, in effect, that the formality condition, viewed in this context, is tantamount to a sort of methodological solipsism.

(Fodor 1981: p. 231)

In light of Wittgensteinian considerations about intentionality and context, the computational model, the guiding insight of cognitivism, can only be preserved by restricting the scope of psychological explanation to formally characterizable entities and operations:

The very assumption that defines their, i.e., cognitive psychologists' field – viz. that they study mental processes qua formal operations on symbols – guarantees that their studies won't answer the question how the symbols so manipulated are semantically interpreted.

(Fodor 1981: p. 232)

Here, then, is Fodor's first major retrenchment: The move from accounting for action, learning, and contentful perception to explaining the fixation and transformations of formally characterized entities or states.

Whereas Fodor comes to this conclusion reluctantly, Stich embraces it readily. Stich endorses the autonomy principle as a foundational principle for cognitive science and argues that it excludes appealing to content (Stich 1983: esp. pp. 164–70). But if semantic objects are excluded from the domain of psychology, syntactic objects are not. Formal operations on the shapes of sentences or words can be described wholly independently of the environment and so of interpretations given the sentences.

Though both come to accept autonomy and formality, they disagree significantly about the relation of explanation in terms of content to formal accounts. Of concern to Fodor is how to preserve content, and so something of our ordinary intentionalist vocabulary, while honoring the requirements of autonomy and formality. Stich takes the bull by the horns and banishes intentionalist vocabulary altogether from scientific psychology in favor of a syntactic theory of mind.

3 The problem of background belief

The extent of the retrenchment that results from Fodor's adopting the formality condition is masked in two ways. The first involves the claim that "the computational theory of the mind requires that two thoughts can be distinct in content only if they can be identified with relations to formally distinct representations" (Fodor 1981: p. 227). In brief, the computational theory requires that differences in content be mirrored by differences in shape.[10]

The second involves taking an opaque reading of propositional attitudes to support (indeed, to be tantamount to) the formality condition:

> in doing our psychology, we want to attribute mental states fully opaquely because it's the fully opaque reading which tells us what the agent has in mind that causes his behavior.
>
> (Fodor 1981: p. 239)

This passage involves an equivocation on the phrase "in mind" that is bridged by the first assumption, namely, that there must be a distinct shape for each distinct content. The first usage of "in mind" concerns what the subject means or intends or understands, and it is this that explains his behavior. The second usage of "in mind" takes us to the idea of mental states as the kind of entities that figure in the causal nexus. It is the crucial first assumption that creates the sense that when we speak of a person's believing or hoping or intending one thing rather than another we are *a fortiori* talking about formal computational states that can stand as causes for subsequently occurring states. As Fodor puts it,

> The form of explanation goes: it's because different content implies formally distinct internal representations (via the formality condition) and formally distinct internal representations can be functionally different – can differ in their causal role.
>
> (Fodor 1981: p. 240)

The misleading step in this summary is Fodor's saying that "different content implies formally distinct internal representations," for nowhere is an argument for this implication or entailment given. On the contrary, it is assumed that this must be the case. His point is that cognitivism can only be saved if this mirroring holds. As Fodor admits, the most he argues is that "taxonomy in respect of content may be compatible with the formality condition, plus or minus a bit. That [it] is compatible is perhaps the basic idea of modern theory" (Fodor 1981: p. 240). It is these two claims – that content is mirrored by form and that opacity entails internality – that make cognitivism plausible despite Wittgensteinian considerations. Deny either of these and cognitivism, as the study of formal operations upon the shapes of representations, loses any connection (save by accident or chance) with the domain of action, belief, and desire.

It is for this reason that I maintain that these two claims mask the extent to which cognitivism has entrenched once the formality condition is acknowledged as necessary for its success.

Stich is more than willing to shed the mask and risk losing our world of action, belief, and desire, a world that took form, he would argue, out of ignorance and superstition. Fodor's is a valiant attempt to create the illusion of compatibility between the domain of action and the scope of scientific psychology. The effort is one that continues to invoke the concepts of belief and desire in a substantive way, but this belief-desire thesis, Stich maintains, is not compatible with an autonomous psychology (Stich 1978). It is part and parcel of folk psychology, a theory of the mind that Stich feels will, in all likelihood, be shown to be false.[11] I shall take up this claim later. For now I want to complete the account of Fodor's concessions.

In *The Modularity of Mind* Fodor concludes that the prospects are "gloomy" for our explaining any of the higher cognitive abilities and capacities, which he refers to as the central systems (including deliberate action, full-fledged perception, language use, and learning). The only systems amenable to scientific study, he argues, are the "modular systems." These systems include the perceptual input and sentence-recognition systems. This second retrenchment results from continued commitment to cognitivism, on the positive side, and from pressure from Wittgensteinian considerations, on the negative side.

Though Fodor discusses a number of features that are criterial for modularity, the single most important one is that modular systems are "informationally encapsulated" (Fodor 1983: p. 64): "The informational encapsulation of the input systems is...the essence of their modularity" (Fodor 1983: p. 71). As the term suggests, these systems are marked by the fact that they have access only to certain information. This is true from two directions, as it were. From the bottom up, each input system is responsive only to a particular stimulus domain. But neither is there penetration from the top down. Higher level beliefs and epistemic principles do not in any way affect the way data is represented and manipulated by the input system. Because of encapsulation, modular systems can readily be described as computational systems – the analogy with computers fits very well here:

> we can think of each input system as a computational mechanism which projects and confirms a certain class of hypotheses on the basis of a certain body of data....The mechanism which solves the problem is, in effect, the realization of a confirmation function: it's a mapping which associates with each pair of a lexical hypothesis and some

acoustic datum a value which expresses the degree of confirmation that the latter bestows upon the former.

(Fodor 1983: p. 68)

Such a confirmation function can be realized within a closed system, that is, with a system in which the data available can be specified in advance and which is impenetrable by higher level cognitive systems. The salient problems for the modularity thesis are problems of individuation – how to individuate the inputs and outputs, how to draw the line between an input system and the central system(s) to which it is related. For Fodor, these problems cannot be solved in the case of the higher cognitive systems, the central systems. That is why they cannot be a subject of scientific theorizing.

The central systems differ from modular systems in two crucial respects. They are domain-inspecific in that they exploit different kinds of information (e.g., visual, tactile, and auditory); and they are unencapsulated (penetrable from background belief, epistemic principles, contextual information) (Fodor 1983: p. 104). This lack of closure prevents the development of the kind of confirmation functions necessary to describe a computational system. Fodor argues this by developing what he sees as a deep analogy with scientific confirmation theory: Central systems and scientific theory building are *isotropic* and *Quineian*.

A modular system is marked by the fact that it is domain specific, that is, one can specify in advance of any particular processing what data are available to the system. Confirmation procedures are not so confined epistemically. There is no way to specify in advance and in principle what range of facts will be evidentially relevant:

> By saying that confirmation is isotropic, I mean that the facts relevant to the confirmation of a scientific hypothesis may be drawn from anywhere in the field of previously established empirical (or, of course, demonstrative) truths.
>
> (Fodor 1983: p. 105)

Input systems are prime candidates for modularity precisely because it seems we can specify what data are relevant, namely, whatever is derivable from the stimulations of each given sensory system.

Not only is the range of materials available for the building and confirming of hypotheses unrestricted, so are the principles of inference and epistemic norms that operate on scientific hypotheses. They cannot be specified in advance of grappling with the concrete problem situation:

By saying that scientific confirmation is Quinean, I mean that the degree of confirmation assigned to any given hypothesis is sensitive to properties of the entire belief system.

(Fodor 1983: p. 107)

What these considerations take us to is the essential open-endedness of theories and hypotheses with regard to both what data and what higher-level and extra-domain beliefs may prove relevant. Contextualist and holistic arguments (if sound, as Fodor takes them to be) explode the idea that epistemic inferential networks have an inherent structure or order that enables one to discover an a priori distinction between non-inferential and inferential belief and to describe a pure logic of induction.[12]

Traditionally these arguments have been used against foundationalist theories of knowledge. Foundationalism is characterized by the two episte-mological commitments that are attacked with and replaced by isotropism and Quineianism, namely, that there is a foundation of privileged belief which can be identified independently of any particular context of justifi-cation or inquiry and a precisely specifiable set of inference rules, principles, or procedures that lead from basic beliefs (or data) to more complex beliefs. These holistic and isotropic considerations are central to Wittgenstein's views on language, meaning, and knowledge. They are what lead him to his scepticism concerning the possibility of a science of cogni-tion. Fodor's endorsement of these views takes him a long way towards the complete Wittgensteinian position.

4 The problem of individuation

One of the outstanding problems Fodor faces, even after this retrench-ment, as he acknowledges (Fodor 1983: p. 91), is the problem of individuation. Where does one draw the line between what is part of a modular system and what is part of a higher-level central "system"?[13] A modular system is a genuinely cognitive system, described in terms of representations and inferential networks, to which holistic considerations are nevertheless irrelevant. Thus, there is considerable pressure (from the top, as it were) to locate the divide between modular and central systems very close to the physiological level. The reason for this is that when it comes to examining any inferential network, it is very difficult not to find oneself quickly embroiled in the problem of background belief, higher-level epistemic principles, and the like. Fodor sketches two possible candidates for modularity – a system that functions to recognize utterances as sentences (Fodor 1983: pp. 64ff.) and a visual system that functions to recognize basic percepts (Fodor 1983: p. 93ff.). The claim to modularity, for both of these, surely warrants careful examination, but that is not my task. What does concern me is that pressure from holistic considerations results, as Fodor acknowledges, in very shallow levels of representation (Ibid.: p. 86ff.), and that "neural architecture...is the natural concomitant of informational encapsulations" (Fodor 1983: p. 99). There is a "characteristic neural architecture associated with each of what I have been calling the input systems" (Fodor 1983: p. 98). Fodor finds this concomitance to be supportive of the modularity of these systems, for

> the intimate association of modular systems, with neural hardwiring is pretty much what you would expect given the assumption that the key to modularity is informational encapsulation.
>
> (Fodor 1983: p. 98)

But there is another way of looking at this concomitance between modular systems and neural hardwiring that is less comforting. That is that it becomes increasingly difficult to see the difference between doing scientific psychology and doing neurophysiology. I strongly suspect that the criterion for demarcation between modular and central systems will have to do with what can be cashed in for physiological terms. But if the line is drawn this close to the physiological, it becomes very difficult to see what the substantive difference is between Fodor's position and a Wittgensteinian position. On the Wittgensteinian view, cognitive capacities cannot be studied in a scientific experimental way, but this does not eliminate neurophysiology. On Fodor's view, we haven't the slightest idea of how to study generalized cognitive capacities scientifically, though we can investigate modular systems that are neurally hardwired.[14]

The problem of individuation arises in a different manner for Stich. This is because Stich confronts the problems of explanatory scope and background belief head on, arguing that a cognitive psychology that appeals to contentful representations cannot succeed. We cannot turn folk psychology into scientific psychology.

Stich's arguments for this radical conclusion come primarily from two directions. First, contentful states do not meet the requirement of autonomy, which is fundamental to a science of psychology.[15] Only a noncontentful theory of mind is compatible with the autonomy principle. Whereas Fodor masks the incompatibility by the claims that shape mirrors content and that opacity is tantamount to formality, Stich opts to sever the connection between the formal and the contentful. This is what distinguishes his syntactic theory of mind from Fodor's rationalist psychology. Stich sees powerful reasons to eschew any but an expedient appeal to contentful representation. These reasons include his view that only a syntactic cognitive psychology can honor the autonomy principle and his very strong suspicion that we are unlikely to find any systematic correlation between the types of entities postulated by scientific psychology and the propositional attitudes hypothesized by folk psychology (cf. Stich 1983: pp. 228–37). Thus, folk psychology is unlikely to be saved by a happy coincidence in which the "gross functional architecture" of a syntactic cognitive theory "cleaves reasonably closely to the pattern presupposed by folk psychology" (Stich 1983: p. 229).

There is a second kind of consideration that weighs very heavily with Stich. This is the argument from "exotic folk," namely, small children, the mentally disturbed, and primitives, all people who are far removed from the typical adult of Western society (Stich 1979; Stich 1983, Ch. 7, section 3). The psychology of these individuals is the concern of developmental, clinical, and comparative theories. The small child who utters "four" upon being asked what two plus two is, but otherwise displays no understanding of what numbers are, can hardly be said to grasp the concept of four in the way that his adult interlocutor does. Stich's own favored example – Mrs. T. who can say of Mr. McKinley only that he was assassinated, but nothing more, not even that assassination involves death – would also elude psychological description if one had to ascribe content to her psychological state (Stich 1983: Ch. 4.1 and Ch. 7.3).[16] And between the extreme case of Mrs. T. and the typical adult are many marginal cases where it is unclear precisely what content to ascribe their statements. There seems something very counterintuitive about a psychological theory that cannot include the more exotic members of our species:

> If we insist on constructing cognitive theories whose generalizations advert to content, then we may well have to do without comprehensive theories of cognitive development and cognitive abnormality....The price for adopting the Strong RTM [representational theory of mind] is that many cognitive generalizations will be beyond our grasp and many of those which we can state will be plagued by the vagueness inherent in the language of content.
>
> (Stich 1983: p. 148)

The syntactic theory of mind, Stich claims, is not subject to these objections. "Four" and "Mr. McKinley was assassinated" can be treated as syntactic objects that result from a more or less complicated set of operations. From a syntactic point of view, it makes no difference whether the person who utters them shows the requisite richness of belief to count as having grasped these concepts.

On Stich's view, the syntactic theory of mind provides a rich research program for psychology. It will develop a proprietary vocabulary that will enable it to describe and explain the behaviors and cognitive capacities of all individuals, not just the typical adult. Stich feels that this research program threatens (although does not entail the elimination of) our folk psychology. Our familiar world of beliefs, desires, and hopes may well prove to be non-existent, the result of ignorance about the real structure of the mind and the causes of behavior.

However, Stich's arguments and views are a much more serious threat to cognitive science than to so-called "folk psychology." In the first place, there are serious questions as to whether a purely syntactic theory of mind is possible. Pylyshyn, for example, argues that the interpretation (providing content) of formal objects is necessary both methodologically (in order to effect an individuation of the relevant syntactic objects and operations) and theoretically (in order to show how formal states explain behavior) (Pylyshyn 1980). Though sympathetic to such objections, I shall not engage in this debate here. Even supposing that syntactic theories can stand on their own, without connection to contentful interpretation, syntactic theories don't pose the serious threat to our ordinary psychological descriptions that Stich thinks.

It is the requirement of autonomy, of the radical separation of the psychological from its external causal and cultural connections, that pushes both Fodor and Stich in the direction of formal entities. The problem of identifying the domain of psychological explanation becomes increasingly pressing given the autonomy principle. For Stich, psychology explains behavior only under *autonomous description*. Like Fodor (in *The Modularity of Mind*), the central problem for Stich becomes the problem of individuating the domain of inquiry:

> psychological theory alone cannot be expected to explain the behavior under the folk description at hand. Rather, psychology can explain the behavior under an appropriate autonomous description.
> (Stich 1983: p. 196)

What constitutes an autonomous description of behavior? Though we have not yet developed this new "descriptive language," we do know that there are certain negative constraints upon its formulation. It can involve neither a physical vocabulary nor a folk psychological vocabulary. Clearly a purely physical description is autonomous, but physically described behaviors call for explanations in terms of physical, and in particular neurophysiological, theories. Thus, physical description cannot constitute the appropriate language of psychology. Folk psychological description, on the other hand, adverts to content and so involves appeal to historical, cultural, and natural facts that violate the requirement of autonomy. What makes a particular behavioral event the act of selling my car is the social context in which the event occurs. As Stich expresses it, the act of selling my car is "a conceptually hybrid act" (Stich 1983: p. 196). The psychological explanation accounts for only one component of this act:

> The explanation of human action as it is described in the everyday language of human affairs is a complex and variegated business. Many different disciplines have a legitimate part to play in this endeavor, including jurisprudence, sociology, linguistics, anthropology, history, philosophy and others....The explanation of human action under commonsense action descriptions is not an endeavor that can be confined within a single intellectual domain.
>
> (Stich 1983: p. 196)

So what is the appropriate descriptive vocabulary for psychology? That, Stich tells us, awaits formulation. We have not yet formed a vocabulary that is autonomous (and so avoids being a folk description) and yet is not purely physical. Stich acknowledges this in a note:

> I am not at all sure just what an appropriate autonomous description of this behavioral event would be. Indeed, perhaps an appropriate autonomous behavioral descriptive language does not yet exist. But no one said psychology was supposed to be *easy*.
>
> (Stich 1983: p. 196)

My suspicion once again is that the formal vocabulary to be developed must be such that we can readily see how that which is formally described would be realized in a physical system. In which case it is not clear what deep explanatory gain is made by going to psychology rather than neurophysiology. This is just the position Fodor found himself in with his defence of the shallow representation of input systems. In narrowing so radically the domain of explanation of scientific psychology, Stich has, like Fodor, come very close to the position espoused by Wittgenstein. These remarks suggest that syntactic theories will occupy a place very close indeed to neurophysiology in the study of human beings. And so psychological theory simply won't explain what we thought it was going to explain, namely, why we engage in the actions we do, what motivates us; the nature of memory, recognition; how we learn.

These last comments, however, run counter to Stich's second defence of the syntactic theory of mind, namely, that only syntactic theories are capable of sustaining developmental, clinical, and comparative psychology.

In short, that exotic folk are as much susceptible to study by syntactic theories as the typical Western adult. My response to this is that I cannot begin to see how explaining the behavior of an individual as the causal result of a series of syntactic operations will generate a developmental or clinical theory. The explanatory power of current theories lies in the content of the states ascribed to the small child or to the mentally disturbed person. It seems that the syntactic theory's relation to these issues is more like the relation of elementary particle theory to auto mechanics or the stability of bridges, namely, that we take it for granted that everything is composed, in some sense, of the elementary particles. But that is far from offering any interesting theoretical connections between explaining why my car broke down and some particulate description of my transmission (if that were possible). At best, the future syntactic theory stands in the same relation to human action and mental life. Let the term "psychology" be reserved for what Stich sees as the only scientific study of the mind possible, but that does not in any way impugn the work and lines of inquiry pursued in connection with the attempt to understand human beings, both the exotic and the non-exotic, in other ways. These other ways would not be scientific ways, according to Stich. That again is just the position Wittgenstein takes.

Yet Stich would see himself in striking opposition to a Wittgensteinian position. Stich sees our ordinary psychological descriptions and explanations as constituting a theory of the inner autonomous causes of behavior. Belief and desire are the two most important theoretical constructs of this theory. As a theory of behavior, folk psychology stands as a rival to current cognitivist theory, and a much inferior rival. Thus, the entities and processes hypothesized by folk psychology (beliefs, desires, weighing of evidence, feeling jealous, etc.) will be shown to be fictions (along with the ether, phlogiston, and the like), on the ground that they are part of a false theory of behavior. Folk psychology is rooted in the superstitious ignorance of primitive humanity. Just as superstitious theories of nature were superseded by a scientific world view, so folk psychology must be overcome.

Stich wants to conclude that beliefs etc. as conceived by folk psychology are the "mythical posits of a bad theory" (Stich 1983: p. 9). But his central arguments show only that they are not autonomous. So how do we get from the failure of autonomy to the conclusion that the states "posited" by folk psychology are mythical? Only by assuming that psychological states must be inner causes and so autonomous. On Wittgenstein's view, this unwavering commitment to the inner does not flow from folk psychology alone but from a misunderstanding of our ordinary psychological talk induced by a misconceived picture of language – the picture of object and designation. Stich's position results from following Wittgensteinian considerations a certain distance while declining to follow them to the end.

5 The place for cognitive science

In seeing how the range of cognitive phenomena open to scientific inquiry is narrowed, two familiar arguments that have insulated cognitivism from criticism are considerably weakened, if not forfeited. It has often been argued that because cognitivism is an empirical thesis, criticism must await the facts. No a priori arguments against this approach to the mind are sound. So the argument goes; or went, for Fodor at least. Having argued for the isotropic and Quineian properties of central systems, Fodor is led to the rather startling conclusion that these systems are not amenable to the methods and models of cognitive science. This is not because their claims and hypotheses about thought and intelligence have been discovered to be false, but that thought and intelligence *cannot* be treated in this way. Thus, the attempt to study the central systems is doomed to failure no matter how ingenious those who seek to force a fit between intelligence and computational models of cognitive processes. As Fodor puts it,

> the difficulties we encounter when we try to construct theories of central processes are just the sort we would expect to encounter if such processes are, in essential respects, Quineian/isotropic rather than encapsulated. The crux in the construction of such theories is that there seems to be no way to delimit the sorts of informational resources which may affect, or be affected by, central processes of problem-solving. *We can't, that is to say, plausibly view the fixation of belief as effected by computations over bounded, local information structures.*
>
> (Fodor 1983: p. 112, my italics)

The upshot of this argument is clear. Given the holistic character of intelligence, intelligence cannot be treated as a closed system, and only a closed system is subject to the kind of articulation that can be studied by the experimental methods of cognitive science:

> the limits of modularity are also likely to be limits of what we are going to be able to understand about the mind, given anything like the theoretical apparatus currently available.[17]
>
> (Fodor 1983: p. 126)

Research that goes beyond these limits can be expected to be stymied in certain characteristic ways, for "nobody begins to understand how such [global] factors [in the fixation of belief] have their effects. In this respect, cognitive science hasn't even started" (Fodor 1983: p. 129).

Despite this rather startling conclusion, that most things cognitive science promised to explain elude such theorizing, Fodor continues to hold that intelligence is a matter of hypothesis formation and confirmation: as if a logic of induction should be forthcoming once we do begin to understand how such global factors (as simplicity, plausibility, conservatism) "have their effects." But appreciation of the significance of these factors leads to a serious questioning of the applicability of the hypothesis-formation model to intelligence (Fodor 1983: p. 105). The hypothesis-formation model can be used only against a background of beliefs and principles that are not themselves elements of the hypothesis-formation system. It seems that what needs to be given up is the hypothesis-formation model itself as the universal exemplar for all cognitive processes. The very considerations that lead to a limiting of cognitive science provide positive grounds against the pervasive and universal applicability of the hypothesis-formation model (or any kind of data-inference model).

The second main line in the defense of cognitivism – the claim that cognitivism is the only remotely plausible theory around ("it's the only game in town" defense) – has also been substantially undermined, and in two ways. First, it is no longer thought to provide a theory for intelligence (deliberate action, learning, or full perception); and second, the considerations that lead Fodor to exclude these from the domain of cognitive science also involve rejecting the idea that nonetheless the cognitivist way of characterizing intelligence is correct.

The only argument left for the cognitivist position is that, until some viable experimentally stable alternative is proposed for intelligence, the only rational thing to do is to continue to support the cognitivist model. But clearly this argument isn't sound. On Fodor's own account, we have no viable theoretical account of behavior or of learning; yet this doesn't induce him to embrace behaviorism, which does purport to provide a theory of behavior and learning. He remains agnostic and uncommitted – quite a rational position to take. My point is that none of the usual reasons for endorsing cognitivism for the central systems remain. And so one must look elsewhere for its support.

For Stich's syntactic theory of the mind, the twin battle cries of "Wait for the facts!" and "It's the only game in town" seem even more remote. It stands only as a promise now, pointing in a direction that is still very obscure. Given the price we are asked to pay to take that direction (namely, to give up "folk psychology"), the insulating arguments simply don't seem that strong. One must look for deeper reasons than these for supporting the syntactic theory of mind.

The reasons why Wittgenstein, Fodor, and Stich draw different morals from the same considerations turn not on the details of what science has or has not achieved, of what has or has not been discovered or tested. This seems especially so in psychology, where experimental results are almost always subject to more than one interpretation. The explanation goes deeper than that; the reasons are to be found in the metaphysical commitments of each. The significance and interpretation of the arguments that lead to retrenchment are provided by commitments more fundamental than giving new empirical theories room to develop. As Fodor reveals, there are three closely related commitments that enable him to hold onto a broadly computational view of the mind, or at least the view that there must be a continuous and uninterrupted processing of data from the input systems to the central systems, even though we haven't the slightest idea how that is achieved. This "optimistic" stance can be taken so long as one is assuming that "the world is a connected causal system" (Fodor 1983: p. 121), and "so long as one is assuming a Realist interpretation of science and a correspondence theory of truth" (Ibid.: p. 121).

Thus, a philosophical interest in cognitive science is in seeing it as placing the mind fully in the "world" as described by science. The mind is wholly continuous with physical stimulations. Beliefs and other propositional attitudes as well as cognitive capacities and abilities pick out entities that can be identified and individuated in a way that shows how they fit into the single connected causal system. The mind is essentially something homogenous; whether at the level of transducers, input systems, or central systems: "all systems that perform nondemonstrative inferences, modular or otherwise, fall together as hypothesis projecting/confirming devices" (Fodor 1983: p. 121). The idea that the mind may be radically heterogeneous is inimical to the conception of cognitive science and its philosophical task. For in viewing the mind as heterogeneous, cognitive science, as the science of information-processing devices, is in danger of becoming, as I have argued, only an extension of the physiological study of perceptual systems. Other domains of inquiry are as disjointed as the mind is heterogeneous. The urge for the unity of science cannot be satisfied.

This urge for a unified vision of the world as a connected causal system plays a different role in Stich's thought. For he sees insuperable obstacles in our intentionalist contentful descriptions being part of cognitive science, that is, the science that shows how human beings are fully part of the connected causal system. So long as our intentionalist explanations are seen as independent in the main of future cognitive science, and as important or even indispensable, in describing and understanding people, the ideal of a unified scientific vision cannot be realized. But if our "folk psychology" itself constitutes a primitive empirical theory of how human beings fit into the connected causal system, then that ideal has not been abandoned; and we have competition between two theories. The appeal to beliefs, desires, and the like constitutes a theory about the causes of human behavior, a theory Stich believes will be shown to be false. To answer Stich fully requires showing why it is mistaken to think of our intentionalist psychological descriptions as being part of a theory. For a full defense of this I would need to expand my remarks on the assumption of autonomy and the picture of language that supports it. So-called folk psychology no more constitutes a theory than talk about mud, rocks, and dirt constitute a theory in opposition to geology. A monistic scientific realism is a specifically modern metaphysical outlook, shared by Fodor and Stich, deeply opposed by Wittgenstein.

10 Vygotsky's social theory of mind

In the last twenty years, there has been an explosion of creative thought about the nature of our ordinary cognitive abilities.[1] This has occurred in psycholinguistics, artificial intelligence, psycho-neurophysiology, and cognitive psychology. Though there are many differences within the cognitive sciences, they for the most part share important fundamental and informing conceptions of cognition. The guiding ideal is that of finding the "internal" rules governing mental function. Implicit in this ideal are four philosophical commitments. These commitments, I would argue, are what bind together the cognitive sciences, forming a new paradigm that I shall call "cognitivism."[2]

The first of these commitments is "Methodological Individualism." Whereas behaviorists equated psychology with the search for relationships between environmental stimuli and behavioral responses, treating the mind as a "black box," cognitivists, who see the behaviorist program as a failure, try to understand the box's inner workings. The essential character of these inner workings is thought to be, in certain crucial ways, independent of the individual's relations to other individuals, to social practices, and to the environment. Thus, psychology becomes the study of the individual mind's inner workings.

The second commitment is to "Methodological Structuralism." What the cognitivist wants is an account of the structure of the fully mature capacity or cognitive structure. Thus, one of the striking features of cognitivism is the relative lack of interest in developmental or learning issues. Where questions of learning arise, learning is often modeled on full adult competency, typically that of hypothesis formation and confirmation or inductive extrapolation.

The third commitment is to "Intellectualism." This is the idea that all behavior is to be explained by some prior act of rule-governed cognition. Such explanation may be couched in terms of a practical syllogism in which the premises are beliefs and desires of the subject with the behavior as the conclusion; or it may be couched in terms of the manipulation of symbols according to the principles of logic or grammar or sound reasoning; or it may be couched in terms of the processing of information. Contemporary cognitivism breaks with the classical Intellectualism of the rationalists in that it is argued that such cognitive acts need not be conscious. Indeed for the most part, it is argued, they are unconscious.

Underlying these first three commitments is a fourth and deeply held philosophical conviction, that of "Psychological Realism." The mind is an arena of cognitive structures that are real and invariant across cultures. Environmental, social, and contextual features are needed only to help discover the nature of the underlying psychological realities; they are not *theoretically* essential to characterizing those structures and capacities themselves.

Developmental issues and learning – once at the very center of psychological theorizing – are of secondary interest theoretically.[3] Moreover, the accounts that are available are already highly delimited by the nature of cognitivist theory itself. For more rationalist oriented thinkers, like Noam Chomsky, developmental questions become "triggering" questions. When and why do certain environmental features trigger an already existent structure or capacity? Or is the triggering itself wholly innate, to be understood in terms of a process of inner maturation? What is triggered – rules, concepts, schemata? What kind of rules and which concepts are triggered? These are the questions addressed to those taking a rationalist approach to cognition. It is important to note that they are all raised from the perspective of the mature adult, in that the concepts and rules to be triggered are the very concepts and rules that characterize the adult performance.

For those who take an empiricist orientation – AI researchers and those using information-flow theory – learning is to be explained in terms of innate inductive extrapolation procedures for which the number of rules and the array of primitive concepts is much smaller than that hypothesized by the rationalist. Yet despite the differences between these two orientations, both accept the idea that what appears to be the development of more sophisticated cognitive abilities from less sophisticated cognitive abilities, can be explained in terms of the cognitive resources of the individual. What a person does is a function of the concepts and/or rules that characterize the psychologically real structures of his or her mind. This is the key idea behind psychological realism: The mind houses psychological structures that are real and invariant, such that what a person does can be explained in terms of the operations of these structures. The recognition of a musical composition, for example, is explained in terms of the ways in which the acoustic properties of the musical performance are encoded and processed in virtue of rules or rule-governed procedures that are internal to the mind itself. Whatever the music is, the explanation of recognition is given in terms of these interior rules of musical analysis.

Lev Vygotsky, a Russian psychologist whose most important work was done from 1926 to 1934, presents a strikingly different view of the mind. Vygotsky's theory, like the theories of the cognitive sciences, grew out of a dissatisfaction with behaviorism and psychological subjectivism. But where cognitivist theories move to the interior of the mind (what was going on to mediate between stimulus and the response), Vygotskian theory moves to the context of the behavior, to the social situation within which the action takes place. At the core of Vygotskian theory is a sustained challenge to the methodological assumptions of the cognitive sciences. On this view, cognitive abilities and capacities themselves are formed and constituted in part by social phenomena. A theory of cognition, then, must be a developmental theory. The individual and personal presupposes the public and intersubjective. For those pursuing a Vygotskian approach to cognition, the individualist orientation of cognitivism distorts the nature of these capacities.

The aim of this chapter is to introduce the reader to the central ideas of Vygotsky's thought and some of the ways in which psychologists and linguists are revising and extending these ideas in their own research. James Wertsch's *Vygotsky and the Social Formation of Mind* (Wertsch 1985a), a powerful but critical explication of Vygotsky's developmental theory, and his *Culture, Communication, and Cognition* (Wertsch 1985b), a collection of essays by psychologists and linguists who support and seek to extend Vygotsky's theory, provide the vehicle for this inquiry. In his book, Wertsch is primarily concerned to explicate Vygotsky's theory of cognitive development and to show how certain weaknesses in the theory can be addressed. The collection of essays represents not only elucidations of Vygotsky's ideas but also the attempts to use his theory as a working hypothesis in pursuing current research.

At the very core of Vygotsky's theory is the idea that psychological structures are not "given" in the individual mind, but are created through interaction with the social environment. Mental functions are the product of social interaction in such a way that they cannot be characterized independently of that interaction. Thus, the study of the development or genesis of cognitive capacities is of primary, not secondary, theoretical concern. This represents a radical break with the paradigm of cognitivism.

1 Vygotsky's theory of mind

In *Vygotsky and the Social Formation of Mind*, Wertsch presents a lucid and concise account of Vygotsky's approach to psychology. He organizes his account around "three themes that form the core of Vygostsky's theoretical framework...(1) a reliance on a genetic or developmental method; (2) the claim that higher mental processes in the individual have their origin in social processes; and (3) the claim that mental processes can be understood only if we understand the tools and signs that mediate them" (Wertsch 1985a: pp. 14–15). All three themes diverge from the methodological commitments of cognitivism. On a Vygotskian view the psychological realism and individualism of the cognitive sciences distorts our understanding of cognitive abilities. Our capacities to conceptualize or categorize objects or to solve problems must be understood developmentally. There is no single set of explanatory principles that explains what recognition is or what memory is or what attention is. There are two reasons for this. First, all such capacities undergo development and so change; and second, there is no such thing as *the* faculty of memory or *the* faculty of attention or *the* faculty of sentence recognition. Psychological realism brings with it an attempt to resurrect a kind of faculty psychology; each cognitive capacity has its structure that can be characterized independently of the other faculties.[4] But on Vygotsky's view relationships among cognitive capacities are such that they cannot be treated as independently existing functions or faculties that stand in certain determinate relationships to each other. Their interrelationship is constitutive of what each is. And central to Vygotsky's view is that the development of these cognitive capacities is social in origin and mediated by *changing uses of language*. The words stay the same from early uses of language to mature speech, but the *word-meanings* of these signs alter with the different stages of development. Thus, word-meaning is at the theoretical heart of his account of cognitive development. It is the basic explanatory element (the unit of analysis) in the explanation of the transition from one stage of cognitive development to another stage. As I hope to bring out, this is a theoretically exciting and rich conception, but one which also faces serious problems, problems being addressed by many who are building upon Vygotsky's basic approach.

With regard to Vygotsky's general developmental approach, Wertsch, drawing on the work of Davydov and Radzikhovskii (Wertsch 1985b),[5] argues that there is a significant gap between Vygotsky the methodologist and Vygotsky the psychologist. Vygotsky the methodologist stands for the more abstract theoretical claims of the theory, e.g., that there are two lines of development, one natural and one cultural, that these two lines of development interact dynamically to give rise to new forms of cognition. Vygotsky the psychologist stands for the detailed explanations given of particular phenomena, e.g., the explanation of early speech forms and the explanation of inner speech. The gap arises in the following way: Methodologically Vygotsky maintains that one cannot understand the emergence of human cognitive skills without understanding the dynamic relation the natural line of development has to the cultural or social line of development. Yet in his detailed explanations, the natural line of development drops out altogether. Thus, Wertsch calls for a more serious look at how the line is to be drawn between the natural and the social. Indeed, current experimental results show that the infant responds to social features of his world very early on, contrary to what is suggested by Vygotsky. This point is well taken, both with respect to how early social life influences the infant and with respect to Vygotsky's ignoring the natural line of development in practice. Of course, once we see how early and how powerfully social factors are involved in the infant's life and development, it becomes increasingly unclear how a line is to be drawn between the natural and the social. Is responding to a smiling face a natural response or a social response? Is "natural" doing what all normal children do under normal circumstances? Then, learning a language is natural. But this clearly doesn't capture the distinction that is intended. What is intended is the old distinction between what is already "within" the child and awaits only inner maturation, and what is provided to the child and shapes the child from outside. Vygotsky retains this distinction in his discussion of the very early development of the infant, but does very little with it. There are certain responses that are instinctual (the sucking reflex, the grip); there is physiological maturation that bears upon cognitive development (the growth of the myelin sheaths of the nervous system). Just how these factors interrelate with the social factors is left unspecified. Though this marks a deficiency in Vygotsky's account, it is not altogether surprising that Vygotsky does not take up this issue. His very account of the social formation of mind brings into question the intelligibility of drawing such a sharp contrast.

Indeed, the real problem here, it seems to me, lies with the simplicity of the contrast between the so-called "natural" line of development and the social line of development. There are at least two dimensions to this contrast. The first is the contrast between the natural as physiological maturation and the social as behavior informed by social interaction (and this would extend to much of the motor-perceptual behaviors of the child). The second is the contrast between pre-linguistic behavior (which would include both physiological maturation and the socially informed motor-perceptual orientation of the child) and linguistic behavior, which is clearly social. Thus, to address the problem of the relations between the natural and the social would require close examination of both of these dimensions of the contrast. This is a problem area that Vygotsky simply does not address adequately.

Having marked this general problem, let us examine the three major stages in cognitive development that Vygotsky identifies. At each stage, word-meaning changes such that the child stands in a different relation to the natural and social environment, and the transition is mediated by social processes that involve a changed use of language. Thus, Vygotsky offers us a heterogeneous theory of cognitive development; there are qualitatively different stages that require different explanatory principles. These three stages are marked by distinctive uses of language: (1) the earliest use of language is expressive and communicative. It is used to express the needs, desires, and interests of the very young child. (2) This is followed by the egocentric speech of the toddler, a kind of on-going commentary that the child engages in that seems to be directed to no one; this is replaced by inner speech by around the time the child is 7 years old. And finally (3) the child comes to use the symbolic speech paradigmatically displayed in mathematical and scientific discourse. Each form of speech marks a stage in cognitive development, and each is progressively more abstract (more "decontextualized," to use Wertsch's helpful phrase). Thus, the 2-year-old's cry of "juice" is directly expressive of her desire for juice, that it be given to her. This is unlike the 4-year-old's ongoing commentary on his blocks as he builds a house; the child's words neither seem directed towards anyone nor immediately tied to some particular desire. And neither of these is like the language of the 12-year-old as she solves a problem in general science.

The transition to each higher stage must be explained. Thus, the central theoretical concern for Vygotsky, on my reading, is a "bootstrapping" problem, namely, a problem of characterizing how more sophisticated competencies arise from less sophisticated competencies. Neither of the traditional approaches to this question, viz. the rationalist conception of the mind as replete with an array of innate cognitive structures or the empiricist conception of the mind as an inductive extrapolator from sensorily given data, is acceptable to Vygotsky. This claim calls for some qualification since Vygotsky does appeal to a strategy of inductive extrapolation, or referential mismatch, as the main impetus for development. It informs one of his more influential experimental techniques. Indeed, in their early work *A Study of Thinking,* Jerome Bruner, Jacqueline J. Goodnow, and George A. Austin (Bruner *et al.* 1965) follow Vygotsky in the use of this experimental strategy. However, this is a technique that can only apply to the later stages of cognitive development and cannot be used to model the early stages. Wertsch argues that "referential mismatches" cannot be the sole developmental mechanism, for they fail to do justice to "the close relationship between the lexical content of a noun phrase and how it occupies a certain propositional role" (Wertsch 1985a: p. 135). There are additional problems with this that I shall take up in the next section, "Refinements and extensions."

In contrast to the traditional approaches, Vygotsky offers a social theory. "Bootstrapping" cannot be explained by considering the child as an individual hypothesis generator and tester. The child as an individual hasn't the resources of the higher levels of cognitive functioning which are necessary to form hypotheses. These abilities are created only through sustained social interaction with adults. Vygotsky's point is not that there are hidden cognitive structures awaiting release through social interaction. His point is the radical one that they are *formed* through social interaction. Development is not the process of the hidden becoming public, but, on the contrary, of the public and intersubjective becoming hidden and private. To see this more clearly, let us look briefly at his three stages of cognitive development.

The first stage marks the transition to first uses of language. In this stage, the natural biological development of the infant becomes supplemented, and superseded in the cognitive domain, by the social development of the infant. The first use of language is purely social. It is an expressive-communicative use in which the words are extensions of the needs, interests, and desires of the child. In this early use of language, the word and the object are fused. Word-meaning is not separable from the particular object indicated by the word. At each stage, Vygotsky attempts to identify the word-meaning available to the child. At this early stage, word-meaning is purely indicative, or referential; this ties the word to the particular situated objects in the child's environment. This gives the word a highly contextualized meaning and use. All subsequent development is, on Vygotsky's view, a process of increased decontextualization of language until words are fully freed from control by the environment in the formation of what he calls scientific, or true, concepts. Since, as Wertsch points out, Vygotsky does little to characterize the relation between natural and cultural development, little is done to address this first bootstrapping problem.

This is not the case, however, with regard to the second stage of development. Here Vygotsky is concerned with the phenomenon of egocentric speech, its function, and its ultimate disappearance by around the age of 7 years. Piaget sets the challenge for Vygotsky. His critical discussion of Piaget's theory of egocentric speech and his own account of its function and importance are excellent. Piaget sees the child's development in terms of decentering, that is, in shifting from a self-centered orientation to the world to a socialized perspective that acknowledges the interests, needs, and viewpoints of others. This, according to Piaget, is achieved due to external social forces. Egocentric speech reflects this fundamental self-centered, or egocentric, thinking of the child in which the child pursues the satisfaction of his desires without regard to others; egocentric speech is not directed to anyone; it does not serve a social purpose. Indeed it seems to serve no real purpose, and so, according to Piaget, with the process of socialization, a process which forces the child to decenter and face reality, egocentric speech disappears.

Vygotsky rejects this entire approach. The child, far from living in an individualistic world of fantasy and fantasy wish fulfillment, is directed outwards to the real satisfaction of his needs. Egocentric speech is not an idle manifestation of self-centered thinking; rather Vygotsky argues egocentric speech serves an indispensable role in development. With egocentric speech, the function of the child's language changes from expressive-communicative to self-directed and self-guiding. It is not idle talk but the emergence of a new form of linguistic usage without which the child remains under the control of the environment.[6] The monologue that accompanies the child's activities is not idle, but is actually a tool for the child to come to guide his own actions. Thus, for Vygotsky development is a process of increased autonomy, i.e., increased voluntary control by the child over his own actions. With increased voluntary control comes increased consciousness on the part of the child, for the two are expressions of the same competence, made possible by a new use of language. Egocentric speech, or primitive self-regulating speech, then, as Vygotsky puts it metaphorically, "goes underground": it becomes inner speech. Inner speech is a later development that is parasitic upon intersubjective public speech.

Thus, any theory that attempts to explain the origin of overt speech in terms of inner thinking is profoundly mistaken. For Vygotsky verbal thinking does not precede speaking; on the contrary, it is made possible by speaking and grows out of speaking. However, Vygotsky is at pains to argue that inner speech or thinking is not speaking *sotto voce* ; it is not public speech spoken softly. It serves a different function from public speaking, though it has its origins in public speaking. It functions as a means of self-control, not communication or expression. This different function is reflected in a different syntax. Inner speech is marked by its striking abbreviation, which reflects the fact that it is used in self-control and not in communicating to others. But for language to function in this self-directed way, it is necessary that the word become separated from the object. The bootstrapping that enables the child to make the shift from the expressive use of language to the self-directed use of language in egocentric speech is achieved through a process of freeing the word from its fusion with the object or objects first indicated. As Vygotsky thinks of it, the word-meaning of a word undergoes a change as a result of the child's social interaction with adults and his peers.[7]

Vygotsky's notion of the "zone of proximal development" helps to

explain how he treats the process of freeing the word. The zone of proximal development is "the distance between the actual development level as
determined by independent problem solving and the level of potential
development as determined through problem solving under adult guidance
or in collaboration with more capable peers" (Vygotsky 1978: pp. 85–6).
Adult guidance in solving problems enhances the child's actual performance and results in enhanced, and at times, qualitatively changed
cognitive abilities. In other words, the child's cognitive growth cannot be
understood as the unfolding of an innate conceptual repertoire of
concepts or schemata; rather it is created in a situation of social interaction. The adult provides the structured context within which the child acts
as though with full understanding or *as though* he recognized the relation of
steps to the goal that he performs.

What is theoretically so important about the zone is that Vygotsky is
introducing an appeal to dispositions as explanatorily basic, rather than an
appeal to categorical structures underlying dispositions which is a foundational commitment of cognitivism. This is a point of great philosophical
divide between the two approaches. Let me elaborate on how this notion
addresses the bootstrapping problem. The child is working on a jigsaw
puzzle for the first time. On the cognitivist view, he needs to come to form
and test the right hypotheses about shapes and color matchings if he is to
learn how to do such puzzles. The wherewithal for forming such
hypotheses is innate. The problem is one of accessing. Vygotsky's description of the situation is quite different. The problem for the child is that he
hasn't the wherewithal to solve this problem. So how are we to explain
how the child shifts from being unable to solve jigsaw puzzles to being able
to do so? The child pulls himself up only within the structured environment and guidance provided by the adult. The right hypotheses do exist –
for the adult, but not for the child. So to focus on the child in isolation
from the social environment is to miss the very element that is crucial for
cognitive development, namely, the social interaction necessary for bootstrapping. It is in virtue of interaction of a certain kind that the hypotheses
come to exist for the child as well as for the adult (though again even in
learning the strategies for solving the puzzle the child may not understand
these strategies in the same way the adult does). The zone identifies the
child's potential relative to the appropriate kind of interaction with an
adult. Vygotsky's appeal to such a potential carries with it an explanatory
principle, namely, that the medium of development is social interaction,
not the intellectualist application of problem-solving strategies on the part
of the child.

Brown and Ferrara's critical examination of the performance of children on IQ tests supports these theoretical claims (Wertsch 1985b). They

present experimental results that show a clear connection between a process of training and performance on IQ tests. Low IQ children gain considerably from training, where training is not simply a matter of practice but of being directed in the use of techniques for solving problems. An important part of what their work shows is that the low IQ performers lack metacognitive skills, i.e., skills in data-collecting, checking, monitoring, and other self-regulatory behavior. Thus, they tend to treat each problem as though it were entirely new, regardless of relevant prior experience. In other words, the retarded performer treats each problem as highly specific, embedded in its particular context. Acquiring metacognitive skills is a matter of decontextualizing specific problems, and this process requires a reflexive use of language which can only be acquired through certain kinds of adult–child interactions.

In answering the bootstrapping problem in the way that he does, Vygotsky's perspective directly challenges two commitments of cognitivism. First, as I have already brought out, it challenges the Intellectualism of the cognitivist approach. The Intellectualist commitment of programs like a Chomskean psycholinguistics or artificial intelligence research reverses the Vygotskian order of development, and treats the metacognitive skills as basic. This is one of the core mistakes of the cognitivist approach. Cognitive development is to be explained in terms of being trained to act in certain ways, not in terms of applying rules, strategies, and the like. In holding this Vygotsky is denying two related but distinct claims. First, he is denying that rules, inductive procedures, and any other formally characterizable logical structures are explanatorily basic in the genesis of cognitive capacities; and second, he is denying that we explain actions by appeal to a prior individual act of theorizing or cognizing or thinking. (And this is not to say that there aren't occasions when actions do follow from such acts; but the ability to do this only comes much later.) Second, Vygotsky's perspective challenges a deeply held view on the nature of explanation itself, namely, the idea that all skills, potentials, abilities, and any other such dispositions must be explained in terms of an *underlying* structure. On Vygotsky's view there is no structural accounting for the dispositions appealed to, and no hint that any such structural accounting is either necessary or wanted.

So how, briefly, is the bootstrapping achieved from the first stage, viz. the expressive-communicative use of language, to the second stage, viz. egocentric speech leading to inner speech? Vygotsky does not himself focus on this problem in his discussion of egocentric speech in *Thought and Language*, as he is much more concerned to refute the Piagetian view and replace it with his own account of the process of internalization. But we can extrapolate the beginnings of such an account. The "mechanism" for growth is found in the zone of proximal development. But, of course, that zone is identified always relative to the cognitive skills of the child at the time. How does work within the zone enable the child's cognitive skills to change qualitatively?

For cognitive growth, there must be a change in the way language functions for the individual; word-meaning itself must change. All such changes involve, according to Vygotsky, the increasing "decontextualization" of words, the freeing of words from the particular contexts in which they are originally used. Two of the essays in *Culture, Communication, and Cognition*, those by Lee (Wertsch 1985b) and Wertsch and Stone (Ibid.), are especially useful in bringing out what is necessary for the decontextualization of words. Both essays focus on the process of internalization whereby social-communicative speech is transformed into inner speech via egocentric speech. The crucial change that makes egocentric speech possible, and with it self-directed behavior, is the separating of the word from its original indicative object. Wertsch and Stone emphasize the role played by child–adult interaction. The communicative speech of the young child is marked by the fact that words have a purely indicative, or referential, function; they do not have a meaning for the child as they do for the adult. The initial stages of the adult–child interaction turn on agreement of reference, but not on agreement of meaning.[8] Thus, the appearance of new words, these authors point out, marks the beginning rather than the end in the development of concepts.

Lee supplements this position very nicely by pointing out that the child's initial use of words is for the effects they can have on others, and that they can have such effects only in virtue of the social structuring of the situation by the adult. Cognitive development then is a matter of the child's coming to structure the situation for himself in which words come to function as causes of the child's own behavior. What is required for this is that the child comes to take words as representative. Words are detachable from their objects, and can be used to guide the behavior of the agent himself. Lee's central point is that the move from the communicative use of words to a self-regulating use of words is made possible by using words representationally. The emergence of egocentric speech is the medium for differentiating the representational use of words from the purely expressive or communicative.

But how does the child come to use words representationally? Wertsch's account leaves out a very important aspect of this early stage in the child's development, namely, play. Play gives a clear exemplar of how the word becomes separated from the object.[9] In play, the word, still fused with the object, becomes the pivot whereby a distinct object is taken for the original object by being designated with the same word. In other words, to detach the word from its object, it is important (paradoxically) that it is originally fused with the object. For example, the word "horse" is viewed as a property of particular horses. A "horse" just is a horse. The child is able in play to take a stick to be a horse by applying the word to it. He is not using the stick symbolically as a horse, and this is seen in the fact that not anything could be designated a horse; only that which can function as a horse, e.g., to be ridden. Thus, on Vygotsky's view children's play is not a function of free creative imagination but is hemmed in by all the constraints that are part of real horses or doctors or mommies (so far as the child has experienced them). Creative imagination grows out of the play of young children, but the two should not be confused. This is a tremendous insight on the part of Vygotsky.

The last of these three significant stages of development is marked by the emergence of what Vygotsky calls the higher mental functions:[10]

> it is precisely during early school age that the higher intellectual functions, whose main features are reflective awareness and deliberate control, come to the fore in the developmental process. Attention, previously involuntary, becomes voluntary and increasingly dependent on the child's own thinking; mechanical memory changes to logical memory guided by meaning, and can now be deliberately used by the child.
>
> (Vygotsky 1965: p. 90)

It is in connection with this change that Vygotsky explicitly introduces his notion of the zone of proximal development, using it in connection with the formal education required for developing these higher mental functions. Thus, it is no accident that Vygotsky's thought is being used and extended in theories of education and learning.[11] However, as I have indicated, it has a much broader theoretical application than this. Vygotsky argues that it is the very institutional structure of formal education that explains the complete decontextualization of words that mediates and makes possible the higher reasoning functions. Formal education in mathematics and the sciences in particular insists upon the pupil's learning and using formal definitions that place the use of a word within a highly structured hierarchy of concepts. Such definitions make the connection with objects in the world quite indirect and remote. The word is decontextualized.

Just as play used the fusion of word and object to make their separation possible, so formal education uses our ordinary everyday concepts (what Vygotsky calls pseudo-concepts) to sever completely the relation between word and object by defining words in terms of other words (what Vygotsky calls true concepts). For example, for the child to learn that force is mass times acceleration (a true concept), he must already have a work-a-day use of the word "force," a use explained by appeal to paradigmatic *examples* of force, like pushing or pulling an object. So there is an important shift from explaining meaning in terms of paradigmatic examples to formal definitions. What we have in Vygotsky's theory is a progression of linguistically mediated cognitive skills that build upon more primitive skills and can only be developed in a socially mediated environment. At this highest stage, the formation of concepts involves the reflexive use of language. Words are used to individuate the use of words.

This reflexive use of language brings with it an increased consciousness of the role of language, and with this increased consciousness comes increased control. Control over one's own behavior, begun with egocentric speech, extends to control over one's own thinking. This changes the character of thinking itself, and with it the ways in which attention, memory, and other central cognitive functions are organized. The mental functions are not static entities, but are individuated in terms of the role they each play within the larger system. That role is affected by, and in part determined by, the relation of each to the operations of other functions. Thus, memory or attention cannot be specified independently of the relations to the other functions. This underscores Vygotsky's deep disagreement with the approaches of the cognitive sciences, which treat these functions structurally. Memory, attention and the other mental functions have a structure, that can be characterized pyschologically or (perhaps) neurophysiologically. For Vygotsky, there is only the functioning with no underlying structure. Take memory for example; a common metaphor for memory is that it is a storehouse of information. Memory then requires as part of its structure a method of categorizing various bits of information, storage bins to keep the information in, and a method for retrieving the bits of information when called upon. A Vygotskian critique would hold that this metaphor reflects the highest mode of thinking. We are already characterizing the objects of memory as pieces of information, as though they were sentences written on pieces of paper and filed away. But this notion of information is a very abstract and sophisticated one, one which Vygotsky argues only arises in certain cultural situations at a relatively late stage in the cognitive development of the child. How then can such a view characterize all of memory? Indeed it is quite plausible to argue that early memories are expressed in action, in repetition, and in acting out, not in terms of information. That they are remembered in repetition or acting out shows that they derive from a more primitive stage in cognitive development, a stage that cannot be characterized by the storeroom metaphor.

So, to summarize the main features of Vygotsky's theory, we see that cognitive development is a process of the decontextualization of word-meanings by means of child–adult social interaction in which the child's zone of proximal development is fruitfully used. Social interaction is the "mechanism" whereby growth occurs, and it is also the source of the content of word-meanings. Just how the child is supported and guided serves to fix word-meanings, even as these evolve through the three stages. However, Vygotsky's account of word-meaning and his identification of it as the unit of analysis (the basic explanatory element of his theory) both suffer from serious difficulties. I shall turn to this now.

2 Refinements and extensions

The difficulties with Vygotsky's theory of word-meaning have provided the catalyst for psychologists and linguists to modify and extend Vygotsky's general approach in theoretically fruitful ways. So we need to look more closely at Vygotsky's notion of word-meaning.

The theoretical apparatus that Vygotsky helps himself to in explaining word-meaning is a familiar one. Word-meaning is to be explicated in terms of reference and sense. The referent of a term is its extension, that is, the set of objects to which it applies. The sense of a term, on the other hand, is its connotation, or meaning more colloquially understood, that is, it is that which fixes the extension of the term. The classic example of this distinction is that provided by the two co-referring expressions "The Evening Star" and "The Morning Star."[12] These two expressions refer to the very same object (namely, the planet Venus) but the senses of the two expressions are quite distinct. For Vygotsky, cognitive development is a process of increased generalization and increased abstraction, a process that Wertsch has described as one of increased decontextualization. Early communicative use of language, it is maintained, involves word-meanings that are purely referential, or indicative, whereas the rational discourse manifesting the higher mental functions requires the use of meaning that is dissociated from its referents ("signs defined in terms of signs"). Thus, word-meaning shifts from the use of the purely referential in expressive speech (e.g., "cat" as Tabby herself) to pure sense in scientific discourse (e.g., "force" as defined by means of a formula).

We clearly need a further account of these two forms of word-meaning in order to assess the adequacy of Vygotsky's account of cognitive development. Up to a point, the distinction between reference and sense is a plausible one to draw, but only up to a point. Vygotsky treats these two terms as basic in explicating meaning. In doing so Vygotsky helps himself to a static theory of meaning that is at odds with the dynamic social character of cognitive development that is indispensable to his theory. This tension in Vykgotsky's work is recognized by him to an extent, but is left unresolved.[13] It becomes the focus of attention for many of those who seek to adopt and modify Vygotsky's theoretical approach to cognition.

Given the importance that word-meaning has for his theory, it is surprising that he never develops a theory of either reference or sense beyond indicating that the referent of a term is established indexically while the sense is established by appeal to other signs. Why isn't this enough for a theory of meaning? Because we are left with the questions, how does the word come to refer to a particular object(s) or to have a particular sense? And how does a word refer to, rather than merely be associated with, an object? What is it for a word to have meaning? A traditional answer is that it is through the activity of the understanding or the intellect that the child is able to discriminate some object, baptize it with a name, and in so baptizing it, generalize beyond the initial object. This is the Intellectualist response. The child is already endowed with the higher cognitive functions and/or with a repertoire of innate concepts. But for Vygotsky concepts and the higher cognitive functions are precisely what are to be explained in terms of their gradual development, a development ushered in by ostension. So he can hardly appeal to a notion of meaning that presupposes these very capacities. Just how do reference and sense presuppose the very phenomena they are intended to make possible?

Vygotsky is quite aware that reference is not mere association. Parrots, dogs, and other animals can be trained to associate words with certain objects, but such association is not reference. Reference carries with it, implicitly, a rule or principle of generalization. Reference, traditionally, plays two roles. It is the means whereby a word is correctly associated with an object or some aspect of an object; and in virtue of so fixing the referent of the term, the object (or aspect) itself becomes the standard for future generalization. But for reference to play these two semantic roles (of naming and generalization), the mind of the agent must be endowed with considerable conceptual apparatus. And this, of course, is the very thesis that Vygotsky is challenging. First, a word can become a name or label for an object only against a background of beliefs about what is being picked out by the word. To fix the referent of a term requires a certain degree of stage setting. To use "cracker" or "salty" or "square" correctly in connection with a cracker, one must understand whether the term applies to the whole object, the taste, or the shape. Pointing, or otherwise ostending the object, does not reveal which of these aspects is being singled out. But if a background of belief is required to set the stage for successful naming, then reference can hardly be semantically primitive in establishing meaning. Second, once the object is named, it is held that the object itself can fix or determine the reference class for the term, and in this way, the object itself is the standard and vehicle for generalization. But no object can play this role by itself. What is required is some method of projection whereby the object can be used as a paradigm or prototype for a general kind. But this normative use of an object is not inherent in the object itself.

The Intellectualist tradition thinks it has an answer. It is through an act of mind that both primitive reference can be established and with it a method of projection or generalization. But again this kind of position is not available to Vygotsky. And indeed left at this level of characterization, appeal to an act of mind explains nothing; rather it is an appeal to a mysterious mental force that creates the very capacities we want to explain, namely, our capacity to generalize and our capacity to use words to refer to objects (as opposed to being uttered in their presence). So if Vygotsky is going to appeal to reference as the primitive or first stage in language formation, he needs to spell out more fully what he means by this. Otherwise he is left with problems to which an Intellectualist answer seems a solution. It is here that we see most sharply the need for a more fully developed account of the perceptual-motor skills of the very young child. It is clear that very early learning or training must build upon the behavioral repertoire of the child. However, even with a more fullsome account of this stage, we will not thereby get an account of the semantic and normative dimensions of reference and generalization. So long as Vygotsky looks to the tripartite relations among the individual child, the word, and the object, he will not be able to avoid the problem I have raised here. Vygotsky attempts to combine a social theory of cognition development with an individualistic account of word-meaning. My view is that the social theory of development can only succeed if it is combined with a social theory of meaning. By this, I mean that there is an ineliminable social element to meaning and reference themselves.

Moreover, Vygotsky wants to retain the connection that referring has to specific objects in a particular context while accommodating that to a process of generalization. And he wants to retain the idea of the distinctive way a child thinks within a social context structured by adults. To do this he needs a more sophisticated account of referring, as reference proper already carries with it a principle of generalization. His very lack of discussion of reference leaves him open to these criticisms.

What about meaning? For Vygotsky, meaning evolves with the developing stages of concept formation. Until the emergence of true concepts, the meaning of our everyday or spontaneous concepts is grounded in ostensive definition, in the appeal to particular situated objects. The concepts that are expressed by the same words throughout development follow a progression that is marked by increased decontextualization until appeal to actually existing objects to explain meaning gives way to definitions in terms of other signs or words (what Vygotsky calls the "true concepts").

How is the shift made from reliance upon an array of actual objects to reliance upon a verbal definition? From Vygotsky, we get no satisfactory answer; we get a shift from talk of reference to talk of sense. Throughout this account of the formation of concepts, no effective answer is given for the objections first raised about the validity of reference in establishing meaning. Now verbal definition is introduced as a mark of higher mental functions without an account of sense. We are left without an account of how generalization and abstraction are achieved. The tools we are given for explaining it – reference and sense – implicate a theory of abstraction that is completely at odds with Vygotsky's general approach, namely, abstraction is thought to be a basic operation of the mind of the individual. Vygotsky was involved in a struggle to extricate himself from the individualist approach, but did not fully succeed.

Wertsch takes Vygotsky to task over these same issues, but hopes to preserve his general account by supplementing his theory of meaning with current work in linguistics and by replacing Vygotsky's use of word-meaning as the unit of analysis with what he calls "activity-setting." Both modifications are welcome changes in Vygotsky's theory. However, the changes, especially the latter, carry a price of their own. But first how does Wertsch address these difficulties in Vygotsky's writings? The inadequacy within Vygotsky's account, according to Wertsch, turns on his reliance on the isolated word and the sign–object relation for word-meaning:

> [Vygotsky] took the word as his basic unit of semiotic analysis and thus overlooked an essential way in which young children's speech may "hook up" with certain aspects of prespeech practical action...
>
> [His] focus on words as isolated units prevented him from recognizing certain crucial aspects of word meaning itself [i.e., its propositional role] and the mechanisms that contribute to its development.
>
> (Wertsch 1985a: p. 134)

Vygotsky's theory can be corrected by supplementing his account of word-meaning with an account of how young children's speech "hooks up" with action ("discourse, or pragmatic, referentiality") and with the grammatical structure of their speech ("propositional referentiality"). Contemporary linguistics offers us the resources for this supplementation, according to Wertsch, resources that were not available to Vygotsky. In brief, the referentiality of speech is more complex than Vygotsky's concentration on the indicative, or purely referential, function of (some) words suggests.

Indicative referentiality, that which is secured through ostensive definition in which a special relation is created between the sign and the object, must be supplemented with discourse, or pragmatic, referentiality and propositional referentiality.

The referring function secured through ostension presupposes for its success these other two kinds of referentiality. First let me take up what Wertsch means by propositional referentiality. In focusing on isolated word–object relations, the propositional, or grammatical, role played by the word is ignored. Is it the subject or the object of an utterance? In using a word as, e.g., the subject, certain broad metaphysical categories are implicated in that use, that the word designates a "mover" that is "animate." So the child, in learning the propositional role that a word plays (its place in the structure of the idealized sentence),[14] is given hints about its lexical content, about what kind of object it picks out. What is being said is that the child masters the indicative function in part by learning the propositional role of the term within the sentence. The propositional role gives the child very general metaphysical categories without which the child cannot succeed in making the indexical identification. Thus, Wertsch concludes there is an essential connection between lexical content of a word and its propositional role.

I think that this is a mistaken way to try to correct a genuine difficulty in Vygotsky's theory. The real problem that it addresses is that ostensive definition by itself cannot secure reference, that is, it cannot secure a principle or rule of generalization. Ostensive definition presupposes a context of background belief on the part of the person who profits from such definition. This is what propositional referentiality is intended to address. If one understands the grammatical role, one thereby grasps some metaphysical categories that enable particular pointings to do the job. There is a twofold error in this view. First, it is a mistake to think that the child, in using words that reflect the categories of activity or passivity, thereby grasps or understands these categories and in virtue of that understanding uses them as he or she does. This leads straight to the Intellectualist position.

Second, even if it is correct that the child's use of language must reflect both lexical content and propositional role (and this does seem indisputable), it doesn't answer the underlying problem first raised about ostension alone. The propositional role, it is claimed, gives the child hints about the lexical content, and so is part of the apparatus that enables the child to grasp what is significant in an ostensive definition. But grasping the active–passive distinction, the animate–inanimate distinction, and the like presupposes an array of background beliefs just as much as grasping that the color is what is intended when one is given an ostensive definition of the word "red." Why should grasping a more general concept be easier than grasping a more particularized one, especially since Vygotsky has argued strenuously to the opposite effect. The most particular and contextualized uses of language are primary. So though Wertsch is correct that propositional role is as importantly descriptive as the indicative function is of a word, it doesn't carry with it an explanation of how ostension works and it doesn't address the stage-setting problem. On the contrary, it becomes part of the description of the problem.

Equally Wertsch's discussion of discourse, or pragmatic, referentiality underscores the problem of stage setting and background belief. The point here is that reference is secured only within a context and against a background of belief. Wertsch draws attention to the fact that even the form of an utterance changes as the context changes. All of this points to a degree of complexity that cannot be grounded in a word ostensively tied to an object. But neither do appeals to propositional and pragmatic referentiality help, though they do enrich our understanding of the phenomena we want to explain. Insofar as propositional referentiality explains (by its tacitly implicating metaphysical categories) it faces the same problems that ostensive definition does. And insofar as pragmatic referentiality draws attention to the complex context within which words are used, it identifies the problem area but does not resolve it. Appeal to both of these linguistic dimensions underscores the inadequacy of the traditional account of meaning Vygotsky appeals to, but neither solve the bootstrapping problem that is central to Vygotsky's developmental theory. Thus, the initial attempt to ground language and meaning in reference (even an enriched understanding of referentiality) has failed. The categories of propositional and pragmatic referentiality, then, do not refine explanation in terms of reference; rather they underscore the failure of reference to explain.

What can current linguistic theory add to our understanding of the (alleged) shift from the contextualized meanings of everyday concepts to the decontextualized meanings of true concepts? Here Wertsch appeals to a very important distinction, that between "extralinguistic context" and "intralinguistic context." True concepts, being defined by other signs, cannot be directly tied to environmental features. To use an archaic, but useful, phrase, they are "under the control" of other signs, not of the environment. Wertsch takes this point and combines it with his critique of the appeal to the isolated "sign–object" relation as basic. All sign–object relations, to be the requisite sort of relations for the use of language, are contextualized, that is, involve both propositional and pragmatic referentiality. Equally sign–sign relations must be contextualized as well. The important difference, according to Wertsch, is that sign–object relations are sustained against the background of an extralinguistic context whereas sign–sign relations are sustained against the background of an intralinguistic context. With the intralinguistic context, the child begins to operate with a new category of objects, objects created through speech. Wertsch gives several examples of such objects that have been studied experimentally. These include the use of pronouns and indexicals to refer back to an object introduced earlier by some descriptive phrase (endorphic reference); the use of direct or indirect speech (metapragmatic function);[15] and the use of theoretical concepts and discourse (metasemantic function). It is the use of theoretical concepts and discourse that marks the use of true concepts. The most important idea that is introduced by this contrast is that the mastery of true concepts, and so full theoretical discourse, requires that the child develop the ability to use language to operate on itself.[16] An important corollary to this account of the relation of theoretical discourse to everyday practical discourse is that the more basic functions of language cannot be explained in terms of a theoretical usage of language, a strategy adopted by many cognitivist theories. For example, the child's early use of language and our own everyday and unthinking use of language are explained in terms of forming hypotheses, garnering evidence, weighing probabilities. All this is part of the structure of theoretical discourse, the abilities for which are acquired only through extensive training.

As earlier in my discussion of referentiality, what we have here is a descriptive apparatus that draws attention to important differences in the use and order of development of language. But we still have our bootstrapping problem: How does the child develop the ability to use words to operate on words? There is a further difficulty with the distinction between intralinguistic context and extralinguistic context. The extralinguistic context is "defined by objects and action patterns" (Wertsch 1985a: p. 145) which provide the pragmatic presuppositions required for even the earliest stage of language use. The intralinguistic context is "created through speech alone" (Ibid.: p. 151). These characterizations will not do as they stand. Objects and actions do not in themselves create the appropriate structuring for the use of language. That structuring or patterning concerns the way in which linguistically competent adults structure the world for the child. And theoretical speech is rooted in skills and techniques of linguistic usage that are tied to practice and activity. Contrary to Vygotsky's way of expressing the progression in the development of concepts, there is no such thing as a fully decontextualized word. All words, like all uses of language, even the most theoretical and abstract, occur within a context of interests, concerns, and beliefs. We see here a second tension created as Vygotsky attempts to combine a static conception of meaning (most evident in his account of true concepts) and the dynamic functional aspects of language usage.

see other articles?

Let us move on to the second modification of Wertsch's. It grows out of the refinements already introduced. Once we accept these refinements, it follows that we can no longer hold onto the idea that the word is the unit of analysis. And indeed Wertsch and many others influenced by Vygotsky do not. In place of the word and word-meaning, Wertsch argues that the unit of analysis must be the activity setting. Several of the contributors to the anthology argue similarly.[17] "Activity-setting" clearly is a technical term, and it designates an activity in which social institutional factors have a fundamental role in defining that activity. This is a significant break with Vygotsky, and in two important ways. First, for Vygotsky, word-meaning still can be characterized in terms of the relation of the individual to an object in the world; in this way Vygotsky holds onto the ideal of a clearly defined explanatory atom (his unit of analysis). For activity theory, the social structuring itself is constitutive of the activity. Second, given Vygotsky's account of word-meaning, we had a fairly good idea of how to specify the meaning of a word in terms of the sign–object relationship (or we thought we did). But with activity-setting, it is much more doubtful that we can find a way theoretically of identifying the basic activity-settings. Wertsch is very clear that he does not want to reduce psychology to sociology[18] nor does he want to reduce psychology to the anecdotal level of cataloguing particular activity-settings. Wertsch hopes that Russian activity-theory psychology will provide the alternative that is needed. There is much that seems promising here and also much that seems unnecessary.

Wertsch completes his book with a chapter on the relation that general socio-historical events have to the development of cognition. He takes it as a lacuna in Vygotsky's work that he never develops the relation of mind to the historical evolution of social institutions. Vygotsky does argue that the decontextualization of concepts is closely tied to participation in formal schooling, but he does not address the question of why the literary practice that gives rise to formal education occurs in our social history. This question, Wertsch suggests, is to be answered along general Marxist lines concerning the emergence of bureaucracy, of a reified commodity structure, and the like. This, it seems to me, leads up a blind alley. It presupposes that there are something like laws of history, which, once known, will complete the account we have of the development of cognition. But certainly the idea that there are such laws of history has been discredited.[19] Appeals to institutional structures like bureaucracy or labor as commodity simply cannot explain the decontextualization of concepts. Moreover, in a very interesting contribution to *Culture, Communication and Cognition,*[20] we see strongly defended a very different and more subtle account of the place of general historical and cultural enquiry in

Vygotsky's thought; one that does not turn on an ideological commitment to Marxism. There is a tendency among some who support a Vygotskian approach to psychology to see Marxist ideology as a necessary component of Vygotsky's theory. Although I do not doubt the importance that the Soviet revolution had for Vygotsky personally and for the development of his thought, I think it no accident that he did not develop the alleged relations between cognitive development and Marxist socio-historical laws.

3 Concluding remarks

Increasingly, there are many psychologists interested in cognition and development, for whom neither behaviorism nor cognitivism is adequate to address the learning and developmental questions they pose for themselves. This, combined with criticisms of Piaget's developmental theory, has made the need to look for an alternative model of the mind more pressing. Vygotsky's dynamic social conception of the mind provides just such an alternative. His two most powerful insights are that language plays an ineliminable role in the constitution and formation of cognition and that inner thought develops from public speech. The greatest subtlety and the greatest weakness of his thought converge in his account of language. The subtlety turns on his understanding that the words themselves change in their semantic role for the child, and it is this change that mediates cognitive growth. This change in the semantic role of the word is made possible by the social structuring provided by the adult. The weakness lies with his theory of meaning, so crucial for his psychological theory. But this weakness is now a source of theoretical innovation that will not only buttress Vygotsky's developmental approach but deepen its explanatory power. My own view, very briefly, is that Vygotsky's approach to the role language plays in cognitive development would be well served by replacing his theory of word-meaning with the account of language and meaning presented in the later work of the twentieth-century philosopher, Ludwig Wittgenstein. Wittgenstein's characterizations of language implicate the ways in which meaning is constituted by the shared judgments and actions of the community. In short, Wittgenstein develops a dynamic conception of meaning that complements the developmental theory offered by Vygotsky.

Notes

Introduction

1 The recent renewal of interest in explaining consciousness testifies to this (Dennett 1991; Searle 1992; Dretske 1995). Functionalist and cognitivist theories of mind have long sidestepped this problem, but it has been remarkably intransigent to attempts to ignore or eliminate it. The argument of this book is directed not only against the classical Cartesian conception of experience and sensations but also against the idea that intentionality is "the easy problem" that current cognitivist theories have adequately solved, as David Chalmers has expressed in his defense of dualism (Chalmers 1996: p. 24).

2 This is much closer, in some respects, to the way in which Quine conceives of the agreement we reach in the use of language. See Quine 1960: p. 59 and Quine 1969b: p. 46.

3 This is an oversimplification of Quine's current views. He has, since the earlier work, especially "Two Dogmas of Empiricism" (Quine 1961), come to hold a modified form of holism, a "moderate" holism that allows for multiple systems of holistically connected beliefs (Quine 1990: pp. 13ff.).

4 Indeed Vygotsky is cited by J. Bruner (Bruner *et al.* 1965) as a forefather to the cognitivist approach that Bruner defends.

1 Wittgenstein on representations, privileged objects, and private languages

1 A.J. Ayer expressed this very well when he argued for the need to recognize two kinds of linguistic rule: "it is necessary that, beside the rules which correlate symbols with other symbols, our language should also contain rules of meaning, which correlate symbols with observable facts" (Ayer 1969: p. 112). Ayer's motivation for this is primarily epistemological; the threat of scepticism can only be removed if it can be shown that there is a direct and immediate link somewhere between language (or some part of language) and the world.

2 Malcolm's interpretation of the private language argument has been repeatedly attacked; one of the most influential of these argues that the private language argument is simply a new application of the Principle of Verification, and, as such, subject to the same difficulties any application of the Principle is. This argument is developed most forcefully by Judith Thomson 1964 and put to considerable work by J.A. Fodor (Fodor 1975: pp. 68–71).

Thomson offers an essentially correct analysis of the argument but she misdiagnoses what goes wrong it. She argues that there are three stages in the development of Malcolm's argument:

1. Classificatory terms must be rule-governed.
2. (1) requires that it be possible to distinguish between following the rule and seeming to follow the rule.
3. (2) requires that if one seems to follow the rule, it must be possible to determine whether the rule is actually followed.

The third stage is crucial, for a private "rule," it is alleged, is not susceptible to such a determination. Thomson treats this third stage as an application of the Principle of Verification – to determine what objects truly fall under the classificatory term. As she puts it, "A sign 'K' is not a kind-name in a man's language unless it is possible to find out whether or not a thing is of the kind associated with 'K' " (p. 137). So, she concludes, the private language argument is just a new version of verificationism.

I have two things to say about this analysis of Malcolm's argument: (1) even if Thomson is right that Malcolm does appeal to the Principle of Verification, it is not necessary for the argument, and so, to construe the private language argument as a reapplication of this Principle misses the point. The third stage of the argument requires only that there be some way of drawing a distinction between following a rule and seeming to follow a rule – it does not require that the distinction be sound. For Malcolm is arguing that it cannot be known whether a private rule is applied *consistently*, and consistent application does not require true application. That this is the fundamental issue can be seen from Malcolm's opening question in the passage quoted above: "Now how is it to be decided whether I have used the word consistently?" (2) To insist that a distinction must make a difference may be a form of verificationism, but it is hardly positivist verificationism. The peculiar flavor of the private language argument comes in showing just how the adherent of private language fails to draw a distinction with a difference.

3 For a detailed and excellent discussion of the various convolutions this line of argument can take, see Saunders and Henze 1967.
4 This point is made especially clearly by Robert Fogelin (Fogelin 1976: Ch. 13). He argues that Wittgenstein is trafficking in what he calls "general sceptical arguments" at this point. Such arguments, he maintains – and correctly so – cannot be safely contained; in as far as they are successful against certain solutions to a problem, they are successful against all solutions to the problem. In PI §265, Wittgenstein seems to think that a public time-table will do the job of determining whether one is correct about the time of departure in a way that memory cannot. To this, Fogelin suggests that we examine Wittgenstein's own method for checking memory reports.

Supposedly, in the time-table example, I can check my recollection by looking at a genuine time-table. To pick one sceptical doubt of any number available what is my criterion for saying they match?: Is it that they seem to match? That doesn't help, for things may seem to match without matching, so we appear to need yet another standpoint for deciding whether my recollection really matches or only appears to match the real time-table.

(Fogelin 1976: p. 163)

5 This point needs some qualification, or perhaps clarification. The issue of uncheckable checks does lead to a blind alley; the issue of whether there are privileged objects of representation which are (to use Sellars' phrase) "self-authenticating" is the real target though it is mistakenly confused with the uncheckable checks issue. I discuss the real target in section 3.

6 Thomson thinks that Wittgenstein holds that there is something especially wrong with private ostension (Thomson 1964: pp. 130–1). This is a mistake. Wittgenstein deliberately reminds the reader of his earlier discussion of ostension in the paragraph (PI §257) immediately preceding his characterization of a private language (PI §258).

7 See note 4.

8 Anthony Kenny (Kenny 1973: especially pp. 192–3) suggests an alternative reading of this passage: the appeal to a "subjective justification" for the use of a private sign "S" is viciously circular, for what is used as a justification (memory of what "S" means) is the *very* thing that is to be justified. In other words, Kenny claims, the independence Wittgenstein insists on is not sceptically motivated but is trivially acceptable: One's ground cannot be the very thing that is being justified. This is a simple logical point, not a sceptical remark about the adequacy of memory as check. This is a promising suggestion; however, I do not think that it is correct. It is not the case, as Kenny claims, that "the memory of the meaning of 'S' is being used to confirm itself" (Kenny 1973: p. 193). This appears to be the case, for if I have remembered the time of departure correctly it will match my memory of the time-table. But this would equally be true if one were matching the memory of the time of departure with a public time-table. The weight of Wittgenstein's argument seems to rest on the claim that the memory of the time-table cannot be checked for correctness. Of course, any attempt to check *this* memory (without appealing to public criteria) would be circular, as Kenny claims, but this is the point at which the empiricist would stop the chain of justification arguing that this memory is in some way self-justificating. So Kenny's interpretation embroils him in the same debate that I argued leads up a blind alley.

9 That Wittgenstein speaks of the standard meter and color charts in the same connection does not mean that he sees no differences between the highly conventional use of the standard meter and the way in which we identify colors. His discussion of the peculiarity of basic color judgments (as both judgments and standards for correctness) in *On Certainty* (OC §522–48 and 624–8) and *Remarks on Colour* displays the way in which color judgments are fully human institutions without being simply given to us in our sensory experience nor being matters of decision, as in the case of the standard meter.

10 Several commentators have been drawn to this interpretation. David Pears (Pears 1969, p. 161) clearly thinks this is the road to the preservation of private languages. He argues in Chapter 8 "Sensations," that Wittgenstein is only successful in showing that meaning cannot be private, but that he cannot show that reference cannot be private. Wittgenstein tackles this problem explicitly and succeeds in showing that private reference is as vacuous as private

meaning. Pears substantially modifies his treatment of the private language argument in his more recent book, *The False Prison*, vol. 2 (Pears 1988: Chs 13–15). Here Pears strives to identify what he calls the "disabling defect" of a private language, which focuses on the unavoidable linguistic incompetence of the solipsist.

The exemplary passage I use here comes from Pears' early work on Wittgenstein, but similar interpretations have been defended by other commentators. For example, see Donagan 1966 and Hintikka and Hintikka (1986. This interpretative strategy, it seems to me, is closely allied to the "two meaning" theory defended by R. Carnap, "Psychology in Physical Language" (Carnap 1932) and A.J. Ayer (Ayer 1946). Instead of talking of the first-person meaning and the third-person meaning of a word like "pain," one talks of public meaning and private reference.

11 Hintikka and Hintikka have construed the "beetle in the box" passage in a similar way though, curiously, they see this argument as supporting their striking interpretive claim that Wittgenstein never rejected a Cartesian metaphysics of mind, only a Cartesian semantics for phenomenological language (Hintikka and Hintikka 1986). This is at best a misleading way to put the point that I am making that Wittgenstein is not rejecting the claim that we human beings experience various sensations including pains. But this commonplace is not thereby an endorsement of Cartesian metaphysics.

12 If one thinks that the private sensation does have a use, namely, to guide the subject in his application of the word "pain," then we have come full circle, for this is the full-fledged version of a private language.

2 Private states and public practices: Wittgenstein and Schutz on intentionality

1 This characterization of consciousness as private is contested by Maurice Natanson in his article "Alfred Schutz on Social Reality and Social Science" (Natanson 1970: p. 111). To so characterize the subjective reflects, Natanson tells us, "the classical error of interpreting 'consciousness' in individual, 'interiorized' terms. It is not private contents of an introspective awareness but the structure of intentionality." Aron Gurwitsch in his "Problems of the Life-World" makes a similar point: "consciousness…must not be taken, as it was by Descartes, for a partial mundane domain, a series or set of mundane events alongside other mundane events…" (Natanson 1970: p. 44). Rather he tells us consciousness should be considered only as "opening up access to objects and entities of every kind" (Ibid.: p. 44). The idea seems to be that the contents of consciousness cannot be treated as empirically occurring episodes but as reflecting the transcendental structure of intentionality. But if a transcendental inquiry into intentionality is just an inquiry into the structure of intentionality, then any account of intentionality could be said to be transcendental. However, whether an account is individualistic or not is a further question. And Schutz, Gurwitsch, and Natanson all agree that the intersubjective mundane world needs to be grounded transcendentally in the subjective, and the subjective is characterized explicitly and implicitly in individualistic terms. Schutz tells us that "[w]e must, then, leave unresolved the notoriously difficult problems which surround the constitution of the Thou within the subjectivity of *private experience*" (Schutz 1967: p. 98, my italics). Gurwitsch hopes for a

transcendental reduction in which consciousness can be seen as "*opening up* access to objects and entities of every kind" (Natanson 1970: p. 44). The argument of my chapter is that these promissory notes cannot be cashed in, and that is because no *individualistic* account of meaning and intentionality can be correct. So denials of privacy are simply beside the point.

2　For Wittgenstein, on the other hand, something analogous to the We-relationship "founds" our *self*-experience as much as our experience of others, and so cannot be derived from our self-experience.

3　Just as Schutz distinguishes between the meaningless stream of consciousness and the meaning endowed through a retrospective act of reflection, so he distinguishes prephenomenal behavior from phenomenal behavior. While engaged in a behavior, it is meaningless: "one's own behavior, while it is actually taking place, is a *prephenomenal* experience. Only when it has already taken place (or if it occurs in successive phases, only when the initial phases have taken place) does it stand out as a discrete item from the background of one's other experiences" (Schutz 1967: p. 56). Wittgenstein, it seems to me, is pointing to something similar when he appeals to "blind obedience" to a rule. However, though the individual agent acts blindly, without reflection or interpretation, his actions are nonetheless meaningful. Schutz, touching on an important point, mischaracterizes behavior as meaningless because he has identified meaningfulness as originating in an act of interpretation. Given that behavior and experience do not emerge from interpretation, the only conclusion he can draw is that they are meaningless. Wittgenstein's view provides an alternative, and it turns on his social view of meaning.

4　This shift takes Schutz much closer to Husserl's account of the sign as expression in his *Logical Investigations*, Vol. 1, "Investigation I Expression and Meaning" (Husserl 1970). Husserl is very careful to distinguish the sign as indication of an object and the sign as meaningful expression. To try to treat meaning as a mental picture "runs counter," he says, "to the plainest facts" (Husserl 1970: p. 299). "The grasp of understanding, in which the meaning of a word becomes effective, is…in a sense an understanding and an interpretation" (Husserl: p. 309). There are "meaning-conferring acts" that provide the interpretation. What is important in this context is that Husserl rejects all accounts of meaning that fail to capture the dynamic, projective aspect of meaning, e.g., meaning as a mental picture, the physical sign itself functioning as a surrogate for meaning, and meaningfulness as no more than a feeling of familiarity. Yet we are left puzzled as to what the meaning-conferring acts do. Insofar as this is to be understood, as Husserl suggests, to involve interpretation, then Husserl's account is also subject to the difficulties raised by Wittgenstein's Paradox of Interpretation.

5　Please note that Wittgenstein is not saying that we don't find the first natural and the others quite counter-intuitive. Part of his view is that we do. But this cannot be appealed to by the advocate of meaning as interpretation.

6　In "Husserl's Perceptual *Noema*," H.L. Dreyfus (Dreyfus 1982b) argues that for Husserl the fulfillment of an empty intention is unintelligible because fulfillment itself is an intentional sense which might be empty or fulfilled. This internal conflict is like the one I bring out in Schutz's account of the relation among sign, interpretive scheme, and object. There I argued that the object cannot be the standard of adequacy for the interpretive scheme as it is itself a meaningful structure and so presupposes the very interpretive scheme for which it is supposed to provide a standard. I want to thank Joe Rouse for bringing this to my attention.

7 See Chapter 8, "Rules, Community, and the Individual," for a fuller discussion of this important point.

8 Also Wittgenstein's view of meaning makes central two ways of characterizing meaning that Husserl, in defense of a subjectivist account of meaning-conferring acts, argues are mistaken. These are what Husserl calls the "surrogative function" of signs (Husserl 1970: p. 304) and the "quality of familiarity" as the mark of understanding (Ibid.: p. 308). Both elements are to be found in Wittgenstein's account: Signs are not related to our actions and the world *via* a meaning-conferring act and understanding is a matter of going on as a matter of course, i.e., in a fully familiar manner.

9 On this point, Schutz comes remarkably close to Frege. Frege distinguishes between the customary sense of a word ("the regular connexion between a sign, its sense, and what it means") and its indirect sense (an "associated idea" that is to be distinguished from the meaning and sense of the sign), when it occurs within an oblique context (Frege 1952: pp. 58–9). Frege and Schutz alike seek to distinguish transparent from oblique contexts in terms of a difference in the objects denoted. Wittgenstein, on the other hand, locates the difference in the contexts of use, not in the objects denoted. For on his view, the sentences in question do not denote objects in the requisite philosophical sense at all, namely, objects cannot fix meaning.

10 This does not commit Wittgenstein to the position that an expecting person must always say aloud what it is that he expects. He may well say it to himself or be disposed to say so. These latter cases, however, are dependent upon the paradigmatic situation in which voice is given to one's expectation.

3 Wittgenstein, Kant, and the "metaphysics of experience"

1 Bernard Williams echoes this view when he argues that Wittgenstein is a transcendental idealist – "the limits of our language mean the limits of our world" – in his "Wittgenstein and Idealism" (Williams 1974: p. 145). Let me note here that Pears has substantially moved away from his strong Kantian reading of Wittgenstein's later work and the puzzles it brings to a much more naturalistic account, one that comes much closer to my own reading of Wittgenstein in its emphasis on the importance of our shared natural reactions and of our training into language games (Pears 1988).

2 The first edition of *Insight and Illusion* (Hacker 1972) defends a strong Kantian reading of the *Investigations*, an interpretation that Hacker later comes to modify substantially in his revised edition of *Insight and Illusion* (Hacker 1986). Importantly, Hacker comes to agree with the main thesis of this chapter that Wittgenstein does not develop transcendental arguments to establish a priori synthetic propositions (Hacker 1986: pp. 206–14).

3 There is a debate in Kant scholarship as to whether the pure concepts are independent of the schematized judgment. There are certainly those who think that the concepts can only be understood as "rules for the performance of mental activities" rather than mental entities of some sort. In *Kant's Theory of Mental Activity*, Robert Paul Wolff puts the point as follows: "Concepts for Kant cease to be *things* (mental contents, objects of consciousness) and become *ways of doing things* (rules, forms of mental activity)" (Wolff 1963: p. 70). Whether one

thinks of concepts as mental contents or rules, Wittgenstein's objection holds. So though I favor Wolff's interpretation, it is not incumbent upon me to resolve this debate as to whether Kant's "concept" is independent of being schematized or not.

4 I am using the way Hacker characterizes the Wittgensteinian project in the first edition of *Insight and Illusion* (Hacker 1972). Pears develops a similar view in his account of Wittgenstein's method as one of oscillation and of Wittgenstein's task as the search for the limits of language (Pears 1969: Chs 5 and 6). And more recent commentators have emphasized what they see as Wittgenstein's search for the limits of sense. What is common to all these transcendental interpretations is that Wittgenstein is seen as seeking to find the limits of the intelligible. In certain ways, I think that Pears offers a more subtle and plausible account, especially in his concern for describing how Wittgenstein's program, which essentially involves citing ordinary linguistic facts, differs from the empirical science of linguistics.

5 Yet even this is a curious example, as I shall show shortly. The claim that Napoleon won the battle of Austerlitz is an empirical historical claim for which there is massive evidence, but it is also a kind of standard itself. It is a paradigmatic historical claim and as such it is not susceptible to serious doubt nor could one be mistaken about it. To doubt this claim is to throw a shadow over all of historical inquiry. If the historian is wrong about this, all historical inquiry is suspect. The only way doubt can be raised about this claim is by raising some general sceptical arguments about the possibility of knowledge *tout court* or by discovering countervailing evidence to the effect that his alleged triumph was a political conspiracy of monumental proportion. Neither of these, however, in themselves provide reason or ground for doubting that Napoleon did win the battle. General sceptical argument, Wittgenstein maintains, is never to the point. And the possibility that counter-evidence will be found does not, as a possibility, provide reason to doubt the claim now.

6 That this is Kant's aim is shown clearly in his famous remark that it "remains a scandal to philosophy and to human reason in general that the existence of things outside us (from which we derive the whole material of knowledge, even for our inner sense) must be accepted merely on faith, and that if anyone thinks good to doubt their existence, we are unable to counter his doubts by any satisfactory proof" (Kant 1964: p. 34, note a (B xl)).

7 One could say that propositions such as "The earth has existed long before my birth" are relatively a priori, i.e., a priori relative to a particular domain of discourse or inquiry. See OC §138. That the earth existed long before my birth is a priori relative to historical inquiry – it is a condition for such inquiry and it stands in need of no justification; in that context it is certain and beyond doubt. For the geologist, on the other hand, how old the earth is is a matter for inquiry. It might be said, in this context, that the "presupposed" proposition in question is an empirical claim standing in need of justification. Yet even in this case there is something odd about saying that the geologist looks for evidence that the earth has existed long before his birth. He doesn't seek to confirm or disconfirm that claim; it is "presupposed" just as much for his task as it is for the historian. It is true that any evidence for the earth's being millennia old is a fortiori evidence for the earth's having existed long before my birth. Again this is a logical relation and not to be confused with the characterization of the target of the investigation.

8 Cf. PI §48–50 for a discussion of the dangers of confusing the object as representation with the representation as object.

9 Though I speak of kinds of propositions that hold fast, this is a family resemblance notion. There are exemplary cases of methodological propositions that are held fast by our activities and judgments (the world has existed since long before my birth), of "judgments of judgment," that is, judgments that are norms (Napoleon was exiled to Elba, $2 + 2 = 4$), and of propositions as rules (the number of primes is infinite). Moreover, a single proposition may change its role given the context of use. I have already indicated two such cases in notes 4 and 5 above.

4 Language learning and the representational theory of mind

1 Of course, ignoring epistemological issues does not in itself eliminate them if they are real problems. Indeed, many philosophers worry (and rightfully so) that the RTM in any of its guises carries with it "veil of perception" problems. I shall not, however, pursue this issue here, but shall allow that a successful distinction can be made between the philosophical problem of knowledge of the external world and the psychological problem of explaining the mechanisms of language learning and the like. Fodor is aware of what he calls an "epistemological version" of the RTM, but hopes it can be avoided (cf. Fodor 1981: pp. 325–6). Fodor later comes to revise this stance of neutrality with respect to epistemological issues. Indeed he comes to argue that the observation–theory distinction that is so important for theories of knowledge as well as theories of scientific explanation can be made "naturalistically" as it were by his computational theory of mind.

2 The expression "computational theory" has been extended in its use to cover connectionist models as well as the classical computational models of Artificial Intelligence. I shall use the expression only in its restricted sense to refer to classical computational models. I do not discuss connectionist models, but it should be clear that such models are much more compatible with the views I defend.

3 I use "cognitive psychology" narrowly (as often happens) to refer to those psychologists who are committed to an inner-process theory of cognitive states and abilities.

4 In Chapter 10, I shall focus on important ways in which Vygotsky resists easy accommodation to the contemporary cognitivist picture of mind. Though Vygotsky's picture is committed, as is cognitivism, to the reality of internal mental processes, he attributes much less innate structure to those processes than cognitivism does. Importantly, he assigns much more explanatory weight to social factors than Fodor, for example, does. But Fodor, insofar as he appeals to Vygotsky and Bruner, is looking for support for his hypothesis-formation model of the higher cognitive capacities.

5 *A Study of Thinking* (Bruner *et al.* 1965) is a classic work that makes the theoretical move from a behaviorist paradigm to the cognitivist paradigm. It is interesting to contrast this book with Bruner's more recent work in which he has come to emphasize the important explanatory role of the social (Bruner 1997).

6 See N. Chomsky, "Review of B.F. Skinner's Verbal Behavior" (Chomsky 1959: pp. 26–58). This argument is made in Section 3 where Chomsky argues that "the word 'stimulus' has lost all objectivity in this usage. Stimuli are no longer

part of the outside physical world; they are driven back into the organism." Also see Kohler 1947: Ch. 3, for an excellent early discussion of the difficulties inherent in behaviorism.

7 Fodor thinks that this kind of objection misfires, for it is directed to the epistemic issue of how we are able to apply concepts successfully in the world. His view is that a sharp distinction between meaning and belief circumvents this kind of objection altogether on the grounds that it is the concepts that are innate, not beliefs about the nature of the world. See Fodor 1975: esp. pp. 62–3. Whether Fodor can so readily disassociate these is part of the discussion of the next section.

8 As we have seen above, for this account of the learning process to be correct, "experience" must be construed very broadly; it cannot be taken to refer to sensory experience only. However, there is reason to believe that Fodor does take it in this narrow way, and insofar as he does, his account of concept learning is mistaken.

9 One of the difficulties in discussing Fodor's views and arguments is that it is not always easy to see what he is saying. Fodor's stance towards Bruner's inductivist model is a case in point. He introduces it in a way that implies that he endorses it: Yet he also suggests that it is intended only as an illustration of the claim that cognitive processes are computational (Fodor 1975: p. 34).

10 Support for the hypothesis formation model of concept attainment comes, not so much from any empirical evidence for it, as from a priori considerations. There are, as Sir Karl Popper has argued in *Conjectures and Refutations*, "decisive arguments of a purely logical nature" against the classical empiricist notion of the completely naive learner:

> This apparently psychological criticism has a purely logical basis which may be summed up on the following simple argument....The kind of repetition envisaged by Hume can never be perfect; the cases he has in mind cannot be cases of perfect sameness; they can only be cases of similarity. Thus they are repetitions only from a certain point of view. (What has the effect upon me of a repetition may not have this effect upon a spider.) But this means that, for logical reasons, there must always be a point of view – such as a system of expectations, anticipations, assumptions, or interests – before there can be any repetition; which point of view, consequently, cannot be merely the result of repetition.
>
> (Popper 1963: pp. 44–5)

These systems of expectations, anticipations, and interests are, so far as Fodor is concerned, computational systems and so systems involving representations. An important line of inquiry, but one that I shall not take up in this chapter, is whether where one finds systems of expectations and the like, there one finds computational systems.

11 To a large extent, Fodor attempts to avoid these difficulties by shifting the burden to others. He maintains that to understand an internal representation is not to understand what determines its truth conditions. Rather understanding is achieved through the fact that there is an interpretative function that maps strings of internal representations onto their truth conditions in the world. This interpretative function is biologically realized in such a way as to guarantee the

appropriate links between truth conditions and concepts. As Fodor puts it, "What takes the place of a truth definition for the machine language is simply the engineering principles which guarantee this correspondence" between use of internal representations and conditions in the world (Fodor 1975: p. 66). So one is just wired up to understand the internal representation #cat#. But this doesn't avoid Wittgensteinian objections concerning the individuation of concepts – it turns them over to the physiologist or the ethologist or whoever is supposed to determine what conditions "trigger" what mechanisms.

12 Two important assumptions are implicit in this discussion: (1) The hypothesis-formation model entails the computational theory; and (2) cognitive phenomena require an explanation in terms of an epistemic model. Both are highly questionable assumptions, but I cannot take them up in this chapter.

13 This expresses a "deeper intuition" with which Fodor is in sympathy, that it is "actually *mandatory* to assume that mental processes have access to formal (nonsemantic) properties of mental representations" (Fodor 1981: p. 325).

14 Hilary Putnam summarizes these difficulties with trying to formulate a purely formal inductive logic in *Reason, Truth and History* (Putnam 1981: pp. 188ff.). As Putnam characterizes this scepticism about constructing a formal inductive logic, "increasingly it is coming to be believed it is not possible to draw a sharp line between the content of science and the method of science" (Putnam 1981: p. 191).

Postscript to Chapter 4

1 This consequence is recognized by many cognitive psychologists who now endorse a strong form of nativism. See, for example, Frank Keil's work on concepts (Keil 1992), Steven Pinker's defense of a strong nativist position with respect to the acquisition and use of language (Pinker 1994), and Henry Wellman's hypothesis that children have an innate theory of mind (Wellman 1990).

2 Fodor also accepts this characterization of the belief system and in particular the relation between hypothesis and confirmation (Fodor and Lepore 1992: Ch. 2).

3 In adopting a causal theory of denotation, Fodor inherits all the problems traditionally associated with denotational theories of meaning. These include the following: the problem of contingent identities; the problem of fixing the referential relation; the problem of distinguishing mere association from referring; the problem of the continued meaningfulness of an expression even if its bearer no longer exists. These long-standing difficulties facing denotational theories have so far not been raised for Fodor's version, as attention has focused on the problem of misrepresentation.

4 Moreover, even if there were this psychophysical basis for mentalese primitive symbols, the asymmetry principle still would not be met. The construction of complex beliefs out of these primitive resources cannot succeed, not even in principle. According to the asymmetry principle, there would not be tokenings of #red# except in a world in which such tokenings are caused by the occurrence of light waves n impinging on the retina of the subject (etc.). But suppose someone were born blind and so the occurrence of light waves n did not cause a tokening of #red# but a certain pressure to the eyeballs would cause it. This is the same problem that haunted the complex concepts like "horse". It looks

like #red# would denote the property of reflecting light waves n or the property of pressure applied to the eyeballs. This is just the problem of misrepresentation all over again. The second problem is that there are principled grounds for rejecting phenomenalism and it is difficult to see any difference with Fodor's causal version of it. The principled objection goes as follows: There can be no complete analysis of a physical object statement into phenomenal experience statements because the phenomenal experience statements supply necessary and/or sufficient conditions for the truth of the physical object statement only if certain conditions specified in material object terms obtain. "This is a penny" is translatable into statements such as "This is round [on condition that it is held at a certain angle in front of my eyes, that my head is turned in the right way, etc.]; this is copper colored [on condition that there is sufficient lighting, etc.]; this is cool [on condition that it has not been left on a hot surface etc.]; and so on." So the real translation is always of the following form: "This is a penny" is true iff "this appears round, copper-colored, and cool under normal conditions." And there is no way to eliminate the appeal to normal conditions expressible in physical object terms. (See R. Chisholm.) Fodor's phenomenalist strategy does not supply a way around this difficulty. A fully naturalized semantics is simply not possible.

5 Social norms and narrow content

1 This is not so for Oscar$_2$, however. He has at best a partial understanding of what the term "sofa$_2$" means.

2 J.A. Fodor commits just this fallacy in "Methodological Solipsism Considered as a Research Strategy in Cognitive Psychology" (Fodor 1981). See Ch. 5 above.

3 Burge acknowledges that Putnam's position is more complicated than the position ascribed to him, but that nonetheless he is justified in his interpretation of Putnam. I am going to follow Burge in this.

4 Like most everyone else, I too will ignore the fact that Oscar and Oscar$_2$ could hardly be "molecule-for-molecule" identical given the different chemical composition of water and water$_2$.

5 Please note that although these second-order intentions concern the use of the word "arthritis," this account of the semantic link of terms of expertise to the experts is not a variant on the objection that Oscar's error is really a metalinguistic error. Burge is quite correct in rejecting this reinterpretation of Oscar's predicament. I am not saying that Oscar's belief that he had arthritis in his thigh is to be reinterpreted as a belief that "arthritis" applied to some ache in his thigh. See Burge 1979: p. 93. Rather Oscar intends that his use of "arthritis" conforms to expert use, such that he is correct in believing that it is arthritis that he is suffering from and not another disease.

6 See Forbes 1987. Forbes emphasizes the need to distinguish between a third-person perspective and a first-person perspective.

7 Also see Loar 1987. I shall use the expression "that-clause content" to mark this distinction.

8 I am not developing the case exactly as Loar does though I do retain the point Loar wanted to make using this case.

9 Let me make two points about this characterization of physicalism. First, I do not equate physicalism with naturalism. Naturalism is best construed negatively

as the denial of the existence of anything supernatural or metaphysical. Second, physicalism does not have to be reductionist. To be explicable ultimately in terms of physical matter does not require that the explanations and vocabulary of one level are replaceable by explanations and vocabulary of another level, though it does require that we can understand how processes and states of the higher level are instantiated at the level of physical description.

10 Andrew Woodfield raises a related objection when he argues that Burge has conflated a theory of content with a theory of content specification. Once these are kept distinct, Woodfield argues, there is space both to acknowledge Burgean points about the social character of content specification and to develop a strongly internalist account of mental content itself (Woodfield 1982a).

11 Moreover, there is no reason to believe that Burge has fallaciously drawn conclusions about the necessity for using relational properties to individuate mental states from arguments against the computational theory of mind.

12 I think that Fodor's use of this "diagnosis" reflects his own commitment to the computational theory of mental processes. In other words, something very close to methodological solipsism tells us what counts as affecting causal powers when it comes to constructing a scientific taxonomy of mental causes.

13 This is, of course, precisely the position of those who argue that there is no real subject matter for scientific psychology to study. See P.M. Churchland 1979 and P.S. Churchland 1986.

14 Stampe (1977) interprets the problem as requiring that we specify the fidelity conditions under which a cause has the requisite effect. Thus, Stampe considers the problem from the point of view of the cause's being sufficient for producing "horse" whereas Fodor treats the problem from the point of view of the cause's being necessary for producing "horse." Also see Dretske 1986.

15 I preface "conceptual role semantics" with "internalist" to underscore the fact that CRS is distinct from a Wittgensteinian view of meaning as use. There are two important differences between CRS and the Wittgensteinian view. First, for CRS, conceptual systems are private and individualist whereas on a Wittgensteinian view, use is public and social. Second, CRS, in excising all relations to the world in specifying conceptual roles, has no place for objects to function as paradigms or exemplars. Though the Wittgensteinian view rejects a denotational theory of meaning, nonetheless exemplary objects play an indispensable role in language use.

16 Loar appeals to Robert Stalnaker's way of doing this (Stalnaker 1987).

17 Loar is aware of this kind of problem. See his remarks on phenomenalism (Loar 1981: p. 128), but he identifies these problems as having to do with epistemological concerns, not concerns of explication. But that is not so. Phenomenalist reductions were introduced explicitly as the analyses of certain sentences.

18 This Gricean account has the virtue of indirectly drawing our attention to the fact that paradigmatic cases of kinds of terms do not rule out marginal or vague or ambiguous uses of the same terms. What I mean is that a word like "arthritis" can be used more like an ordinary word like "sofa," in which case it is not used as a term calling for expert knowledge. Folk wisdom can have it that arthritis is any kind of joint or muscle ache and can be alleviated by wearing a copper bracelet. It is quite clear that terms of art can also become assimilated

into general usage and become interchangeable with some non-technical word or descriptive phrase. "H_2O" is a clear example of this; and in philosophical circles "the firing of C-fibres" became a virtual substitution for "being in pain," and *not* because the identity theory was found to be true. Such devaluing of the technical term is not what is intended in the discussion of the linguistic division of labor.

19 For a fuller discussion of this argument, see Chapter 4 "Language learning and the representational theory of mind."

20 See Chapter 7 "The philosophical significance of learning in the later Wittgenstein" for a more complete defence of the claim that the fact that we learn language has important philosophical implications for our understanding of language.

21 For a more detailed account and defense of this social view of normativity, see Chapter 6 "Rules, community, and the individual."

22 This is a central argument of Chapter 4 "Language learning and the representational theory of mind."

23 As a hypothesis, this deviant belief is much more difficult to state and sustain than Burge allows for in his description of earth and twin-earth. Indeed, if it is really true on twin earth that sofas$_2$ are religious objects, then it is simply not possible that they could have been used, bought, and sold in just the same ways as sofas are on earth.

6 Rules, community, and the individual

1 These are the considerations that Kripke develops as the "new sceptical problem" Wittgenstein poses for us (Kripke 1982: Ch. 2). Robert Fogelin also offers a Humean interpretation of Wittgenstein's discussion of understanding and rule-following (Fogelin 1976: Ch. 10).

2 This fact, like any other, is itself subject to multiple interpretations. Kripke takes the failure to find any privileged isolated fact about the individual or his history to establish a sceptical conclusion.

3 Robert Brandom in *Making It Explicit* also distinguishes these two arguments, referring to what I have identified as the argument of the Paradox of Interpretation as, quite perspicuously, "the gerrymandering argument" (Brandom 1994: p. 41).

4 See PI, esp. §160 (on the sensations of reading), §169 (on feeling the causal connection), and §§176–7 (on the "experience of the because").

5 A full defense of the Wittgensteinian position requires careful examination of these arguments. For the sake of the argument here, I am taking for granted that these points are sound.

6 In this chapter, I am sketching only those features of Kripke's interpretation of Wittgenstein that bear upon how to understand the community view of rule-following.

7 This is the picture embodied in the Classical View of a rule as something that can be "grasped in a flash" and serve as guide to action and standard of correctness.

8 The authors also make use of "containment" metaphors (Baker and Hacker 1984: p. 102) and suggest a conventionalist reading of grammar as well (Ibid.: p. 124).

9 Also see RFM Part VI.21: "The application of the concept 'following a rule' presupposes a custom. Hence it would be nonsense to say: just once in the history of the world someone followed a rule (or a signpost; played a game, uttered a sentence, or understood one; and so on)."

10 Certainly Baker and Hacker 1984 support this, but also see McGinn 1984, Tait 1986, and Budd 1984.

11 McGinn (1984), esp. pp. 126–33.

12 It is not clear that even this example provides us with a case in which the grasped rule does not manifest itself in practice. After all, his understanding is displayed in the fact that he does not challenge the right of his opponents to so move their pawns; in the discussion of games he does not question the legitimacy of moving pawns two squares (though presumably he will not discuss the effectiveness of such moves), and so on. In cases like this one, we are led to the idea that he has tacit understanding of this rule.

13 See Wright 1986: esp. pp. 16–23 and Essay 1, "Truth-Conditions and Criteria."

14 This is one of Baker and Hacker's internal relations, that between a rule and its applications.

15 To complete the argument against McGinn, I need to show that some neural state of the individual does not constitute understanding or provide the *appropriate* causal basis for use. This issue requires separate treatment.

16 I would want to distinguish the normativity provided by standards and representations from other more naturalistic ways of "going wrong." The rat that nibbles the poisoned cheese has gone wrong, but not in the way that someone playing chess badly goes wrong. There is a kind of natural teleology expressed in the behaviors of animals, but it is not behavior that is guided by a standard.

17 Additional textual support for the community view comes from three sources. First, throughout his discussion of rule-following, Wittgenstein appeals to what we say, to instances of teaching, explaining the meaning of a word, or engaging in games, all of which are treated as involving more than one person. Second, Wittgenstein holds that a number of key concepts are interwoven – "agreement," "rule," "same," and "regularity" (see §208 and §§224–5) – and cannot be explained independently of each other. "Agreement" quite explicitly, and the others implicitly, is construed as agreement among human beings (§241). Lastly, Wittgenstein repeatedly draws an analogy between following a rule and obeying an order. This analogy only makes sense if we suppose that more than one person is involved.

18 This statement needs modification, but the purposes of explication are best served by putting this in strong form. The modification allows that individuals *who have already mastered a practice or language* can exercise that capacity independently of a social context. This independence of the individual is parasitic upon community.

19 See section 3, pp. 169–172 for a discussion of the manifestation argument.

20 For an excellent discussion of this, see Blackburn 1984a. Blackburn argues that the community view of rule-following cannot provide even a sceptical solution to the new problem of meaning, and so the individual rule-follower is vindicated. A more detailed examination of why Blackburn's argument fails is called for, though I haven't room to provide it here.

21 This is, of course, B.F. Skinner's own view of the relation between the true explanation of behavior and the evaluative gloss we project upon behavior (Skinner 1974).

7 The philosophical significance of learning in the later Wittgenstein

1 The passages from Wittgenstein that I rely most heavily on are the rule-following discussion of the *Investigations* (PI §138–242) and Part VI of the *Remarks on the Foundations of Mathematics*. In the background of the argument are those passages from *On Certainty* that are concerned with the idea of propositions that hold fast and the distinction between the normative and the empirical.

2 The discussion of this chapter is restricted to the learning of the novice or initiate learner. Matters alter significantly when one considers the kind of learning in which the linguistically competent and cognitively sophisticated can engage. Indeed, matters have already changed considerably when one considers the differences between the preverbal child and the child who can ask for names.

3 This is precisely what Wittgenstein would take to be a paradigmatically vacuous argument. In PI §32, he dismisses just such an explanation: "Augustine describes the learning of human language as if the child came into a strange country and did not understand the language of the country; that is, as if it already had a language, only not this one."

4 In distinguishing these three kinds of regularity or uniform behavior, I am drawing heavily on the work of Wilfrid Sellars, particularly his "Some Reflections on Language Games" in Sellars 1963.

5 This distinction between pattern-governed behavior and rule-obeying behavior is allied to the distinction drawn in the context of the cognitive sciences between following rules explicitly and implicitly. The reason that I prefer to follow Sellars' way of drawing the distinction is that it does not commit one to the view that every structured practice can be described as a series of moves governed by a set of rules. It is an attempt to avoid the ubiquity of descriptions and explanations of behavior in terms of rules and representations. I think that it is doubtful, if not impossible, for all behavior to be so described or explained.

6 Fodor defends a causal denotational theory of meaning. One of the central problems facing this theory is the problem of misrepresentation, which is a variant on what I am calling the problem of normativity. Fodor's attempt to build normativity into his causal theory of denotation fails. See Cummins 1989: Ch. 5; Dretske 1986; Jones *et al.* 1991; as well as Chapter 5 , "Social norms and narrow content" above.

7 Being public and being social need not go together. See Bilgrami 1987 who argues for the public character of understanding but rejects the social.

8 Wittgenstein's arguments are directed against the notion that conscious mental states can embody knowledge or rules without their ever being manifested publicly in the behavior of the subject. The matter is complicated if one attempts to apply this Wittgensteinian strategy against contemporary theories of mind that hypothesize unconsciously held and used knowledge and rules. The central problem that Wittgenstein raises is nonetheless a problem for these theories of mind as well. To restate the problem: No object, whether an

acoustic sound, a string of letters, patterned paper, pole, bird, or flower, has representational content, or more broadly, normative content, in its own right. No object has a normative role in virtue of the way that it is used and the background against which it operates. This is the argument that Wittgenstein makes repeatedly against different candidates for being that which is inherently representational or normative: An ordinary object used as an exemplar for ostensive definition (an apple), a specially made object stipulated to play a particular normative role (the standard meter), a mental image, a formula, an interpretation. The problem of misrepresentation for Chomsky/Fodor-like theories is a variant on this key problem as is the "thickness of slice" problem for theories of natural teleology. The hope of current theories of mind and mental content is that the causal order will solve the problem whereas, for Wittgenstein, only the social order can solve the problem. For the debate on the problem of misrepresentation, see note 6 above. For the debate on the problem of thickness of slice, see Dretske 1988; and Dennett's articles "When Frogs (and Others) Make Mistakes" and "Evolution, Error, and Intentionality" both in Dennett 1987.

9 This is hardly a non-controversial claim. There has been considerable debate over whether Wittgenstein's account of rule-following requires both public and social regularities of behavior or only publicly accessible regularities. See Kripke 1982 for a defense of the social or community view of rule-following; Baker and Hacker 1984 for a lively defense of the alternative; and Holtzman and Leich 1981 for arguments on both sides of the issue. My own view is that neither of these interpretations is fully adequate. For a full defense of my interpretation of the social view of rule-following, see Chapter 6, "Rules, community, and the individual."

10 Wittgenstein makes the same point in several places in the *Philosophical Investigations*: "What sort of connexion is there here [between my actions and a rule]? Well, perhaps this one: I have been trained to react to this sign in a particular way, and now I do so react to it" (PI §198); and "Following a rule is analogous to obeying an order. We are trained to do so" (PI §206).

11 Also see Dreyfus 1972 and Searle 1992: Ch. 8. Both defend the indispensability of a background of skills and capacities without which rules and representations cannot be used.

12 I think that there are two good reasons for taking his discussion of learning in Part VI as having general import. First, though most of the discussion of learning, technique, concept and rule uses mathematical examples, Wittgenstein explicitly extends the discussion to language in general (RFM VI.31–49):

> To what extent can the function of language be described? If someone is not master of a language, I may bring him to a mastery of it by training. Someone who is master of it, I may remind of the kind of training, or I may describe it; for a particular purpose; thus already using a technique of the language.
>
> (VI.31)

Second, his discussion of these matters here resonates with the discussion of rule-following in the *Investigations* and with much of the discussion of belief and certainty in *On Certainty*, even to the point of particular passages in the *Remarks* having their counterparts in the *Investigations* (e.g., compare VI.3 with PI §193, VI.21 with PI §199 and §240, VI.32 with PI §204, VI.38 with PI §201, VI.39 with PI §242).

13   This is, of course, Lewis Carroll's problem of Achilles and the Tortoise all over again.

8 The etiology of the obvious: Wittgenstein and the elimination of indeterminacy

1   This disjunction suggests that the two expressions "representational" and "normative" can be used interchangeably. This really is not correct. "Normative" is the more basic and general of the two expressions. Representations are one kind of norm, but not the only.

2   Vygotsky makes a very similar argument with respect to naming (Vygotsky 1965). He too thinks that naming is a more sophisticated cognitive act that can only come after some mastery of language use. However, many who recognize that the ostensive definition picture of language acquisition presupposes significant cognitive competence on the part of the child nonetheless draw a very different conclusion. They take these considerations to support a strong nativist position. The child has an innate array of cognitive capacities, concepts, and theories that enables her to respond appropriately to ostensive definitions. See, for example, Fodor 1975; Keil 1989; Pinker 1994; and Wellman 1990. But Wittgenstein sees the strong nativist solution as explanatorily bankrupt. On his view it engenders an explanatory regress by reproducing in the child the very mastery of norms – epistemic, logical, and conceptual – for which we are seeking an explanation. The nativist psychologist takes the mastery of norms as unproblematic, but that is precisely what Wittgenstein takes to be the key philosophical issue. What is troubling to Wittgenstein is the very idea that the initiate learner can supply all that is required to turn an association between a word and an object into a normative meaning relation.

3   This mixing of physical causal descriptions with logical or normative ones has been pointed out and criticized by many. See, for example, Rorty 1979: Ch. IV.

4   Consider Wittgenstein's discussion of the various ways in which the rules of chess can be learned (PI §31).

5   Part VI of the *Remarks* was written during the period (1941–4) just before Wittgenstein worked on Part I of the *Investigations* (1945). It is important to note that of all the *Nachlass* material collected together in the Revised Edition of RFM, only Parts I and VI are presented complete as Wittgenstein wrote them without editorial revision or rearrangement. All the other parts have been subject to varying degrees of editorial revision. I want to thank David Stern for drawing this to my attention. See Biggs and Pichler 1993: pp. 60–9.

6   It is a proof that Wittgenstein cites in Part VI.6 where he draws attention to an important affinity between instances or examples of finding a prime number $>p$ and the algebraic proof:

> It will now be said that the algebraic proof is stricter than the one by way of examples, because it is, so to speak, the extract of the effective principle of

these examples. But, after all, even the algebraic proof is not quite naked. Understanding—I might say—is needed for both.

(RFM.VI.6)

7 Let me enter two caveats to my use of Euclid's proof. First, Wittgenstein's interpretation of Euclid's proof is in fact more complicated than is indicated in the text of this chapter. I want to highlight certain points which would only be lost if all the complications of a full explication were introduced. The most important of these complications is that Euclid's proof is an indirect proof by contradiction – a reductio ad absurdum. It involves a conspicuous use of the Law of Excluded Middle. Many interpret Wittgenstein as endorsing an intuitionist mathematics and so as rejecting the use of indirect proof by contradiction and of course denying the validity of the Law of Excluded Middle. See Wright 1980: esp. Part 2; and Shanker 1987: esp. Chs 2–3. This is an important issue, but one that can be avoided for the purposes of this chapter. The proof could be reconstructed to avoid this. But the difficulties involved in interpreting Wittgenstein's views on this proof (and the law of non-contradiction itself) can be sidestepped for the purposes of introducing the proof in this chapter. What is crucial is that the proof constitutes a set of instructions for finding a new prime number for any finite set of prime numbers. The second caveat concerns treating Euclid's proof as a constructive proof. The modern proof for the infinity of prime numbers is not a constructivist proof. Again, this is a matter I do not want to take on in this chapter. What is important is that Wittgenstein did take it to be a constructive proof and that taking it as such helps elucidate Wittgenstein's notion of background technique. *That* is the goal of this chapter.

8 If one performs the formal test by actually applying the transformation rules step by step, it becomes quite clear that, as Wittgenstein says, the concept of a proof presupposes the concept of transformation rules. We'll follow Euclid in specifying a set of prime numbers as the total set. This is the hypothesis that will generate the required contradiction.

Let 2, 3, and 5 be the prime numbers.
Take the product of 2, 3, and 5, and add 1. $\quad 2 \times 3 \times 5 = 30 + 1 = 31.$
Then 31 is either a prime number and not a prime number.

1 If it is, we have added another prime number to the list of prime numbers, and so it was not complete.
2 If it is not, 31 must be divisible by some prime number, p.

Now if p is identical with any of the prime numbers 2, 3, 5, it will (evenly) divide 30. Since p is also to divide (evenly) 30 + 1, then p must divide 1 evenly which is impossible.
Thus we get the contradiction that p divides 31 evenly and that p does not divide 31 evenly.

On the basis of this contradiction, we reject the hypothesis we began with (that 2, 3, 5 are the only prime numbers) as the source of the problem.

9 David Pears makes a closely related point when he states that "We discover the regularities in nature's behaviour only by first establishing regularities in our own behaviour" (Pears 1988: p. 371).

10 This is an oversimplified account of the relation between self-regulation and judgments of sameness. There are many cases of rule-following, even quite simple cases, that are not repetitive in the way that has been emphasized here. Teaching children to share is teaching a rule, but one that can be realized in a variety of ways, from sharing toys by dividing them up to sharing a swing by waiting in line. I owe this point and example to John Deigh. The mathematical example is useful precisely because so many of the techniques involved are not multifaceted in this way. Even if there is more than one technique for, say adding or multiplying, whichever technique is used, its mastery is mastery of addition.

11 Wittgenstein is particularly drawn to Euclidean proofs in geometry precisely because geometry is, as it is said, "the mathematics of all plane figures constructible with a straight edge and compass." Euclidean proofs are recipes for constructing geometric figures.

12 This will have implications for how Wittgenstein sees the relation between behavior and an intentionally describable action. Behavior itself can be seen and isolated from the background against which it is intelligible as an intentional action. This is one of the points of analogy between psychology and mathematics.

13 Wittgenstein develops this point as follows in the *Remarks* VI:

> How do you test for a contrapuntal property? You transform it according to *this* rule, you put it together with another one in *this* way; and the like. In this way you get a definite result. You get it, as you would also get it by means of an experiment. So far what you doing may even have been an experiment. The word "get" is here used temporally; you got the result at three o'clock.—In the mathematical proposition which I then frame the verb ("get," "yields" etc.) is used non-temporally.
> The activity of testing produced such and such a result.
> So up to now the testing was, so to speak, experimental. Now it is taken as a proof. And the proof is the *picture* of a test.
>
> (RFM VI.2)

14 In putting the matter this way, I intend to draw attention to the similarity in what Wittgenstein says about objects and states of affairs in the *Tractatus* and propositions and proofs in the RFM. As Wittgenstein tells us in the *Tractatus*, the world is all that is the case, that is, the totality of states of affairs, not the totality of objects. Similarly mathematics, and by extension any rule-governed practice, is the domain of proofs and not propositions.

15 Even the use of the exclamation point by each of them differs. For Quine, it indicates that the linguist is making a report on the current state of affairs (rather than a question). For Wittgenstein, it indicates a command to do something.

16 S.G. Shanker argues for a similar interpretation in *Wittgenstein and the Turning Point in the Philosophy of Mathematics* (Shanker 1987: esp. Ch. 7).

17 Examples include "Only you can know if you had that intention" (PI §247), "Every rod has a length" (PI §251), "One plays patience by oneself" (PI §248), and "Another person can't have my pains" (PI §253).

18 Examples from *On Certainty* include "Here is a hand" (OC §1ff.), "the earth has existed since long before my birth" (OC §84ff.), and "every human being has two human parents" (OC §239ff.).

19 Baker and Hacker, for instance, prefer this way of characterizing the relation between rule and its application (Baker and Hacker 1984).

20 This is what leads Merrill B. Hintikka and Jaakko Hintikka to maintain that central to Wittgenstein's philosophy is "the ineffability of semantics" (Hintikka and Hintikka 1986: p. 17). They pursue this idea by characterizing "the role of language-games as the basic semantical links between language and reality" (Hintikka and Hintikka 1986: p. 212). They are certainly on to something correct in Wittgenstein. Though the techniques cannot be described, they can be shown. It is in this way that the Doctrine of Showing survives.

21 See J. S. Mill, *A System of Logic* (Mill 1873), of course. And for a contemporary version, see P.S. Churchland, *Neurophilosophy* (Churchland, P.S. 1986).

22 See, for example, PI §80, PI II.xii; RFM I.5.

23 Historically, Wittgenstein can be seen to reject Frege's strong distinction between the logical and the psychological, but not by a return to the old forms of psychologism represented by J. S. Mill in the nineteenth century.

24 See R. Carnap, "Empiricism, Ontology and Semantics" (Carnap 1956) and M. Foucault, *The Archaeology of Knowledge* (Foucault 1972).

25 There is this much to the anti-realist interpretation of Wittgenstein. It is part of Wittgenstein's rejection of the idea of logical form, of an eternally given range of possibilities within which all contingencies occur.

26 This needs some elaboration as there are places where Quine seems to be saying something quite similar to this. In "Ontological Relativity," he says that "in practice we end the regress of background languages, in discussion of reference, by acquiescing in our mother tongue and taking its words at face value" (Quine 1969b: p. 49).

9 Wittgenstein's rejection of scientific psychology

1 In case my exposition of Wittgenstein seems oversimplified, I shall note that the primary aim of the chapter is not full-scale exegesis but rather the use of certain key arguments of the *Investigations* to assess critically some central claims of cognitivism.

2 I focus on the work of Fodor and Stich because each is exemplary of important, but distinct, positions within cognitivism. I shall mention other advocates of cognitivism only in passing or in footnotes. For Fodor's work, I shall rely most heavily upon the following: *The Language of Thought* (Fodor 1975); "Methodological Solipsism Considered as a Research Strategy in Cognitive Psychology" (Fodor 1981b); and *The Modularity of Mind* (Fodor 1983). For Stich's position, I rely on his *From Folk Psychology to Cognitive Science: The Case Against Belief* (Stich 1983).

3 It seems to me that one can distinguish four basic objections that Wittgenstein raises to any form of mentalism (i.e., the view that behavior is to be explained by inner mental causes). In addition to the two I shall discuss in this chapter, there are also his attack on introspectible feelings and his argument that inner-

process accounts are pseudo-explanatory. The former is applicable to an introspectionist psychology and so of no concern in this chapter. The latter can be
directed against cognitivism but does not constitute a very strong objection,
though in understanding the replies to it, much that is illuminating about
cognitivism emerges. See my article "Beyond the Infinite Regress" (Williams,
Meredith 1980).

4 The debate concerning the nature of mental representations (whether they are
linguistic entities or images) makes no difference to the Wittgensteinian
critique. See Barbara Von Eckardt, "Comments and Criticism, Cognitive
Psychology and Principled Skepticism" (Von Eckardt 1984), for a clear statement distinguishing a number of theses that often are run together.

5 This is misleading in the following respect. It suggests that there are only two
alternatives: Wittgensteinian nihilism and cognitivism. This is, of course, not
the case. There is the work of those who are attempting to develop a scientific
psychology that rejects the autonomy of cognitive life in favor of a social
conception or at least a strong externalist component. Those who favor a social
conception include Rom Harre, *Personal Being* (Harre 1984); and Alan Gauld
and John Shotter, *Human Action and Its Psychological Investigation* (Gauld and
Shotter 1977). Those who favor including an externalist component with
cognitive scientific theories are numerous, including D.C. Dennett's cognitive
ethology (Dennett 1987), F. Dretske's information-processing model (Dretske
1981), and the biological approaches of R. Millikan (Millikan 1984) and D.
Papineau (Papineau 1987). In this chapter, however, I am not concerned with
canvassing all positions but with assessing the claims of adherents of cognitivism.

6 Patricia and Paul Churchland, who share many of Stich's views, are quite sceptical even of this claim (Churchland, P.M. 1979; Churchland, P.M. 1981; and
Churchland, P.S. 1986).

7 I am claiming to characterize a certain development in Fodor's work. I do not
claim that Fodor so describes his progress nor that he would endorse this characterization.

8 For a full characterization and defense of this interpretation of the development of Fodor's work, see Chapter 4 above.

9 It seems to me that a considerable part of what makes this objection plausible
is the way in which Fodor interprets this position as contrasting conceptual
stories with causal stories, where conceptual stories are a matter of offering
logically necessary and/or sufficient conditions. Wittgenstein's notion of a
grammatical investigation is not a matter of citing logically necessary and/or
sufficient conditions nor of pointing out trivial logical connections of the sort
evinced by the conceptual story concerning Wheaties. This is a different and
perhaps deeper way of answering Fodor's objection, but it is not one that I
shall take up in this chapter. Rather I shall argue in conceding that there are
two different kinds of story to tell, Fodor eventually gives up the possibility of
giving causal stories for most of the questions raised.

10 There is also the issue of whether such mirroring is a plausible conjecture.
Fodor requires it in order to maintain some connection between scientific
psychology and the human mind. This requires that all aspects of cognitive life
be made to fit the data inference model if a purely formal treatment is to be
given. This very central assumption is, I think, one of the more dubious. See
Chapter 4 above.

11 Paul Churchland agrees completely with the view, arguing that folk psychology has become, in Lakatos' phrase, a "degenerative research program." Pace Stich, however, he argues that the only science of the mind is neurophysiology. He would agree with the Wittgensteinian conclusion that there is no scientific psychology, but it would be a mistake to see any further affinities between the two positions. I will address some important aspects of the gap in my discussion of Stich later in this chapter.

12 For a full critical examination of the idea that knowledge has an inherent structure or order, see Michael Williams, *Unnatural Doubts* (Williams, Michael 1992).

13 I put "system" in scare quotes to indicate that we need not take at face value the implication that intelligence or general cognitive capacities are to be realized computationally.

14 It can be objected that this convergence is only apparent. The methodologies of neurophysiology and cognitive psychology are recognizably distinct and so constitute distinct approaches to understanding the mind. This, it seems to me, is not a telling objection, for my point is that cognitive psychology, on Fodor's revised view, is a close continuation of neurophysiology. I reach this conclusion in part on the suspicion that the only way to draw the line between the modular systems and the central systems will be in terms of what can be cashed in physiologically.

15 See Stich 1978 and Stich 1983: esp. pp. 160–70. It is interesting to note that Stich takes the autonomy principle to be fundamental and indispensable to the cognitive sciences whereas Fodor is led to the autonomy principle by his commitment to the computational model of the mind.

16 A crucial part of Stich's argument for this conclusion turns on his account of our folk psychological concept of belief. The ascription of content to another's belief (or any other propositional attitude) implicitly involves assigning to the other a content similar to the speaker's own. This is a debatable account of how content is assigned, but even without it, Stich's conclusion is quite plausible, for a contentful psychology does take the mature Western adult as the standard and treats the child, in any case, as a small adult, competent in mentalese though just beginning to master his new natural language. One must think of animals that display cognitive abilities in a similar light. See Stich 1979; and Churchland 1980.

17 This is not a new argument. Herbert Dreyfus developed this in great detail in *What Computers Can't Do* (Dreyfus 1972).

10 Vygotsky's social theory of mind

1 See Howard Gardner's *The Mind's New Science* (Gardner 1985) for an excellent and very readable account of this important development in the study of cognition.

2 In putting forward these four commitments, I am not claiming that all proponents of cognitivist models and theories explicitly avow them or avow them in exactly the form in which I present them. The field is much too fluid for this to be true. But I do hold that the work that created and sustains this revolution in thinking about the mind – namely, artificial intelligence research, Chomskean linguistic theory, computational theories of vision and categorization – does reflect these commitments.

3 For a more recent defense of a strong nativist view of natural language acquisition, see Pinker 1994.

4 To make this more vivid, let me briefly characterize two examples. First, on Chomsky's view there is an innate linguistic competence that is characterized in terms of a set of transformational rules of grammar. The structure of this linguistic competence is independent of an array of other cognitive capacities that effect our actual linguistic performances, like perception, motivation, past learning, and the like. What is involved in actually uttering anything is vastly more complicated than the characterization of the linguistic competence itself. A second example can be given from artificial intelligence models. From a flow-chart perspective, a motor-control routine can be distinguished from a memory system from a perceptual system from transducers from executive control unit (and so on). All of these systems work together to produce a single utterance, but the structure of each can be characterized relatively independently of the others.

5 V.V. Davydov's and L.A. Radzikhovskii's paper "Vygotsky's Theory and the Activity-Oriented Approach in Psychology" (Wertsch 1985b) is one most interesting of the papers in the collection. The authors spell out Vygotsky's methodological analysis of psychological theories. Vygotsky has some very interesting reflections on the relation between a psychological theory and the general philosophical orientation it expresses. The formation of a theory is a two-fold process: (1) The theory begins with some object of study, or unit of analysis, e.g., a reflex, an introspectible subjective state, a behavior, a cognitive capacity. It then develops a general explanatory principle, e.g., appeal to conditioning, introspection, flow-chart model, and so defines itself within the philosophic tradition, as reductionist, dualist, rationalist, and so on. (2) Then the psychological theory verifies itself from the perspective of the logic of this philosophic tradition. This view of the relation between psychological theories and philosophical perspectives underscores the importance of developing a critical awareness of the presuppositions that support the content of a particular theory.

6 Though I use this behaviorist language to describe Vygotsky's position, it is not intended to carry with it the full theoretical baggage of psychological behaviorism. The most important point to note is that the environment is a social and cultural one; it is not an environment of behaviorist stimuli.

7 Grasping word-meaning is the indispensable element in human consciousness. Thus, Vygotsky concludes the unit of analysis, i.e, the basic explanatory element of his theory, is word-meaning. This is an error, and I shall come back to this later in section 2.

8 This distinction between the reference and the meaning of words itself is subject to difficulties that I shall bring out in section 2.

9 In *Thought and Language* (Vygotsky 1965), Vygotsky does not discuss the role of play. His primary focus is on mounting a successful critique of Piaget's account of egocentric speech. However, later in his career he wrote on play in such a way as to complete, it seems to me, the account of the "mechanism" whereby the very young child using language expressively comes to use language representationally. And without coming to use language in this latter way, cognitive development is simply stymied. I think that without this we do not have an account of how words become detached from the objects with which they are originally fused. See Vygotsky 1976.

10 This way of characterizing the third stage oversimplifies Vygotsky's account, but such oversimplification is useful in trying to give an overview of his position.

11 This is certainly true of several of the contributors to *Culture, Communication, and Cognition* (Wertsch 1985b). Indicative of the growing influence of Vygotsky's ideas is Gerald Coles' book, *The Learning Mystique, A Critical Look at "Learning Disabilities"* (Cole 1987), which is explicitly influenced by Vygotsky.

12 Drawing this distinction between reference and sense comes from Gottlob Frege, the late-nineteenth century logician, whose work is foundational for contemporary philosophy of language. See his "On Sense and Meaning" (Frege 1952). This article is better known as "On Sense and Reference"; the translation was changed in the third edition.

13 Thus, we find a peculiar tension between Chapter 5 and Chapter 6 in *Thought and Language* (Vygotsky 1965). Chapter 5 classifies the kinds of concepts there are in their order of development. It gives a picture of concepts as relatively static entities. Chapter 6, on the other hand, offers a dynamic account of how scientific, or true, concepts are acquired that is at odds with the characterization given in Chapter 5.

14 I speak of the "idealized sentence" because the young child, of course, does not speak in such full sentences, but rather uses single words to express the full proposition. Indeed this is why the language of proposition is used, for "proposition" is alleged to be that entity expressed by a "sentence" where a sentence is the physical string of sounds or marks. This notion of "proposition" is problematic itself.

15 Wertsch draws on the terminology and means for distinguishing these interlinguistic uses of language from Michael Silverstein, "The Functional Stratification of Language and Ontogenesis" (Wertsch 1985b). I find both "metapragmatic function" and "metasemantic function" somewhat infelicitous expressions for referring to the linguistic phenomena that Wertsch is concerned with. The metapragmatic function is direct and indirect quotation. The metasemantic function of language is not, as seems the most natural reading, a concern with the concepts of "truth," "reference," "meaning," and the like, but with theoretical discourse.

16 This builds on the cognitive skills developed during egocentric speech, namely, the ability to use the word as representative rather than just expressive or communicative.

17 See, for example, Davydov and Radzikhovskii, "Vygotsky's Theory and the Activity-Oriented Approach in Psychology," V.P. Zinchenko, "Vygotsky's Ideas about Units of Analysis of Mind," and David McNeill, "Language Viewed as Action" (Wertsch 1985b). Davydov and Radzikhovskii don't so much argue that activity ought to replace word-meaning, as that Vygotsky's notion of word-meaning already implicates activity. The word as tool is already embedded in a context of practical activity. Here I agree with Wertsch that this is too strong a claim to make; at best one might argue that Vygotsky is himself unclear about word-meaning and its relation to the social context. This unclarity is expressed in the tension I have referred to in the text of this chapter.

18 Such a position is associated with Herbert Mead, *Mind, Self, and Society from the Standpoint of a Social Behaviorist* (Mead 1934).

19 See Sir Karl Popper, *The Poverty of Historicism* (Popper 1986) and Isaiah Berlin, "Historical Inevitability" (Berlin 1969). For a contemporary critique, see Roberto Unger, *False Necessity* (Unger 1988).

20 Sylvia Scribner, "Vygotsky's Uses of History" in Wertsch 1985b.

Bibliography

Arrington, R.L. and Glock, H.-J., eds. (1996), *Wittgenstein and Quine*, London, Routledge.

Ayer, A.J. (1946), *Language, Truth and Logic*, 2nd ed., New York, Dover Publications.

—— (1969), *The Foundations of Empirical Knowledge*, New York, St. Martin's Press.

Bach, K. (1986), "Burge's New Thought Experiment," *The Journal of Philosophy*, vol. 85, no. 2, pp. 88–97.

Baker, G.P. and Hacker, P.M.S. (1984), *Scepticism, Rules, and Language*, Oxford, Blackwell.

Baker, L. (1989), "On a Causal Theory of Content" in Tomberlin 1989.

Berlin, I. (1969), *Four Essays on Liberty*, Oxford, Oxford University Press.

Biggs, M. and Pichler, A. (1993), *Wittgenstein: Two Source Catalogues and a Bibliography*, Working Papers from the Wittgenstein Archives at the University of Bergen No. 7.

Bilgrami, A. (1987), "An Externalist Account of Psychological Content," *Philosophical Topics*, vol. 15, no.1, no. 3, pp. 191–226.

Blackburn, S. (1984a), "The Individual Strikes Back," *Synthese*, vol. 58, no.3, pp. 281–301.

—— (1984b), *Spreading the Word*, Oxford, Oxford University Press.

Block, N. (1986), "Advertisement for a Semantics for Psychology," P. A. French, T. E. Uehling, H.K. Wettstein eds, *Midwest Studies in Philosophy; Studies in the Philosophy of Mind*, vol. X, pp. 615–78.

Bloor, D. (1983), *Wittgenstein A Social Theory of Knowledge*, New York, Columbia University Press.

—— (1997), *Rules and Institutions*, London, Routledge.

Bogdan, R.J., ed. (1986), *Belief: Form, Content, and Function*, Oxford, Clarendon Press.

Brandom, R. (1994), *Making it Explicit*, Cambridge, MA, Harvard University Press.

Bruner, J.S., Goodnow, J.J., and Austin, G.A. (1965), *A Study of Thinking*, New York, John Wiley & Sons, Inc.

Bruner, J.S., Jolly, A., and Sylva, K., eds. (1976), *Play, Its Role in Development and Evolution*, New York, Basic Books.

Bruner, J.S. (1997), *The Culture of Education*, Cambridge, MA, Harvard University Press.

Budd, M. (1984), "Wittgenstein on Meaning, Interpretation, and Rules," *Synthese*, vol. 58, no. 3, pp. 303–323.

—— (1989), *Wittgenstein's Philosophy of Psychology*, London, Routledge.

Burge, T. (1979), "Individualism and the Mental," *Midwest Studies in Philosophy*, IV.

—— (1982), "Other Bodies" in Woodfield 1982b.

—— (1986a), "Intellectual Norms and Foundations of Mind," *The Journal of Philosophy*, vol. 83, no. 12, pp. 397–720.

—— (1986b), "Individualism and Psychology," *The Philosophical Review*, vol. LCV, no. 1, pp 3–45.

Carnap, R. (1932), "Psychology in Physical Language" ("Psychologie in physikalische Sprache"), *Erkenntnis* vol. 11, no. 2, pp. 107–42.

Carnap, R. (1956), *Meaning and Necessity*, 2nd Edition, Chicago, The University of Chicago Press.

Chalmers, D. (1996), *The Conscious Mind: In Search for a Fundamental Theory*, Oxford, Oxford University Press.

Chisholm, R.M. (1948), "The Problem of Empiricism," *The Journal of Philosophy*, vol. 45, no. 16, pp. 512–17.

Chomsky, N. (1959), "Review of B.F. Skinner's Verbal Behavior," *Language* 35.

—— (1980), *Rules and Representations*, New York, Columbia University Press.

Churchland, P.M. (1979), *Scientific Realism and the Plasticity of Mind*, Cambridge, Cambridge University Press.

—— (1981), "Eliminative Materialism and Propositional Attitudes," *The Journal of Philosophy*, vol. 78, no. 2, pp. 67–90.

Churchland, P.S. (1980), "A Perspective in Mind Brain Research," *The Journal of Philosophy*, vol. 77, no. 4, pp. 285–307.

—— (1986), *Neurophilosophy: Toward a Unified Theory of Mind/Brain*, Cambridge, MA, The MIT Press.

Coles, G. (1987), *The Learning Mystique, A Critical Look at "Learning Disabilities"*, New York, Pantheon Books.

Cummins, R. (1989), *Meaning and Mental Representation*, Cambridge, MA, The MIT Press.

Dennett, D.C. (1971), "Intentional Systems," *The Journal of Philosophy*, vol. 68, no.4, pp. 87–106; also in Dennett 1978a.

—— (1978a), *Brainstorms*, Cambridge, MA, The MIT Press.

—— (1978b), "Skinner Skinned" in Dennett 1978a.

—— (1987), *The Intentional Stance*, Cambridge, MA, The MIT Press.

—— (1991), *Consciousness Explained*, Boston, Little, Brown and Co.

Descartes, R. (1972), *The Philosophical Works of Descartes*, Vol. 1., tr. Elizabeth S. Haldane and G.R.T. Ross, Cambridge, Cambridge University Press.

Donagan, A. (1966), "Wittgenstein on Sensation" in Pitcher 1966.

Dretske, F. (1981), *Knowledge and the Flow of Information*, Cambridge, MA, The MIT Press.

—— (1986), "Misrepresentation" in Bogdan 1986.

—— (1988), *Explaining Behavior*, Cambridge, MA, The MIT Press.

—— (1995), *Naturalizing the Mind*, Cambridge, MA, The MIT Press.

Dreyfus, H.L. (1972), *What Computers Can't Do*, New York, Harper and Row.

——, ed. (1982a), *Husserl, Intentionality and Cognitive Science*, Cambridge, MA, The MIT Press.

—— (1982b), "Husserl's Perceptual *Noema*" in Dreyfus 1982a.

Dummett, M. (1973), *Frege Philosophy of Language*, London, Duckworth.

—— (1993a), *The Seas of Language*, Oxford, Clarendon Press.

—— (1993b), *Origins of Analytical Philosophy*, Cambridge, MA, Harvard University Press.

Euclid (1956), *The Thirteen Books of the Elements*, Vol. 2, tr. Thomas L. Heath, New York, Dover Publications.

Fodor, J.A. (1968), *Psychological Explanation*, New York, Random House.

—— (1975), *The Language of Thought*, New York, Thomas Y. Crowell.

—— (1981a), *Representations*, Cambridge, MA, The MIT Press.

—— (1981b), "Methodological Solipsism Considered as a Research Strategy in Cognitive Psychology" in Fodor 1981a.

—— (1983), *The Modularity of Mind*, Cambridge, MA, The MIT Press.

—— (1988), *Psychosemantics*, Cambridge, MA, The MIT Press.

—— (1990), *A Theory of Content and Other Essays*, Cambridge, MA, The MIT Press.

Fodor, J.A. and Lepore, E., (1992), *Holism*, Oxford, Basil Blackwell.

Fogelin, R. (1976), *Wittgenstein*, New York, Routledge & Kegan Paul.

Forbes, G. (1987), "A Dichotomy Sustained," *Philosophical Studies*, vol. 51, no.2, pp. 187–211.

Foucault, M. (1972), *The Archaeology of Knowledge*, tr. A.M. Sheridan Smith, London, Tavistock Publications.

Frege, G. (1952) "On Sense and Meaning" in Geach and Black 1952.

Gardner, H. (1985), *The Mind's New Science*, New York, Basic Books, Inc.

Gauld, A. and Shotter, J. (1977), *Human Action and Its Psychological Investigation*, London, Routledge & Kegan Paul.

Geach, P. and Black, M. (1952), eds., *Translations from the Philosophical Writings of Gottlob Frege*, Third Edition, Oxford, Basil Blackwell.

Hacker, P.M.S. (1972), *Insight and Illusion*, London, Oxford University Press.

—— (1986), *Insight and Illusion*, Revised Edition, Oxford, Clarendon Press.

—— (1990a), *Wittgenstein, Meaning and Mind, Part I Essays*, Oxford, Basil Blackwell.

—— (1990b), *Wittgenstein, Meaning and Mind, Part II Exegesis §§243–427*, Oxford, Basil Blackwell.

Hacker, P.M.S. and Baker, G. (1984), *Scepticism, Rules & Language*, Oxford, Basil Blackwell.

Hardwick, C. (1971), *Language Learning in Wittgenstein's Later Philosophy*, The Hague, Mouton.

Harre, R. (1984), *Personal Being*, Cambridge, MA, Harvard University Press.

Harries, K. (1968), "Two Conflicting Interpretations of Language in Wittgenstein's *Investigations*," *Kant-Studien*, vol. 59, no. 4, pp. 397–409.

Heal, J. (1989), *Fact and Meaning, Quine and Wittgenstein on Philosophy of Language*, Oxford, Basil Blackwell.

Hintikka, M.B. and Hintikka, J., (1986), *Investigating Wittgenstein*, Oxford, Basil Blackwell.

Holtzman, S. and Leich, C., eds. (1981), *Wittgenstein: To Follow a Rule*, London, Routledge & Kegan Paul.

Husserl, E. (1970), *Logical Investigations*, Vol. 1, New York, Humanities Press.

Johnston, P. (1993), *Wittgenstein, Rethinking the Inner*, London, Routledge.

Jones, T., Mulaire, E. and Stich, S. (1991), "Staving Off Catastrophe," *Mind & Language* 6, 58–62.

Kant, I. (1964), *Critique of Pure Reason*, Norman Kemp Smith, tr., London, Macmillan & Co., Ltd.

Keil, F.C. (1989), *Concepts, Word Meanings, and Cognitive Development*, Cambridge, MA, The MIT Press.

Kenny, A. (1973), *Wittgenstein*, Cambridge, MA, Harvard University Press.

Kohler, W. (1947), *Gestalt Psychology*, New York, Liveright.

Kripke, S. (1979), "A Puzzle about Belief" in Margalit 1979.

—— (1982), *Wittgenstein on Rules and Private Languages*, Oxford, Blackwell.

Lear, J. (1982), "Leaving the World Alone," *The Journal of Philosophy*, vol. 79, no. 7, pp. 382–403.

Loar, B. (1981), *Mind and Meaning*, Cambridge, Cambridge University Press.

—— (1987), "Subjective Intentionality," *Philosophical Topics*, vol. 15, no. 1, pp. 89–124.

—— (1988), "Social Content and Psychological Content" in Merrill and Grimm 1988.

Malcolm, N. (1963), *Knowledge and Certainty*, Ithaca, Cornell University Press.

—— (1966), "Review of Wittgenstein's *Philosophical Investigations*," in Pitcher 1966.

Margalit, A., ed. (1979), *Meaning and Use*, Dordrecht, D. Reidel.

McDowell, J. (1984), "Wittgenstein on Rule Following", Synthese, vol. 58, no. 3, pp. 325–63.

—— (1994), *Mind and World*, Cambridge, MA, Harvard University Press.

McGinn, C. (1984), *Wittgenstein on Meaning*, Oxford, Basil Blackwell.

McGinn, M. (1989), *Sense and Certainty, A Dissolution of Scepticism*, Oxford, Basil Blackwell.

Mead, H. (1934), *Mind, Self, and Society from the Standpoint of a Social Behaviorist*, Chicago, University of Chicago Press.

Merrill, D. and Grimm, R., eds. (1988), *Contents of Thought*, Tucson, University of Arizona Press.

Mill, J.S. (1873), *A System of Logic*, London, Longman.

Millikan, R. (1984), *Language, Thought, and Other Biological Categories*, Cambridge, MA, The MIT Press.

Morawetz, T. (1974), "Wittgenstein and Synthetic *A Priori* Judgments," *Philosophy*, vol. 49, no. 190, pp. 429–34.

—— (1978), *Wittgenstein & Knowledge, The Importance of On Certainty*, Atlantic Highlands, NJ, Humanities Press.

Natanson, M., ed. (1970a), *Phenomenology and Social Reality*, The Hague, Martinus Nijhoff.

—— (1970b), "Alfred Schutz on Social Reality and Social Science" in Natanson 1970a.

Papineau, D. (1987), *Reality and Representation*, Oxford: Basil Blackwell.

Pears, D. (1969), *Ludwig Wittgenstein*, New York, Viking Press.

—— (1987), *The False Prison*, vol. 1, Oxford, Clarendon Press.

—— (1988), *The False Prison*, vol. 2, Oxford, Clarendon Press.

Pinker, S. (1994), *The Language Instinct*, New York, William Morrow and Co., Inc.

Pitcher, G., ed. (1966), *Wittgenstein*, Garden City, NY, Doubleday & Co.

Popper, K. (1963), *Conjectures and Refutations*, London, Routledge & Kegan Paul.

—— (1986), *The Poverty of Historicism*, London, ARK.

Putnam, H. (1975a), "The Meaning of 'Meaning'" in Putnam 1975b.

—— (1975b), *Mind, Language, and Reality*, Cambridge, Cambridge University Press.

—— (1981), *Reason, Truth and History*, Cambridge, Cambridge University Press.

Pylyshyn, Z. (1980), "Cognitive Representation and the Process-Architecture Distinction," *The Behavioral and Brain Sciences*.

—— (1980), "Computation and Cognition," Behavioral and Brain Sciences, vol. 3, no. 1, pp. 111—32.

Quine, W.V.O. (1961), *From a Logical Point of View*, Second Edition, New York, Harper & Row, Publishers.

—— (1960), *Word & Object*, Cambridge, MA, The MIT Press.

—— (1969a), *Ontological Relativity and Other Essays*, New York, Columbia University Press.

—— (1969b), "Ontological Relativity" in Quine 1969a.

—— (1990), *Pursuit of Truth*, Cambridge, MA, Harvard University Press.

Rorty, R. (1979), *Philosophy and the Mirror of Nature*, Princeton, Princeton University Press.

Saunders, J.T. and Henze, D.F. (1967), *The Private Language Problem*, New York, Random House.

Schulte, J. (1993), *Experience and Expression, Wittgenstein's Philosophy of Psychology*, Oxford, Clarendon Press.

Schutz, A. (1967), *The Phenomenology of the Social World*, Evanston, IL, Northwestern University Press.

Searle, S. (1992), *The Rediscovery of the Mind*, Cambridge, MA, The MIT Press.

Sellars, W. (1963a), *Science, Perception and Reality*, London, Routledge & Kegan Paul.

—— (1963b) "Empiricism and the Philosophy of Mind" in Sellars 1963a.

Shanker, S.G. (1987), *Wittgenstein and the Turning Point in the Philosophy of Mathematics*, Albany, NY, SUNY Press.

Skinner, B.F. (1957), *Verbal Behavior*, New York, Appleton-Century-Crofts.

—— (1974), *About Behaviorism*, New York, Vintage Books.

—— (1984), *Beyond Freedom and Dignity*, New York, Bantam.

Stalnaker, R. (1987), *Inquiry*, Cambridge, MA, The MIT Press.

Stampe, D. (1977), "Towards a Causal Theory of Mental Representation," P.A. French, T.E. Vehling, H.K. Wettstein, *Midwest Studies in Philosophy, Studies in the Philosophy of Language*, vol. II, pp. 42–63.

Stich, S. (1978), "Autonomous Psychology and the Belief-Desire Thesis," *The Monist*, vol. 61, no. 4, pp. 573–91.

—— (1979), "Do Animals Have Beliefs?," *Australasian Journal of Philosophy*.

—— (1983), *From Folk Psychology to Cognitive Science: The Case Against Belief*, Cambridge, MA, The MIT Press.

Stroll, A. (1994), *Moore and Wittgenstein on Certainty*, Oxford, Oxford University Press.

Tait, W.W. (1986), "Wittgenstein and the 'Sceptical Paradoxes'," *The Journal of Philosophy*, vol. 83, no. 9, pp. 475–88.

Thomson, J. (1964), "Private Languages," *American Philosophical Quarterly*, vol. 1, no. 1, pp. 20–31.

Tomberlin, J., ed. (1989), *Philosophy of Mind and Action Theory, 1989* (Philosophical Perspectives 3), Atascadero, CA, Ridgeview Publishing Company.

Unger, R. (1988), *False Necessity*, Cambridge, Cambridge University Press.

Vesey, G., ed. (1974), *Understanding Wittgenstein*, Ithaca, NY, Cornell University Press.

Von Eckardt, B. (1984), "Comments and Criticism, Cognitive Psychology and Principled Skepticism," *The Journal of Philosophy*, vol. 81, no. 2, pp. 67–88.

Vygotsky, L.S. (1965), *Thought and Language*, Cambridge, MA, The MIT Press.

—— (1976), "Play" in Bruner *et al.* 1976.

—— (1978), *Mind in Society: The Development of Higher Psychological Processes*, Cambridge, MA, Harvard University Press.

Watson, J. (1930), *Behaviorism*, New York, Norton, 1930.

Wellman, H.M. (1990), *The Child's Theory of Mind*, (Cambridge, MA, The MIT Press.

Wertsch, J.V. (1985a), *Vygotsky and the Social Formation of Mind*, Cambridge, MA, Harvard University Press.

——, ed. (1985b), *Culture, Communication, and Cognition, Vygotskian Perspectives*, Cambridge, MA, Cambridge University Press.

Williams, B. (1974), "Wittgenstein and Idealism" in Vesey 1974.

Williams, Meredith (1980), "Beyond the Infinite Regress," *Journal for the Theory of Social Behavior*, vol. 10, no. 3, pp. 67–88.

Williams, Michael (1977), *Groundless Belief*, Oxford, Basil Blackwell.

—— (1992), *Unnatural Doubts*, Princeton, NJ, Princeton University Press.

Wolff, R.P. (1963), *Kant's Theory of Mental Activity*, Cambridge, MA, Harvard University Press.

Woodfield, A. (1982a), "Thought and the Social Community," *Inquiry*, vol. 25, pp. 435–50.

——, ed. (1982b), *Thought and Object*, Oxford, Clarendon Press.

Wright, C. (1986), *Realism, Meaning & Truth*, Oxford, Basil Blackwell.

—— (1987), *Wittgenstein on the Foundations of Mathematics*, Cambridge, MA, Harvard University Press.

Index of quotations

Philosophical Investigations II

Remarks on the Foundations of Mathematics

Index